COMPARING NEW DEMOCRACIES

NEW DIRECTIONS IN COMPARATIVE AND INTERNATIONAL POLITICS

Series Editors
Peter Merkl and Haruhiro Fukui

Comparing New Democracies: Transition and Consolidation in Mediterranean Europe and the Southern Cone, edited by Enrique A. Baloyra

Comparing Pluralist Democracies: Strains on Legitimacy, Mattei Dogan

No Farewell to Arms? Military Disengagement from Politics in Africa and Latin America, Claude Welch

ABOUT THE BOOK AND EDITOR

The transition to democracy has been a significant trend in Mediterranean Europe and Latin America during the last ten years. This book presents comparative analyses that offer a theoretical synthesis of the dynamics of recent democratization processes on both sides of the Atlantic. The contributors argue that transition is a response to fundamentally political factors. They describe how dictatorships deteriorate and collapse, how key events in the early stages of transition may encourage the military to withdraw from politics, and what the requirements are for a democratic outcome. The second part of the book focuses on the specific processes of transition and consolidation occurring in Argentina, Brazil, and Uruguay. Finally, a crucial dilemma of democratic consolidation—the issue of governability—is examined within the framework of the relationship between social structure and political institutionalization.

Enrique A. Baloyra is associate dean of the Graduate School of International Studies, University of Miami, Coral Gables, Florida.

COMPARING NEW DEMOCRACIES

Transition and Consolidation in Mediterranean Europe and the Southern Cone

---

EDITED BY
ENRIQUE A. BALOYRA

WESTVIEW PRESS / BOULDER AND LONDON

New Directions in Comparative and International Politics

Published in 1987 in the United States of America by Westview Press, Inc.; Frederick A. Praeger, Publisher; 5500 Central Avenue, Boulder, Colorado 80301

Library of Congress Cataloging-in-Publication Data
Comparing new democracies.
(New directions in comparative and international politics)
Bibliography: p.
Includes index.
Contents: Democratic transition in comparative perspective / Enrique A. Baloyra—Democratic establishments / Leonardo Morlino—Mass and elite perspectives in the process of transition to democracy / Rafael López-Pintor—[etc.]
1. Democracy—Case studies. 2. Latin America—Politics and government—1948- . 3. Spain—Politics and government—20th century. I. Baloyra, Enrique A., 1942- . II. Series.
JC 423.C665 1987 321.8 86-33996
ISBN 0-8133-0396-6

Printed and bound in the United States of America

The paper used in this publication meets the requirements of the American National Standard for Permanence of Paper for Printed Library Materials Z39.48-1984.

10 9 8 7 6 5 4 3 2 1

TO LUIS QUIROS VARELA
IN MEMORIAM

CONTENTS

PART THREE: ON GOVERNABILITY

TABLES AND FIGURES

Figures

Tables

ACKNOWLEDGMENTS

Many wonderful people deserve special thanks: the contributors, for a confidence that I hope has been rewarded; Virginia Barton and Carmen Bradley of the Graduate School of International Studies of the University of Miami, for preparing the different versions of the manuscript; Bill Smith, for his chapter and his invaluable editorial suggestions; Lauri Fults and Janice Murray of Westview Press, for their fine editing; and most fundamentally, Barbara Ellington, senior acquisitions editor at Westview, for believing from the start.

Enrique A. Baloyra

ACRONYMS

ABI	Associação Brasileira de Imprensa (Brazilian Press Association)
ACF	Adelante, con Fé! (Forward, with Faith!)
AD	Alianza Democrática (Democratic Alliance)
ADENA	Acuerdo Democrático Nacional (National Democratic Accord)
ANP	Acção Popular Nacional (Popular National Action)
ARENA	Aliança de Renovação Nacional (National Renovating Alliance)
ASIMET	Asociación de Industrias Metalúrgicas (Association of Metal Working Industries)
BA	bureaucratic authoritarian
CBI	Corriente Batllista Independiente (Independent Batllista Tendency)
CDU	Convergencia Democrática Uruguaya (Uruguayan Democratic Convergence)
CEB	Comunidades eclesiais de base (Christian base communities)
CFP	Concentración de Fuerzas Populares (Concentration of Popular Forces)
CGT	Confederación General de Trabajadores Confederação Geral dos Trabalhadores (General Confederation of Workers)
CIE	Centro de Informações do Exército (Army Information Center)
CIS	Centro de Investigaciones Sociológicas (Center for Sociological Research)
CNBB	Conferência Nacional dos Bispos do Brasil (National Conference of Brazilian Bishops)
CNT	Comando Nacional de Trabajadores (National Workers Command)
CONAPRO	Concertación Nacional Programática (National Democratic Agreement)
COPCON	Comando Operacional do Continente (Continental Operations Command)

CORFO	Corporación de Fomento de la Producción (Development Corporation)
CPN	Corriente Popular Nacionalista (Popular Nationalist Tendency)
CR	Conselho da Revolução (Council of the Revolution)
CUT	Central Única dos Trabalhadores (United Workers Central)
DC	Democracia Cristiana (Christian Democracy)
DGS	Direcção Geral de Segurança (Directorate General of Security)
DOI-CODI	Divisão de Operações Internas–Centro de Operações de Defensa Interna (Division of Internal Operations–Center for Internal Defense Operations)
EEC	European Economic Community
ESG	Escola Superior de Guerra (Superior War College)
ESNI	Escola Nacional de Inteligência (National Intelligence School)
ETA	Euskadi ta Askatasuna (Basque Organization for Direct Action)
FA	Frente Amplio (Broad Front)
FEUC	Federación de Estudiantes Universitarios Católicos (Federation of Catholic University Students)
	Federación de Estudiantes de la Universidad de Chile (Student Federation of the University of Chile)
FEUU	Federación de Estudiantes Universitarios de Uruguay (Federation of Uruguayan University Students)
FIESP	Federação das Industrias do Estado de São Paulo (Federation of Industries of the State of Sao Paulo)
FNC	Frente Nacional Constitucionalista (National Constitutionalist Front)
FPI	Frente Popular de Izquierda (Popular Left Front)
FUD	Frente de Unidad Democrática (Democratic Unity Front)
GAU	Grupos de Acción Unificada (Unified Action Groups)
GDP	Gross Domestic Product
GNP	Gross National Product
IDI	Izquierda Democrática Independiente (Independent Democratic Left)
IMF	International Monetary Fund
INCRA	Instituto Nacional de Colonização e Reforma Agrária (National Institute of Colonization and Agrarian Reform)
IOP	Instituto de Opinión Pública (Public Opinion Institute)
MAN	Movimiento de Acción Nacional (National Action Movement)
MAPU	Movimiento de Acción Popular Unitario (Unitary Popular Action Movement)

MDB Movimento Democrático Brasileiro (Brazilian Democratic Movement)
MDP Movimiento Democrático Popular (Popular Democratic Movement)
MFA Movimento das Forças Armadas (Movement of the Armed Forces)
MID Movimiento de Integración y Desarrollo (Integration and Development Movement)
MIR Movimiento de Izquierda Revolucionaria (Movement of the Revolutionary Left)

OAB Ordem dos Advogados Brasileiros (Order of Brazilian Lawyers or Brazilian Bar Association)

PC Partido Comunista (Communist party)
PCB Partido Comunista do Brasil (Communist Party of Brazil)
PCP Partido Comunista do Portugal (Communist Party of Portugal)
PDC Partido Demócrata Cristiano (Christian Democratic party)
PDP Partido Democrático Popular (Popular Democratic party)
PDR Partido Derecha Republicana (Republican Right party)
PDS Partido Democrático Social (Social Democratic party)
PDT Partido Democrático Trabalhista (Democratic Workers party)
PEM Programa de Empleo Mínimo (Minimum Work Program)
PFL Partido da Frente Liberal (Liberal Front party)
PI Partido Intransigente (Intransigent party)
PIDE Policia Internacional e de Defensa do Estado (International and State Defense Police)
PLP Por la Patria (For the Fatherland)
PMDB Partido do Movimento Democrático Brasileiro (Party of the Brazilian Democratic Movement)
PN Partido Nacional (National party)
POJH Programa de Empleo para los Jefes de Hogar (Work Program for Heads of Household)
PP Partido Popular (Popular party)
PPD Partido Popular Democrático (Popular Democratic party)
PR Partido Radical (Radical party)
PS Partido Socialista (Socialist party)
PSB Partido Socialista do Brasil (Socialist Party of Brazil)
PT Partido dos Trabalhadores (Workers party)
PTB Partido Trabalhista Brasileiro (Brazilian Workers party)
PVP Por la Victoria del Pueblo (For the People's Victory)

SD Social Demócrata (Social Democrat)

SMATA Sindicato de Mecánicos y Afines del Transporte Automotor (Union of Mechanics and Kindred Workers of Automotive Transportation)
SNI Serviçio Nacional de Informações (National Intelligence Service)
TP traditional party (Uruguay)
TSE Tribunal Superior Electoral (Superior Electoral Tribunal)
UCD Unión de Centro Democrático (Union of the Democratic Center)
UCR Unión Cívica Radical (Radical Civic Union)
UDI Unión Democrática Independiente (Independent Democratic Union)
UN Unión Nacional (National Union)

INTRODUCTION

Enrique A. Baloyra

Since the mid-1970s students of the politics of transition to democracy have struggled to keep pace with their subject matter. Beginning with Portugal, Greece, and Spain in Mediterranean Europe and the Dominican Republic in the Caribbean, and followed by Ecuador, Peru, Bolivia, Argentina, Uruguay, and Brazil in South America, an impressive number of authoritarian regimes have been replaced by democratic ones.

These transition processes began, almost coincidentally, when very sophisticated studies seeking to explain the breakdown of democratic regimes in Latin America were being published. Those studies were based on four paradigms dominating the study of Latin American politics and society: cultural revisionism, dependency analysis, liberal sociologism, and critical Marxism. Each offered a very different perspective on democratic breakdown.[1] Thus, scholarly efforts had concentrated on a kind of regime change opposite the one about to take place.

The first few cases of authoritarian breakdown occurred in countries at intermediate levels of development or in those under traditional types of domination or both—and not in those under the domination of the "new type" of authoritarian regimes inaugurated in the mid-1960s in South America. The breakdown did not lead to a process of transition in all cases. In the late 1970s Bolivia had a false start, and in Central America civil war broke out in both Nicaragua and El Salvador. Every student of Latin America knows that political regimes have changed relatively frequently. These considerations may have formed the basis of the initial reticence and well-founded skepticism that greeted the early cases of authoritarian breakdown. These feelings perhaps were reflected in the language of a U.S. Department of State paper intended to solicit bids for a research project entitled "Democracy in Latin America, Prospects and Implications." The department requested that the study ". . . examine what is perceived by many observers to be a genuine movement toward democratic government throughout the hemisphere. This assumption should be tested and the findings should be analyzed in terms of implications for U.S. policy and for hemispheric affairs in general."[2]

In their proposal to the department, three academicians from the University of North Carolina at Chapel Hill suggested that the ongoing process reflected (1) favorable sociohistorical circumstances, (2) the support and encouragement of external actors, (3) the agreement of key elites on the desirability of democracy, and (4) the availability of alternative leadership committed to democratic politics.[3] But those elements changed dramatically from one situation to another and produced unexpectedly favorable outcomes in some cases, delayed the process in others, and apparently left some countries behind altogether.

Old stereotypes die hard. It took Portugal and Spain ten years from the beginning of democratization efforts to gain entrance to the European Economic Community (EEC). More than commercial selfishness delayed their entrance. Other European nations appeared unable to accept the notion of a democratic Spain and Portugal. North American visions of Latin America may be equally unprepared to encompass the implications of similar changes in the Western Hemisphere.

An initial problem in constructing a credible explanation of democratization in Latin America is how to progress beyond the "polarized patheticism" of extant views about U.S. foreign policy. By this I mean the enduring, shaping influences of the metaphors of Cuba and Vietnam on the domestic political debate about U.S. foreign policy. Despite obvious differences, both liberal and conservative interpretations assume that nothing politically relevant occurs in Latin America without the active participation of the United States. It may be harder to argue against this proposition than to create a consensus on the likely impact of U.S. foreign policy on the democratization of Latin America.

A second problem is that until very recently contemporary mainstream social science had relatively little to say about democracy and democratization. If anything, this much-abused topic appeared to have lost its validity. To make matters worse, one of the most conservative U.S. administrations in the twentieth century embraced the agenda of democratization as one of the emphases of its foreign policy. As a result, defense of democratization in Latin America suddenly has become a "conservative" position in U.S. academic circles. Fortunately, this malaise has not spread to Latin America itself where the "beastly, blind years" of authoritarian repression, as Carlos Floria calls them, have had a profound, sobering, and maturing impact on wide segments of the academic community, the political class, and the public.

In addition, the U.S. obsession with Central America tends to belittle the significance of democratization in South America. A wide variety of

U.S. citizens—policy influentials, single-issue activists, solidarity lobbies, and conservative free-lance benefactors supplying war materiel to the Nicaraguan guerrillas—appear incapable of seeing anything but the crisis in Central America. To be sure, what is going on in Central America is extraordinarily important. However, the dynamics of a process that has had a direct impact on the lives of more than 200 million South Americans is equally important and no less deserving of attention. But the dynamics of political change in South America have little to do with revolution and with romanticized, drugstore paperback visions of the Third World, so they may be less appealing. It is easier to deal with the convenient, facile (albeit misguided) dichotomies awash in analyses of Central America. In summary, we are talking about probably the most significant political trend in the Western Hemisphere since the mid-1960s.

This book presents the theoretical and empirical perspectives of a group of scholars that began to meet in December 1979. At that time President Jimmy Carter was grappling with a hostage crisis in Iran. Ronald Reagan was merely an aspirant to the presidential nomination of his party. U.S. attention was beginning to turn toward the unfolding crises of Central America. Argentina, Brazil, and Uruguay were still solidly under authoritarian domination.

The group expanded and has continued to meet ever since and to test its initial assumptions and propositions against a reality that has forced all its members to refine our ideas. The chapters contained herein are the result of that discussion, evaluation, and refinement, and each chapter shares many of the assumptions of contemporary political science, defined broadly. However, the only element of intellectual agreement among us is the desire to avoid simplistic Manichaeism and to provide a comparative perspective on the dynamics of genuine processes of change. We seek to present a perspective on democratization that extends beyond the demonology of the familiar metaphors of Cuba and Vietnam and that is founded on a keen understanding of the historical frustration of the democratic project in the Latin countries of Europe and America and on the conviction that the only solutions to the dilemmas of democratization are political. Our perspective addresses a process that holds more promise than the brave new world of the technocratic military juntas and the redemptive community profferred by armed revolutionaries in power. More than anything we utilize the contemporary tools of our discipline to illuminate the dynamics of what we consider a major watershed in the political history of our countries. This requires a predominantly political explanation. Nothing else will do.

The comparative analyses presented in Part 1 offer a theoretical synthesis of the dynamics of recent processes of democratization on both sides of the Atlantic. Baloyra (Chapter 1) offers a series of propositions about processes of political transition, a model for the comparative analysis of the resolution of the "game" of transition, and a description of the "logic" of political transition. Morlino (Chapter 2) offers a more taxonomic model of the causal dimensions of a crisis of transition adding a very strong European component. Using the case of Spain, López-Pintor (Chapter 3) describes how the exertions of elites involved in a process of transition must result in outcomes congruent with the demands and aspirations of the masses. Huneeus (Chapter 4) explains why a society with a solid democratic tradition and a very sophisticated system of political parties has been unable to break down the personalistic, authoritarian regime of General Augusto Pinochet.

Part 2 focuses on the processes of transition and consolidation in Argentina, Brazil, and Uruguay. Floria (Chapter 5), a historian and political commentator, traces the background and context of the Argentine transition by underlining the attitudinal and political reasons for previous failed attempts. He suggests that only a party-based democracy anchored in liberalized political perspectives will work in Argentina. Smith (Chapter 6) describes the Brazilian process of transition as a dynamic contradiction between a scheme of controlled liberalization, which as conceived originally by military planners would relegitimize the regime, and an attempt to regain autonomy for civil society that eventually acquired a dynamism of its own. Rial (Chapter 7) explains how an incredibly complex electoral system and a system of parties whose decadence contributed to the collapse of democracy in Uruguay were precisely the springboards for a restoration of the traditional democratic model. Floria, Smith, and Rial suggest that we have witnessed what Morlino would call weak democratic consolidations in those countries.

In Part 3 Waldino Suárez turns our attention to some vexing questions that have not been resolved by the inauguration of these new democracies and that will haunt their chances for consolidation (Chapter 8). Suárez discusses governability in reference to what has to be considered one of the most difficult cases in the hemisphere—Argentina. In the conclusion (Chapter 9), Baloyra recasts the arguments in reference to a model that has been utilized for comparative and diachronic analyses of transitions and that may be useful for the analysis of consolidation. The Glossary and List of Acronyms are intended for the student as well as for more-seasoned readers unfamiliar with the topic or the area.

NOTES

1. For a discussion of these paradigms and of their possible contribution to a theory of democratization, see Enrique A. Baloyra, "La transición del autoritarismo a la democracia en el Sur de Europa y en América Latina: Problemas teóricos y bases de comparación," in Julián Santamaría (ed.), *Transición a la democracia en el Sur de Europa y América Latina* (Madrid: Centro de Investigaciones Sociológicas, 1982), pp. 290–303.

2. U.S. Department of State, *Democracy in Latin America, Prospects and Implications* (Washington, D.C.: U.S. Department of State, March 24, 1980), p. 1.

3. Federico G. Gil, Enrique A. Baloyra, and Lars Schoultz, "Decompression, Democratic Transition and United States Foreign Policy Toward Latin America" (research proposal, August 1980), p. 1.

PART ONE

THEORETICAL AND COMPARATIVE PERSPECTIVES

1
DEMOCRATIC TRANSITION IN COMPARATIVE PERSPECTIVE

Enrique A. Baloyra

Anyone who has studied democratic transition, as have the contributors to this book, knows that the similarities among the cases, at least those similarities observable at the national level of analysis, prove to be poor predictors of a democratic outcome.[1] Preliminary comparative analyses of transition have suffered from a failure to look at this process from the "inside" to determine what separates success from failure (a contrast between the chapters on Brazil and Chile will be very instructive in this regard). Nevertheless, there is a need for some kind of framework against which to evaluate the maze of details and contradictory evidence concerning a particular process of transition. The chronological sequence of events must be broken down into some more or less discrete, meaningful stages; and the substantive and procedural aspects of the process of political transition, especially the issues that precipitate its "endgame" phase, need to be described. Any discussion of democratization in Latin America must refer to the basic arenas where politics takes place, particularly in a situation in which one system of authority is unraveling while a substitute is not yet in place. Definitional rigor should prevail at the nominal and operational levels so that the ambiguities and contradictions found at the empirical level may be interpreted correctly and may not be confused with descriptive gaps resulting from chaotic semanticism. Basically, this chapter is an attempt to clarify these concepts. It is a comparative exercise (with some reference to cases not included in this volume) as well as a guide to the chapters that follow.

THE DIMENSIONS OF POLITICAL TRANSITION

A succinct review of the more prominent characteristics of these transitions would suggest that they have been more frequent in the more advanced forms of authoritarian domination; that they have responded primarily to endogenous impulses; that they have been managed by military coalitions seeking to liberalize and reequilibrate the current regime or to extricate themselves gradually through a strategy of free and competitive elections; that they have required the neutralization of extremist obstructionism in endgame episodes; and that the failure to address the agenda of transition in full has resulted in weak consolidations and incomplete democratizations. The review of the cases will show that these "partial victories" did not come easily, as they required extraordinary exertions of political will.

The point of departure in these processes has been a capitalist state with a *regime d'exception* (regime of exception) maintained by a dictatorial government seeking to contain the society and to control an exclusionary political community.[2] The end result is the disappearance of the authoritarian regime (defined here as the arbitrary rule imposed by a dictatorial government). The disappearance of this regime does imply the emergence of a new regime in which the government does not abuse its powers because it is constrained by autonomous intermediary institutions (I offer this as a concise, generic definition of democratic regimes). These are the most basic elements that these processes have in common.

By a process of *democratic transition* I mean, (1) a process of political change (2) initiated by the deterioration of an authoritarian regime (3) involving intense political conflict (4) among actors competing (5) to implement policies grounded on different, even mutually exclusive, conceptions of the government, the regime, and the state; (6) this conflict is resolved by the breakdown of that regime leading to (7) the installation of a government committed to the inauguration of a democratic regime and/or (8) the installation of a popularly elected government committed to the inauguration of a democratic regime.

The temporal dimension implicit in this operational definition is presented in Figure 1.1. Whatever sequence is implied in the figure does not presuppose an orderly, irreversible progression through neatly differentiated stages. What is depicted in the figure is a series of major, albeit distinct in some instances, recurrent events that takes place during the transition. The events themselves are conceptualized in terms of the following definitions.

Deterioration is the loss by an incumbent government of its ability to cope with the policy agenda, particularly the two key concerns of political economy—security and prosperity—and other salient issues of high symbolic appeal to the public. Deterioration is the situation in which governments find themselves when they are unable to conjugate minimally acceptable levels of efficacy, effectiveness, and legitimacy.[3] Governments and regimes deteriorate, but this is not conducive to a process of transition unless there is a *breakdown*—that is, a collapse of the incumbent government followed by a marked discontinuity in the nature of the regime. Breakdown can

FIGURE 1.1 Stages of the Process of Regime Transition

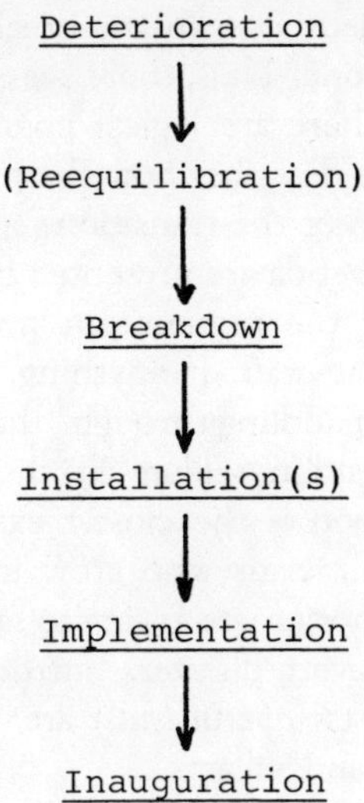

Note: See the text and the glossary for the definition of these terms. Liberalizations are not considered part of implementation in this model. The latter is utilized in connection with events occurring after breakdown. The process may include the installation of several caretaker governments, each of which may address different aspects of the agenda of transition.

occur without deterioration as a result of the sudden death or assassination of the head of state, a scandal of major proportion, or other events that paralyze the government and bring about its downfall. The evidence suggests that in most cases deterioration is not followed immediately by breakdown because most governments institute measures designed to reequilibrate their regimes and keep them in power. Many authors refer to the dynamics surrounding the deterioration of authoritarian regimes as an authoritarian crisis (crisis is a perfectly viable although much-abused term).

The *installation* of a new government creates a more appropriate context in which to begin implementing a process of transition that will change the nature of the regime. Use of the future tense is fully intended here for regimes are not installed—they must be inaugurated, and this requires time and effort. In most of the cases reviewed here, the governments installed after breakdown have contented themselves with restoring the rule of law and implementing the electoral timetable of the transition. Only in the case of Portugal does one find a major attempt on the part of a transition government to address an agenda of major socioeconomic changes. Several governments may be installed between the breakdown of a regime and the crystallization of a different one. Thus, there are as many empirically different varieties of transitions as there are logical possibilities.

The term *implementation* describes how the protagonists of the transition address the different aspects of the transition's agenda. The substantive and procedural aspects of that agenda are presented in Table 1.1. Implementation does not imply or require the presence in power of a benevolent actor capable of extraordinary statecraft. If anything, the evidence suggests that implementation is more a "muddling through" than an epic story. In addition, the protagonists of a transition seldom fit the mold of the philosopher king—Juan Carlos de Borbón is the closest example one finds—and tend to be relatively obscure politicians who grow in stature—a Raúl Alfonsín, for example—scheming authoritarians trying to save the day, or dour, taciturn military officers trying to avert disaster. Furthermore, obstructionists (*obstruccionistas*) and aperturists (*aperturistas*) are roles played by the actors, not metaphors for heroes and villains.

One problem with usage of the term implementation is that it refers to a competitive situation in which democratic rules are introduced into a context that remains very authoritarian.[4] Another is that implementation may begin as part of a reequilibration strategy of liberalization that was not designed for a genuinely democratic outcome. In addition, in most of the cases reviewed here implementation of the electoral agenda is what precipitated the endgame of the transition. Basically, no one is fully in charge, and the outcome of the transition depends on how its protagonists utilized their resources to implement their own versions of transition. This being the case, we must assume that implementation will be conflictual. But conflict is reduced dramatically past the point of the endgame of the transition. The *endgame* is that relatively short, complex, and crucial episode of the transition in which the balance of power changes decisively in favor of the aperturists following a confrontation with the obstructionists. The timing of the endgame is the most relevant determinant of the length of the transition. Our evidence shows that implementation is very similar in all cases once the endgame has taken place. This similarity reduces the utility of a typology of transitions based on stages.

Installation—and subsequent implementation—may lead to the *inauguration* of a democratic regime. By this I mean the crystallization of a pattern of relations among society, political community, government, and state that conforms to the democratic blueprint and results from the installation of a government committed to democratization. The weakness of these inaugurations may be related directly to the outcomes of implementation. For example, in South America (1) judicial restorations, for the most part, have not included prosecution and conviction of those primarily responsible for

TABLE 1.1
Procedural and Substantive Aspects of the Agenda of Transition

PROCEDURAL ASPECTS	SUBSTANTIVE ASPECTS
1. Restoration of the rule of law	Credibility and authenticity of the transition
a. Government acting consistently within the law	Who, in effect, is the government?
b. Judicial restoration	Legitimacy of the transition
Government not abusing power	End of Arbitrary rule
Government acting within the limits of its own legality	Opposition actors decide to participate
Amnesty	Identity of beneficiaries
Account for the disappeared	Clarification of circumstances and sanctions
2. Constitutional Revision	Adjustments deemed necessary to relations among state, society, government, and political community
a. Reform of the state	Governability Democratization of capitalism Respect for basic rights
b. Review of the economic model	Balance between public and private sectors Property relations
c. Formula of representation	Inclusiveness of the political community
d. Ideological space afforded	Incorporation of the Left and of antidemocratic actors
e. Presidential model	Civilian supremacy Executive-legislative balance
3. Electoral Process	Identity of the government
a. Basic electoral statute	Characteristics of the contest
b. Electoral timetable	Ability of the parties to organize the public
c. Validity and efficacy	Degree to which outcome is favorable to democratization
4. Transfer of Power	Can the government attempt to
a. Timing of endgame b. Degree to which (1) and (2) require further action	...inaugurate and/or consolidate democracy?

abuses of authority under the military governments; (2) constitutional reform has not altered the political economy; (3) the installation of a republican government and the inauguration of a democratic regime may not have put an end to military interventionism; (4) there may not have been a "transfer of power" accompanied by the appearance of a new hegemonic actor in society; and (5) there certainly has not been a satisfactory solution to the issue of governability. However, it does not follow that these processes were a "gift of the dictators."[5]

The cases reviewed here show a succession of several transitional governments; the vagaries of several electoral contests; the intense, sometimes violent conflict between *aperturistas* and *obstruccionistas;* the different configurations of breakdown; the intricacies of implementation and the remarkable similarity among endgames; and the eventual dissipation of uncertainty about the final outcome. The transition is a complicated process, with numerous setbacks, obstructionism, and great ambiguity about some of the rules and the timetable of the transition. The lack of a consociational agreement about the desirability of a democratic inauguration gives rise to an open confrontation that results in the neutralization of the obstructionists. Without a doubt, competitive and conflictive implementations have been the norm. As a matter of fact, it is hard to detect any elements of consensualism in the South American cases; it would appear that in the absence of a consensual blueprint elections actually proved to be the backbone of these fully competitive albeit relatively peaceful variants of implementation.

The actual variants emerging from the "ideal" model suggested by Figure 1.1 are basically a result of when and how the endgame takes place. Obstructionism may be neutralized at the time of breakdown, or this may come relatively late in the implementation phase. In either case the endgame only can take place if the "logic of transition" prevails. That logic does not require that antidemocratic obstructionists be "liquidated," only that their use of violence be rendered ineffectual.

As is always the case, not all is well with the proposed analytical framework. For example, one may argue endlessly about the periodization of the stages in each of the cases reviewed here.[6] Although it would be useful to treat particularly bitter periods of confrontation as discrete stages, the entire sequence of transitional events is replete with confrontations. Likewise, given the fact that only in Portugal does one find something close to a *ruptura* (rupture), it is sometimes difficult to pinpoint the breakdown. To be sure, even though most democratic inaugurations examined here were not predicated upon a rupture, they were made possible because the logic of transition prevailed, and therefore, implementation led to endgame. The experience in Chile suggests the determinants required to bring about the endgame, as the emphasis here is on transition as a game of conflicts and confrontation.

What follows is an attempt to make some semblance of order and reason out of a series of very involved, convoluted processes. I am well aware of the inevitability of distortion but confident that this is within tolerable bounds and that the logic of these comparisons is valid. I will describe the Argentine, Ecuadoran, and Portuguese cases very briefly in reference to their main events. These events will be used as analytical benchmarks to distinguish qualitatively different periods in the process. Deterioration, breakdown, implementation, and endgame will be featured most prominently. Then I will propose some substantive comparisons utilizing all the cases included in this book.

COMPARATIVE PERSPECTIVES

A comprehensive comparative discussion of recent processes of transition should include the deterioration (1980–1983) and collapse of the Process of National Reorganization in Argentina; the liberalization that became a transition in Brazil (1974–1985); the recalcitrant case of the Dominican Republic (1966–1978); the violent transition in Ecuador (1972–1979); the dismantling of the Peruvian "experiment" (1973–1980); the spring of freedom in Portugal (1973–1976); the "optimal" transition in post-Franco Spain (1973–1977); and the restoration of the traditional democratic model in Uruguay (1980–1985). Each one of these processes had elements unduplicated elsewhere.

The Spanish transition is unique in terms of the military's secondary role, the low level of violence, the degree of agreement among the transition's protagonists, and a mechanism of transition based on the monarchy. These factors made the breakdown of the regime coincidental with the endgame of the transition, led to a smooth implementation, and made Spain perhaps the only case in which one may properly speak of "transition from above." All of these make the Spanish case relatively optimal and, by the same token, hard to imitate. This is an important consideration because there has been a very strong, explicit tendency to utilize the Spanish case as a role model for actual (Argentina, Uruguay, and Brazil) and possible (Chile) transitions in South America. Yet this in itself adds one more element of uniqueness to the case of Spain—namely, that its tremendous psychological and cultural impact in Latin America cannot be paralleled by any other. Rafael López-Pintor discusses why and how, despite forty years of dictatorship, the Spanish public was ready for democracy and against extremist experiments.

Although all other cases of transition involved a common scenario of military retreat, each was singular in some respect. The "movement of the captains" in Portugal came closest to a *ruptura* of the old order. In Portugal the transition process resembled a revolution because some of its protagonists tried to utilize mass mobilization to impose their radical blueprint of transition. Portugal's similarity with Peru is belied by the fact that the transitional coalition of the Peruvian military was engaged in an entirely different ideological, and thus political, change. This coalition was dismantling the remnants of the Velasco Alvarado experiment in "inclusionary corporatism."[7] The Peruvian transition put an end to the only clearcut case of military reformism in a major South American country in the last twenty years.

There is nothing comparable to the defeat suffered by the Argentine military in the Falklands-Malvinas War and to the direct connection between this defeat and the breakdown of the regime. In his chapter, Carlos Floria complains that this factor has been downplayed in too many analyses of the Argentine case. That case is also unique given the extremes of brutality and thoroughness with which the military put down the leftist insurgency in the country.

The Dominican case is perhaps the hardest to integrate into the proposed analytical scheme. It is difficult to believe that President Joaquín Balaguer wanted to initiate and implement a genuine process of transition. But he was forced to accept such a transition. The United States successfully pressured Balaguer to abide by his word and accept the electoral triumph of the opposition.

Although there are civil-military alliances in all processes of transition, the Ecuadoran case highlights a problem that may mark the difference between success and failure in these cases. I am referring to the active collaboration between the most recalcitrant military leaders, who were placed in strategic positions in the intelligence and security services, and reactionary conservatives in the private sector.[8] Ecuador offers the only recent case of bloody confrontation and actual combat among military factions. Finally, the Ecuadoran regime did not conform to the "new" authoritarianism.

Brazil witnessed a deterioration that began at the moment of greatest triumph of the most successful bureaucratic authoritarian (BA) regime, the longest process of transition, the largest number of elections between deterioration and breakdown, the most complex, prolonged conflict within the military, and the most convoluted of endgames. Like its Brazilian counterpart, the Uruguayan military wanted to legitimize its regime from below and were similarly unsuccessful. Yet once the transition began the Uruguayan regime unraveled in record time.

However, there are important similarities among these cases as well as a group of common causal determinants. Although I cannot describe the dynamics of transition for all the cases that have not received chapter-length treatment herein, I will illustrate how to utilize the proposed analytical model in the cases of Argentina, Ecuador, and Portugal. All other cases discussed in some detail in this book will be included in the comparative analysis but without further discussion or elaboration.

TABLE 1.2
Patterns of Democratic Transition

Type	Sequence of Events	Cases
Early-internal	Deterioration is resolved by an endgame contributing to breakdown. Implementation by first government installed following breakdown.	Spain
Delayed-external	Deterioration and reequilibration considerably short of liberalization. Endgame is precipitated by external factors that produce the breakdown as well. Short period of implementation.	Argentina Dominican Republic Peru
Delayed-internal	Deterioration with a liberalization that gradually escapes the control of a military government. Endgame takes place within military institution itself but with overt civil-military alliances.	Brazil Uruguay
Late-external	Deterioration leads to breakdown and one or more installations. Very conflictual implementation contested by more explicit civil-military alliances. Late endgame.	Ecuador Portugal

Note: This typology of patterns of transition results from the combination of the following dichotomies: (1) outcome of deterioration: breakdown/reequilibration; (2) outcome of breakdown: liberalization/implementation; (3) outcome of reequilibration: breakdown/liberalization; (4) outcome of liberalization: implementation/inauguration. The most significant causal agent at work here is the timing and locus of the endgame: early/delayed/late and internal/external.

The logic of the comparison is straightforward. Spain and Chile are deviant cases and represent, respectively, the extreme cases of success and failure among those considered here. All other cases involve a military extrication through a liberalization linked to elections. The basic distinction among them is posited in Table 1.2 in terms of four patterns of transition (early-internal, delayed-external, delayed-internal, and late-external). The first involves cases in which there was a genuine project of *apertura/abertura* (aperture, opening) from the very beginning, with endgame at breakdown followed by relatively untroubled implementation (Spain and perhaps Peru).[9] The second is somewhat hard to distinguish from the first given the simultaneity of endgame and breakdown. But, in reality, these come at the end of a fraudulent process of liberalization that fails to stabilize the regime (Argentina and Dominican Republic). The contingency of external determinants of endgame is unique, although fortuitously so in all probability. The third pattern involves a project of reequilibration through a real but limited liberalization that escapes the control of the military. It is difficult to perceive the exact moment of breakdown in these cases (Brazil, more likely Peru, Uruguay). The fourth pattern involves cases of breakdown, rancorous conflict among relatively evenly matched factions, and a very problematic, uncertain implementation with a late endgame (Ecuador and Portugal).

Despite obvious contextual, ecological, and social differences among these cases, the proposed analytical model efficiently explains the reasons for the different patterns and identifies how the logic of transition sets the stage for an endgame favorable to a democratic outcome. These uses justify the validity of the model. More importantly, the exercise will force us to revise some currently held beliefs about the inadequacy of democracy for the politics of late, dependent capitalism. If a logic of transition could prevail under such adverse circumstance, there is reason to believe that these weak inaugurations could be consolidated if the lessons of transition were assimilated in full.

THE POLITICS OF CATASTROPHIC ENDGAME: TRANSITION IN ARGENTINA

There were some symptoms of discontinuity in the final stages of the government of General Jorge Videla, who had been installed by the military coup of March 23, 1976, and who had inaugurated the Process of National Reorganization.[10] The discontinuity becomes more obvious when we contrast the years 1979 and 1980. Such a contrast exposes a government capable of maintaining control in 1979 but already in a more compromised position in 1980.

The regime experienced some instability in 1979. The Commission of the 25 trade unions tried to organize a general strike on April 27, but the government forestalled it. In May the government moved quickly to prevent private political gatherings and incarcerated leaders of the Frente Popular de Izquierda (Popular Left Front, or FPI) and of the Movimiento de Integración y Desarrollo (Integration and Development Movement, or MID). In September, with a delegation of the Inter-American Commission of Human Rights in the country, the government admitted that it had 1,438 political prisoners who had not been charged. It also admitted responsibility for forcibly seizing about three thousand signed depositions concerning disappeared persons from the offices of a human rights organization. The

Interior Ministry continued to ignore writs of habeas corpus. In late September General Banjamín Menéndez protagonized an abortive rebellion against the army commander in chief General Roberto Viola in Córdoba.[11] In late 1979 the government issued a vague blueprint for a return to civilian rule attributed to the recently retired General Viola, the most likely successor of Videla. The document made no reference to any timetable, except to emphasize that the junta of commanders in chief would remain in power until 1985.[12] Although this announcement of a gradual return to constitutionalism was greeted with skepticism, the timing and context of the announcement suggested an ongoing conflict within the military about a policy of liberalization.[13] However, the accumulation of these incidents fell considerably short of inducing a deterioration of the regime.

Deterioration (early 1980–November 1981)

But 1980 was a different story. Serious economic setbacks and widespread condemnation of human rights abuses by the regime put the government on the defensive precisely at the time when it needed to orchestrate an orderly succession of military presidents. The government lost the initiative as the economic situation worsened and it became necessary to impose harsh measures. In turn, these developments had a negative repercussion on opinion within the military and contributed to a paralysis of the outgoing government.

The anniversary of the coup brought forth more evidence of contradictory opinions within the military institution. General Leopoldo Galtieri, Viola's successor as commander in chief of the army, stated that the military would remain in power until 1990. Viola argued that a return to democracy would have to forget the war against subversion and include the military in any scheme of government.[14] The government pronounced itself ready to initiate a dialogue with the country's political parties, but they did not show much enthusiasm for the idea.

The government was shaken badly by two developments related to the disappeared. In February 1980 Amnesty International released a report on the situation in Argentina. In April the Inter-American Commission on Human Rights released its own. Both admitted a decrease in the incidence of torture, kidnappings, and disappearance but condemned the government for using these systematically. Although the local media and wide sectors of opinion did not yet react favorably to these "foreign" condemnations, much of the information in the reports came from the Catholic Church, which was about to take issue with the government on the question of the disappeared.

In March the government was confronted with a series of financial scandals that began with the bankruptcy of the Banco de Intercambio

Regional (Regional Trade Bank), second largest among private banks.[15] In April the Central Bank had to take over the Banco de los Andes (Bank of the Andes), the largest private bank in the country. It was necessary to intervene the Banco Odonne (Odonne Bank), the Banco Internacional (International Bank), and several large conglomerates.[16] During that month a large part of the speculative capital attracted by high interest rate was repatriated. Numerous firms staged massive layoffs. Others stopped meeting their financial obligations or simply shut down. The first stirrings of labor activism resulted in a series of strikes.

During June the government endured great pressures to devaluate the peso, but economic superminister José Luis Martínez de Hoz insisted on the soundness and validity of the economic model. On July 10 the government announced a package of economic measures that brought back speculative capital but did not address the structural flaws of the model. Despite the protests of local entrepreneurs, import duties were lowered even more.[17] Inflation remained at greater than 100 percent. In August the government tried to regain the initiative by pledging that the overall course of the regime's economic strategy would not change during 1981–1984. A visit to Brazil by President Videla did not go well. He was questioned by the media about alleged Argentine participation in the coup staged by Bolivian general García Meza and about the disappeared. The Brazilians were cold to his proposal to organize a crusade against subversion in South America.[18]

September offered further proof of military divisiveness and of the incoherence it engendered. On the one hand, the Interior Ministry prevented a series of political party gatherings and showed a relatively hardline posture. On the other, General Viola continued his attempts to widen and deepen his contacts with trade unionists and politicians. September 29 went by without the expected official announcement. On the 30th a brief, confused communiqué announced that an official proclamation of the new president would be made in ten days, but seventy-two hours later a carefully worded statement announced Viola's designation as president (the statement avoided using the term *unanimous* to describe the decision that led to Viola's accession). Apparently the navy led the opposition to Viola within the junta.[19] In October about fifty officers who had opposed Viola's designation were retired, but it was Galtieri, not Viola, who benefited more from these changes.[20] During November the president-designate supported the official interpretation on the question of the disappeared but showed more flexibility regarding the economy.[21]

In January 1981 Martínez de Hoz admitted the depth of the economic crisis, which featured a record number of industrial failures, a doubling of the fiscal deficit, an increase in foreign indebtedness to $27.2 billion, a trade deficit of $2.4 billion, and a 1.6 percent drop in the Gross Domestic Product (GDP).[22] Given this picture, Viola's weak position vis-à-vis the junta (whose members would not retire until the end of the year), Galtieri's December appointment of hardliners to the army High Command, and the emergence of a more determined opposition, General Viola initiated his term in a very precarious situation.

Viola's difficulties amounted to more than a crisis of government. Except for a brief period in summer 1981, Viola could not really govern the country; he had his back against the wall all the time. He never seized the initiative and could not convince the opposition of the truthfulness of his promise of a political change. One observer described the situation as "a comedy of errors, equivocations, doubts and intrigues that did irreparable damage to the regime."[23] Despite his pardon of former president Isabel Perón, he could not engage the Peronists in a dialogue for they already had decided to join the Multipartidaria (a coalition consisting of the Peronist, Radical, Intransigent, and Christian Democratic parties and the MID). Viola, however, was not confronted with mass mobilization; the Multipartidaria gained momentum from mid-year on but did not challenge the government on the street. Instead, the leaders of the Multipartidaria maintained their pressure on the government to issue a call for elections and return to constitutionalism.[24]

Viola's economic policies did not enjoy any more credibility than his overtures to the opposition. On March 31, 1981, his minister of economics, Lorenzo Sigaut, introduced a series of measures—including a 22.9 percent devaluation, new export surcharges, and even lower import duties—that was not received well.[25] In May there was a $400 million outflow of hard currency, and in July a financial panic ensued. The worsening economic crisis stimulated political activism among labor and business organizations. On June 17 the Sindicato de Mecánicos y Afines del Transporte Automotor (Union of Mechanics and Kindred Workers of Automotive Transportation, or SMATA) mobilized a few thousands members in Greater Buenos Aires for a thirteen-hour protest. The government arrested about one thousand persons to control the situation. However, only 10–15 percent of the labor force responded to a call for a July 22 general strike by the Confederación General de Trabajadores (General Workers Confederation, or CGT).

Despite his June counteroffensive Viola's neck was already under the ax of his comrades in the junta. He failed to engage the political parties in a dialogue, could not convince the hardliners of the advantages of a liberalization, could not control the economic crisis, and projected an image of incompetence.[26] In essence, General Viola could not consolidate his presidency, and with him in power, the regime could not reequilibrate itself.

Breakdown (November 9–December 22, 1981)

On November 9 General Horacio Liendo replaced Viola but refused to remain as president when it became public that Viola had been overthrown.

The junta appointed Rear-Admiral Carlos Alberto Lacoste as provisional president. On December 22 General Leopoldo Galtieri was installed as president in an eight-minute ceremony. Galtieri remained commander in chief of the army and kept his seat in the junta.[27]

I lack the intimacy of detail to clarify two crucial issues concerning Viola's overthrow, which is described here as a breakdown of the regime. One has to do with the nature of the coalition that opposed Viola and installed Galtieri. Ostensibly, Viola was removed because his government was unable to reverse the economic decline and his colleagues were impatient with Viola's very tentative scheme for liberalization. In economic terms, Galtieri intended to steer a middle course between nationalist and liberal options, but it is doubtful that this or any other combination would have worked because the public had lost faith in the military's ability to run the economy.

With respect to the question of liberalization, which could not be postponed much longer without considerable cost, Galtieri cannot be considered an aperturist. Thus, the second issue concerns Galtieri's real motives with respect to the situation prevailing at the time of his installation. Galtieri's installation was more likely a reequilibration attempt supported by the more hardline element. Galtieri did not come to power to initiate the process of transition delayed by Viola's ineptitude. If anything, Galtieri intended to restore and prolong a more "decisive" type of military rule, and shortly after his installation he began to implement a series of hardline policies.[28]

Reequilibration and Breakdown (December 22, 1981–June 14, 1982)

Galtieri gave early signs of favoring a more thorough program of economic austerity. His minister of economics, Roberto Alemann, asked and apparently received permission to include state enterprises in the program. These were, for the most part, under military management. Alemann's request was made in light of the dismal performance of the economy in 1981: a drop of between 5 and 6 percent in GDP; a decline of 15 percent in industrial output and a level of industrial activity between 40 and 50 percent of installed capacity; 5 percent unemployment, according to the government, and 13–16 percent according to unofficial sources; 1 million unemployed workers without any kind of benefits; 130 percent inflation; a 456 percent decrease in the value of the peso between March 1981 and February 1982; and foreign indebtedness reaching $32 billion, of which $20 billion was from the public sector.[29] The government saw the economic crisis as one of the engines propelling the deterioration of the regime.

Alemann focused on lowering inflation, which originated, he believed, in the public sector. He froze the salaries and pensions of public employees and tried to decrease public expenditures and the fiscal deficit. He discontinued the indexation of salaries to the level of inflation and warned that, beginning in mid-year, he would not print money to cover the deficit. He maintained free convertibility and high interest rates, readjusted export surcharges, and ordered a series of studies to investigate the liquidation of insolvent state enterprises.[30]

Politically Galtieri could not advance very far. His flamboyant personality and populist rhetoric could not tone down the increasing demand for a return to constitutionalism. The Multipartidaria remained firm in this respect and presented an economic program of its own. Galtieri threatened to impose sanctions on the parties. He showed little inclination to discuss elections except at the municipal level. The Multipartidaria called the government a dictatorship marching to the north while the country was going south. On March 30 the CGT organized a protest demonstration in Buenos Aires that ended in violent repression, with more than one thousand persons detained and one person dead. On April 2 the Argentine military invaded the Malvinas.

Endgame (April 2–June 18, 1982)

The Argentine transition is somewhat anomalous and deviant in that the decisive confrontation marking the endgame of the transition was exogenous to the process itself. By this I mean that the reequilibration attempt of the hardline factions of the Argentine military ended in disgrace with the Argentine surrender on June 14 and with the removal of Galtieri on June 18. The consequences and power implications of this breakdown generated the momentum for implementing the transition (that hitherto had been rejected by the military). So profound was the crisis that one could talk about the period between the surrender and the reconstitution of the junta on September 10 as a crisis of the state itself because the country, in effect, was leaderless.

We will never know whether the Argentine Process of National Reorganization would have been ended by a democratic transition without the Falklands-Malvinas War. Although anything advanced on that score must be treated as speculation, it can be argued that the action of the Multipartidaria, the mass mobilization instigated by the labor organizations, and the economic crisis imposed the logic of the transition on domestic Argentine politics. This might have made Argentina no different than, say, Brazil and Uruguay. Maybe Galtieri's boundless ambition and the weight of the "dirty war against subversion" were too much of an obstacle to get the transition going without an "extraordinary" impetus. What is certain is the military could not implement a strategy of reequilibration, a failure that only accelerated the deterioration of the regime. Basically, the regime was already in the grip of the logic of transition, and if anything, the second breakdown put the regime beyond retrieval.

Implementation (July 1, 1982–March 1984)

During the brief interregnum following Galtieri's ouster it was announced that General Reynaldo Bignone (retired) would be the new president. Bignone had excellent relations with the top military brass and very good connections with the political class. His government was identified as a government of transition and was rumored to be controlled by the new army commander in chief General Cristino Nicolaides. Bignone's government did not receive the support of the two other branches of the armed forces, which felt that the army's performance in the war had been disgraceful and no longer entitled it to preside in the junta. Therefore, at the time of his installation on July 1, Bignone lacked an effective support coalition, he did not have a consensus to extricate, and he was not even considered in control.[31]

All of these circumstances should have put Bignone in a weak position vis-à-vis General Nicolaides, a reputed hardliner. But Nicolaides could not do to Bignone what Galtieri did to Viola. The elements contributing to the deterioration of the regime continued to operate, and the defeat in the Malvinas and its aftermath provided further impetus to deterioration. The economy remained beyond control, labor activism increased, the political parties became even more assertive and, worst of all, the armed forces remained sorely split.[32] Therefore, Bignone, who was in favor of extrication, and Nicolaides, who apparently was not, had considerable trouble consolidating. The condition of statelessness affected Bignone and Nicolaides more directly, but it also affected those who conspired against them.

Despite these difficulties Bignone was able to take some initial steps toward a transition even before the reconstitution of the junta in early September 1982.[33] Given the prior occurrence of the endgame, Bignone did not have to deal with a very complicated transition agenda. Constitutional revision was not at all an issue, and there was little Bignone would or could do regarding the disappeared. Eventually, his government approved an amnesty that aroused a storm of protest from the opposition, which considered this a "decision of state that should be taken by a Constituent Power."[34]

The transition was implemented because the opposition decided to seize the initiative, to take the government at its word (a situation that had not prevailed during the Viola and Galtieri governments), and to participate fully in the process. The Radical party called for a demonstration on July 20, 1982, before the government had restored the legality of public partisan gatherings (the government then lifted the restriction). On August 26 the government released the text of a new statute on political parties that for the most part was acceptable and allowed the parties to register voters (incidentally, voter registration was very successful; the parties were able to induce 31 percent of the voters who registered to affiliate with them, a percentage far above the historical mean).[35] Labor union activism created a measure of mass mobilization that had been absent from the process as well. In August there was a transportation strike. On September 22 there was a general strike led by the "62" Peronist-controlled labor unions. General Bignone held talks with the rival factions, CGT-Azopardo and CGT-Brazil, and decreed a salary increase that was considered insufficient. The government refused another increase, and on December 6 labor staged a general strike.[36] On December 18 the Multipartidaria staged a march attended by 150,000 persons in Buenos Aires that ended in violence. Basically the transition took place without much improvement in the economic situation.[37] But the space opened up by the Bignone government did not close, and the logic of transition came fully into play.[38]

"MUDDLING THROUGH": TRANSITION IN ECUADOR

In the case of Ecuador, the military called the process of transition a *restauración* (restoration), which it sought to control from the very beginning.[39] Unlike the Peruvian and Portuguese cases, the Ecuadoran military's justification for controlling the transition could not be the defense of the revolution's ideals. The military's appetite for control stemmed from a desire to extricate itself from a situation of its own creation with a minimum loss of prestige and from the need of senior officers to keep an eye on everyone, including each other.

Deterioration (February 1972–January 1976)

The Ecuadorian military came to power in a preventive coup against the government of José María Velasco Ibarra in order to forestall the anticipated victory of Assad Bucaram in the June 1972 elections. The military government of General Guillermo Rodríguez Lara was unable to define its goals or the nature of the regime through which it sought to function. Polarized by Brazilian and Peruvian options, the Ecuadoran military decided to call itself "nationalist and revolutionary."[40] This contradiction hampered the design and execution of policy, including relations with the opposition. The nationalists were attracted by the Peruvian experiment and wanted a firm stance on the development of the country's oil resources. They also favored welfare policies, including agrarian reform. Their conservative colleagues wanted no part of these; they believed the country had been spared greater trouble by the preventive coup and saw little merit in policies "designed to pacify the Left." So severe was this split within the Ecuadoran military and so delicate the balance of power among these factions that the implementation of the transition could be characterized as a protracted confrontation.

Rodríguez Lara's early reformism (1972–1974) did not go far enough for the opposition, which had created a Democratic Restoration Front in July 1972 and continued to demand free elections. However, the reforms that were implemented proved too threatening to the conservatives, who in July 1974 forced Rodríguez Lara to discard his reformism and suspend all political activities for an additional period of five years.

In 1975, after three years in office, the government remained ineffective, the economic situation continued to deteriorate, and there was alarm about the regime's lack of ideological definition. In late August most of the opposition parties lined up behind the Civic Junta for Institutional Restoration, which called for a return to constitutional government.[41] On September 1, 1975, troops loyal to General Raúl González Alvear, head of the Joint Chiefs of Staff, captured the defense minister General Marco Almeida Játiva and the army chief of staff General Angel Vega and surrounded the presidential palace demanding the resignation of Rodríguez Lara and pledging to return the country to constitutional rule within two years. After a bloody encounter the rebels seized the palace briefly but were overwhelmed by the government's counterattack.[42] The military leaders of the rebellion were allowed to leave the country, and more than thirty officers were retired from active service. However, the government detained Abdón Calderón Muñoz, president of the Frente Radical Alfarista (Radical Alfarista Front); José Vicente Ortuño of the Movimiento Nacionalista Revolucionario (Nationalist Revolutionary Movement), led by former president Carlos Julio Arosemena; and Carlos Cornejo of the Movimiento Velasquista (Velasquista Movement). It was assumed that the more conservative elements of the Civic Junta had advance knowledge of the rebellion (a right-wing coup attempt had been anticipated for some time) but only the Velasquistas had come out overtly in favor of the coup on September 1.[43]

Rodríguez Lara tried to reequilibrate with a cabinet reorganization that brought more military men into the government. More significantly, on September 8 the military announced the creation of the Ecuadoran Armed Forces Joint Command. The new general commander of the army, General Guillermo Durán Arcentales appointed the general commander of the navy, Rear-Admiral Alfredo Poveda Burbano, "provisional chief" (*jefe accidental*) of the Joint Command.[44] Durán was a more conservative figure than Rodríguez Lara; Poveda represented the most leftist of the branches. This lineup probably reflected a desire to keep the peace among the different military factions at a particularly difficult moment. Finally, the government introduced a series of economic reforms.

Apparently, the military was debating two options: extrication and institutionalization. Extrication implied the risk of an eventual return to office of traditional political figures loathed by the military. Institutionalization implied further serious divisiveness within and among the branches. On October 9 Rodríguez Lara made a reference to institutionalization in a speech in Guayaquil. But the relentless pressure of the opposition continued to exacerbate tensions within the military institution. On November 23 the Catholic Church came out in favor of national reconciliation. On November 26 the Interior Ministry issued a decree introducing limited press censorship "to protect the interests of national security and guarantee the normal development of the institutionalization plan being pursued by the government."[45] This was clearly a defensive institutional move on the part of the military. On December 6 Rodríguez Lara announced that the Plan de Institucionalización (Institutionalization Plan) would be published in February and that he would step down.[46] Apparently, Rodríguez Lara was trying to reconcile the two basic options, but the main problem for the military was that his government proved unable to reequilibrate the regime. His continued presence in power made them all the more vulnerable to another internal confrontation.

Breakdown (January 11, 1976)

It is a little daring to talk about the breakdown of a regime that could not consolidate itself, which seems to have been the case in Ecuador. But it is possible to identify the moment of the collapse of the Rodríguez Lara government, following his removal from office in a subsequent, bloodless coup. At the time of the coup (January 11, 1976) a transportation strike had paralyzed the country, and controversy about the government's handling of the oil question had reached a dangerous level. The government could not define its priorities and lacked a minimum of civilian and military support. With the country at a standstill Rodríguez Lara was forced into retirement, and a triumvirate representing all factions assumed office. The new government pledged to carry out the military program of 1972 and to turn power over to an elected government at the end of 1977.[47] To be sure, these were contradictory aims.

Implementation (January 14, 1976–August 10, 1979)

Eventually, the *aperturistas* were able to count on Admiral Poveda Burbano while the *obstruccionistas* linked up with General Durán Arcentales. In this case aperturist and obstructionist are not simply metaphors for left and right or liberal and conservative respectively.[48] For example, the leaders of the September rebellion were considerably to the right of General Durán, whom the Ecuadoran Left initially viewed as their most likely ally in the new government. Admiral Poveda, on the other hand, may have come to support the extrication option as the lesser evil. Therefore, the positions of different military factions changed during the transition.

Three alternative paths for the return to constitutional government were discussed in talks between the government and the opposition. These talks took place between early February and mid-March.[49] The more conservative politicians, arrayed behind a new civic junta, favored a constituent assembly that would select a provisional president in order to keep the process of change under elite control. They were very disturbed by inclusion of a number of figures known for their support of leftist policies in the new cabinet. The less traditional parties and more progressive elements preferred the enactment of a new constitution followed by elections. Obstructionists with close links to coastal economic interests wanted the whole exercise stopped for they saw very little gain in it.

Uncertainty prevailed through March 1976, when the *aperturistas* managed to initiate the transition process through a government decision to update the Civil Registry and begin the process of voter registration. In June the government announced that two commissions would consider separate constitutional options: whether to amend the document of 1945 or to draft and enact a new one. The obstructionists did their homework by placing one of their own, Colonel Bolívar Jarrín, in the position of spokesman for the government. They were able to slow down the process by delaying the appointment of the members of the two commissions until December. Additional delays in the completion of the Civil Registry and in the *empadronamiento* (registration) of voters made it clear to everyone that civilian rule would be technically impossible until late 1978.

The process continued despite delays, scandals involving high officials, and labor agitation, which included a general strike on March 18, 1977, a month-long teachers' strike, a strike in October by sugar workers that ended with the death of at least twenty-five workers, and riots in Quito in April 1978.[50] These were the elements of mass praetorianism in the Ecuadoran process. In April 1977 the *aperturistas* scored a modest victory when former president Galo Plaza was appointed to head the Tribunal Supremo del Referendum (Supreme Tribunal of the Referendum). On May 23 the two constitutional commissions delivered their drafts. Despite some liberalizing amendments added to the 1945 document, there was little question that the draft of the new constitution provided for a more democratic regime. On June 23 a third commission presented its report on the statute of parties and elections, and Admiral Poveda used the occasion to reiterate the government's commitment to an electoral transition.

On January 15, 1978, the constitutional referendum was held. Despite a campaign by wealthy Guayaquil businessmen for a "null" vote against both constitutional options, the outcome was a serious blow to obstructionist hopes: 90 percent of the eligible voters participated, 75 percent of whom expressed a preference, and a plurality of 43 percent favored the new constitutional draft.[51] Following the referendum the armed forces announced that they would retain control of the process of transition. In February 1978 Colonel Jarrín rejected the parties' contention that the process should be governed by the transitional regulations of the new constitution and stated instead that the military would be bound by the new document only after a duly elected president had been inaugurated. Apparently, military hardliners and progressives had agreed that they should retain control.[52]

After their defeat in the referendum, the obstructionists embarked on defamatory, dilatory tactics through the Supreme Court and the Tribunal Superior Electoral (Superior Electoral Tribunal, or TSE). These were presided over by obstructionists Gonzalo Karolys and Rafael Arízaga respectively. They banned the presidential candidacies of seven individuals, including Bucaram, and proscribed two "dangerous" political parties from participating in the election.[53] To make matters worse, the military refused to restore habeas corpus and release all political prisoners before the election. While these tactics were put in practice a separate crucial battle was occurring within the armed forces. In a struggle about promotions, General Durán's entire slate of candidates was rejected, with the exception of Jarrín. Apparently, senior officers saw through Durán's efforts to place his own men in top military commands.

On July 16, 1978, the presidential elections finally were held. The results gave a plurality of 30.6 percent of the vote to the Concentración de Fuerzas Populares (Concentration of Popular Forces, or CFP) ticket of Jaime Roldós and Osvaldo Hurtado. The relatively small margin separating the second and third positions—Sixto Durán of the Frente Nacional Constitucionalista (National Constitutionalist Front, or FNC), with 22.9 percent; and Raúl Clemente Huerta of the Frente de Unidad Democrática (Democratic Unity Front, or FUD), with 21.7 percent—helped make matters worse for the obstructionists.[54] The FNC had its principal source of support in the highlands; the FUD drew its strength from the coast.[55]

Endgame (August–December 1978)

Judge Arízaga reacted very swiftly against this adverse outcome. He mounted a series of maneuvers transparently designed to reduce the credibility of the result, to reduce the margin of the Roldós-Hurtado victory, to buy time in order to organize a rightist coalition, and to bring the process to a standstill. Supreme Court chief magistrate Karolys contributed by declaring his availability to serve as provisional president. In the meantime, the Chambers of Production orchestrated a vicious campaign against Roldós and his running mate Hurtado and against the "socialist ideology" of Hurtado's Democracia Popular (Popular Democracy) party.

The tone and tenor of the Arízaga-Karolys effort had all the characteristics of reactionary conservatism. Both men seemed to speak for conservative sectors fearful that a democratic transition was threatening in itself. However, as was the case in Portugal, the audacity and irresponsibility of the obstructionists proved to be their undoing. Using the incredible charge that the CFP had engaged in fraudulent electoral practices, Arízaga threatened to annul the election on the basis of "evidence" he would present later.[56] When unable to produce such evidence, Arízaga was forced to resign on September 22, thus clearing the way for Admiral Poveda to form a new TSE. To his credit, Durán disassociated himself from the Arízaga-Karolys campaign and concentrated on preparing for the runoff election.

A final serious attempt by obstructionists with direct links to military officers occurred on November 29, when former presidential candidate Abdón Calderón was assassinated in Guayaquil. Bucaram and Roldós claimed that a destabilization effort was afoot and that assassination squads had entered the country to hunt down opposition leaders.[57] Vice presidential candidate Hurtado accused interior minister Jarrín of trying to sabotage the transition. Abel Salazar, a lawyer of questionable reputation connected to terrorist activities in Guayaquil, was identified as the main suspect in the Calderón murder. It appeared that Salazar and his associates were linked to military and police officers, including Guayaquil chief of police Jorge Castro, and an assistant to Jarrín, Major Jaime Hermosa, who later implicated Jarrín in the murder.[58]

This tense confrontation led to Jarrín's resignation and to the resolution of the endgame; the more violent obstructionists were removed from contention. The new interior minister, Rear-Admiral Víctor Gardós removed all of Jarrín's close associates from their posts, including General Alberto Villamarín Ortiz, the chief of police, and Colonel Silvio Arias Torres, the head of the Servicio de Investigaciones Criminales (Criminal Investigations Service) in Guayaquil. Although the very cautious manner in which Jarrín and his associates were prosecuted in early 1979 suggests that the military did not want to suffer further embarrassment or division as a result of this incident, it is clear that the incident not only destroyed the credibility of the obstructionists but also unified military leaders in their acceptance of the outcome of the upcoming elections. In short, reaction to Calderón's murder tilted the resolution of the Ecuador transition in favor of a democratic outcome. The removal of Jarrín and his associates opened the way for a full-fledged implementation of the transition. This removal neutralized a very vicious element, limited the options of actors who could have benefited from the success of the obstructionists, and induced those actors to participate in the process through the legal avenues open to them. By year end the momentum for implementation was growing impressively strong as former presidents Galo Plaza and Clemente Yerovi called for no further delays.

On January 19, 1979, the new electoral code was approved, and it appeared that the election would be all but impossible to stop. To be sure, the TSE managed to complicate things with inept and confused rulings on eligibility. As the case against Jarrín dragged on the military found it necessary to stifle a media campaign regarding the Calderón affair and military mismanagement in the public sector.[59] But a comment by General Durán suggested that a firm military consensus for extrication had crystallized. In a public appearance designed to minimize the impact of the resignation of the comptroller general, General Durán, at best an unenthusiastic supporter of the *apertura,* stated that "there was no power on earth capable of stopping the *restauración.*" On April 22, 1979, the runoff and the congressional election were held. Roldós defeated Durán by 69 to 31 percent of the presidential votes, and the CFP received slightly less than 30 percent of the congressional vote.[60] Roldós was installed on August 10, 1979.

PORTUGAL: THE POLITICS OF RANCOROUS TRANSITION

The Portuguese case is particularly relevant to the study of transition in Latin America because, unlike the Spanish case, the military was in control of the entire process and was the effective agent for the breakdown of the Salazarist regime.[61] The deterioration of the regime included most of the features attributed to the syndrome of democratic breakdown in Latin America: economic crisis, labor unrest, an unresponsive and ineffectual government, and a situation perceived by the military as a threat to their institutional integrity.

Deterioration (late 1973–April 1974)

The Salazarist regime deteriorated dramatically during the government of Prime Minister Marcelo Caetano (1968–1974). Early in his term of office, Caetano failed to deliver on his promise of liberalization. His version of *abertura* went no further than changes in the names of the official party from União Nacional (National Union) to Acção Nacional Popular (Popular National Action, or ANP); of the security police from Policia Internacional e de Defensa do Estado (International and State Defense Police, or PIDE) to Direcção Geral de Segurança (Directorate General of Security, or DGS); and of the official title of the Salazarist state from *estado novo* (new state) to *estado social* (social state). Following these cosmetological adjustments Caetano failed to alter a protectionist economic policy that served primarily the interests of a few well-connected firms. Under Caetano, the poorest country in Western Europe saw little improvement in its standard of living: Per capita income remained less than $1,000; illiteracy hovered around 35 percent; and between 1963 and 1973 Portugal's population experienced a net loss of 1 million persons.[62]

The government seemed equally unable to solve the colonial question; it doggedly pursued a colonial war that spread to all the Portuguese possessions in Africa. The war consumed an ever-increasing share of public expenditures, and the human toll became unbearable. Between 1961 and 1974, in proportional terms, the Portuguese casualties in Africa exceeded the number of U.S. casualties in Vietnam.

The deterioration of the regime began in late 1973. The first ten months of that year witnessed a decline of 4.1 percent in GDP compared to the first ten months of 1972. Mounting inflation and unemployment led to a more defiant labor attitude. Between December 1973 and April 1974 the country was paralyzed by frequent strikes led by the better-paid and most-qualified workers. July 13, 1973, marked a turning point in the attitude of the military toward the Caetano government. On that date the government issued Law Decree 353, which redefined and eased the standards of promotion and advanced to officer status a number of previously ineligible noncommissioned officers. Most officers perceived this relaxation of standards, intended to replenish the attrition caused by war, as a threat to the integrity of their institution. On December 6, 1973, a "movement of captains" crystallized among young officers, who formed a coordinating committee in Lisbon. Inevitably, discontent with the implications of Decree 353 turned into discontent with the performance of the government and to questions about the legitimacy of the regime.[63] On March 5, 1974, the movement of captains became the Movimento das Forças Armadas (Movement of the Armed Forces, or MFA), and Major Otelo Saraiva de Carvalho was asked to develop and coordinate plans for a military coup. A March 16 initial attempt ended in failure, but a second attempt succeeded on April 25 without bloodshed.

Breakdown (April 25–May 15, 1974)

Once in power the MFA began to promote a series of comprehensive changes in the government in order to change the nature of the regime. The MFA's Junta of National Salvation moved quickly to dissolve or reorganize the Council of State and the National Assembly, the ANP and its ancillary organizations, and the DGS. The military also took some far-reaching steps to change the regime. The first proclamation of the junta committed the MFA to hold an election, by universal suffrage and within a period of twelve months, for a constituent assembly that would decide the nature of the new regime. In addition, the MFA vowed to guarantee civil liberties, to respect the independence of the judiciary, and to abolish censorship.[64] The military's commitment to this blueprint set the Portuguese transition in motion.

Given their monopoly of public power during these early days, the junta and the MFA were able to implement a series of structural reforms with relative ease. Given the military's perception of the national crisis, the MFA and the junta felt justified in assuming a supervisory, tutelary role that included the right to determine whether the provisional government—still to be organized—was adhering to the principles of their proclamation. In addition, the MFA insisted that the junta remain in existence through the entire period of transition, that it select the president of the provisional government, and that the military dominate the Council of State. In order to protect itself from "rightist ideological abuse" the junta created a commission to control the media.

Inevitably, the role assumed by the armed forces led to a duality of power between the provisional government and the MFA. This duality persisted until the MFA redefined its role in the process of transition and abandoned the revolutionary alternative. In a way this decision responded to cleavages within the armed forces that resulted from attempts on the part of civilian protagonists of the transition to influence the MFA. Aperturists and obstructionists fought bitterly about the blueprint of the transition within the government, within the MFA, and on the streets.

Implementation (May 15, 1974–November 25, 1975)

In May the junta selected General Antônio de Spínola provisional president. He had played a part in the redefinition of the political role of the military with the publication of his book *Portugal e o Futuro.*[65] Although relatively compatible with the confused blend of liberal, corporatist, and progressive tendencies found in the first manifesto of the junta, Spínola's instincts were conservative, and his actions became obstructionist. His version of *abertura* featured the direct election of a powerful president, a referendum on the transition, and a delay in the elections for the constituent assembly. His proposals were defeated soundly by the Council of State. His preferences on the colonial question (continued antagonism toward the guerrilla movement and the development of a Portuguese commonwealth) were not received well within the MFA, and his economic policies fell considerably to the right of those of the more moderate sectors. Following the resignation of his prime minister, Palma Carlos, Spínola's isolation increased as the MFA adopted a position in favor of nationalization and agrarian reform and developed a complex organizational structure that branched out to the entire country.

Life was difficult for the socialist and social democratic *aberturistas* during this period. Party oppositions increasingly were polarized, with the principal contradiction pitting the Partido Comunista do Portugal (Communist Party of Portugal, or PCP) against the Partido Socialista (Socialist party, or PS) on practically every issue. Spínola's clumsy maneuvers strengthened the hand of the Communists early on. On September 10 Spínola made the mistake of challenging the MFA directly by inviting Portugal's "silent majority" to a mass demonstration on September 29. The MFA banned the demonstration, and Spínola was forced to resign on September 30. In March 1975 he attempted a military coup that was a complete failure.

Armed with this evidence of rightist obstructionism, the PCP could agitate against its adversaries by trying to implicate them in efforts to stop the "revolution."[66] In January 1975 the Council of State had approved, by a close vote, a new labor statute that helped the Communists tighten their control of the labor movement. They forged a close alliance with the now general Otelo Saraiva de Carvalho who, as head of the powerful Comando Operacional do Continente (Continental Operations Command, or COPCON), had access to all military intelligence, direct command of elite troops, and privileged access to the new premier, Vasco Gonçalves. The PCP also had control of several dailies and very good contacts with the commission that regulated the media, which gave the party a good measure of influence on public opinion. In short, the PCP had a very solid position during the early stages of the transition.

In the meantime the MFA found it necessary to adopt some defensive measures in order to protect the integrity of the armed forces. In December 1974 the Council of State issued a declaration proclaiming the nonpartisan nature of the MFA. In February 1975 the MFA announced a program that made explicit its intention to continue overseeing the actions of the government, now controlled by the radical Left, and to remain in operation as a special institution. On March 15 Constitutional Statute 5 created the Conselho da Revolução (Council of the Revolution, or CR), which replaced the junta and the Council of State. On March 17 the CR presented the political parties with a new blueprint for transition in which it would retain the right to direct the revolutionary program and control the armed forces for the next three to five years. This implied that although the armed forces may have been divided and unwilling to become involved in the ongoing struggle between Socialists and Communists, those who favored an activist role for the MFA in a more radical version of the transition appeared to have gained the initiative. The MFA remained interested in economic and social changes that only could be brought about by a change of regime and implied more than a political reform. Shortly after its creation, the CR nationalized a number of banks and insurance companies that had effective control of the economy.

Spring and summer 1975 were an extremely critical period for the Portuguese process of democratic transition. On April 25, after a short and intense campaign, the Socialist party won 38 percent of the vote in the election, which gave the Socialists a total of 115 (or 46 percent of the) seats in the Constituent Assembly.[67] With only 13 percent of the vote the Communists could not match the influence of the Socialists, who with the support of the 80 delegates of the Partido Popular Democrático (Popular Democratic party, or PPD) created a very solid majority in the assembly. These results practically assured that the new Portuguese constitution would mandate a democratic regime. Therefore, the April 1975 elections settled one of the principal questions of the transition.[68]

The Communists' reaction to their electoral defeat was to shift toward a strategy of mass praetorianism that would enable them to preserve the revolutionary alternative. The pursuit of this strategy put them on a frankly obstructionist course and eventually contributed to their marginalization from the process. Their Stalinist secretary general, Álvaro Cunhal, denounced the strategy of Eurocommunism and questioned the validity of the election results by affirming that the PCP's strength went beyond votes. Cunhal could have accepted the defeat by minimizing its significance and pledging continued support for the democratic version of transition, while seeking to preserve his excellent contacts with the MFA and his strong position in the labor movement. Instead, he tried to utilize those contacts to impose his own version of transition, which included the creation of a militia and committees for the defense of the revolution; a "strong unity" between the working class and the MFA; direct challenges to the government of Admiral José Pinheiro de Azevedo (when Pinheiro replaced Gonçalves); disruption of the work of the Constituent Assembly; and, finally, direct appeal to the rank and file of the armed forces. These actions by the Communists ran parallel to efforts by radical military officers to transform the MFA into a national liberation movement.[69]

Beginning in May 1975 the Socialists and the CR drew closer. The CR began to adopt a more moderate line thanks in no small measure to a group of officers led by Major Melo Antunes. On June 21 the CR came out in favor of democratic socialism and warned that armed militias would not be tolerated by the military. On July 15 the Socialists staged a massive demonstration in support of the CR. Attempts by leftist obstructionists to counter the improved fortunes of the Socialists proved ineffectual. Their allies in the government did not fare well. Premier Vasco Gonçalves could hardly offer them much support. His government was unable to maintain order, cope with recession and unemployment, or reequilibrate through a reorganization of the cabinet. The government's base of support narrowed down to the Communists while the Socialists confronted Gonçalves with his inability to govern. On August 21, under intense pressure from the Antunes faction, President Costa Gomes (Spínola's successor) took steps to defuse the situation. Costa Gomes already had voiced his preoccupation with the speed of the revolutionary process and his dissatisfaction with attempts to antagonize Portugal's Western allies. He began by removing a number of key military units from Saraiva de Carvalho's COPCON. On August 29 Costa Gomes appointed Admiral Pinheiro de Azevedo prime minister.

Endgame (Fall 1975)

The final major attempt of the leftist obstructionists came in the fall 1975. In September, using its labor strength and supported by seven small parties of the extreme Left, the PCP tried to bring Gonçalves back as prime minister. Having failed in this attempt, the PCP defied the Pinheiro government openly. In October the CR created a new security force, the Agrupação Militar de Intervenção (Military Intervention Group), which paralleled the COPCON, and began to purge the armed forces through a reduction of personnel in active service. On November 19 Premier Pinheiro suspended the operations of the government to protest the communist-instigated takeover of the building where the constituent assembly functioned. Two days later General Saraiva de Carvalho was removed as commander of the Lisbon garrison. On November 25 Saraiva de Carvalho made a last-ditch effort to impose his radical version of transition by staging a coup. Troops under the command of Lieutenant General Antônio Ramalho de Eanes defeated the rebellion.

Needing to preserve internal unity and having neutralized rightist and leftist obstructionism, the Portuguese military decided to redefine its role in the process of transition. The CR was made the sole representative of the MFA, and its powers were reduced to those of a consultative organ. On February 26, 1976, the MFA and the main political parties, including the PCP, pledged their support for the draft of the new constitution prepared by the assembly. Once the duality of powers between the MFA and the transition government disappeared, the Pinheiro government was able to implement the last stages of the transition. On April 2, by a vote of 250 to 15, the Constituent Assembly approved the new constitution. On April 25, exactly two years from the beginning of the Portuguese "spring of freedom," the Socialists won a plurality of 35 percent of the vote in the parliamentary elections. In June their presidential candidate, General Ramalho Eanes, won 61.5 percent of the vote.[70] The Portuguese democratic regime was inaugurated formally on July 14, 1976. President Eanes was sworn in as the first democratically elected president of Portugal in fifty years. Two days later he asked socialist leader Mario Soares to form a new government.

THE LOGIC OF POLITICAL TRANSITION

Direct Causes of Deterioration

Do authoritarian regimes deteriorate and break down in a fashion similar to that of democratic regimes? The evidence reviewed thus far and the discussion in subsequent chapters will show that any similarities are somewhat superficial. The two modes of domination have different vulnerabilities. On the surface, authoritarian regimes appear more stable because they can prevent effective opposition and can exclude from participation in the political community those actors who only express themselves adequately through mass political organizations.[71] It would appear, therefore, that the stability of authoritarian regimes hinges on the need to compensate a low level of institutionalization with a high degree of political control. Authoritarian control is implemented through a selective use of violence, which normally will be low even in semiconsolidated regimes; a corporatist strategy of interest representation conducive to the "limited pluralism" described by Juan Linz;[72] and, especially in more traditional regimes, a relatively minimalist approach to public policymaking.

The "new" authoritarian regime counterpart to these mechanisms is a treatment of public policy issues as if these were merely technical—a tendency detectable also in the more traditional types but elevated to a doctrine of "effective government" by the architects of the "bureaucratic authoritarian" regimes of the Southern Cone. In essence, I am talking about a balancing act that requires a strategy of containment predicated on a selective use of violence and a relatively tolerable performance on the part of the government.

It should be stated, lest we lose sight of the evidence, that deterioration and breakdown do not result automatically from arbitrariness, abuse of power, government inefficiency, corruption, widespread poverty, and low living standards. If this were the case, one would be hard pressed to explain the longevity of the more enduring forms of authoritarianism, which incidentally appear to be those associated with personal dictatorships: Francoism, Salazarism, Castroism, Somocism, and the like. In essence, "objective conditions" of tyranny alone do not suffice, even if these are at particularly intolerable levels. Through the ages people have learned to feign acceptance of authority and to devise strategies of survival, even under the most onerous circumstances.[73] In addition, if left alone people will not become involved in politics, at least not in a very militant fashion. This is precisely the secret of authoritarian domination—to create a climate of ostensible "normality" that only "extremists" and "politicians" will find unsatisfactory.

This would suggest that authoritarian regimes are particularly vulnerable to sudden increases in different modes of political participation, but this is not as simple as it sounds. An extension of the determinants of democratic breakdown will not do here. For example, much was made of the vulnerability of democratic regimes to "praetorianism," described in the literature as a situation in which a regime with a low level of institutionalization is confronted by a high level of political participation.[74] Yet if low institutionalization is an endemic problem of Latin American government—the result of a lack of consensus on procedural norms, low regime legitimacy, low levels of governmental efficiency, or all of these factors—it only would take an upsurge in unregulated participation to break a regime down. One may imagine, then, that authoritarian regimes are very vulnerable to mass praetorianism, but the case of contemporary Chile, examined in this book by Huneeus, suggests otherwise.

Were this true in the cases reviewed in this book, authoritarian deterioration and breakdown should have led to chaos given the presumably low degree of party discipline and cohesion (Uruguay); the presence of traditional clientelistic structures (Brazil, Ecuador, Dominican Republic, and Uruguay); the avatars of decades of authoritarian suppression (Portugal and Spain); patterns of cleavages conducive to fixed electoral outcomes (Argentina, Ecuador, and Peru); and "tired" leadership (practically all), not to mention the disarray of other institutions of political intermediation. Yet this did not come to pass, and, somehow, political parties were able to intermediate and channel the energies unleashed by breakdown into peaceful processes of implementation. In fact, praetorianism does not figure very prominently among the direct causes of deterioration listed in Table 1.3 (direct causes are processes and events that help reduce the legitimacy, efficiency, and efficacy of the incumbent governments). Factors related to elite conflict appear to be more relevant than any configuration conjuring up a vision of masses rushing to the barricades. To be sure, one may readily identify a growing inability to govern, but a symptom, even a most relevant one, does not a cause make.

In cases in which the opposition roused the public and where this action became one of the determinants of deterioration, such activism did not create a praetorian context. Even when the syndrome of deterioration appears linked to a crisis of regime consolidation, praetorianism does not appear as an important determinant of deterioration. In the relatively more complex and newer authoritarian regimes of Argentina, Brazil, Ecuador, Peru, and Uruguay, deterioration appears related to military disunity about the nature of the project that deserved to be consolidated. In all cases, especially in Argentina and Uruguay, the military became disoriented past the point of suffocating the "internal threat," the aspect of intervention for which military leaders could find the greatest consensus. In Ecuador, the Rodríguez Lara government failed to take a discernible direction, even after the September 1975 coup. In Peru, General Velasco's failing health put the already difficult consolidation of the "experiment" practically beyond reach. The "activist" military governments of Argentina, Brazil, Chile, and Uruguay engaged in serious attempts to reorganize society "from above." But only in the case of Brazil, where Smith suggests the economic model was a "savage capitalism" and not liberal monetarism, could the regime find some legitimacy in the

TABLE 1.3
Direct Causes of Deterioration of Authoritarian Regimes

ARGENTINA Growing disunity within the military as a result of (1) inability of General Videla to create support for his successor; (2) inability to agree on the most sensible course for the regime following the internal war; and (3) inability to reverse the adverse trend of the economy.

BRAZIL Growing disunity within the military concerning (1) how to react to the electoral defeat of 1974; (2) the economic model; and (3) the military's presence in power. Growing political activation of civil society and inefficiency of electoral *casuismo*.

CHILE Activation of the opposition as a result of adverse economic conditions; scandals about mismanagement and corruption among the economic advisers to the president; condemnation from abroad; and "demonstration effect" of transitions in neighboring countries.

DOMINICAN REPUBLIC Gradual estrangement between the government of Joaquín Balaguer and groups benefiting from economic prosperity. Low legitimacy of the government as a result of successive electoral frauds.

ECUADOR Inability of the Rodríguez Lara government to consolidate the regime following the overthrow of Velasco Ibarra. Growing disunity within the military about appropriate economic strategies and ways to treat the political opposition.

PERU Inability of the government of General Velasco Alvarado to consolidate the "experiment" in inclusionary corporatism. Growing economic difficulties: collapse of fisheries, lack of support from major international financial institutions. Velasco's failing health.

PORTUGAL Lackluster performance of the government of Marcelo Caetano in failing (1) to deliver on promises of liberalization; (2) to continue very costly colonial wars; (3) to cope with stagflation and unemployment. Growing politicization of the military.

SPAIN Inability of the government of Carlos Arias Navarro to maintain the continuity of the regime following the assassination of Admiral Luis Carrero Blanco and the death of General Francisco Franco. Dwindling base of elite support for the regime.

URUGUAY Inability of the armed forces to agree on a course of action following their successful eradication of the urban guerrillas. Inability of the military to legitimize a revamp of the traditional democratic model "from above."

performance of the economy. Essentially, the regimes of Argentina, Chile, and Uruguay did not create new economic wealth.

By contrast, men like Marcelo Caetano, Joaquín Balaguer, and Carlos Arias Navarro typified the "reactive mentality" of the leadership of the more traditional authoritarian regimes. Their preference to let things take their course but to resist change, and their inability to reduce the distance between their governments and the societies that grew increasingly estranged from them eroded their base of support substantially, even to a "bunker element" or "palace guard." Unable to implement but a few cosmetic changes, to rejuvenate the traditional formula of domination, or to adjust to the demands of the times, they were finally overcome by their opponents. In these cases political activation was, at best, an element of secondary importance before breakdown, and deterioration was in fact a crisis of regime continuity. This crisis was punctuated by a gradual, eventually irreparable estrangement between government and society that was accompanied by intergenerational conflict. In summary, then, paramount in the logic of transition is a very strong component of elite conflict, which results from very serious disagreements about the nature of the regime and leads to a paralysis that contributes to the deterioration of the regime.

A question must be raised at this point concerning strategies of reequilibration and the degree to which the governments of authoritarian regimes undergoing deterioration will utilize violence. The impression that the more traditional regimes deteriorate more peacefully is an artifact of the cases selected for analysis, which only include successful cases of transition. This leaves out a number of violent transitions affecting precisely those regimes. Why and in what circumstances do the elites of an authoritarian regime decide to forego more repression and opt for a change of regime? Is this part of the logic of transition?

One may hypothesize that because the repressive capacity of a regime is not inexhaustible there will come a point at which, given the sustained impact of deterioration and the increasing cost of repression, a consensus for extrication may emerge.[75] As it is very difficult to talk about, much less measure, consensus within an institution as secretive as the military, it may be more prudent to adopt an alternative approach based on factors that are likely to produce a decision to extricate on the part of senior military officers.

Six such determinants may be identified in the cases reviewed in this book: (1) military perceptions of the strength of the opposition; (2) the choices available to the military; (3) the balance between military aperturists and obstructionists; (4) the extant pattern of societal cleavages; (5) the substantive programs of the opposition; and (6) the presence of actors traditionally antagonistic to the military. The first three are related very intimately to the military's perception of the situation. First among these perceptions is the military's impression of the strength and commitment of the opposition. I am not speaking here about the level and nature of organized protest, at least at the outset, but primarily of opinion among different segments of the elite, among governments friendly to the regime, and within sectors particularly close to the military. In other words, I am discussing the impact of credible interlocutors on the military's perception of the situation. For example, Carlos Floria comments on the solitude of the Argentine military after Malvinas, when even the sectors that supported the military in 1976 left it alone, with devastating results.

A second, closely related factor is the calculus of actual costs and benefits of alternatives available to the military. Elements such as the prestige of the institution and the likelihood of a breakdown of discipline and morale come into play here. The third factor in this group, which could be given the status of an intervening variable, is the balance between aperturists and obstructionists within the military. As we are dealing for the most part with successful cases of transition, we must be very careful; the roles of a transition's actors change during different stages of that transition. This is particularly true of the military. One suspects that, given the idiosyncrasies of the institution and the uncertainty surrounding the process of transition, most officers do not have a clear schedule of preferences and are guided primarily by institutional concerns. This would imply a dispute between two minority factions for the hearts and minds of their colleagues, as illustrated very vividly by the cases of Ecuador and Portugal discussed in brief here. The case of Brazil suggests a similar, albeit more tortuous, prolonged process.

A second group of three factors seems to have the status of determinants exogenous to the military institution. One factor here is the pattern of cleavages prevalent in the society at the time of deterioration and the extent to which these cleavages are represented by different political forces that have become mobilized and would become contestants in an electoral process. Theoretically, the more efficacious the repression conducted by the regime, the less likely are all the relevant forces to retain a political identity and emerge as alternatives. But most of our cases belie this logical premise and attest to the resilience of more or less organized partisan loyalties.

The nature and feasibility of the substantive policies proffered as alternatives is second among these exogenous factors. I am referring here not only to platforms or programs but also to the extent to which there is a new project that could help legitimize an alternative regime. There were such projects in Spain and Portugal in a relatively ample sense, but this was less clear in the Latin American cases, except for the obvious political differences. The third factor would focus on the presence of an actor considered antagonistic by the military. One constant in all the processes of military extrication reviewed here has been the proscription of parties considered dangerous by the military. Without exception, all military governments of transition proscribed actors whom they identified as security risks.

These six factors constitute an important causal background to any decision on the part of the military to remove a government trying to preserve the deteriorating regime or to choose between reequilibration and extrication. We have been able to document four different patterns of transition dictated, in large part, by how these decisions were made (see Table 1.2). Prior to these two decisions the six factors in question must have led to an evaluation of the situation on the part of the military as well as to the emergence of public or quasi-public factions capable of engaging in a deliberative mode of behavior outside the chain of command. In response, a military coalition may crystallize and begin to implement a transition. This carries us into the terrain of determinants of breakdown, from which we will exclude Chile, a case in which (for the reasons discussed by Carlos Huneeus) the military has remained obedient and has refrained from such activities.

Effective Causes of Breakdown

There are some analytical difficulties resulting from the fact that deterioration is a process and breakdown is an event. One is that the effective cause of breakdown may be a previous event relatively removed in time. This was the case in Ecuador, where the government of Rodríguez Lara never recovered from the impact of the abortive coup of September 1975. However, there may be other cases, particularly those with a "late" endgame (patterns 2 and 3 in Table 1.2) in which this causal link is far less obvious. A very large sample of cases would facilitate identification and specification of commonalities or even a modest degree of quantification. But to extend the sample would require including cases from other cultural areas (which might complicate the analysis) and cases in which there is no correspondence among the key analytical variables.[76] What is important is not to assume that events closer to a breakdown are necessarily more causally relevant or to confuse the act of deposing a government with the cause of that government's downfall.

An inventory of effective causes of breakdown is presented in Table 1.4. Effective causes of breakdown are those events or actions (or both) that lead to the collapse of the regime. A contrast with the determinants of deterioration listed in Table 1.2 suggests three kinds of breakdown scenarios. The first scenario involves crises of continuity, where there was either a commitment to liberalization or even a carefully designed mechanism for leadership succession that rightist obstructionists refused to honor. In the Dominican Republic the United States forced President Joaquín Balaguer

TABLE 1.4
Causes of Breakdown of Authoritarian Regimes

ARGENTINA Military defeat in Falklands-Malvinas War (Galtieri). Unwillingness of the institution to allow the government to function (Viola).

BRAZIL Exhaustion of electoral casuismo. Unwillingness of President Figueiredo to assume a leading role in choosing his successor. Inability of the official PDS to agree on a presidential candidate.

DOMINICAN REPUBLIC U.S. pressure forcing President Balaguer and senior military officers to accept the outcome of the 1978 election.

ECUADOR Heightened tensions within the military resulting from the bloody military rebellion of September 1975. Praetorianism: strikes paralyzing the country; Rodríguez Lara government unable to maintain order; united opposition demanding return to constitutionalism.

PERU Praetorianism: bloody army repression of police strike in Lima, rioting, state of emergency; moderate and populist opposition leaders demand apertura.

PORTUGAL Law Decree 353 leads to the creation of the Armed Forces Movement.

SPAIN Growing isolation and obstructionism of Arias Navarro leads to his confrontation with King Juan Carlos.

URUGUAY Ability of the opposition to resist a "transition from above." Pact of the Naval Club commits the military to negotiated transition.

to accept the outcome of the 1978 election. In Spain King Juan Carlos literally flushed Premier Arias Navarro out of the palace and precipitated a confrontation. Ideally, Portugal should fit this pattern, and to a certain extent it does if one focuses on the collapse of the Caetano and Spínola governments. But in Spain and in the Dominican Republic the military was in a relatively subordinate role, and there was no serious leftist obstructionism. In a second group of cases deterioration led to a paralysis of the incumbent government and to an inability to maintain order. These are the cases in which praetorianism makes a belated, albeit effective, appearance, and the collapse is produced by a coalition that installs a government at least vaguely committed to a transition (Argentina, Ecuador, and Peru). Finally, in other cases involving military extrications, there was a "surrender" of sorts to the outcome of a process of liberalization that had escaped the control of the military (Brazil and Uruguay).

The fact that the military played a leading role in most of these cases cannot be overemphasized. Very deep, bitter disagreements surfaced and led to negotiations in which different factions auctioned their preferences. In different ways Argentina and especially Portugal represent extreme cases in which disagreements within the military threatened literally to blow up the very foundations of the state. However, circumstances did not have to get so much out of control to become a direct threat to the institution. In Brazil the military nearly came to blows, and in Ecuador it actually did. In Peru and in Uruguay the military could not agree on why it should continue in power. It is here that we find one other important aspect of the logic of transition at work—that is, a situation in which the military decides to dismantle the regime and install a new government for fear of its own institutional integrity. It should be noted that with the exception of the coup against Caetano, all the military coups and conspiracies taking place in the cases under review pitted one military faction against another. Consequently, the decision to install a new government and to extricate are essentially defensive military responses to authoritarian deterioration.

The Politics of Endgame

Having reviewed the logic of transition in the context of deterioration and breakdown, I now turn to find that combination of elements that leads to endgame and makes possible a successful implementation of the transition. In this context there are basically two configurations: endgame simultaneous with breakdown and a late endgame with a very conflictual implementation.

Conflicts of transitions are not merely systems of oppositions between civilians and military, even in cases of military extrication. There is, to be sure, one constant source of civil-military friction in those processes: the military's insistence on maintaining overall supervision of the process. This is an extension of the military's defensive response, not necessarily an institutional attempt to compromise the transition. Even in cases where the distance between the military and civil society is large, as in Argentina in 1983 or in Peru in 1979, there are other very relevant cleavages within the military that may be ignored only at great analytical cost. Military institution versus military government, aperturists versus obstructionists, and nationalists versus moderates (not to mention leftists versus rightists in Portugal) were three types of relevant military oppositions in the cases reviewed here.

The main patterns of oppositions found in the different cases at the time of the endgame are depicted in Table 1.5. The most significant events leading to endgame are excluded because they have been discussed already and involve, in most cases, some kind of obstructionist reaction to adverse electoral outcomes. Cleavages among civilian actors have been excluded

TABLE 1.5
Patterns of Oppositions Between Major Actors in Different Cases of Transition

Country	Civil-Military (Major Actors)	Intramilitary (Major Actors)
Argentina	demand for transition (Multipartidaria) the disappeared (human rights organizations) the economy (labor and employers organizations) amnesty (Multipartidaria and human rights organizations)	transition: aperturists vs. obstructionists (Viola, Bignone vs. Galtieri, Suárez Mason, Menéndez, Nicolaides); disaster of Malvinas (army vs. navy and air force)
Brazil	<u>distensão/abertura</u> executive-legislative relations rules of electoral competition (regime vs. opposition) economic model (labor and local entrepreneurs) amnesty (human rights organizations) treatment of marginal groups (Church, interest organizations)	choice of next president (government vs. military institution) restoration of rule of law (government vs. military hardliners)
Ecuador	tutelary role of the military in the transition (opposition parties) mechanics of transition (conservatives vs. populists)	oil policy and economic model (nationalists vs. moderates) transition (aperturists vs. obstructionists)
Peru	tutelary role of the military in the transition (political parties) economic policies (labor, students, peasants)	political economy model (Velasquista nationalists vs. moderates led by Morales Bermúdez)
Portugal	duality of power nature of the revolution mechanics of transition (MFA/junta/CR) tutelary role of the military (MFA/junta/CR)	transition, the new society (moderate and radical officers)
Uruguay	tutelary role of the military nature and mechanics of transition	transition (aperturists vs. obstructionists)

because these are focused on electoral contests and are described in considerable detail elsewhere in this text. The cases of Spain and the Dominican Republic have been excluded because they did not involve significant civil-military oppositions.

Whatever similarities may be gleaned from the details offered in Table 1.5 say little about how the logic of transition applies to endgames. Given the relatively small number of cases, the relationship between types of cleavages and patterns of transition (see Table 1.2) is not entirely clear. For example, there is a simultaneity in the case of Uruguay between cumulative civil-military cleavages and a negotiated transition. We find similar cleavages in Argentina where the transition was anything but a *salida pactada* (negotiated withdrawal). There is room for conjecture here but probably at the risk of missing more vital connections. I am referring to certain structural preconditions that narrow the choices of strategies of extrication and create relatively comparable scenarios of extrication through elections. Our evidence shows that elections tilt the process of implementation in favor of a democratic outcome.

Despite its aversion to politics and its loathing of certain political figures, the military of the different countries discussed herein did not have many choices in terms of legitimate strategies of extrication. Once the military settled on elections, it more or less decided the transition in favor of a democratic oucome. This was not a resolute, insightful action but rather a product of circumstance. With the exception of Brazil, no "official party" was in any kind of condition to put on a convincing electoral performance in favor of a continuation of the regime. There were no official parties to speak of in many cases, or if there were, they and the parties closer to the regime had suffered the onslaught of deterioration. Therefore, the electoral aspect of the logic of transition was dictated by the strength of the "revived" democratic parties as well as by the dearth of decent alternatives for continuism. The Brazilian military put on the most convincing show in this regard, but eventually it had to accept the inevitable. In essence, therefore, a genuinely competitive election is most likely to lead to a democratic outcome. But how does an election called for in less than ideal circumstances become genuinely competitive?

The government's ability to guarantee the physical integrity of the participants in the electoral process is a crucial element in ensuring a genuinely competitive election. This element appears to be a major difference between the successful cases reviewed here and others overcome by violence. The restoration of the rule of law is another critical aspect of implementation, an acid test of the transition, and an arena where the opposition may turn a controlled liberalization into a genuine transition. The indifference curves of risks for government and opposition may meet, and uncertainties about the authenticity and outcome of the process may be reduced.

Elections may and do become "efficacy tools" of transition if the government is able to fulfill this minimal obligation and if it begins to act more consistently and within the limits of its powers. Opposition reluctance to accept a process of transition as valid depends on many things, but opposition can be reduced if the government keeps its word regarding relatively modest commitments such as electoral timetables, campaigning, and voting safety. Even before the endgame has neutralized the more obnoxious obstructionists, an effective restoration of the rule of law—including, at least, a partial political amnesty and the return of exiles—will put a transition government on a collision course with the obstructionists and, by the same token, offer concrete proof to opposition democrats that the old regime is being dismantled. Our evidence suggests that a successful implementation of these measures is essential in order to increase the legitimacy and credibility of the transition; induce the opposition to participate; broaden the potential base of support for a coalition of aperturists; and create favorable conditions for the endgame. These conditions cannot be mimicked nor kept away from the public. They show whether there is a transition or not.

In addition, the very exertions of the obstructionists and the intensity of the ideological cleavages depicted in Table 1.5 suggest that even though the process of implementation may not have addressed substantively the entire transition agenda, the transition itself was not trivial. A detailed analysis of the conflicts involved in the endgames of these transitions should prove this point.

In essence, a decision to move away from a regime of exception in a capitalist state that does not imply a profound change in the political economy is bound to be linked to a strategy of extrication through elections. Given minimum guarantees about the integrity and authenticity of the elections and the simultaneous restoration of the rule of law, the opposition is bound to engage in the transition effort, make the elections competitive, and ultimately derail whatever project for a limited, controlled liberalization that may have existed. If and when this leads to confrontation with obstructionists, particularly in endgames taking place outside the military institution, the logic of transition prevails, and the obstructionists eventually are thwarted in their purpose. What follows, then, is a great irony not because it restores power to those civil actors who held it last (Fernando Belaúnde and his Acción Popular [Popular Action] party in Peru, the Socialists in Spain, or the Radicals in Argentina) but because it vindicates the lesson that there are no truly viable alternatives to civilized politics. This is the most important lesson of the logic of transition.

NOTES

1. The comparative analysis of transition has benefited from a number of important contributions. See, for example, Juan Linz, "The Transition from Authoritarian Regimes to Democratic Political Systems and the Problems of Consolidation of Political Democracy" (Paper presented at IPSA Tokyo Round Table, March 29–April 1, 1982), especially pp. 23–35. Leonardo Morlino, *Come Cambiano i Regimi Politici* (Milan: Franco Angeli, 1980); and, more recently, Leonardo Morlino, "Le instaurazioni democratiche nell' Europe Mediterranea: Alcune ipotesi comparata" (Revised version of a paper presented to the seminar, "La política comparada de la transición democrática" (University of Belgrano, Buenos Aires, August31–September 2, 1983), pp. 17–30. Adam Przeworski, "Some Problems in the Study of the Transition to Democracy" (Paper delivered at the workshop Prospects for Democracy in Latin America and Latin Europe, Wilson Center, Washington, D.C., September 24–26, 1979), pp. 4–11. Carlos Huneeus, "La transición a la democracia en España: Implicancias para América Latina" (Paper presented to the seminar La Eleción Española de 1982 y Sus Implicancias, Institute of Latin America Studies, University of North Carolina at Chapel Hill, May 22–26, 1983). Karen Remmer "Redemocratization and the Impact of Authoritarian Rule in Latin America," *Comparative Politics* 17, no. 3 (April 1985): 253–276. Eduardo Viola and Scott Mainwaring, "Transitions to Democracy: Brazil and Argentina in the 1980s," *Journal of International Affairs* 38, no. 2 (Winter 1985): 193–219. Salvador Giner, "Economía política y legitimación cultural en los orígenes de la democracia parlamentaria: El caso de Europa del Sur," in Julián Santamaría (ed.), *Transición a la Democracia en el Sur de Europa y América Latina* (Madrid: Centro de Investigaciones Sociológicas, 1982), pp. 11–58. Also see Federico G. Gil, Enrique A. Baloyra, and Lars Schoultz, "The Peaceful Transition to Democracy: Elections and the Restoration of Rights"; and Enrique A. Baloyra, "The Deterioration and Breakdown of Reactionary Despotism in Central America," Democracy in Latin America: Prospects and Implications, Papers no. 1 and 2 (Washington, D.C.: Department of State Contract 1722-020083, August and September 1981 respectively).

2. *Government*, *regime*, and *state* are defined in the Glossary.

3. For a discussion of these concepts, see Juan J. Linz, *Crisis, Breakdown, and Reequilibration* (Baltimore, Md.: Johns Hopkins University Press, 1978), pp. 16–23.

4. For more on this see Rafael del Aguila and Ricardo Montoro, *El Discurso Político en la Transición Española* (Madrid: Centro de Investigaciones Sociológicas and Siglo XXI de España, 1984), Chapter 2, especially pp. 35–63.

5. This is Carlos Floria's expression in *Guía para una Lectura de la Argentina Política* (Buenos Aires: ATEC, S.A., 1983), p. 72.

6. As with many aspects of the topic of transition, Dankwart A. Rustow pioneered the idea of stages in "Transition to Democracy: Toward a Dynamic Model," *Comparative Politics* 2, no. 3 (April 1970): 337–363. Carlos Huneeus followed this approach in "La primavera democrática en Portugal" and in "El reencuentro de España con la democracia," in Natalio Botana (ed.), *Los Caminos de la Democracia* (Santiago de Chile: Editorial Aconcagua, 1978), pp. 91–141 and 143–198 respectively. We followed this approach in Gil, Baloyra, and Schoultz, *op. cit.*, Part II, pp. 35–111, and found it useful in the discussion of cases but unwieldy and of diminishing

utility for comparative purposes. Basically, one almost has to differentiate as many patterns as there are cases. This compromises the validity of typologies of transition derived from the idea of stages.

7. Usage of inclusionary corporatism follows Alfred Stepan, *The State and Society: Peru in Comparative Perspective* (Princeton, N.J.: Princeton University Press, 1978), Chapter 3, particularly pp. 74–81.

8. Only Bolivia, El Salvador, and Guatemala offer comparable cases of conspiratorial alliances engaged in comparably high and effective levels of rightist violence against the transition. Not surprisingly, these cases are the most controversial and weakest of the recent cases of transition in Latin America. Their complexity requires separate, in-depth treatment exceeding the space available in this book.

9. This pattern is identified in the literature as a "transition from above." For example, Mainwaring and Viola apply this to the case of Brazil, *op. cit.*, pp. 202–206. Although essentially correct in identifying the origin and impetus for a particular blueprint of transition, this characterization may be misleading because it presumes a degree of control of the process that is not actually there.

10. This analysis of the Argentine case is a condensed version of Enrique Baloyra-Herp, "Argentina: ¿Transición o disolución?" (Paper delivered at the international seminar Transición a la Democracia en la Experiencia Comparada, University of Belgrano, Buenos Aires, August 31–September 2, 1983; and at the international seminar Procesos de Democratización y Consolidación de la Democracia, Center for the Study of Contemporary Reality, Academy of Christian Humanism, Santiago de Chile, April 9–12, 1984).

11. *Latin American Political Report* (LAPR) 13, no. 39 (October 5, 1979): 306, 308.

12. See *Latin America Regional Reports, Southern Cone,* (LARR-SC), RS-80-01 (February 1, 1980): 6.

13. This conflict emerged because hardliners such as Menéndez and General Carlos Suárez Mason, a rival of General Leopoldo Galtieri, to succeed Viola, became alarmed by the possibility of a transition. *LAPR* 13, no. 35 (September 7, 1979): 276.

14. *LARR-SC,* RS-80-03 (April 18, 1980): 2.

15. *Ibid.*, p. 5.

16. *Latin America Weekly Report* (LAWR), WR-80-16 (April 25, 1980): 7; *LAWR,* WR-80-17 (May 2, 1980): 1; and *LAWR,* WR-80-27 (July 11, 1980): 7.

17. *LAWR,* WR-80-28 (July 18, 1980): 1.

18. *LAWR,* WR-80-34 (August 29, 1980): 1.

19. See *LAWR,* WR-80-40 (October 10, 1980): 1; and *LARR-SC,* RS-80-08 (October 10, 1980): 6.

20. *LARR-SC.* RS-80-09 (November 14, 1980): 2; and *LAWR,* WR-80-42 (October 24, 1980): 7–8.

21. *LARR-SC,* RS-80-10 (December 19, 1980): 5–6.

22. *LARR-SC,* RS-81-01 (January 30, 1981): 1.

23. See Félix Luna, "El 'proceso' (1976–1982)," *Criterio* 55, nos. 1894–1895 (December 24, 1982): 742–743.

24. For the perspectives of the leaders of the Multipartidaria see Oscar Alende et al., *El Ocaso del Proceso* (Buenos Aires: El Cid Editor, 1981).

25. *LARR-SC*, RS-81-03 (April 10, 1981): 1–2. Also see *LAWR*, WR-81-14 (April 3, 1981): 10.

26. For a sample of Viola's difficulties during his "best moment" in June and July 1981, see *LAWR*, WR-81-24 (June 19, 1981): 4; *LAWR*, WR-81-27 (July 10, 1981): 2; *LAWR*, WR-81-28 (July 17, 1981): 3; *LAWR*, WR-81-29 (July 24, 1981): 4; and *LAWR*, WR-81-34 (August 28, 1981): 1.

27. See *LAWR*, WR-81-47 (November 27, 1986): 1; *LAWR*, WR-81-49 (December 11, 1981): 1; *LARR-SC*, RS-81-10 (December 18, 1981): 1–2; and *LAWR*, WR-81-50 (December 18, 1981): 1–2.

28. See *LAWR*, WR-82-01 (January 1, 1982): 1–2; and *LARR-SC*, RS-82-01 (January 29, 1982): 4–6.

29. *LAWR*, WR-82-02 (January 8, 1982): 1–2; and *LAWR*, WR-82-06 (February 5, 1982): 5–6.

30. *LARR-SC*, RS-82-02 (March 5, 1982): 4.

31. See *LAWR*, WR-82-25 (June 25, 1982): 1–2; *LAWR*, WR-82-26 (July 2, 1986): 1–2; and *LAWR*, WR-82-28 (July 16, 1982): 7–8.

32. *LAWR*, WR-82-29 (July 23, 1982): 7–8; *LARR-SC*, RS-82-06 (July 30, 1982): 7; *LAWR*, WR-82-33 (August 20, 1982): 5; *LAWR*, WR-82-34 (August 27, 1982): 1; and *LAWR*, WR-82-37 (September 24, 1982): 7.

33. *LARR-SC*, RS-82-07 (September 10, 1982): 2–3.

34. See Dardo Pérez Gilhou, "La amnistía," *Criterio* 56, no. 1901 (May 12, 1983): 190–191.

35. Figures from Alberto Spota, "Transición y pretensión de salida a la democracia en la Argentina" (Paper delivered at the international seminar La Elección Española de 1982 y Sus Implicancias, Institute of Latin American Studies, University of North Carolina at Chapel Hill, May 22–26, 1983), p. 71.

36. See *LAWR*, WR-82-38 (October 1, 1982): 7; and *LAWR*, WR-82-48 (December 10, 1982): 1.

37. *LARR-SC*, RS-82-09 (November 19, 1982): 7.

38. For the electoral aspect of the process and the installation of Raúl Alfonsín, see Chapter 5 in this book.

39. This is a revised version of the section on Ecuador featured in Gil, Baloyra, and Schoultz, *op. cit.*, Part II, pp. 73–80.

40. John D. Martz, "Ecuador: Authoritarianism, Personalism, and Dependency," in Howard J. Wiarda and Harvey F. Kline (eds.), *Latin American Politics and Development* (Boston: Houghton Mifflin, 1979), pp. 305–306.

41. The parties demanding a return to constitutionalism included the Conservative, Social Christian, Christian Democratic, Socialist, and Liberal parties plus the Partido Nacionalista Revolucionario (Nationalist Revolutionary party), the Federación Nacional Velasquista (National Velasquista Federation), and the Izquierda Democrática (Democratic Left). The Communist party continued to support Rodríguez Lara. *Latin America* 9, no. 35 (September 5, 1975): 1–2.

42. For the communiqués issued by both sides during the day, see *Foreign Broadcast Information Service, Latin America* (FBIS-LA), LAT-75-170 (September 2, 1975): G1-G11.

43. *Latin America* 9, no. 36 (September 12, 1975): 284–285.

44. *FBIS-LA*, LAT-75-175 (September 9, 1975): G2.

45. *Latin America* 9, no. 48 (December 5, 1975): 378.

46. *Latin America* 9, no. 49 (December 12, 1975): 385.

47. *Latin America* 10, no. 3 (January 16, 1976): 17.

48. For speculation about the ideological make up of the new government and of the members of the triumvirate, see *Latin America* 10, no. 4 (January 23, 1976): 29; and *Latin America* 10, no. 18 (April 30, 1976): 134–135.

49. *Latin America* 10, 7 (February 13, 1976): 53; and *Latin America* 10, 14 (April 2, 1976): 110–111.

50. *Latin America* 11, no. 19 (May 20, 1977): 146; *Latin America* 11, no. 41 (October 21, 1977): 326–327; *Latin America* 11, no. 42 (October 28, 1977): 329; and *Latin America Political Report* (LAPR) 12, no. 14 (April 14, 1978): 111.

51. *LAPR* 12, no. 3 (January 20, 1978): 20.

52. *LAPR* 12, no. 8 (February 24, 1978): 58.

53. *LAPR* 12, no. 24 (June 23, 1978): 186, 188.

54. *LAPR* 12, no. 28 (July 21, 1978): 217–218. For a more detailed discussion of the preelectoral maneuvers of the parties, the shortcomings of the Ecuadorian party system, and the implications of these elections, see John D. Martz, "The Quest for Popular Democracy in Ecuador," *Current History* 78, no. 454 (February 1980): 67–70.

55. This split coincided with one of the most enduring cleavages in Ecuadoran politics. See John D. Martz, *Ecuador: Conflicting Political Culture and the Quest for Progress* (Boston: Allyn and Bacon, 1972), pp. 16–41, 57–76, 147–163, 191–209. For a more comprehensive analysis of the elections of the Ecuadoran transition, see Facultad Latinoamericana de Ciencias Sociales, *Elecciones en Ecuador, 1978–1980: Análisis, Partidos, Resultados* (Bogotá: La Oveja Negra, 1982).

56. *LAPR* 12, no. 31 (August 11, 1978): 244.

57. *LAPR* 12, no. 49 (December 15, 1978): 391.

58. *LAPR* 13, no. 1 (January 5, 1979): 5–6; *LAPR* 13, no. 3 (January 19, 1979): 23; and *LAPR* 13, no. 7 (February 16, 1979): 55.

59. *LAPR* 13, no. 13 (March 30, 1979): 102–103.

60. *LAPR* 13, no. 17 (May 4, 1979): 1–2.

61. This is a revised version of the section on Portugal featured in Gil, Baloyra, and Schoultz, *op. cit.*, Part II, pp. 58–66. For contrasting views on the Salazar regime, see Michael Derrick, *The Portugal of Salazar* (New York: Campion Books, 1939); Peter Fryer and Patricia McGowan Pinheiro, *Oldest Ally: A Portrait of Salazar's Portugal* (Westport, Conn.: Greenwood Press, 1961; reprinted 1981); and Antonio de Figueiredo, *Portugal: Fifty Years of Dictatorship* (New York: Holmes and Meier, 1975). Also see Philippe C. Schmitter, "The 'Regime d'Exception' that Became the Rule: Forty-Eight Years of Authoritarian Domination in Portugal," in Lawrence S. Graham and Harry M. Makler (eds.), *Contemporary Portugal: The Revolution and Its Antecedents* (Austin: University of Texas Press, 1979), Chapter 1.

62. Jorge Campinos, "La transición del autoritarismo a la democracia en la Europa del Sur: El ejemplo portugués," in Santamaría, *op. cit.*, pp. 159–166. Also see de Figueiredo, *op. cit.*, Chapter 10.

63. For the dynamics within the armed forces that led to the coup see Douglas L. Wheeler, "The Military and the Portuguese Dictatorship, 1926–1974: 'The Honor

of the Army'"; and Lawrence S. Graham, "The Military in Politics: The Politicization of the Portuguese Armed Forces," in Graham and Makler, *op. cit.*, Chapters 6 and 7. Also see Philippe C. Schmitter, "Liberation by Golpe," *Armed Forces and Society* 2, no. 1 (January 1974): 85-131; and Rona M. Fields, *The Portuguese Revolution and the Armed Forces Movement* (New York: Praeger, 1976), especially Chapter 4.

64. See the Program of the MFA in Campinos, *op. cit.*, pp. 193–197. For an English version of this program and of other important documents of the time, see the appendices in Fields, *ibid.*, pp. 239–288.

65. For an English summary of this book, see U.S. Congress, House of Representatives, Committee on Foreign Affairs, Subcommittee on Africa, *The Complex of United States—Portuguese Relations: Before and After the Coup*, 93rd. cong., 2d. sess. (Washington, D.C.: U.S. Government Printing Office, 1974), Appendix 5, pp. 222–230.

66. The best discussion of the role of the PCE is still Eusebio Mujal-León, "The PCE and the Portuguese Revolution," *Problems of Communism* 26, no. 1 (January–February 1977): 21–41.

67. Campinos, *op. cit.*, pp. 185–188.

68. For further interpretation of the preferences of the Portuguese electorate during the transition, see John L. Hammond, "Electoral Behavior and Political Militancy," in Graham and Makler, *op. cit.*, Chapter 8.

69. Campinos, *op. cit.*, pp. 189–190; and Huneeus, *op. cit.*, pp. 127–128.

70. Huneeus, *ibid.*, p. 138.

71. For more on this, see Maria Helena Moreira Alves, *State and Opposition in Brazil* (Austin: University of Texas Press, 1985). Also see Juan J. Linz, "Opposition In and Under an Authoritarian Regime: The Case of Spain," in Robert A. Dahl (ed.), *Regimes and Oppositions* (New Haven, Conn.: Yale University Press, 1973), pp. 172–259.

72. Juan J. Linz, "An Authoritarian Regime: Spain," in Erik Allardt and Yrvo Littunen (eds.), *Mass Politics: Studies in Political Sociology* (New York: Free Press, 1970), pp. 255–257.

73. James C. Scott, *Weapons of the Weak: Everyday Forms of Peasant Resistance* (New Haven: Conn.: Yale University Press, 1986), especially pp. 289–303.

74. The classical formulation of this thesis was made by Samual P. Huntington, *Political Order in Changing Societies* (New Haven, Conn.: Yale University Press, 1968), Chapter 4.

75. For more on this see Chapter 2 in this book, and Przeworski, *op. cit.*, pp. 8–11.

76. For a discussion of these kinds of issues, see the two classic articles by Arendt Lijphart, "The Comparable-Cases Strategy in Comparative Research," *Comparative Political Studies* 8, no. 2 (July 1975), especially pp. 163–165; and "Comparative Politics and the Comparative Method," *American Political Science Review* 65, no. 3 (September 1971), especially pp. 685–690. Also see the discussion of "equivalence" in Adam Przeworski and Henry Teune, *The Logic of Comparative Social Inquiry* (New York: John Wiley & Sons, 1970), Chapter 6.

2
DEMOCRATIC ESTABLISHMENTS: A DIMENSIONAL ANALYSIS

Leonardo Morlino

This chapter is of necessity a synthetic analysis of a puzzling topic. How can we deal with as complex a phenomenon as the establishment of democracy in Western Europe and Latin America? The topic becomes even more puzzling if we intend to pay close attention, as we must, to several variations that occurred in each country during the process under scrutiny and if we seriously take into account the Western cases during the 1940s (Italy, Austria, West Germany, and France) and the 1970s (Portugal, Spain, and Greece) and a few Latin American cases since the mid-1970s (Argentina, Brazil, Peru, and Uruguay) at the same time.

The thesis developed here tries to overcome these various methodological problems by means of a dimensional analysis of the processes of establishment. Each dimension can be considered a sort of continuum with two poles, along which we may place each country. From the point of view of an individual country, the result is a unique configuration that emerges from such a multidimensional analysis. To put it another way, I suggest that in order to understand and explain those establishments in a comparative framework we should analyze the dimensions identified here. This chapter also intends to set the parameters of possible, future research.

SOME DEFINITIONS

In its initial phase the process of establishment overlaps the process of transition. By *transition* I mean, in a strict sense, the ambiguous, intermediate period when the previous regime has abandoned some of its nondemocratic structures without having acquired all the structures of the soon-to-emerge regime. This is a period of institutional flux and uncertainty during which the actors involved confront each other with different interests, projects, and political strategies. As in most cases one might consider and in all cases taken into account here (except for Germany), the "previous" regime is authoritarian.

The transition begins when the political and civil rights that characterize any liberal-democratic arrangement begin to gain open recognition and several formal and actual constraints on the manifestations of political pluralism are overcome. The transition period can be considered concluded when it becomes evident that the process of regime change has been undertaken or, more precisely, when the concrete possibilities of establishing a democracy appear clearly. This usually occurs when the first open, fair, and competitive elections are held in the country. However, in a few cases, the democratic direction of the process surfaces even earlier because some other key event, such as the legalization of the Communist party, occurs.

A *democratic establishment* is the process of installing a set of structures and rules that are common to and recurring in democratic regimes. Such a process of democratization begins during the transitional period and ends when all the structures and rules characterizing a democracy are in place. To clarify the point of arrival or, in other words, the result of the process, I will offer the following definition of *democracy*. By such a term I mean a mass, liberal democracy—that is, a set of institutions and rules that allow competition and participation for all citizens considered as equals. Empirically, such a political arrangement is characterized by free, fair, and recurring elections; male and female universal suffrage; multiple organizations of interests; different and alternative sources of information; and elections to fill the most relevant offices.[1] Behind such a set of institutions lies an accommodation, a compromise among social and political actors on the method and the rules for peaceful conflict resolution. Mass, liberal democracy also means the acceptance of opposition; acceptance of the possibility that lower social groups may mobilize; and acceptance of uncertainty regarding the outcomes of conflicts of interests.[2] Speaking in procedural terms, democracy implies certainty produced by predictable rules compounded by uncertainty on the outcome of decisions.

Transitions to democracy and processes of democratic establishment or democratizations characterize all the cases of regime change mentioned at the beginning of the chapter. But if we take into account some other recent (or fairly recent) Latin American cases, we should consider not only the transition to democracy, but also to "something else." Such a "something else" includes a limited democracy, a protected democracy, or an institutional hybrid. By *limited democracy* I mean a democratic arrangement where there are partial constraints on or limits to political rights (for example, the Communist party is illegal). A democracy can be considered *protected* when (whether limited or not) the armed forces support and condition the democracy, thus betraying a core rule of any democratic arrangement—civilian supremacy over military elites. The *institutional hybrid* is characterized by some change and opening of the previous authoritarian regime, but in this case the old elites and institutions basically do not change their roles.

In spite of the relevance of these three different results, they are not within the purview of this chapter.[3] Such alternative possibilities must be mentioned in order to stress that transitions to "something else" cannot be differentiated empirically from democratic transitions. Therefore, I am compelled to speak of only one process, which can be labeled liberalization. Given that in some cases mentioned previously liberalization was a prelude to democratization, let me define liberalization and democratization in relation to each other. *Liberalization* is the process of concession from above of greater and larger civil and political rights, never too large and complete, but of such a nature that allows authoritarian elites to control the civil society, both at elite and mass levels. Basically, liberalization brings about partial institutional change in an attempt to overcome the authoritarian crisis. Such a goal is attained by enlarging the regime's base of social support without giving up military rule completely. Actually, military leaders very often remain in key positions, at least in the economic structure of the country. In order to ensure some success, such a political hybrid must be able to count on the support of social and political elites, on the government's ability to limit mass participation, and on a possibly tenuous appeal of the Western democratic model among the elites. Such a process had notable success in Brazil, where liberalization was initiated after the elections in 1974, which showed the unpopularity of the military government at the mass level, and concluded with democratization at the beginning of 1985.

The term *democratization* refers to a very different process, which can be alternative or subsequent to liberalization. This process is marked by the real recognition of civil and political rights and, where necessary, by a complete transformation in the service of a reconstruction of civil society. Political parties and a party system emerge. The organization of interest groups, such as labor unions, takes place. The elaboration, or adoption, of the principal democratic institutions and procedures that will characterize the regime, such as electoral laws and a specified relationship between executive and legislative powers, occurs.

LESSONS FROM PREVIOUS DEMOCRATIZATIONS

Before examining the main aspects of and variations in the democratization process, it is useful to consider the lessons that may be drawn from the first democratizations, such as the Northern European cases. Four crucial conditions relevant in every establishment can be identified.[4] First is national unity. All the complications deriving from regional, autonomist, or even separatist demands must be overcome. In fact, societies comprising plural and multiethnic states have had to face many virtually insuperable difficulties as a result (for instance, Africa at the time democratic regimes were established following decolonization). On the other hand, this problem also existed (and continues to exist) in Spain, but a successful establishment and consolidation occurred nevertheless. Therefore, the existence of national unity is an important condition, but neither a necessary nor a sufficient one.

The second condition is social equality. By this I mean how a plural society can manage the social question and rectify or prevent extreme inequality through the diffusion and distribution of resources. At issue here is whether agreement and compromise will prevail in handling this politically relevant issue and thereby avoid extreme polarization and conflict that could lead to civil war.

The third condition—elite agreement—requires the formation and reproduction of consensus regarding democratic compromise among the key decisionmakers in the society. We look here for a pact made possible by elites realizing the harmful effects of the "negative games" resulting from their failure to compromise. (The Venezuelan experience of 1957–1960 is instructive in this regard.) In addition, elites must perceive viable solutions that do not include civil war or separation. Such perceptions (and subsequent acceptance of these solutions) can occur if a strong sense of national community exists, as is the case of plural societies supported by consociational democracies;[5] if there is a cultural tradition in which the use of violence has been discarded; or if recent, diffuse memories of violence and its related moral costs still are deeply embedded in the psyche of the elite.

In the fourth condition—democratic viability—it is not necessary that democratic compromise be considered the best possible solution by all the actors. It is only necessary that the transition's protagonists accept that compromise as an expedient, pragmatic, and preferable solution.

THE MODALITIES OF DEMOCRATIC ESTABLISHMENT

Table 2.1 attempts to identify the ways in which democratic establishments take place. As can be seen, such identification requires the consideration of at least nine dimensions, their constituent categories, and their combinatory probabilities, all of which enable us to discern the particular multidimensional configuration of each establishment as well as each resulting democratic arrangement. The dimensions and their categories do not correspond to abstract hypotheses; on the contrary, I have included only the relevant empirical aspects of the cases that have taken place in Western Europe and in Latin America.

TABLE 2.1
Dimensions in Democratic Establishments

Dimensions
A. Duration brief (one year) or long (more than three years)
B. Extent of violence absent or present
C. Actors c1 external or c2 internal in power or c3 internal in power + internal opposition or c4 opposition or c5 external + opposition
D. Presence of military d1 completely absent or d2 passive neutrality or d3 favorable politicization or d4 unfavorable politicization
E. Type of agreement e1 implicit or explicit or e2 procedures only or procedures and policies
F. Degree of formalization of the agreement constitutional or other
G. Degree of participation high or low
H. Spectrum of emerging political forces wide and complete or partial and incomplete
I. Structure and personnel in administration and judiciary continuous or discontinuous

Beginning with the modalities and forms of establishment, the duration of the process is relevant only to the extent that it serves as a basic frame of reference for the other aspects of the process. A proposed interval of between one and more than three years contrasts the ease and rapidity in reaching institutional solutions and the delays that had to be overcome. In Greece, for example, a few months (July–December 1974) were sufficient to conclude the establishment. In Spain almost two years passed from the Ley de Reforma Política (Law of Political Reform) approved by referendum in December 1976 to the definitive approval of the constitution on October 31, 1978. The importance of the degree to which the process has been peaceful or filled with violence cannot be overstated. A peaceful process makes a successful establishment more probable and thus brings a successful regime consolidation to fruition.

With regard to the actors—the core feature of democratic establishment—one must distinguish clearly between the actors leading the transition and those who are the protagonists of the democratic establishment. Actually, in a few cases, different actors played different roles or different roles were played by the same actors during the two phases. For Western Europe, the obvious examples of external and international actors during and after World War II are Germany, Italy, and France.

The international factor catalyzes actors inside the existing nondemocratic regime and pushes them to initiate the transition and, eventually, the establishment. I have in mind, for example, the impact of colonial war on the lower-ranking officers in the Portuguese army. In April 1974, in response to the long duration of the colonial wars in Guinea-Bissau, Mozambique, and Angola; the costs of these wars; the lack of prospects for success; and the inability of high-ranking officers and government officials to break such an impasse, lower grade officers deposed the old regime. In July 1974, as a result of the immediate and disruptive effect of their military defeat in Cyprus, high-ranking Greek military leaders turned over the reins of government to an exiled civililan leader, Constantin Karamanlis. A third case is provided by the defeat of Argentina in the 1982 Falklands-Malvinas War, which accelerated the disintegration of the military regime in that country. Another kind of external influence, which is much more difficult to clarify empirically, is the role played by democratic regimes in the democratization of countries under authoritarian rule in their own geopolitical area.

Domestic institutional actors include the armed forces, the government, the bureaucracy of the authoritarian regime, and, generally, authoritarian political forces that decided to try managing and controlling the process of establishment. Institutional actors tend to play a more central and leading role during the transition than during the establishment. In the final phases of the installation process, forces such as the monarchy are not always able to control the changes. Frequently, the moderate governmental and non-governmental actors of the authoritarian regime and a part of the opposition forge an effective coalition dedicated to change. Both groups are beset by problems among themselves and with other authoritarian forces and more extreme oppositions. The formation of such a coalition can lay the foundations of the transition and, subsequently, of the establishment. Once the establishment already has begun and the first elections have taken place, political actors of the previous regime have to be integrated fully into the democratic process and must achieve their representation through the electoral mechanisms of the new regime.

It is rare to see opposition forces take over the process of transition to democracy during a period of authoritarian domination and become the protagonists of change. If the opposition becomes the main actor in the transitional phase, it is invariably an armed opposition, and the result is not a democratic regime. Opposition forces have become the leading actors of establishment in several cases when the transition has been led by external forces or by domestic institutional actors. In the clearest example of this type, the opposition led the establishment of the French Fourth Republic following World War II. Cases of transition led by domestic institutional actors are Greece, where the establishment was conducted by rightist moderates led by Karamanlis; Argentina, when Raúl Alfonsín assumed the presidency following the election of October 1983; and other Latin American cases such as Ecuador in 1979, Peru in 1980, Bolivia in 1982, and Uruguay and Brazil in 1985.[6]

Beyond the first four possibilities contemplated in category C in Table 2.1, it is possible to see mixed paths—for example, the interaction of external actors (C1) and a domestic coalition (C3). But it is more likely that such an interaction would join external actors with the domestic opposition during both the transition and the establishment. For example, despite contrary indications, this could be a probable path to democratization in Chile. In this scenario, the United States would play an unusual role as active promoter of democratization.[7]

Whatever its role in the establishment, leading or secondary, active or passive, the military is important in this process because, among other things, it holds a monopoly on coercive power. The least complicated cases of establishment are those that proceed from military defeats (Greece and Argentina), profound internal division (Portugal), or even a completely disorganized structure (Italy). The most difficult cases are those in which the army remains intact and untouched during the change, particularly with regard to status and social prestige. In fact, after an initial, passive neutrality, factions of the armed forces can become politicized in opposition to the democratic regime. One may recall, for example, the confused attempt to overthrow the government in Spain on February 23, 1981. Whatever the case, a completely successful democratic establishment is unthinkable unless the military accepts a subordinate role to that of the civilians. Thus, even if military leaders support the democratic regime, they are potentially dangerous, and they may try to maintain at least partial control of the political process. Such a result is more probable if there is a serious crisis during establishment or if there are recurring crises in its aftermath. The classically unfortunate case, in this regard, is that of Turkey in the 1960s and 1970s.

When military leaders hold the establishment process under their control, thereby conditioning its various phases, or when they leave political power in the hands of the civilians but maintain the armed forces' internal structure, the most likely result is a difficult establishment that is long and complicated—Portugal after the "coup" in 1974, or, more recently, Brazil—or else an unstable democratic regime, such as in Bolivia, Peru, and Ecuador. Thus, if there is a politicization of the army contrary to the democratic regime, a successful democratization is impossible. Indeed, such a politicization would compromise the establishment from the very beginning. It is worth repeating that democratization only may be initiated and carried out if the coercive arena does not become a battleground. Problems in this arena, for the most part, must be solved previously or, in the worst cases, in the initial stages of transition. The use of coercion must be abandoned a priori. This is one of the key features of the democratic compromise.

Another crucial aspect of the process is the formation of the founding coalition of the regime. Such a coalition is factual, and it results from the coming together of diverse political and sociopolitical actors during the transition. The term *coalition* is used here in a broad sense inasmuch as the agreement that is at the base of the coalition may be tacit and implicit, accepted factually, or imposed by other political forces (in a few recent Latin American cases such an agreement or pact was not explicit). Establishment has a much greater chance for success and the possibility for consolidation increases in an analogous manner when the founding coalition is broad and when all the present, politically active forces of the country are participating in the agreement.

Philippe Schmitter has described the main features of such accommodations or pacts. They are the result of a bargaining process between elites and institutions; they tend to reduce competition and conflict, at least at the beginning; they strive to control the policy agenda; they distort the democratic tenet concerning the equality of citizens; they change power relationships in the long run; they start a new political process; and they have different, even unintended, results.[8] Such agreements, even when implicit, acknowledge the possibility and legitimacy of different political and ideological standpoints; these agreements constitute the moment and the place where the "mutual guarantees" described by Robert Dahl are requested and granted.[9] Such guarantees are at the core of democratic compromise.

The degree of formalization of the agreement about the electoral rules depends on the scope and articulation of the constitutional process, the diversity of the political forces, and the nature of the formal document that concludes the agreement. Significant formalization will be more likely if the previous authoritarian regime lasted a long time and if another constitution, which was not abrogated by the authoritarian regime, still is considered valid. The constitutional arena and other more informal arenas create opportunities for stipulating institutional compromise and for proclaiming a set of values, whether ambiguous or well articulated, with which the various political actors identify. Finally, the more formal arena of the constitutional process or other less official, less visible arenas can provide opportunities for reaching a consensus on substantive political issues; for a partial accommodation of class conflict (including monetary, wage, and fiscal matters); or for an acceptable solution to center-periphery conflicts regarding regional autonomy.

Not every political force will participate when the constitutional process is weak or poorly organized at the beginning of establishment. The constitutional act also may be concerned with solving a few substantive, actual conflicts as well as articulating the rules of the game. In this case, there might be additional reasons for political conflict. In fact, the actors harmed by those provisions immediately will begin to institute a procedure for revising and redrafting the constitutional document. This is exactly what took place in Portugal between the end of 1976 and June 1982.

There are two other qualifying elements of establishment that are related strictly to each other but also are connected with the previous dimension. In the case of the spectrum of emerging political forces (category H in Table 2.1) it is necessary to determine what political forces are more or less present and organized when the transition begins and what exist when the establishment begins. If one assumes—as can be done plausibly in most of countries with such experiences—that class conflict is the most relevant political cleavage and that it prevails over other cleavages, it is necessary to determine which actors on the left-right spectrum are present and active as protagonists or partners in the mentioned agreements. Cases may arise in which actors of the political Left are present and organized, while those of the Right are not; or the exact reverse might be true. There may be cases in which leftist and rightist actors are present. From the point of view of the success (if not the rapidity) of establishment and of the probability of consolidation, only the last hypothesis is empirically the most favorable one.

This consideration leads to another that has not received careful attention. The coalition founding the regime can modify itself during the period of establishment, which leads to outcomes different from those foreseen initially. Portugal is the clearest example in this regard. When the establishment began, almost immediately after the overthrow of the authoritarian government in April 1974, the coalition at the base of the regime that was being formed consisted of lower-ranking military leaders with communist leanings, Socialists, and leftist parties. Within two years the situation changed radically. In fact, the Right and the moderate center-right organized politically, and an alliance was formed among civilian forces that included Socialists and the moderate sectors of the military. The result was the marginalization of the military, communist sympathizers, and the Communists led by Alvaro Cunhal, who left the coalition. The regime itself veered more clearly toward a classic democratic course. Therefore, the terms and the forms of the agreements, the protagonists, and the political resources in the political arena can be modified, partially or deeply (during the establishment), with consequences that are relevant for the entire process of establishment.

During the process that I have been analyzing, elites play the central role, including the elites of the previous regime and those of the opposition. New elite forces also enter the scene. Therefore, the "game" is being played by a few leaders whose choices count enormously for the future of the country. Very often, however, in the transitional phase and in the initial phases of establishment, or in the subsequent phase, there is a more or less extensive and intensive degree of mass participation. When this occurs, that participation usually manifests as demonstrations, strikes, and sometimes, acts of collective violence. Thus, it is relatively easy to measure the trends and styles of mass participation accompanying the transition. Mass participation can introduce influences that will be used by the elite actors in the confrontations maintained during the establishment in spite of the agreements already in effect. The campaign for the first elections are the best occasions for those "shows of force," particularly when the real depth of support for various actors is not yet clear.

The last aspect that characterizes the establishment is the degree of continuity that is maintained with the administrative and judiciary structures of the previous regime, particularly as that continuity is linked with the mode in which the crisis of the old regime and its transformation took place. Various problems appear at this stage that include purging high-level officials in the administrative and judiciary sectors as well as in the apparatus of suppression (intelligence agencies, police, and military) and placing in key positions persons whose loyalty toward the new institutional arrangements will not be in question. The resolutions to these problems have profound implications for the legitimation of the regime.

These problems are without expedient, clearcut solutions. On the one hand, greater continuity with the previous regime can make the new regime more palatable and less painful to those sectors more closely identified with the former. On the other hand, a major normative discontinuity makes the new institutions more legitimate for the social groups connected with the previous opposition and, therefore, excluded from the previous regime. The solution is very often a nonsolution, an accommodation between the two, or a continuity. The other solution, a much rarer one, is found only in the case of change characterized by a strong break or rupture with the past. Portugal in 1974 is again a good example, and one might add the German case, although with various elements of continuity.

As I suggested at the beginning of this chapter, a close, deeper analysis of these dimensions would yield the specific multidimensional configuration of the democratic establishment in each country and a full account of the process of establishment. In my opinion, this is a sound way of analyzing this phenomenon. However, it also is possible to sketch out two "polar" models of establishment—a *reforma* (reform) model and a *ruptura* (rupture) model—and then to place each empirical case within the continuum defined by these two poles.

Before illustrating the two models, I would like to stress, first, that these models cannot establish a clearcut distinction between transition and establishment. As a result, these two partially overlapping phenomena are considered together. Second, I do not see any necessary empirical consistency among the various dimensions that characterize the models. However, the *reforma* model would be marked by (1) a long duration; (2) a relative absence of violence; (3) a key role played by internal actors and incumbents of the previous regime; (4) a (possibly) relevant role for the armed forces; (5) an implicit agreement with little formalization; (6) little mass participation; (7) a partial, incomplete presence of political forces at the beginning of the process; and (8) strong continuity of the structures and personnel of the previous regime (see Table 2.1). By contrast, the *ruptura* model would be characterized by (1) a short duration; (2) a high incidence of violence; (3) a key role played by the democratic opposition; (4) the absence of the armed forces; (5) an explicit, highly formalized agreement; (6) a high level of mass participation; (7) a wide spectrum of political forces active in the process; and (8) a strong discontinuity in the structures and personnel of the previous regime.

One could stress that the two most distinctive features of the models are the roles played by different actors and the continuity/discontinuity dimension. In all probability the transition period is the ideal context in which to make this distinction. In other words, change may begin by following the rules of the previous authoritarianism, as in Spain, or by breaking them with a coup d'état, as in Portugal, or in some other way. As is normally the case in empirical analysis, most of the actual cases show elements of both that could be labeled *rupturas pactadas*—a sort of "agreed upon ruptures"—or *reformas* with *ruptura*—that is, reform with some strong elements of rupture.

Typologies of Democratic Establishments

Recent empirical attempts to build typologies of democratic regimes have focused on democratic systems established a long time ago.[10] Such analyses are very helpful, but we still lack a comparable attempt that emphasizes the new democracies of Southern Europe and Latin America. The first step in such an attempt would require an empirical analysis of each democratic arrangement in which the establishment has been completed. Given this lack of comparative, preliminary spadework, I shall not pay attention to the democratic systems effectively established in the countries mentioned at the beginning of this chapter. I shall not consider, for example, the

TABLE 2.2
Democratic Establishments: Developmental Factors

A. Political tradition
- a1 form of government: monarchical or republican
- a2 conflictual experience: scant and remote or frequent and recent

B. Previous experience with mass politics
- b1 intensity and diffusion
- b2 duration

C. Type of previous regime
- c1 competitive oligarchy
- c2 colonial
- c3 military authoritarian
- c4 bureaucratic authoritarian
- c5 corporate authoritarian
- c6 mobilizational authoritarian
- c7 totalitarian

D. Duration of previous regime
less than ten years or more than forty years

E. Reasons for collapse/change of previous regime
- e1 profound socioeconomic transformations
- e2 economic failure
- e3 military defeat
- e4 divisions in the dominant coalition for other reasons

F. Degree of organization of opposition in the previous regime
low or high

G. Modalities or transition
- g1 continuity or discontinuity
- g2 participation: low or high
- g3 violence: low or high
- g4 duration: brief or long

concrete modalities through which the channels of articulation of interests are restructured, particularly those interests that succeed in organizing collectively and profit from the new areas of freedom and action assured by respect for civil rights; the organization of party structures; the characteristics of the electoral system; the institutions that specify the relationships between the legislative and executive powers; or other features that could be taken into consideration.

I shall try to address the major problem of how to explain variations in outcomes in the democracies actually established, especially the variations in the modalities of development of the establishment itself (see Table 2.2). The empirical studies that analyze this problem in depth are very few. Therefore, I will utilize my own research to identify what I believe are some prominent explanatory factors. First, it is necessary to mention the political traditions of the country, particularly two specific aspects of those traditions. One is the form of government, which in the European cases may be reduced to the presence or absence of a monarchical tradition. This is intimately related to the classical institutional problem of monarchy versus republic. Although this institutional problem is not relevant in Latin America, it did exist in Japan after World War II and was resolved by means of a substantial transformation of the imperial institution into a formal power without the divine right that it previously enjoyed. This same problem was resolved positively in Spain during 1975–1976 with the maintenance of the monarchy in a seemingly formal position. Actually, this resolution legitimized the new democratic regime among high-ranking military officers and the most conservative social sectors. In Italy and Greece this issue was resolved in favor of a republican outcome through referenda. In Italy the 1946 referendum was hard fought, and the outcome was uncertain until the very end. In 1974 another referendum posed the question with results more favorable to the republican option. Italy thus became the only country with one and then two small monarchical parties and with a monarchical component still embedded in the political Right thirty years after the democratic establishment.

The second aspect—whether any previous violent and conflicting experiences, perhaps as extreme as civil war, remain deeply rooted in the collective memory—is of more general importance. Such experiences tend to have a moderating impact on the behavior of the elites of the future democracy. The more significant cases involving civil war are Spain in the 1930s and Greece in the 1940s. There is little doubt that memories of the enormous human costs of those past experiences were determining influences on the elites' willingness to compromise. At the mass level, memories of such previous experiences, even if conflict did not escalate to civil war, can have that moderating impact as well. It is also possible that the previous authoritarian experience may have been the result of a failure to reach a compromise that avoided violence and civil war, especially if the previous regime emerged in the aftermath of such traumatic events.

Previous experiences with mass political participation deserve a separate analysis. In cases where such participation was sustained consistently for relatively long periods of time we should treat the new establishment as a redemocratization. The distinctive term *redemocratization* indicates that there has been a mass, liberal democracy characterized by civil liberties; universal male suffrage (at least); mass parties (which were substantially organized at a local or national level); labor unions and other interest associations; mass mobilization; party identifications; and relatively structured mass political involvements. The key point to stress is that such a liberal democratic experience legitimized a conception of politics different from the notion of politics as a "business" for an oligarchy with a higher social status.

Previous democratic experience, therefore, affects deeply the new democratic arrangements; it is part of the historical memory of the people preserved, in turn, by the mechanisms of political socialization. These memories are difficult but not impossible to measure empirically. For example, one could study the continuity between the previous democratic experience and the new one in terms of party leadership, party organization, electoral strength, or even the continuities of other collective organizations that characterize every mass democracy.

A more accurate evaluation of this macrofactor is possible if one simultaneously considers two intervening variables. These are the duration and type of the authoritarian experience that took place in between democratic regimes. The time elapsed since the previous democratic experience and the characteristics of the subsequent authoritarian regime affect the current experience with mass politics. It is more significant for the new democratic regime if the last one was long-lasting, very diffuse, and deep and if the authoritarian parenthesis was shorter and its regime weaker.

The importance of this macrofactor is analogous to the hypothesis known in the literature on political parties as the "freezing proposition." According to Seymour Martin Lipset and the late Stein Rokkan, the Western European party systems of the 1960s (with few significant exceptions) reflect the cleavage structures of the 1920s. Lipset and Rokkan contended that the party organizations themselves were older than the majority of their national electorates.[11] The extended version of the Lipset-Rokkan hypothesis proposed here is that a political experience with party organizations of a mass nature "freezes" allegiances and alignments in such a way that they are able to survive, as if in hibernation, throughout the authoritarian period; they then reappear in the initial phase of the new regime and manifest themselves clearly in the first democratic elections. It seems worthwhile to be more precise about this complex phenomenon.

The influence of past experiences with mass politics on a democratic establishment can be viewed in two ways. The first is through the representative institutions that emerge and the second through the parties and the party system that are formed. The institutional choices made at the beginning of an establishment are influenced by the restoration of the old institutions or by the "lessons" derived from the deficiencies and failures of the previous democratic institutions. The myths and propaganda of the subsequent authoritarian regime are also at play here, particularly among the leadership. The example of West Germany illustrates this point more clearly. In fact, Germany had a deep, extensive experience of mass democracy before the Nazi seizure of power. It is sufficient in this regard to recall the controversy about how the pure proportional system may or may have not been at the origin of the crisis and fall of the Weimar Republic. The strongly negative evaluations regarding those institutions suggest why, for example, the new democratic leadership in West Germany adopted a system that established a minimum threshold of 5 percent for party representation in Parliament. It also is easier to understand why the leadership introduced innovations such as the constructive vote of "no confidence" and the increased powers of the prime minister. All these improvements over the Weimar system were designed to limit the incidence and impact of parliamentary crises and to make the parliamentary institution more efficacious.

In the case of parties and the party system, some of their leadership is likely to consist of leaders from the previous democratic period—perhaps persons who have been in opposition for a long time, even in exile or in prison. In addition, the population still will hold the memory of the parties and their newspapers and propaganda as well as maintain identifications transmitted through the family. Finally, in the political turmoil created by the fall or change of the authoritarian regime the most natural occurrence will be the recreation of the old democratic-era parties, some of which may have survived underground during the authoritarian interlude.

The reconstitution of parties with the same names, even with the same leaders and similar bases of electoral power, does not signify, however, the formation of the same party systems. Duration and type of authoritarian experience will influence party formation. It is difficult to imagine that the authoritarian experience could pass without leaving a deep imprint in this regard. Usually, the authoritarian regime (and the miliary intervention that gave rise to it) had a strong antiparty bias that took the form of relentless propaganda and the repression of party activists. Thus, the lessons derived from the crisis and collapse of the previous democratic regime act to moderate the renewed political forces. Finally, other elements, such as profound socioeconomic transformations, have a bearing on the configuration of the parties and the party system.

Argentina provides an interesting example of these dynamics. There, the short time since the last democratic experience (which ended in 1976); the type of military regime; the profound experience with mass politics (which also was democratic in character and began as early as 1955); and the application of similar electoral formulas and institutional arrangements augured a strong continuity of parties and the party system. It turned out just that way in the sense that the two leading parties remained the same: the predominantly middle-class Unión Cívica Radical (Radical Civic Union) and the labor-based Peronist (also known in Argentina as Justicialist) party. But the traditional correlation of electoral strength was reversed. The ambiguous, sometimes conniving actions of the unions at the beginning of the last authoritarian period and the economic crisis caused by the military regime (to mention but two important factors) contributed to a Radical victory in the elections of October 1983 that reversed a Peronist electoral dominance of forty years.

PREVIOUS AUTHORITARIANISMS AND THEIR CRISES

The impact of the authoritarian regime on the process of establishment is obvious but requires some elaboration. Suffice it to note that the first element listed in Table 2.2 that describes this impact (C1, or competitive oligarchy) corresponds to the experience of the first democratization and, therefore, should be brought back to this ambit. The second corresponds to the usually fruitless attempts at democratization following decolonization. Among the rare examples that one can cite to the contrary is India, which would deserve a separate analysis. The only case of transition from totalitarianism to democracy is that of Germany. Nevertheless, the Germany of Hitler, in terms of territory and population, was a completely different entity from present-day West Germany. The majority of the other cases of transition to democracy have, as a starting point, authoritarian regimes of diverse types.[12] Regarding the significant characteristics of authoritarian regimes and their possible interaction with different modes of establishment, the possibilities are too vast to discuss here. Attention will be limited to the two significant variables and their impacts: namely, the degree to which an authoritarian regime mobilizes, organizes, and controls the civilian society and its participation; and the extent to which the regime has altered not only the social structure but also its patterns of political identification.

An official party with its diverse articulation is the principal vehicle of participation. Through socialization and resocialization processes new political allegiances and identifications are created that may be very persistent. Such identifications overlap with the possible preceding democratic experience, and they can survive in the new, equally democratic reality. In Italy, for example, the participation and loyalty elicited by the Partito Nazionale Fascista (National Fascist party) for twenty years and then repeated in the few months of the Repubblica Sociale di Salo (Social Republic of Salo) are found again in the electoral followers of the Movimento Sociale Italiano (Italian Social Movement), which has continued to survive for several decades after the end of the war.

The authoritarian regime also can be characterized by a complex set of structures that, on the whole, may be labeled authoritarian corporatism. In Portugal the articulated corporate apparatus was renovated after 1974 but not dismantled altogether. The new associations and the cooperatives that have substituted for the various *gremios* (guilds) in commerce or in agriculture—the *gremios da lavoura* (labor guilds) and the *casas de povo* (people's homes)—have the patrimony and the social and economic tasks of the old corporate organs. Sometimes, the same personnel remained in those organs. If for more than forty years, as happened in Portugal, a similar, capillary state structure has performed functions of representation and articulation of interests, the dismantling of that structure does not result in a vacuum; instead, the previously existing mechanisms remain, and an analogous form of corporatism will survive, but without the previous aura of state legitimacy.

The second variable measuring impact of a previous regime on the partisan aspect of politics refers to the extent to which the authoritarian regime was able to destroy previous social and political identifications through the single official party and through a systematic suppression of opposition of any kind. Such destructions affect the following establishment because they make the activation of civil society after the authoritarian breakdown a more difficult, slow, and uncertain process. In other words, these destructions can leave a weakened civil society behind that really is not ready to reorganize itself and to find patterns of solidarity and cohesion. In this case it is more likely that the extent of participation during the transition and establishment will be minimal and that political forces will emerge only partially (see "G" and "H" in Table 2.1). The problem of societal weakness has important interactive effects with problems of continuity/discontinuity of the repressive apparatus, and an analysis of the former helps clarify how purging and transforming these structures complicate the democratic establishment.

The importance of the duration of the authoritarian regime as an intervening variable already has been mentioned. Salazar's Portugal constitutes the example of the longest duration of an authoritarian regime: forty-eight years between the coups of 1926 and 1974. There are also cases of brief authoritarian interruptions and cases in which a short authoritarian interlude is attached to an equally brief democratic experiement. These are really cases of chronic incapacity for consolidation of any regime, particularly in Latin America after World War II.[13]

The reasons for the collapse or the gradual deterioration of authoritarian regimes require elaboration in order to identify the contingencies of a democratic establishment and to anticipate the problems the new regime will encounter. The key question is what are the actual operative causes of the authoritarian crisis. The first likely answer is suggested by what may be construed as a general hypothesis: The conditions for an authoritarian crisis are set up when the dominant coalition of actors that supports the regime begins breaking down or already has broken down. Stated differently, when the pact that forms the basis for the authoritarian regime has broken down, the regime is likely to deteriorate.

This hypothesis requires further elaboration. To begin with, I exclude the logical, but empirically indefensible possibility that in a relatively short period an alternative coalition could arise that is endowed with new coercive resources sufficient to engage in a victorious struggle against the established authoritarian regime. This would be the case, for example, if a rapid, overwhelmingly armed mobilization of numerically substantial rural or urban masses, headed by a leader or a small group and capable of defeating the armed forces, occurred. One also may exclude the possibility that the coalition in crisis may reequilibrate itself simply by removing certain actors and replacing them with others.

It is necessary to bear in mind the connections among the actors in a coalition as well as the process of institutionalization that might have taken place in the regime and the subsequent estrangement between state institutions and some politically relevant social groups in the coalition. State institutions will seek to consolidate themselves, which implies that military and bureaucratic elites will tend to separate themselves from the other actors in the coalition, thereby rendering it less cohesive. For example, this separation will have limited impact if the regime really has institutionalized itself and gained complete control of the coercive arena, some sort of mass legitimacy, or, in any case, passive support or diffused apathy. This is not, however, a recurrent, common case in Latin American countries. Instead, these coalitions are not very cohesive, they remain fluid, and they are poor in terms of resources. Objective, internal conflicts of interest further weaken and make ambiguous the pacts at the base of the coalition; and there are divisions and potential conflicts among the institutional agents themselves and among the military in particular. This is all the more true when the regime has difficulty in securing its own mass legitimization because middle- and working-class social groups already have created their own organizations and developed democratic forms of political participation. However, in such a case authoritarian rulers may pursue a pseudodemocratic legitimization through bogus elections, forced referenda, or puppet parliaments.

The Causes of Authoritarian Crises

What are the causes of authoritarian crisis in these kinds of situations? If the authoritarian regime was able to consolidate itself, one should consider long-term causes as well as factors more close at hand. Conversely, if authoritarian consolidation was not achieved, then the middle- and short-run factors should be emphasized. In the former case the crisis may stem from three possibilities. First, if there are transformations in the structure and then in the preferences and choices of social and economic groups that participate in the dominant authoritarian coalition, then those groups will strive to transform the coalition. Second, these transformations may bring some actors out of that coalition who then may become active or passive opponents of the regime. The transformations also may cause internal strains, conflicts, and demands for a restructuring of the regime. Third, socioeconomic transformations may make previously excluded actors more influential and increase their coercive capability, which they may use to mobilize against the regime.

Basically, one must look at how socioeconomic transformations may have affected the dominant coalition and its political structures. Analysis of the Spanish and Portuguese crises would illustrate the analytical possibilities of this approach. I am referring, for example, to social and economic changes that transform the resources of some actors in the potentially dominant coalition and that can induce them to seek a renegotiation within the coalition or even to ask for transformations in, or of, the regime. There can be drastic attitudinal changes on the part of relevant actors in the coalition together with an actual change of the leaders in power.

In the case of short- and medium-run factors, the breakdown or gradual erosion of the dominant coalition is due primarily to four causes. First are divisions within the armed forces that result from private struggles for power, leadership problems, or difficulties in carrying out certain policies. This might be the case in Chile, if the military institution should turn against the policies and the person of General Augusto Pinochet.

Second, divisions between the armed forces as a whole and civilian actors in the coalition may cause regime breakdown. Civilians may want to affirm their rule inside the coalition; policies supported by civilians may fail to attain the law and order objectives of the armed forces; or once those objectives are attained, the military no longer is willing to bear and to impose upon others the economic and human costs of those civilian policies. Thus, the military may reconsider the costs of its presence in power and may withdraw its support of the regime provided alternative satisfaction for corporate military demands is available. This might have been one of the determining elements of the democratic *abertura* (opening) in Brazil.

Third, military defeat can ignite disagreements within the armed forces or cause the separation of the civilian elites from the military, which would remain isolated even at a mass level. Subsequently, passive dissent or support or even apathy among the citizenry could transform into open, intense opposition. This is undoubtedly the case most pertinent to the Argentine situation after the disaster of the Falklands-Malvinas War.

Fourth, civilian elites may exit the dominant coalition because of policy failures, especially in the economic realm, or because the time seems ripe for other policies that do not require the support of the coercive power of the military. This specific "cause" obviously is more probable where there is a developed industrial infrastructure and a capitalist bourgeoisie that previously had participated in the coalition in support of the regime.[14] In fact, this can be seen in the background situations mentioned already—Brazil, Argentina, Uruguay (and perhaps Chile).

The enormous, potential relevance of the international factor must be considered next. This may be the crucial "intervening variable" that accounts for the crisis and the breakdown. I already have considered the salience of this factor in conditioning the transition and establishment in certain

Western European cases. This factor had a major, short-term disruptive impact in the case of Greece with Cyprus and in the Italian case, with Mussolini's military defeat at war. In the Portuguese case, it operated in the middle and long term in the transformation of the regime brought about by military concern with the trajectory of colonial wars.

It is very difficult empirically to identify only one effective "cause." It is more realistic to frame hypotheses based on more than one of the reasons for crisis discussed herein. However, given the importance of the coercive factor, its determining impact on the outcome of the crisis, and the fact that these constitute the focus of military concern, the conflicts and the eventual isolation of the military from other political actors and from society weigh more heavily than other causes.

On the question of whether recurring mechanisms in the crises of authoritarian regimes exist, especially in those regimes adopted here as empirical references, an answer already has been provided, if only implicitly. First, it is necessary to distinguish between cases in which, despite everything, the crisis continues for a long time and others in which it rapidly leads to the collapse and transformation of the regime. There is no need here to elucidate the intuitively clear difference between a process of prolonged crisis and one of collapse. Nevertheless, it seems necessary to emphasize certain aspects and manifestations of the crisis and the additional necessary conditions that can lead to the breakdown of an authoritarian regime.

The breakdown of the dominant coalition supporting the regime has overt consequences and manifestations at the policymaking level. The exacerbation of the conflict among the elites makes decisionmaking more difficult, even to the point of outright paralysis. This is the case precisely in those sectors where the disagreements were more profound and where the inability to resolve them may lead to the breakdown of the coalition pact. To be sure, if this were the case, the divisions would deepen until they became unmanageable. There would be a serious loss of regime legitimacy at the elite level.[15]

A second consequence of growing divisions inside the coalition, especially if they specifically involve the military, can be the undermining of the repressive capacities of the regime, especially if this is accompanied by the activation and mobilization of social groups previously favorable or neutral toward the regime or a growth and organization of the opposition.

At this point a few elements become relevant, although they do not lead to collapse of the regime but rather to its gradual, continual transformation into a different sort of regime. I am referring here specifically to three related, particularly important aspects that in turn are connected with the crisis of the dominant coalition. First, sectors of the dominant coalition may separate from the regime and adopt attitudes of indifference and, later, of active opposition. Second, certain groups that were undecided or previously indifferent—for example, organized groups belonging primarily to the middle classes—may move toward an active opposition to the regime, thereby strengthening the opposition. This crystallization of active, organized opposition has serious destabilizing effects; it reinforces the latent opposition that the regime never had succeeded in eliminating completely or because it gives birth to new organized movements unfamiliar to the regime. Third, the opposition may regain its vigor and become capable of increased activity, which is more or less clandestine and more or less extremist, having managed all along to resist authoritarian repression. This third scenario has occurred where there have existed solid social bases for the opposition—for example, the Church and a sufficiently strong working class with prior organizational traditions.

The capacity for organized activity and the actual distribution of attitudes and coercive resources, influence, and pressure among the different opposition groups are not terribly important when the second phase of the crisis begins, which lays the basis for the transformation of the regime. These become so later on and will condition the success or failure in establishing the new regime, which probably no longer will be authoritarian in nature. The characteristics and diversity of the opposition vary, obviously, from country to country.

In this phase what is particularly important is that opposition to the regime exists and becomes capable of modifying the balance of power in the political arena; it also is important that the opposition foreshadow the possibility of a political alternative—otherwise, the crisis might go on indefinitely. There is one restraining condition that is absolutely necessary for a change of regime. Mobilization must be such that it does not frighten the actors who belong to the previous, dominant coalition, especially the military. The military instead must see all the disadvantages of remaining in government in terms of the deepening divisions within its organization, if not the undermining of the hierarchical principle, and in terms of all the advantages of a return to the barracks. These advantages include lessened political responsibilities and perhaps heightened social prestige, as the military now would be the protector and guarantor of change. If this were not the case, the effect would then be the easing of existing tensions within the dominant coalition, a recreation of the conditions that brought about the establishment of the authoritarian regime in the first place, and the strengthening of the regime coalition.[16] As we can see, the dilemma at this stage of the crisis is that, on the one hand, a political alternative has to exist and, on the other, a delicate equilibrium has to be maintained that eases the transformation through very serious difficulties. Here, the capacities of the leadership in facilitating the process of change will be put to the test.

At this point one might ask if the general conditions for a transformation of the regime exist, what other factors are necessary for such a change actually to take place? Is it necessary for some "accelerating" event to occur that precipitates the situation? Or does the progressive, at first tacit but well-understood need among the more crucial actors to suscribe to a pact help usher in the transformation? Although any answer to these questions only could be offered on a case-by-case basis, a leadership that is able and committed to bringing about the change of regime and the creation of a pact to which that leadership itself can contribute could be sufficient. This does not exclude other favorable contingencies that might present themselves.

In summary, Table 2.2 enumerates the most recurring motives for the collapse or change of authoritarian regimes. These are military defeat; disastrous economic failure and related crises; profound socioeconomic transformations that gradually modify the social base of the authoritarian regime; and, finally, the breakdown of the dominant coalition of the regime. The causes of the authoritarian crisis are influential determinants of the nature of the following democratic establishment. For example, the new elite may have to deal with problems that are not favorable to a democratic consolidation, such as a deep economic crisis. The role of the military in the new regime may be very problematic. It might be necessary to accommodate, or at the very least deal with, protagonists of the transition and establishment who really are not democratic.

Table 2.2 highlights the degree of organization of the opposition during the authoritarian regime. Having already discussed this aspect in the previous section, I only will stress that the presence of a more or less organized opposition in the last phase of the authoritarianism crisis makes a great deal of difference for a democratic establishment. In fact, when opposition exists and is organized, the political parties will be able to occupy the political spaces created by liberalization right from the initial phases of transition and establishment. Thus, from the very beginning, the parties can be influential in the main choices made by the provisional organs of government regarding urgent problems left unsolved by the authoritarian regime and in the choices that determine the future institutional arrangements of the democratic agenda. In fact, the degree of preexisting organization of the opposition can condition all the dynamics of establishment: the actors who are the protagonists, the agreements they reach, the spectrum of political forces that emerge, and the stimulation of major or minor public participation in this phase.

Modalities of Transition

The last factor considered here, modality of the transition, is linked so intimately to the establishment that often it is not possible to establish a clear analytical distinction between the modalities of one and of the other one. Factors such as the degree of continuity, participation, use of violence, and duration come into play as well. Some observations regarding the continuity/discontinuity problem are in order here. *Discontinuity* refers to a change brought about when the rules of the previous regime are broken. There is, therefore, an act that causes the regime to collapse and the transition to be initiated: a coup, a passage of the government into civilian hands, or similar events. If during such a phase there was a harsh, although not necessarily violent, conflict that brought down the old regime, then even this event may forge new solidarities. These, in turn, may facilitate not only the foundational agreements but also the whole process of democratic establishment.

By *continuity* I refer to a situation in which the authoritarian regime begins to change gradually by complying with the same rules envisioned by that regime for its internal self-transformation. Up to a certain point, the process of change remains consistent with the institutions of the old regime. Then those rules are implemented or betrayed in order to reach a different goal from that for which they were created. To be sure, the main condition and characteristic of a continual change is the central role played by the governing elite of the authoritarian regime. Such an elite leads the transition and uses the old norms to proceed to a controlled change, which might not necessarily bring about a democracy, at least if the plans of that elite are carried out in full. Additionally, such continual change will increase the legitimacy of the new regime among the social sectors tied to the previous one. Those sectors will be less afraid of the change, and, therefore, more readily disposed to approve and accept it. The reasons such an elite decides to commit apparent political suicide are similar to those at work in the first democratization. Actually, the mechanism described by Carl Friedrich's "law of anticipated reaction" is at work here. One part of the governing elite perceives, for various reasons, that the change cannot be stopped without using coercive force to an extent that it cannot, or does not want, to use. Or else a sector of the authoritarian leadership may believe that it is even more profitable to approve the change; thus, this sector separates itself from the more reactionary, declining sector of the authoritarian coalition. Whatever the case, this separating elite reacts by trying to direct the transformation, which enables the elite to obtain the support of the moderate opposition, isolate the more extreme opposition, and avoid the dangers of a breakdown or of direct confrontation.

It would be interesting to make a comparison between Spain and Brazil utilizing this scheme. In fact, after the death of Franco in Spain, a continual transition was initiated along the lines of a *reforma*; it respected the rules of the regime up to the approval of the Ley de Reforma Política by the Francoist Cortes in November 1976 and then by a referendum, equally foreseen by the ley orgánica (organic law) of 1945. From February to June 1977 a series of laws was approved that allowed the organization of parties, the legalization of the Communist party, the dissolution of the one-party system, and other measures. From that moment on in early 1977 Spanish politics took place outside the logic of the previous regime. Democratic establishment had started. The transition was remarkably continual, but it led to a genuine democratic establishment.

A similar continuity can be found in the case of Brazil, although the project of the military elites may have aimed at a protected democracy. However, the military regime was never effectively consolidated. It did not have a forty-year duration as did the Franco regime in Spain. There did not exist, as in Spain, a series of *leyes orgânicas* that articulated an apparatus of norms. The Brazilian military regime was born following a coup in 1964 as a provisional military intervention in order to give order to a confused political situation. Therefore, the continuity of the transition was contradicted by a refined manipulation of electoral rules, which were changed several times in the years leading to the elections of November 1982, the first relatively competitive election since 1964. In those elections the opposition, with a percentage of the vote equal to or larger than that of the governmental party, received a smaller number of seats for governors, for the Senate, and in the federal and state houses. The disproportion was obvious and notable. The military succeeded in surviving the enormous popular mobilizations of March–April 1984. It continued to be present in the cabinet and in the key public economic agencies and continued to oversee the indirect election of the president of the republic. Despite all this, in late 1984 the candidate of the opposition, Tancredo Neves, was elected with an overwhelming majority of the votes. Only at this point can it be said really that the transition was completed because the democratic direction of the establishment was clarified.

SOME CONCLUDING REMARKS

Tables 2.1 and 2.2 offer a synopsis of factors and phenomena that anyone concerned with the analysis of democratic establishments should take into consideration. As I affirmed at the beginning of this chapter, my primary goal only was to sketch out those factors and phenomena that are relevant at a comparative level. Here, I would like to stress again that a case-by-case analysis would compel us to go into more detail in our hypotheses and to explore other more specific hypotheses.

If, then, from the analysis of establishment we would like to move to the results of the process, the next step is to consider other processes that can be described as consolidation, maintenance, and crisis. In other words, there are three possible outcomes at the end of a democratic establishment: a more or less complete consolidation; maintenance of the democratic regime; and a more or less sudden crisis that puts in jeopardy the preservation of the recently installed democracy. Although all European cases followed the first path, some of the Latin American countries followed the second or the third one. However, for the leaders of every newly established democracy, the priority is always how to consolidate the new regime. Thus, the first path deserves to be explored fully.[17]

NOTES

1. I refer to the classic empirical definition of liberal, mass democracy. For more details, see Robert A. Dahl, *Polyarchy, Participation and Opposition* (New Haven, Conn.: Yale University Press, 1971), pp. 1–5.

2. See Adam Przeworski, *Capitalism and Social Democracy* (Cambridge: Cambridge University Press, 1985); and also his "Some Problems in the Study of Transition to Democracy," in Guillermo O'Donnell, Philippe C. Schmitter, and Laurence Whitehead (eds.), *Transitions from Authoritarian Rule* (Baltimore, Md.: Johns Hopkins University Press, 1986).

3. I believe these are the configuration that Finer had in mind when he referred to "facade-democracy" and "quasi-democracy" in Samuel E. Finer, *Comparative Government* (Harmondsworth: Penguin, 1970), pp. 441–531. For a more detailed analysis of the institutional hybrid, see my "Autoritarismi," in Gianfranco Pasquino (ed.), *Manuale de Scienza Politica* (Bologna: Il Mulino, 1986).

4. Dankwart A. Rustow, "Transitions to Democracy: Toward a Dynamic Model," *Comparative Politics* 2, no. 3 (1970): 337–363.

5. For the definition and discussion of consociationalism cited most frequently, see Arendt Lijphart, *Democracy in Plural Societies* (New Haven, Conn.: Yale University Press, 1977).

6. There are some legitimate questions about whether in the cases of Uruguay and Brazil the intent of the institutional actors was to evolve toward a protected democracy. See Chapters 6 and 7 in this book.

7. For contrasting perspectives of the role played by different actors in the establishing process see the essays in O'Donnell, Schmitter, and Whitehead, *op. cit.*

8. Philippe C. Schmitter, "Patti e transizioni: Mezzi non-democratici a fini democratici?" *Rivista Italiana di Scienza Politica* 14, no. 3 (December 1984); 363–382.

9. Dahl, *op. cit.*, Chapter 7.

10. For an excellent illustration of this, see Arendt Lijphart, *Democracies* (New Haven, Conn.: Yale University Press, 1984).

11. Seymour Martin Lipset and Stein Rokkan, "Cleavage Structures, Party Systems and Voter Alignments: An Introduction," in Seymour Martin Lipset and Stein Rokkan (eds.), *Party Systems and Voter Alignments: Cross-National Perspectives* (New York: Free Press, 1967), p. 50.

12. The best typology of authoritarian regimes is still that formulated by Juan J. Linz in "Totaliltarian and Authoritarian Regimes," in Fred I. Greenstein and Nelson W. Polsby (eds.), *Handbook of Political Science*, vol. 3 (Reading, Mass.: Addison-Wesley, 1975), pp. 175–411.

13. For an extended discussion of this topic, see Chapter 8 in this book.

14. Robert H. Dix offers a different, empirically interesting but somewhat perplexing analysis of the crisis and collapse of authoritarian regimes in Argentina (1955), Peru (1956), Colombia (1957), Venezuela (1958), Cuba (1959), and the Dominican Republic (1961). See Robert H. Dix, "The Breakdown of Authoritarian Regimes," *Western Political Quarterly* 35, no. 4 (December 1982): 554–573.

15. One may suppose that, in most cases, legitimacy at the mass level is always weak. For more on this see the Chapters 4 and 5 in this book.

16. One must not forget that fear of the ostensible threat implied by activation of the popular classes was at the root of the genesis of bureaucratic-authoritarian regimes. See Guillermo A. O'Donnell, "Tensions in the Bureaucratic-Authoritarian State and the Question of Democracy," in David Collier (ed.), *The New Authoritarianism in Latin America* (Princeton, N.J.: Princeton University Press, 1979), pp. 285–318.

17. I have begun to explore this in Leonardo Morlino, "Consolidamento democratico: Definizione e modelli," *Rivista Italiana di Scienza Politica* 16 (1986).

3
MASS AND ELITE PERSPECTIVES IN THE PROCESS OF TRANSITION TO DEMOCRACY

Rafael López-Pintor

The focus of this chapter is on transition to democracy as a converging process of mass needs and aspirations with elite decisions and behavior. These factors mutually reinforce each other in the opening of a system of representative government. Spain after Franco is the central empirical reference of this investigation; it is also the case most familiar to me, and it is largely paradigmatic of the incremental and legalistic reforms intrinsic to the transition to democracy. Spain is also the most recent case of such a transition in Europe.

I intend to avoid the sort of facile determinism implicit in vulgar Marxism or in the political development literature as well as in voluntaristic decisionmaking paradigms. In this way I avoid the two opposed and most common interpretative obfuscations that proceed from these analytic perspectives: uniformity as a product of socioeconomic determinism and uniqueness as a product of the absolute free will of individual decisionmakers. (The former vision is more frequent among social scientists, the latter among political historians, politicians, and opinionmakers). Instead, I search for a contextual explanation as supported in middle-range or partial theories, some of them available from classical political thought, some others from our own time.

There are several guidelines worth articulating given this intellectual perspective. First, following Machiavelli, one may describe the establishment of a given type of regime as a function of a certain necessity in the society (*necessità*), of a constellation of favorable events (*fortuna*), and of the capability of available leadership (*virtù*).[1] Second, a representative system of government is more likely to succeed in a society without severe social inequality

(Aristotle, Machiavelli).[2] Third, the fear of reverting to a situation of generalized violence or civil war fosters the acceptance of a given type of regime.

A Spanish version of Hobbes' *Leviathan* was edited amid the transition atmosphere of the 1970s. In a one-hundred-page introduction, chief editor Carlos Moya repeatedly states—as if for therapeutic purposes—an argument clearly summarized in the opening paragraph.

> To reconsider the role of the State is a theoretical imperative for a country whose national history now puts an end to two hundred years of civil war with a democratic outcome. Thus the opportunity for a new reading of Hobbes' *Leviathan,* where the objective discourse on the State has become the thought of the *ultima ratio* of its physical existence. This is the abolition of civil war as the collective foundation of that sovereign power whose universal respect and fear induces the peace of all citizens in a civil society finally secure from the violent avatar of war. To have comprehended the political substance of the nation state . . . is to have understood the objective argument for civil war and, thereby, the ritualistic over-determination of what has happened until now.[3]

Fear is frequently dealt with as a political factor in Machiavelli's works, both in *The Prince* and in *The Discourses,* and can be considered a component of *necessity.*

When a society has reached a certain degree of complexity in its socioeconomic structure and its state apparatus, a change of regime may leave both largely untouched. Important changes at both levels have helped remove the old regime. In other words, structural transformations already have taken place that have undermined the regime. It was de Tocqueville's argument that after the revolution so much remained unchanged, particularly within the state administration, and that so much had changed under the *ancien régime* in a path that was to be fully opened by revolutionary events.[4]

Some additional approaches from contemporary writers also shall be taken into account in this chapter. On the one hand, it is fruitful for political analysis to identify major political actors, the nature and amount of their resources, their strategies, and the constraints on the viability of different political alternatives. These factors have been conceptualized in a different manner by such authors as Albert Hirschman and Robert Dahl.[5] On the other hand, it may be pertinent to look at the interplay of different political actors within the broader network of relationships among the powerful, the powerseekers, the political stratum, and the apolitical stratum of a given system.[6] Consider the axiom that political opposition will be permitted if the government feels that an attempt to repress it would fail or that, even if it succeeds, the cost of coercion would be higher than the benefits.[7] Once the barriers to opposition are reduced, organized political pluralism will spring up to the extent that there are latent groups and subcultures in the polity striving to get into the open. In a sense, "organizational pluralism is ordinarily a concomitant, both as a cause and effect, of the liberalization and democratization of hegemonic regimes."[8] At the same time, once political pluralism is institutionalized, there is no guarantee that a high degree of equality will follow in the distribution of resources—political, economic, or any other kind. Hence, a change toward democracy or the stabilization of a pluralistic polity are not sufficient conditions for a society to enter the path of uninterrupted progress toward equality.[9]

THE SPANISH CALENDAR OF TRANSITION

Spain's system of government evolved from dictatorship to democracy during a three-year period (1976–1979). Most importantly, parliamentary democracy in Spain was fashioned as a reform strategy and occurred without any formal—either rapid or violent—breakdown of the Franco regime.

It has been argued that successful political reform is an even rarer phenomenon than revolution.[10] Hence, there has been considerable surprise and much curiosity about contemporary Spanish politics. The increasing amount of literature and concern about Spanish politics among social scientists illustrates this fact, not to mention the attention the Western mass media have devoted to the Spanish political process after Franco.[11]

Table 3.1 lists the main institutional events that defined the process of transition to democracy in Spain. My explanation of this process will advance through the structural changes in society, the mass political aspirations and mobilization, and the internal conflicts of the Francoist elite, all mediated by the event of Franco's death and the performance of King Juan Carlos. All of these events took place without any formal breakdown of previous authoritarian legislation or any important political denunciation of the Franco regime—although it also must be said that they occurred in an atmosphere in which neither localized violence nor a certain amount of general suspense were absent.

Why was it that the Spanish people, both the elites and the public, chose to transform their polity peacefully? The thesis argued here is that the way in which the transition toward democracy took place in Spain was as much a function of the internal dynamics of the ruling sectors of the Franco regime as it was of pressures from outside those sectors. The conjunction of both sets of factors precipitated the change of regime once two catalytic elements, without which Spain's transition hardly could be understood, took place. These were the natural death of General Francisco Franco and the actions of a king who had been appointed by Franco and enjoyed the loyalty of the armed forces. All these occurred in a society

TABLE 3.1
The Main Events of the Spanish Political Transition

Date	Events
November 1975	The death of Franco and the swearing-in of King Juan Carlos as prescribed under Franco's law.
March 1976	All major opposition forces united in the Coordinación Democrática (an opposition front broader than the Junta Democrática set up in Paris in 1974).
July 1976	Premier Carlos Arias---a former premier under Franco---is dismissed by the king after failing to gain acceptance of his proposals for limited democracy. Adolfo Suárez appointed new premier. First limited amnesty decreed.
November 1976	The Francoist Assembly (Cortes), on the initiative of the Suárez Government, passes the Law for Political Reform, which dissolves the Assembly, thereby formally opening the way for free general elections.
December 1976	Disavowing the campaign for mass abstention waged by most opposition forces (and the campaign for a negative vote waged by the most reactionary opposition forces), more than 70 percent of the Spanish electorate backs the Reform Law in a referendum.
February-April 1977	Most political parties are legalized. The movement and official unions are dissolved. An electoral coalition of fourteen minor parties (Unión de Centro Democrático) is formed under the leadership of Prime Minister A. Suárez.
March 1977	Second amnesty decreed.
June 1977	First general election of a parliament (consisting of the Congress of Deputies and the Senate), which is meant to be "ordinary" but in fact is bound to draft a constitution as its main endeavor. In this sense, the Parliament serves as a constituent assembly.
December 1978	A constitution is approved in Parliament and voted on in a referendum.
March-April 1978	First general election and local elections take place under the new constitution. Adolfo Suárez of the UCD becomes President of the new government. Statutes of self-government are negotiated for Catalonia and Basque country; these are approved in referendum in October 1979.

that had been undergoing profound structural transformations since the 1950s; that had rapidly reduced its traditional levels of inequality; that had passively accepted the Franco regime; and that was highly depoliticized. Against a recent historical background of civil war, repression, and absence of civil rights, the majority of Spaniards witnessed, with no small amount of fear and anxiety, how government and opposition fulfilled the democratic covenant more or less peacefully. Probably the staunchest Francoists (civil and military) did not feel strong enough to maintain the authoritarian system without paying high costs. On the other hand, the political opponents of the regime may not have felt strong enough to attempt its overthrow without risking failure.[12]

THE POLITICAL EFFECTS OF STRUCTURAL CHANGES IN SOCIETY

History shows that economic prosperity and development are ambivalent in their political effects. Economic expansion may work to the enhancement of freedom but also may be responsible for its deterioration.[13] A similar argument could be made with regard to the political effects of economic deterioration or recession. There are many cases of economic crises positively affecting or, in any case, accompanying a process of redemocratization; the reverse also is true.

For example, consider the multiform political scenario in the West after the crisis of the 1930s. More recently, there have been transition processes to democracy in the midst of economic recession in Spain and Portugal for Southern Europe and in Ecuador, Peru, Brazil, and Argentina for Latin America. It behooves the political analyst to determine the linkage mechanisms between politics and the economy in different circumstances. Specific objective conditions must be identified where feelings of relative deprivation arise, spread throughout the society, and consequently bring political change in one direction or another. Still, the relationship between decreasing social inequalities resulting from a period of economic prosperity and the increasing likelihood of successful democratization remains unchallenged—as *Political Man* has recorded persistently since 1959 down to its lastest edition (in 1981).[14] This was certainly the case in Spain in the 1970s.

It would require excessive space to describe the socioeconomic and cultural transformations undergone by Spanish society during the last two decades. Yet some facts are relevant to the political questions being posed here. First, Spanish society underwent some structural changes during the second half of the Franco regime as a result of rapid industrialization. This does not imply that these changes happened primarily *because* of the policies of the authoritarian regime, although they obviously were promoted by and concomitant with them. Rapid industrialization would have taken place ten to fifteen years earlier had Spain joined the Allies in World War II, as was the case in other European countries. The point is that these changes reduced social inequalities largely to a question of historical significance. They had a positive effect on the maintenance and at least passive legitimation of the Franco regime as well as on the kind of political change that occurred after Franco.

By the mid-1970s, Spanish society was less inegalitarian than ever before in contemporary history. As a result, more social sectors were concerned with keeping what they had gained than ever before. In addition, most Spaniards had little interest in politics but rather strong socioeconomic concerns. Given these circumstances, the society at large offered an appropriate cushion for the maneuvering of the political elites (government and opposition) to settle their historical differences peacefully. Most people were not prepared to become involved in risky actions either to maintain the authoritarian regime or to topple it. They even were willing to suffer patiently the violence of minority groups of the extreme Right and Left. The aim of most people was to maintain a rather affluent society, with open opportunities of all kinds.

This hypothesis concerning the political effects of reduced inequalities is closer to the thought of Aristotle and Machiavelli than to the theories of de Tocqueville, Marx, or modern political-development theorists such as Daniel Lerner or Karl Deutsch. I am not proposing that economic development need have a linear relationship to the growth of democracy, nor that the enlargement of the Spanish proletariat accompanying industrialization was likely to foster a classical Marxian revolution. However, the relative deprivation theory of revolution (de Tocqueville) might have applied to Spain had the Franco regime remained in existence until the present day when economic recession is having a strong impact on the prosperity of many individuals, who currently feel that they have less now than they had before. My hypothesis is closer to Aristotle and Machiavelli in the sense that democracy is more likely to be established successfully and maintained when there is little social inequality.[15] This is a rather modest proposition, but one that—in today's industrial Spain, as in preindustrial history—might be a fruitful one.

Although the industrialization of the Spanish economy began in the last quarter of the nineteenth century, it stalled several times due to internal and international crises. The last and, for our purposes, most significant of these was the world crisis of the 1930s, which was followed by civil war and an international economic boycott lasting into the early 1950s. From this point until the present international economic crisis, rapid industrialization took place in Spain and affected the country's social structure to the most significant extent in modern history. A contrast of some conventional economic indicators illustrates this. For example, per capita income increased from about $500 in the early 1960s to more than $3,000 in the late 1970s.[16] Agricultural labor, which accounted for almost 50 percent of total employment in 1950, fell to 42 percent in 1960 and to less than 20 percent in 1980.[17] This was accompanied by a rapid increase in urbanization. In 1960, 34 percent of the population was living in towns of more than 100,000 inhabitants; this figure had increased to 44 percent by 1970.[18] These socioeconomic changes implied higher standards of living as well as a better distribution of resources among Spaniards. As a result of the expansion of the industrial and service sectors of the economy, the middle economic strata of society became the majority.

It is my hypothesis that these changes fostered the legitimation of (or at least a consent to) the regime under which they occurred. They relegated political discontent to minor segments of the society, to the well educated, and well off.[19] Actually, the Spanish economy began to deteriorate at the end of the Franco regime as a consequence of the first oil crisis. Spaniards became aware of the economic crisis, but by the time of Franco's death, they did not seem to think that the regime under which they had prospered was to blame. The opinion surveys of that time reflected the objective decrease in consumption standards but expressed a rather hopeful outlook that things were going to improve both for the country and for the individual. In contrast, by 1979 the Spanish people seemed less optimistic, but there was no authoritarian regime to be toppled nor a political force—either in government or opposition—that could credibly offer the people a rapid, successful way out of the economic crisis.

The data in Tables 3.2–3.4 clearly show that during the transition period, even when consumption rates and the wealth of the nation had been increasing at a slower pace than in previous years, average wages and salaries kept rising above inflation rates. In addition, although ordinary citizens perceived the country's economic deterioration, they thought their own situation was better than that of the country. Concerning the country and themselves, many people were relatively optimistic and hopeful about the future. All of these support the hypothesis that by the end of the Franco regime and during the transitional period, there was more conformity and concern about maintaining hard-won gains than there was deprivation and its potential for political action.

POLITICAL ASPIRATIONS AND EXPECTATIONS

A number of reasons have been advanced to explain why the Spanish people were depoliticized under Franco. Unlike the fascist regimes of Hitler and Mussolini, the Franco regime was concerned particularly with keeping the people uninvolved in politics. This was compounded by a certain (historical) political skepticism, by the fact that 70 percent of Spain's

TABLE 3.2
Material Conditions of Life in Spain, 1960-1979
(in percentage)

Year	Intergenerational Occupational Mobility (from manual to nonmanual)	Wages and Salaries as percent of Total National Income	Households with			People Who Believe They are Better or Worse Off than Years Earlier	
			TV	Refrig-erator	Car	Better	Worse
1960	-	-	1	4	4	-	-
1966	27.6	53	-	-	-	-	-
1970	-	-	-	-	-	-	-
1973	34.3	58	85	82	38	-	-
1976	-	-	-	-	-	42	14
1977	-	64	-	-	-	-	-
1979	-	-	-	-	-	36	20

Sources: For occupational mobility, see *Informe Sociológico sobre la Situación Social de España 1970* (Madrid: Euramérica, 1970), pp. 586-588; *Estudios Sociológicos sobre la Situación Social de España 1975* (Madrid: Euramérica, 1976), p. 740. For wages and salaries, see *Estudios Sociológicos, 1975*, p. 959; *Informe Mensual, Abril 1980* (Madrid: Caja de Pensiones "La Caixa"), p. 23. For households, see *Estudios Sociológicos, 1975* p. 975. Opinion data for 1976 are from the Instituto de Opinión Pública (IOP) and belong to a national survey conducted in May; data for 1979 are from a national survey by the Centro de Investigaciones Sociológicas (CIS) and were published in *Revista Española de Investigaciones Sociológicas* (REIS), no. 6 (April-June 1979): 239.

TABLE 3.3
Objective Indicators of Spanish Economic Conditions, 1970-1979

Year	Annual Rates of Increase Per Capita GNP[a]	Annual Rates of Increase in National Consumption[b]			Annual Rates of Increase in the Cost of Living[c]	Annual Rates of Average Increase in Wages and Salaries Per Hour[d]	Wage increase Greater than Inflation Rates[e]
		Total	Private	Public			
1970	-	-	-	-	100	100	-
1971	-	-	-	-	109.7	113.9	3
1972	7.0	7.5	7.8	5.5	117.6	133.7	9
1973	7.0	7.7	7.8	6.7	134.1	160.5	5
1974	4.7	4.6	4.1	8.3	158.1	203.5	8
1975	0.0	2.3	2.0	5.2	180.4	256.5	10
1976	2.0	4.4	4.3	5.3	216.1	334.5	8
1977	1.3	2.1	1.9	3.7	273.1	435.4	3
1978	-	-	-	-	318.4	549.5	8
1979	-	-	-	-	367.9	675.3	6

[a] In constant prices, 1970.
[b] In constant prices, 1970.
[c] Consumption prices constant, 1970.
[d] Monthly, 1970=100.
[e] Percent of constant prices, 1970.

Note: These figures come from Boletín Mensual after the formula $\frac{D1}{D2}:\frac{C1}{C2} \times 100 - 100$ where D1 is the wage increase in a given year and D2 is the increase in the previous year; C1 and C2 represent cost-of-living increase rates for a given year and previous year.

Sources: España, Anuario Estadístico 1979 (Madrid: INE, 1979), p. 295; Boletín Mensual de Estadística, several issues (Madrid: INE, 1979).

Table 3.4
Subjective Indicators of Spanish Economic Conditions, 1968-1979 (in percentage)

Year	Economic Situation of the Country is		Future of the Country Will Be		Individual Economic Situation has not Changed or is Better	Opinion About Individual Future	
	Very Good or Good	Very Bad or Bad	Better	Worse		Optimistic	Pessimistic
1968	56	24	-	-	-	-	-
1973	-	-	-	-	-	49	6
1974	32	22	-	-	-	-	-
1975	25	24	40	25	62	-	-
1976	27	27	42	9	61	54	9
1979	6	41	27	12	-	40	13

Sources: Data for economic situation in 1968, 1975, and 1976 belong to IOP and were published in *REOP*, no. 14 (1968):186, and no. 44: 283; data for 1979 belong to CIS and were published in (REIS) no. 6 (1979): 304. Data for 1975 and 1976 country future were published by *REOP*, no. 44 (1976): 283; data for 1979 were published by *REIS*, no. 6 (1979): 305. Data for individual economic situation from *REOP*, no. 44 (1976): 285. Data for 1973 individual future were published by *REOP*, no. 36 (1974): 249; data for 1976 belong to IOP and have not been published; data for 1979 were published in *REOP*, no. 6 (1979): 305.

population had not lived under any other kind of political system; and by the traditional backwardness of the country.[20] To these could be added a certain degree of political anomie, which reflected a general cultural anomie that sprung from the rapid structural changes in the economy and society. Almost one-half the adult population consisted of first- or second-generation migrants.

The low level of political interest among a "silent majority" of Spaniards coexisted with the increasing politicization of some social segments: the young, the more educated, skilled and professional labor, and so on. For most Spaniards, the Franco regime was a given for which they felt neither enthusiasm nor animosity. Yet at the same time, democratic ideas were considered the more reasonable alternative, more suited to the times and unfolding circumstances (see Tables 3.5 and 3.6). After all, democracy was the system prevailing in the more-developed neighboring nations and was the banner being held aloft by the younger generation, by professionals and intellectuals, by the Church, and by even businessmen—in a word, "those who know better."

On the eve of Franco's death, most people were worried about the future, and they remained anxious during the transition period. Public uncertainty also was reflected in the population's negative evaluation of the country's political situation. The rather high level of political confidence exhibited by the public after the appointment of Premier Adolfo Suárez in 1976 had not existed since 1973 (two years before Franco's death). This mood was accompanied by an increase in political interest and in the expression of democratic aspirations—mostly in Catalonia and the Basque country—where a defense of regional identity and a demand for self-government always had been incompatible with the Franco regime. These regions were spearheads in the process of change. In these well-developed areas of Spain, the existence of regionalist attitudes was in itself a challenge to Franco's authoritarian rule. There always had been more people in these regions than in any other part of Spain favoring federalism and even independence. They were first in rejecting the Franco regime. In addition, they were very suspicious of the first reform steps that King Juan Carlos and President Adolfo Suárez took in 1976 and 1977 (see Tables 3.7, 3.8, and 3.9).

Available opinion data are highly illustrative of these phenomena but are not used here as evidence that democratic ideals were springing automatically from the society at large. Much to the contrary, there was an increasing interaction among powerholders, powerseekers, the politicized strata, and the depoliticized public. Each political actor was looking at the others and anticipating reactions. A climate of uncertainty accompanied by a considerable amount of violence was reached in the last months of the Arias government, due to generalized rejection of his timid reform proposals.

TABLE 3.5
Public Interest in Politics and Political Involvement Before and After Franco's Death
(percentages of national samples and electorate)

Year	Political Situation of the Country is Very Good or Good	People in Favor of		Do Not Have Any Interest in Politics	Voting turnout in Referenda and Elections
		One-man Rule	Democratic Representation		
1966	-	11	35	-	
1971	-	-	-	51	
1973	54	-	-	62	
1974	42	18	60	-	
1975	32	-	-	-	
1976 (May)	29	8	78	35	
1976 (Dec)	52	-	-	-	
1977 (June)					77
1978 (Dec)					78
1979 (Mar)					68
1979 (Apr)					69
1979 (June)	-	9	76	36	61

<u>Sources</u>: Political situation data from IOP, published in <u>REOP</u>, no. 44 (1976): 290; data for December 1976 from <u>Consulta</u>, published by <u>Cambio 16</u> (January 9, 1977): 14.
Political rule data for 1966 and 1976 belong to IOP and have not been published; those for 1974 belong to Consulta S.A. and were published by <u>Cambio 16</u> (June 3, 1974); data for 1979 belong to CIS and were published in <u>REIS</u>, no. 6 (1979): 275. The wording of the question in all these surveys was not strictly the same, although basically comparable. In all surveys, the subjects were asked if, in politics, they would prefer an outstanding person to make all important decisions or the people's representatives to make these decisions.
No interest in politics data for 1971 and 1973 belong to ICSA/Gallup and were published by <u>Informaciones</u> (February 15, 1974); data for 1976 and 1979 belong to IOP and CIS respectively. The wording of the question in all these surveys was basically the same: "How much interest do you have in politics: very much, somewhat, little, none." Voter turnout data are from the records of the Ministry of the Interior.

TABLE 3.6
Public Acceptance of Political Parties Before and After Franco's Death (percentages of samples, national and largest cities)

1971 (national sample) Percentage of people who said the existence of political parties would be	
. beneficial	12
. neither beneficial nor harmful	9
. harmful	23
. did not know (DK)/did not answer (DA)	56
1973 (national sample) Percentage of people who said they were	
. in favor of the existence of freedom for political parties	37
. against it	34
. did not know (DK)/did not answer (DA)	29
April 1975 (national sample) Percentage of people who said political parties	
. should be permitted in Spain	56
. should not be permitted	22
. did not know (DK)/did not answer (DA)	22
January 1976 (national sample) Percentage of people who said political parties	
. should exist in Spain	41
. should not exist	25
. did not know (DK)/did not answer (DA)	35
May 1976 (sample of four major cities) Percentage of people who said political parties	
. should exist in Spain	67
. should not exist	3
. did not know (DK)/did not answer (DA)	30

Sources: For 1971 and 1973, Estudios Sociológicos Sobre la Situación Social de España (Madrid: Euroamérica, 1976), pp. 1259, 1277. For 1975, El Europeo (April 19, 1975); data from Consulta S.A. For 1976, IOP.

The same occurred during the early months of the first Suárez government. There were strikes, mass demonstrations, political murders and kidnappings, mounting pressures by the press, and visible signs of a split in the military and in the elite of the ailing regime. This was a period during which it became particularly evident that at no time is a regime weaker than when it first attempts to reform itself. Machiavelli and de Tocqueville were very clear on this.

> It should, however, be noted that [states with a capacity for improvement] will never introduce order without incurring danger, because few men ever welcome new laws setting up a new order in the state unless necessity makes it clear to them that there is need for such laws; and since such a necessity

TABLE 3.7

Public Attitudes on Desirability of Democracy After Franco's Death (percentages of samples, national and largest cities)

December 1975 (national survey) Percentage of people who said they would like the king to grant (or follow)	
. more freedom of speech	72
. universal suffrage	70
. more regional autonomy	61
. amnesty	61
. more political freedom	58
. more democratic policies than previously existed	58
May 1975 (sample of seven largest cities) Percentage of people who said	
. the system should evolve toward a democracy of the Western kind	74
. this evolution is not possible without reforming fundamental laws	60

Sources: Data for December belong to Consulta and were published by Cambio 16 (December 1, 1975); data for May belong to Metra Seis and were published by *Informaciones* (May 31, 1975).

> cannot arise without danger, the state may easily be ruined before the new order has been brought to completion.[21]

Ironically, danger also may result from people's awareness of the contrast between the previous and the emerging conditions of life.

> Experience shows that the moment of greatest danger for a bad government is ordinarily that at which it begins to reform itself. Only a great genius might save a Prince who embarks on relieving his subjects after a long oppression. The evil which they patiently suffered as inevitable seems insufferable once the idea of escaping it is conceived. Whatever has been alleviated of the abuse, it seems better to discover what is left and injures the sensibilities; the evil has lessened, to be sure, but the feelings are very much alive.[22]

Theoretically, the situation during these early stages of the Spanish transition could have led to either a revolution or a coup d'état. Why did neither happen? Why did the government not lose control of the situation? Why did every major actor run a risk but never attempt to play a trump card? Of course, these questions are being answered a posteriori and are not free of an ex post facto bias.

In looking at the state of Spanish society, I propose that decreasing social inequality fostered both passive support for the Franco regime and a prudent extrication from it upon Franco's death. At the same time, the democratic alternative was becoming more popular among the public at

TABLE 3.8
Democratic Aspirations and Public Opinion in Catalonia, Basque Country, and Other Spanish Regions Before the 1977 Election
(in regional percentages from national samples)

Public Opinion of Government	Barcelona	Catalonia-Balearic Islands	Basque Country-Navarra	Galicia	Andalusía	Center
The current government is not democratic.	35	25	35	14	13	14
The current government is not an advocate of freedom.	26	17	29	12	11	13
The performance of the king is positive.	65	73	51	73	87	76
Freedom is better than order.	--[a]	22	25	14	13	--
A republic is better than a monarchy.	--	30	33	14	13	--
Respondent considers him/herself anti-Franco.	--	51	56	28	28	--

[a]Dashes indicate data were not disaggregated.

Source: Data are from Juan Linz, Informe Sociológico (Madrid: Euramérica, 1981), pp. 130-144.

TABLE 3.9
Public Attitudes Toward Self-government in Certain Spanish Regions, 1976 (regional percentages of a national sample)

	Respondent Preference			
Region	Centralism	Autonomy	Federalism	Independence
Basque Country-Navarra	28	49	11	9
Catalonia-Balearic Islands	48	42	7	-
Barcelona	20	61	12	4
Galicia	45	44	6	3
Andalusía	64	30	3	1

Sources: J. Jiménez Blanco et al., La Conciencia Regional en España (Madrid: Centro de Investigaciones Sociológicas, 1977), p. 80.

large. The younger, more cultivated, and more politicized sectors of the society, which were undermining the regime from within and without, increasingly were committed to the democratic alternative.[23] As to the way in which this changing opinion could affect the emergence of democracy after Franco's death—nobody thought democracy could emerge before—I quote myself, in the spring of 1975, in order to partly correct the ex post facto bias.

> Will this emerging, democratically oriented generation guarantee a democratic future for Spain? In the long term, an affirmative answer could be ventured. In the short term, this would seem more than problematic. The possibility for a democratic evolution may arise from two sorts of circumstances: well planned reform—what the regime doves call *apertura* [opening]—or uncontrolled disintegration of the regime. From a mass culture perspective it is hard to foresee which way the Spanish future will go. At the outset it will mostly depend on elite factors—particularly conflicts within the authoritarian coalition, and attacks from radical opponents. Yet, since the regime's active social base is a rather limited one, any important crisis may work as a catalyst for the mobilization of opponents, and also of previously passive supporters who will not identify anymore the regime with the person of Franco. . . . The Portuguese experience is highly illustrative of how fast a regime structure may disintegrate without anyone shot dead. But it also illustrates how difficult it is to build a democracy upon the debris of a long-lived authoritarian regime.[24]

THE MOBILIZATION OF THE POLITICIZED AND THE INTERPLAY BETWEEN POWER HOLDERS AND POWER SEEKERS

A description of the mass mobilizations and the elite maneuvering during the Spanish transition has been provided by various authors.[25] The point to be stressed here is that the staunchest Francoists chose not to play their trump card—coup d'état—to preserve the regime, nor did the opposition play its card—revolution. Possibly neither side was sure of success. Both had to consider the state of the society, which was rather conformist and apathetic, and the final uncertainty of how much support they could obtain from it. Both also feared either uncontrollable social violence and protest (the Francoists) or indiscriminate repression (the opposition).

The contradictions of the regime had clouded the perception of civil society held by the most adamant rightists. The more politicized among the Francoists, by contrast, knew from experience in government how difficult and costly it was to mobilize a few thousand people. They were aware of the increasing organizational capacity of the unofficial unions. Finally, they realized that intellectuals, public officials, professionals, and businesspeople suspected that the people in decisionmaking positions in and out of the government administration no longer constituted a united authoritarian bloc as they had in the 1940s and 1950s. For the opposition forces as well, there was much uncertainty regarding the amount of mass support obtainable and the intensity of the support available from liberals in the educated middle class. These could be put to a serious test in a violent confrontation. Most importantly, the opposition was afraid of outright repression.

This is not to suggest that the democratic covenant had smooth sailing or that there was a well-planned blueprint shared by the government and by an opposition willing to adhere to it after its enactment. This was partly the case in some specific issues, but on the whole there was much trial and error by both government and opposition. There were some visible signs of splits within the Francoist civil and military elites. These have been described elsewhere, but some of the most apparent deserve mention here.[26] First, and most important, leadership of the reform was appropriated by men who had served as ministers under Franco. There were also politicians who had served under Franco but who joined the opposition platform of Coordinación Democrática (Democratic Coordination). There were, to be sure, leading actors of the Franco regime who strongly opposed reform and continued to campaign against it in open elections. Yet this split was numerically disproportionate. For example, only 15 percent of the deputies in the Francoist Assembly voted against the Law of Political Reform in 1976. As for the military, there were dismissals and resignations affecting the higher positions as well as public statements against reform following certain governmental decisions. Most conspicuous among these were the Suárez bill for political reform in 1976 and the legalization of the Communist party in 1977. Yet on the whole, the military stressed allegiance to the king, who was the overseer and final arbiter of the process.

I know of no in-depth study about the relations between the monarch and the military—even at the level of formalized public communications such as speeches. The king did pay utmost attention to cultivating his personal contacts with the military at all levels. High military officials were very parsimonious in their public declarations concerning the political process up to the first general election. From then on, they were more expressive; they almost always reemphasized their manifest support for the constitution and for the people's will and stressed their loyalty and obedience to the king and their independence from party politics. Finally, as far as the monarch himself was concerned, King Juan Carlos' speeches at the annual January 6 Pascua Militar (Christmas observance by the military) parade constitute the best formal indicators of his messages to the military. The political process always was given considerable attention in those speeches, and there was a consistent leitmotiv in the king's words during these years: unity and discipline.

On different occasions, the king addressed matters that seem to have been particularly salient to civil-military relations at the time. At the 1976 Pascua Militar he appeared to be concerned mostly with the future. In 1977 he asked the military to ignore those who sought to promote its demoralization and disunity. In 1978 he called political change a necessary part of the march of history; he considered it "absurd" not to advance and defended the depoliticization of the military. In 1978 he also acknowledged military cooperation in the political process, which he termed "necessary." In 1980 he expressed his deep identification with the military institution and asked the military not to delude itself with the idea of protagonisms—that is, of leading the nation—which were "inopportune."[27] The inopportunity of such protagonisms was vindicated by the failure of the coup attempt in February 1981.

On the opposition side, one must stress the threat posed by the persistent lack of commitment to democracy by the most extreme wing of Basque nationalism. As the transition process unfolded, violence by Euskadi ta Askatasuna (Basque Organization for Direct Action, or ETA) continued to increase. Between 1974 and 1977 ETA's yearly death toll was less than twenty. This figure tripled between 1977 and 1982. The electoral expression of this extreme nationalism, the Herri Batasuna coalition, invariably received around 15 percent of the vote in the Basque country. (See Tables 3.10 and 3.11.)

TABLE 3.10
Support for Independence for the Basque Country and Navarra, 1976-1981

Dates	Percentage in Favor of Independence (from regional samples)
June 1976	11
June 1979	26
December 1980	18
April 1981	12

Source: CIS.

King Juan Carlos chose Adolfo Suárez premier and inspired his program, which served as a transitional mechanism between past and future. Juan Carlos was in a position to legitimately demand the allegiance of Franco loyalists. The late general had appointed him and had left rather loose institutional arrangements. At the same time, Juan Carlos expected the support of the opposition forces because he was allowing them to enter the political game as legitimate actors.[28] The performance of the king is crucial to understanding how the entire process of change took place. If there was any individual actor who had the capacity to make the process turn one way or another, it was the king. It is hard to imagine a breakdown of the Spanish authoritarian regime under the conditions prevailing at the time without the mediating role of the monarch, both as an institution and as a person. In the 1970s Spain was not under the influence of some of the factors that contributed to the collapse of other European authoritarian systems. Paramount among these was military defeat, which simply destroyed the regime—as with Nazi Germany and Fascist Italy—or at least a serious setback that undermined the cohesion of the military—as in Greece under the colonels and in Caetano's Portugal. Lacking these the king seemed to be the horse on which both the Spanish people and interested observers had to place their bets.

Once Franco died the reform process was launched. This process occurred in an atmosphere of violence and uncertainty. But with the king massively acclaimed in his almost continual trips throughout the country, the Spanish people anticipated that Franco's nondemocratic Cortes (parliament) would pass the Law of Political Reform. The people massively supported this bill later on in a referendum, not only because it was the best thing for the country but also because there was a need for change and democracy (see Table 3.12). Some people consciously, and most of them unconsciously,

TABLE 3.11
Deaths from Political Violence, 1968-1979

Year	Killings by ETA (Basque leftist separatists	Killings by GRAPO (Marxist-Leninist group)	Killings by Groups of the Extreme Right	Killings by Police and Civil Guard	Total
1968	2	-	-	-	2
1969	1	-	-	-	1
1971	-	-	-	1	1
1972	1	-	-	2	3
1973	6	-	-	1	7
1974	18	-	-	-	18
1975	14	7	-	2	23
1976	18	2	1	22	43
1977	11	8	8	23	50
1978	64	6	4	15	89
1979	67	29	10	20	126
Total:	202	52	23	86	363

In 1973 L. Carrero Blanco was killed by ETA. Consistently, the largest percentage of killings by ETA were policemen and civil guards. The largest percent of killings by police and paramilitary forces were people engaging in public demonstrations and protests.

Source: This table has been compiled from information made available from the files of the daily newspaper *El País*. As assistant at CIS Emilia Nasarre is to be recognized for her patient work.

TABLE 3.12
Public Attitudes Toward the Bill of Political Reform
(percentage of national samples)

November 1976	Percentage of people who said that the reform bill	
	. will be passed by the Cortes......	58
	. will not be passed...............	6
	. did not know (DK)/did not say (DA)	36
December 1976	Percentage of people who said they voted Yes in the reform referendum because	
	. it was the best thing to do.......	29
	. it was for good of the country....	10
	. there is need for change and democracy.........................	29
	. of influence by P.V. and the government........................	10
	. of influence by others (spouse, friends)................	3
	. other............................	3
	. did not know (DK)/did not say (DA)	16

Source: Estudios del CIS: La Reforma Política (Madrid: Centro de Investigaciones Sociológicas, 1977), pp. 17, 34. The November poll was conducted on the 16th and 17th from a sample of 976 individuals. The December poll was conducted after the referendum of the 16th and 18th from a sample of 1,008 individuals.

might have felt that in voting for reform they were saving themselves from the unknown.

THE PACTS OF MONCLOA

There is no formal document underwriting the new democratic covenant of Spain. The constitution of December 1978 was approved in referendum two years after the Law of Political Reform also had been approved and more than one year after the first general election. If there is a transition document, it must this law. But this law was opposed by the democratic forces at that time. The so-called Pactos de la Moncloa, named after the residence of the Spanish prime minister, therefore did not constitute a foundational agreement for the Spanish transition to democracy. They dealt with socioeconomic and political matters and were signed by the representatives of all significant parties upon the initiative of Premier Suárez in October 1977, four months after the first general election. The pacts came midway between the referendum for approval of the Law of Political Reform in December 1978 and the beginning of the Constituent Assembly elected in the 1977 election.

The political relevance of the Moncloa agreement was somehow independent of its content. The agreement provided an opportunity for all parties to stand together at the center of power as if they were taking part in a coalition government inaugurating the new regime. This was also a gesture of mutual goodwill prior to the drafting of a constitution that would take more than one year to formulate. The pacts also were endorsed by both houses of Parliament. By signing these pacts, the opposition parties formally shared the leadership of the transition. As for the new democratic cabinet of Premier Suárez, the pacts provided much needed support for the new economic policies designed to combat the recession, but this support did not last long. By the end of 1978 the opposition parties were accusing the government of noncompliance with the pacts. After the December 1978 referendum for approval of the new constitution, Premier Suárez was ready to call for a new general election in March 1979.

The Pacts of Moncloa had a political as well as a socioeconomic aspect. On the political side, the Moncloa agreement basically enlarged freedom of speech, the right to meet and act in public demonstrations, and the right of association. With regard to freedom of the press and the issue of prior restraint, the obligation of an "administrative deposit" prior to publication still remained. Yet distribution only could be prevented by judicial authority upon demand of the government or of private citizens. On state secrets, a promise was made by the government to interpret their legal premises less restrictively. A legislative reform was promised through which the concept of "private meetings" would be enlarged to include up to fifty persons without any administrative approval required. Public meetings could be held following previous notice to competent administrative authorities but without any explicit approval being necessary. Official permission would be required for public demonstrations, but in case of nonresponse, approval would be assumed.

The promised legal reform also would implement the following changes: All associations were to adopt an organizational structure consonant with democratic principles; legal registration of political parties would take place within a specified time period once their bylaws were presented to the government, unless judicial action had been undertaken against the parties; only a court of justice could suspend or dissolve any association; and, finally, a system of public financing for political parties would be established based upon the principle of support proportional to the electoral returns of each party.

The Pacts of Moncloa also sought to create consensus for a set of policies that could adjust the Spanish economy to the new conditions of the world crisis. Some policies would aim to reduce inflation and balance the trade deficit, and others would restructure sectors of the economy and distribute the costs of the crisis more equitably. The policies of readjustment, or *saneamiento*, of the economy were to include a monetary policy based on a progressive reduction of the money supply; a budgetary policy that reduced public spending on the consumption side while favoring capital investment; public deficit reductions; a new, more realistic exchange rate for the peseta, which would continue to float in order to favor exports; and an incomes policy based on estimated, instead of past inflation rates. Social security costs also would be reduced.

The reform of the economic structure was to include a budgetary reform to improve the control mechanisms on public spending, which were practically nonexistent in the area of social security and amounted to about 50 percent of the total national budget; a tax reform that would deal with the general income tax, an income tax on corporations, and the value added tax; a reform of the financial system to promote an active, continual control of the money supply, to liberalize the system, and simultaneously to supervise the solvency of financial institutions; a new legal framework for labor relations and a new labor code; a reform of public enterprises to increase their efficiency; and an energy program to rationalize and nationalize consumption. Industrial and agrarian policies would be devised to improve the Spanish position in international markets.

Although the Pacts of Moncloa did not constitute a foundational agreement, they defined the arena where government and opposition would meet—first to agree on an agenda, and then to engage in the public contestation characteristic of democratic procedures. The opposition subscribed to the pacts because the transitional government kept its promise and implemented the political reform that put in place the structure of the new regime. With the procedural mechanisms in place, the opposition exercised its right to offer alternative policies and present itself as a viable option.

THE HERITAGE OF AUTHORITARIAN REGIMES: LESSONS FROM THE SPANISH EXPERIENCE

There are factors that play an ambivalent role in the political process; in the case of Spain these were economic recession and regional nationalist demands during the Spanish transition. First these circumstances favored democratization; then they obstructed the consolidation of the new regime. There were other factors that stemmed from the previous authoritarian experience and that had a sustained effect upon the new polity. They represented a more or less burdensome inheritance. Significant political change takes place in any given society only at the price of equally significant costs. Sometimes such costs are paid in a swift, drastic, and very visible manner. This usually happens with war. At other times costs are paid over a longer term and are less visible. Some long-standing consequences of authoritarian rule are to be seen more clearly in the realms of political culture, the mobilization structures of the society, and the recruitment and behavior of political leadership.

Regarding the political culture of democracy, it is important to note that democratic values can be preserved and transmitted through family and adult agents of socialization even under long-lasting dictatorships, if a previous experience with representative government has been rewarding to the society. Furthermore, these values spread quickly as the public realigns itself politically once the goals for change are clearly posed by a successful democratic coalition. It is then that the weaknesses of a regime in transition look more prominent. I have shown empirically how rapidly the democratic realignments of the public were progressing as the Franco regime entered the 1970s; these realignment become massive by the end of 1976, when Premier Suárez clarified the direction of political change.[29]

Democratic realignments are still more rapid and more efficient if the breakdown of dictatorship has taken place during demonstrations of force or when there was a clear failure to make force a decisive factor. In Spain democratic attitudes were tested severely four years after the first general election, when a coup attempt failed in February 1981. The king assumed direct control of the situation and neutralized the revolt; Spanish society rallied behind him and reaffirmed its support for the new regime. Other plots were discovered on the eve of the October 1982 elections, which gave the Socialist party an absolute majority. In February 1981, 9 percent of adult Spaniards showed some sympathy toward coups. By October 1982 the figure was only 5 percent.[30]

Although these findings may be cause for some optimism among democrats, one cannot overlook the negative effects of dictatorial rule upon the political culture of a people. This rule not only disrupts early socialization agencies, such as the family and the school; dictatorship also destroys the democratic mechanisms for political intermediation (parties and other linkages) and substitutes other less visible, nonaccountable agents that enhance corruption and cynicism.

The need for adult democratic resocialization results in part from the fact that the family breaks down as an agent for the transmission of political values. The political conflicts of the society frequently find a reflection within the family. Repression and political success affect family behavior mostly by depoliticizing it. In order to preserve family cohesion parents may foster attitudes of apathy and skepticism. Such values run counter to the needs of mobilization, party membership, and elite recruitment that are essential to democracy.

There is also the breakdown of party structures and democratic linkages, which leaves political intermediation in the hands of irresponsible actors who can play power games without any ideological justification or public accountability. This in itself brings out corruption, which is hard to eliminate even after a change of regime and harder when change takes place incrementally and in a legalistic fashion.[31] Corruption also is most likely to persist under conditions of economic recession, as is often the case during a transition to democracy. Scarcity reinforced the networks of favoritism and personal benefit between the bureaucracy and society.[32]

Finally, a few observations are necessary concerning the recruitment and behavior of politicians when democracy is reinaugurated. On the one hand, the availability of democratic leadership will depend largely on the survival of politicians from previous democratic experiences, as was the case in postwar Europe and is currently the case in Latin America. On the other hand, there always will be problems with new recruits not because of a shortage of supply, but due to the quality of their previous political experience. After a long period of democratic interruption, people schooled under authoritarian rule will not make the best democratic politicians either in government or in opposition. The Spanish case is paradigmatic of a failure of transition leadership to adapt to the normal democratic game. Suárez and his transition party Unión de Centro Democrático (Union of the Democratic Center, or UCD) practically were swept from the political arena five years after the first general election. The Socialist party, once in government, soon showed governing styles not too different from those of the UCD.

Each regime has its own logic both of government and opposition. Outstanding players in a game are not by definition equally competent at other games. It is up to these players to demonstrate a capacity for other games. Apparently, the UCD could not outlive its own success at managing the transition in Spain. Any party with an interest in survival in a democracy must fight against the persistence of rules alien to the game of competitive politics. These include overt behavior against the rules and institutions of popular government and the rule of law; resistance to popular pressures through refusal to resign from public positions when politically necessary to cope with certain problems; not offering explanations acceptable to constituents when resigning from a position or making shifts in policy; a lack of interest in or ability to strengthen ties with specific constituencies, if only to secure their vote; and more intense conviviality with advocates of authoritarianism (both civil and military) than with supporters of democracy. These types of behavior result in weakness and ambiguity in matters of policy as well as in alienation of party activists and voters.

This antidemocratic behavior brings to the fore two aspects of political action that are strategically important in the consolidation of a democratic system of government. First, if democracy is to succeed, the sons of Brutus must be kept under strict control. The founder of the Roman Republic was bound to kill his own children, who were supportive of the Tarquinian restoration of authoritarian monarchy. The first few years of that republic were filled with troubles and difficulties, but once those were surmounted, the regime lasted for more than five centuries. The people may be sensible to the weakness of the transition leadership and thus may look for a less ambiguous government either of the Right or of the Left.

Second, the strength of democracy largely depends on the weakness of its opponents, and this, in turn, depends on the capacity of democratic leaders to keep their opponents under control. Democracy only can be defended by democrats, and democrats are those who have learned the rules of the game of popular support.

In practical terms, there may be occasions in which the leadership for a transition may be found among politicians that do not come from the womb of the authoritarian system. If this is feasible the outcome could be an asset for the democratic consolidation. More frequently, however, conditions are not ripe for the promotion of the best leadership, and the polity must play trial and error for a period of time. Yet this shortcoming should not be an obstacle to the political analysis of the ideal conditions for democracy nor to the practice of democracy, which is predicated on the assumption that civilized politics does not require perfection.

NOTES

1. Niccolò Machiavelli, *The Discourses* (Harmondsworth: Penguin, 1970), Book 1, pp. 16–18, 25–27, 38, 39, 46–55, and Book 3, pp. 1–9.

2. Aristotle, *The Politics* (Harmondsworth: Penguin, 1966), Book 4, Chapter 11, pp. 171–174; *ibid.*, Book 1, pp. 55, 243–248.

3. See Carlos Moya, "Thomas Hobbes: Leviatán o la invención moderna de la razón," in Carlos Moya and A. Escohotado (eds.), *Thomas Hobbes, Leviatán* (Madrid: Editora Nacional, 1979), p. 9.

4. See Alexis de Tocqueville, *L'Ancien Régime et la Revolution* (Paris: Gallimard, 1967), Book I.5, Book II.2–6, Book III.1, .3, .4, .5, .8.

5. Albert O. Hirschman, *Journeys Toward Progress: Studies of Economic Policy-Making in Latin America* (Garden City, N.Y.: Doubleday, 1965), Chapters 1, 5; Robert A. Dahl, *Modern Political Analysis* (Englewood Cliffs, N.J.: Prentice Hall, 1967), Chapters 3, 4, 5; Charles W. Anderson, *Toward a Theory of Latin American Politics,* (Nashville, Tenn.: Graduate Center for Latin American Studies, Vanderbilt University, 1963).

6. Dahl, *ibid.*, p. 78.

7. Robert A. Dahl (ed.), *Political Oppositions in Western Democracies* (New Haven, Conn.: Yale University Press, 1966), Preface.

8. Robert A. Dahl, "Pluralism Revisited," *Comparative Politics* 10, no. 2 (January 1978): 196, 197.

9. *Ibid.*, p. 199.

10. Samuel Huntington, *Political Order in Changing Societies* (New Haven, Conn.: Yale University Press, 1968), Chapter 3.

11. Among the vast literature on the Spanish transition the following should be mentioned: Juan J. Linz, "La frontera del Sur de Europa: Tendencias evolutivas," *Revista Española de Investigaciones Sociológicas,* no. 9 (January-March 1980): 7–53; Juan J. Linz et al., *Informe Sociológico Sobre el Cambio Político en España, 1975–1981* (Madrid: Euramérica, 1981); John F. Coverdale, *The Political Transformation of Spain After Franco* (New York: Praeger, 1979); Peter McDonough et al., "The Spanish Public and the Transition to Democracy" (Paper delivered at the 1979 annual meeting of APSA, Washington, D.C., August–September 1979); José M. Maravall, "Transición a la Democracia: Alineamientos Políticos y Elecciones en España," *Sistema,* no. 36 (May 1980): 65–105; José M. Maravall, *La Política de la Transición* (Madrid: Taurus, 1982); Carlos Huneeus, "Transition to Democracy in Spain: Unión de Centro Democrático as a Consociational Party—An Exploratory Analysis" (Paper delivered at a workshop of the European Consortium for Political Research, Brussels, April 1979); Salvador Giner, "Political Economy and Cultural Legitimation in the Origins of Parliamentary Democracy: The Southern European Case" (Paper delivered at a workshop of the Centro de Investigaciones Sociológicas, Madrid, December 1979); Giuseppe di Palma, "¿Derecha, izquierda o centro? Sobre la legitimación de los partidos y coaliciones en el Sur de Europa," *Revista del Departamento de Derecho Político,* no. 4 (Fall 1979), 125–145; Michael Roskin, "Spain Tries Democracy Again," *Political Science Quarterly* 93, no. 4 (Winter 1978): 629–646; Jonathan Story, "Spanish Political Parties: Before and After the Election," *Government and Opposition* 12 (1977): 474–495; Julián Santamaría (ed.), *Transición a la Democracia en el Sur de Europa y América Latina* (Madrid: Centro de Investigaciones Sociológicas, 1982); Rafael López-Pintor, *La Opinión Pública Española: Del Franquismo a la Democracia* (Madrid: Centro de Investigaciones Sociológicas, 1982); Raymond Carr and Juan P. Fusi, *España de la Dictadura a la Democracia* (Barcelona: Planeta, 1979).

12. Ostensibly, the opposition to Franco was not able to overthrow him while he lived. Before the referendum on the Law of Political Reform in December 1976, the opposition forces asked voters to abstain from voting, but voter turnout was 77.4 percent, of which 94 percent voted for ratification.

13. See Albert O. Hirschman, *The Passions and the Interests: Political Arguments for Capitalism Before Its Triumph* (Princeton, N.J.: Princeton University Press, 1977), pp. 119–128.

14. Seymour Martin Lipset, *Political Man: The Social Bases of Politics* (Baltimore, Md.: Johns Hopkins University Press, 1981), pp. 469–476.

15. See note 2.

16. Fundación FOESSA, *Estudios Sociológicos Sobre la Situación Social de España, 1975* (Madrid: Euramérica, 1976), p. 1976; *Anuario Estadístico de España, 1979* (Madrid: INE, 1979), p. 294.

17. *Encuesta de Población Activa, 1980* (Madrid: INE, 1980), p. 143.

18. Anuario Estadístico, *op. cit.,* p. 56.

19. As has been illustrated by many surveys, the opinions most critical of the Franco regime and most favorable to democracy were found among the younger generation, mostly the educated middle and upper middle class and a smaller segment of skilled labor. To mention but a few sources, see the *Informes FOESSA* on the social situation of Spain (1966, 1970, 1975), or the survey research appendices in

the *Revista Española de la Opinión Pública* and *Revista Española de Investigaciones Sociológicas* (the former running from 1965 to 1977; the latter from 1978 to the present). A typological construction of cultural outlooks—political included—among urban Spaniards under the Franco regime can be found in Rafael López-Pintor and Ricardo Buceta, *Los Españoles de los Años 70: Una Versión Sociológica* (Madrid: Tecnos, 1975).

20. On the nature of the Franco regime, see Juan J. Linz, "Totalitarian and Authoritarian Regimes," in Fred I. Greenstein and Nelson W. Polsby (eds.), *Handbook of Political Science,* vol. 3 (Reading, Mass.: Addison-Wesley, 1975) pp. 175–411; Eduardo Sevilla-Guzmán, Manuel Pérez Yruela, and Salvador Giner, "Despotismo moderno y dominación de clase: Para una sociología del régimen franquista," *Revista de Sociología,* 8 (1978): 103–141. The skepticism of Spanish political culture recently has been pointed out by Maravall, *op. cit.*, p. 27; and McDonough et al., *op. cit.*, pp. 13, 14.

21. Machiavelli, *op. cit.*, pp. 105–106.

22. De Tocqueville, *op. cit.*, pp. 277–278.

23. Changes in these sectors—largely a result of the nature and contradictions of the authoritarian regime—have been described by different authors. See Sevilla-Guzmán et al., *op. cit.*, pp. 121–141; Giner, "Political Economy and Cultural Legitimation," pp. 31–37; Coverdale, *op. cit.*, Chapter 1; Amando de Miguel, *40 Millones de Españoles 40 Años Después* (Barcelona: Grijalbo, 1976).

24. Rafael López-Pintor, "The Political Beliefs of Spaniards: The Rising of a More Democratic Generation" (Paper presented at a meeting of the Latin American Studies Association, Atlanta, 1975).

25. Coverdale, *op. cit.*, Chapters 1, 3, 4; Maravall, *op. cit.*, pp. 13–22.

26. *Ibid.*

27. This brief account has been based on a perusal of Madrid newspapers and is but an outline of what would be required by a more formal content analysis of documentary materials.

28. Giusseppe di Palma has seen the leadership function in the Spanish transition as one of building up legitimacy toward the past as well as toward the future, *op. cit.*

29. See opinion data above and also Rafael López-Pintor, "Opinión Pública," Chapters 2, 3.

30. Survey data are from the data bank of the Centro de Investigaciones Sociológicas.

31. For a theoretical review and summary conclusions of comparative research on clientelistic relations, see an introduction by L. Graziano and a review by Carl H. Lande in the monographic volume "Political Clientelism and Comparative Perspectives," *International Political Science Review* 4, no. 4 (1983): 425–434, 435–454.

32. See the Introduction in Michael Clarke (ed.), *Corruption: Causes, Consequences and Control* (London: Frances Pinter, 1983), pp. ix, x, xiii, xvi.

PART TWO

SOUTH AMERICAN CASES

4

FROM DIARCHY TO POLYARCHY: PROSPECTS FOR DEMOCRACY IN CHILE

Carlos Huneeus

The study of change of political regimes cannot be separated from an analysis of internal changes in the regimes that have been replaced. Recent political science studies have tended to emphasize changes from one type of political regime to another; there have been considerably fewer studies of changes within a political regime that may lead to its transformation.[1] Interest in this topic originated with the eruption of the "new authoritarianism" in the early 1960s, when the military initiated a cycle of coups that affected a number of Latin American societies, including stable democracies such as Chile and Uruguay and large countries such as Brazil and Argentina.[2] Initially, political scientists studied the causes that led to the installation of these regimes, an enterprise that began with an analysis of the crisis and breakdown of democracy, a task in which Juan Linz had a leading role.[3] The apparent consolidation of authoritarianism encouraged the study of the crisis of democracy, particularly for those who may not have valued it sufficiently when it prevailed. However, the authoritarian regimes began to fall, starting with the Revolução das Flores (Flower Revolution) in Portugal on April 25, 1974, followed later on by Greece and Spain.[4] This initiated a wave of democratizations that involved these Southern European countries and the "new authoritarian" regimes of Latin America: Ecuador, Peru, and Bolivia in 1977–1978, and, later, Argentina, Brazil, and Uruguay.

This wave also reached Central America, and decades of traditional dictatorships, transmitted from fathers to sons or from general to general—such as Somoza in Nicaragua, the Duvaliers in Haiti—collapsed and enabled transitions to regimes that were not necessarily democratic. Only the Paraguay of General Alfredo Stroessner and the Chile of General Augusto Pinochet have survived this wave of democratization. Nowadays there is little interest in studying an experience that no one wishes to see repeated again. The main concern of actors, analysts, and the general public is to consolidate these democratic systems that have to elude skillfully the numerous, serious constraints and burdens inherited from the authoritarian regimes.

Concerning the deterioration and breakdown of authoritarian rule one must describe the preconditions for regime change, identify the phenomena that have triggered the transition from authoritarianism to democracy, and determine the rate and scope of this process. The colonial war in Angola was a determinant of the intensive and extensive politicization of the armed forces in Portugal, which caused the strong military assumption of leadership during the transition. Analysis of the economic and social changes experienced during the Franco regime in Spain and the institutional mechanisms that were adopted as a result is indispensable for understanding why after the death of the Caudillo, there was a *reforma* (reform) and not a *ruptura* (rupture).[5] In Brazil changing politico-institutional conditions after 1974 illustrate how a pluralist system was attained by means of the *abertura* (process of opening up) and through elections.[6]

In addition, the study of the changes in the political regimes is very closely related to the study of political regimes. Rainer Lepsius describes changes of political regimes in terms of two strategies: *Machtübergabe* (handing over power) and *Machtübernahme* (taking power).[7] Before and after the event associated with regime change, coalitions are formed that express agreements and alliances among elites, sectors of elites, and power groups. These coalitions carry out the change of power, determine the principal direction of the politics of the new regime, generate high stability in the governing elite, and condition the continuity of tenure of some of the government personnel. Even in a change of regimes as radical as that in Hitler's Germany after January 30, 1933, the continuity of subsystems such as the bureaucracy and the armed forces prevailed. Consequently, the study of the previous regime is indispensable for understanding the dynamics of the new one. It also is useful to remember the pain and suffering associated with the former regime in order to defeat attempts to restore the authoritarian system.

This chapter will analyze the authoritarian regime in Chile under the leadership of General Augusto Pinochet, who, in 1986, had completed twelve years in power—the equivalent of two presidential periods of the long Chilean democratic era.[8] My objective is to calibrate changes in the regime that may have been determined by the political transformations that began in 1983 with the *protestas* (protests) and the policy of *apertura* (process of opening up) and to assess the impact of these changes on the prospects for democratization.

In fact, commencing on May 11, 1983, various sectors of the opposition affiliated with the trade unions and the political parties convened the first public protest; they called on the people to express their rejection of government policies. Subsequently, Chile lived through a period of intense, prolonged political mobilization that led to important transformations in the system of authoritarian rule.

Initially, the government was dumbfounded by the magnitude of the protest and by the pressure of an extremely serious economic situation that led the government on January 13, 1983, to intervene in a significant part of the financial system. Political pressure from the opposition and economic crisis moved the regime on August 12 to initiate a policy of liberalization and economic patronage. This policy was sparked by a new cabinet presided over by ex-president of the Partido Nacional (National party, or PN) and former senator Sergio Onofre Jarpa. By virtue of this policy, which was known as the *apertura*, numerous prominent politicians who had been exiled by the regime were able to return to Chile. The press enjoyed extensive freedom with the emergence of new weekly publications that strongly criticized the regime and Pinochet. The political parties, which had been obliged to survive clandestinely (in family circles, study centers, and voluntary institutions that provided a cover for party members and activists) and had to confine political action to defending human rights and to criticizing economic policy, were able to come out into the open. The parties enjoyed a wide margin of action that enabled them to hold mass functions on closed premises and in open areas, such as the demonstration by the Alianza Democrática (Democratic Alliance) at O'Higgins Park in November 1983, which brought together between 150,000 and 200,000 people. Pressure groups that had been controlled from above by official leaders and severely constrained by legislation and authoritarian policy unexpectedly opened up and were penetrated by a strong political fervor. This fervor expressed itself in trade union elections, student federations in each of the universities, and professional associations that enabled the opposition to present itself as a powerful political actor. This organized interest also found its way into social groups which hitherto had adopted an indifferent attitude. The result was the emergence of new institutions that fought to defend their own interests and those of the organizations in which they operated: for example, the associations of university professors.

Thus, there was intensive and extensive political mobilization, which brought about an abrupt expansion in the political arena of collective political action. An overbearing political confidence had led the government to declare that it had "goals and not timetables" and that it would construct a new democracy for a new generation of Chileans. This project was buoyed up by an economic euphoria created by foreign loans, but eventually the euphoria collapsed like a sand castle under the weight of a huge foreign debt. Politics, which hitherto had been ignored, excluded, and even despised, suddenly became a central element in Chile. Until that moment, the prime concern had been the economy. From the moment of the *protestas* and *apertura*, however, primacy belonged to politics.

The government applied a strategy of drastic politico-military control. The *protestas* and the *apertura* were marked by intense political conflict that produced high casualties. This significantly weakened the opposition's capacity to mobilize, which stirred up public opinion. In the space of eighteen months, there were more than one hundred deaths; hundreds of people were injured, including civilians, uniformed officials, and members of the Catholic Church (see Table 4.1).[9] There were also violations against Church premises, such as the bomb that exploded in a church in Punta Arenas causing the death of an army lieutenant who might have been involved in planting it there.

The Pinochet regime did not fall, but it was forced to introduce numerous, important transformations. The current political regime is the same one, but it is different; the same constitution is in force as are the same laws, but these laws now are even more drastic with a constitutional law on *estados de excepción* (states of exception); the same coalition governs, but the opposition has numerous, important spaces of freedom that previously were unknown in this kind of political regime.[10]

In order to study the changes in the Chilean authoritarian regime and evaluate their possible future implications, it is not particularly appropriate to use a functional, consensualist approach, but rather to adopt a genetic approach.[11] Lewis Coser and Ralf Dahrendorf have made contributions to the theory of conflict that seem particularly appropriate here.[12]

Adoption of a functionalist vision of authoritarianism implies that any serious problem the regime faces will be interpreted as an indicator of "crisis," whose outcome should be either the fall of the regime or its restoration to stability. When there is a prolonged crisis but it apears that the regime will not collapse, the situation is treated as "crisis management." This approach is unsuitable for analyzing changes under authoritarian domination for if the crisis is long, it simply means that the regime has succeeded in restoring its stability.

A functionalist approach in analyzing politics tends to exaggerate the role of the opposition, thereby producing a vision of authoritarianism under pressure. This leads to what Bolivar Lamounier has called a "heroic vision of the masses," which is characterized by a triumphalistic view of the imminent, inevitable fall of authoritarianism.[13] Authoritarian regimes seldom fall because of the role played by the opposition; they fall instead because of tensions and conflict within the governing coalition. An analysis of the dynamic trends of the authoritarian regime can be best made using an approach based on conflicts within the regime's coalition. A focus on the

TABLE 4.1
Indicators of Violence During the Political *Apertura*, August 1983-November 1984

Indicators	Number of Incidents
Nonterrorist civilian deaths	78
Armed forces deaths (including secret police)	5
Carabinero deaths	18
Terrorist deaths	25
Nonterrorist civilian injuries	464
Armed forces injuries (including secret police)	22
Carabineros injured	144
Nonterrorist civilians detained	5,615
Terrorists detained	126
Attacks against armed forces (including secret police)	4
Attacks against *carabineros*	31
Attacks against diplomatic premises	2
Attacks against government premises	12
Attacks against municipal premises	50
Attacks against opposition political leaders	4
Attacks against the judiciary	2
Attacks against the Catholic Church	17
Attacks against newspapers and magazines	6
Attacks against radio stations	13
Attacks against TV channels	2
Attacks against information agencies	3
Attacks against educational establishments	17

Table 4.1

Attacks against financial institutions	66
Attacks against the railways	46
Attacks against the metro	5
Buses burned	37
Vehicles burned (excluding buses)	18
Attacks against buses	29
Attacks against electricity transmission pylons	63
Attacks against street lampposts	170
Others	142

Sources: The following Chilean newspapers: El Mercurio, La Tercera, Las Ultimas Noticias, La Segunda, and La Nación.

regime's strategy for conflict regulation enables us to make this dynamic analysis and fathom the implications of changes under authoritarianism, particularly those that may facililtate a democratic transition at a later time.[14]

CONFLICT REGULATION AND THE DYNAMICS OF AUTHORITARIAN REGIMES

Political systems may be understood in terms of their basic strategies of conflict regulation. Gerhard Lehmbruch suggested that these are the hierarchical-authoritarian, which is analogous to authoritarian regimes; the majority strategy, which is analogous to the winner-take-all version of competitive elections; and the consociational formula analogous to democracies established by consensus, having a multiparty system and proportional representation.[15] In turn, the constituent elements of a political system may be analyzed "inward" and "outward." Observed inwardly, political systems show much heterogeneity in the strategies of conflict regulation utilized by their subsystems. Bureaucracies and the armed forces are governed by hierarchical-authoritarian strategies, both under authoritarian and democratic regimes. However, in certain subsystems structural determinants of a political or cultural nature require the adoption of a strategy different from that which has been generally adopted in the political system.[16] Klaus von Beyme demonstrated that in Franco's Spain an authoritarian regime may adopt consociational or proportional criteria for establishing the government in order to ensure the participation of people from the different power groups that form the governing coalition.[17]

The constituent mechanisms of the strategies of conflict regulation are institutional or personal. Some authoritarian regimes achieve high levels of institutionalization and low levels of personalization. Others can be highly personalized, with a weak, changing institutional profile.[18] It has been shown consistently that an authoritarian regime with an extremely high institutional profile, such as Mexico, also operates under the influence of personalistic factors.[19] Among these personal powers, the leader's role as mediator and arbiter stands out and is utilized particularly when institutions are unsuccessful in regulating conflict.[20] Thus, authoritarian stability does not depend solely on its institutional gestalt but also on personal elements.

An analysis of conflict regulation and subsystem functioning in authoritarian regimes enables us to have a more complete, differentiated perception of the elements of power and of the decisionmaking process. Thus, the political system is a *Polykratie* (a system with some diffusion of power) or a *Monokratie* (monism).[21] A regime described as a *Polykratie* is distinguished more by the complexity and heterogeneity of its constituent parts and by the intensity of conflicting interests rather than by its strength and stability.

THE LEGITIMACY OF POLITICAL SYSTEMS

The constituent elements of a political regime also may be defined outwardly. Outwardly, the regime must meet some requirements of legitimacy—that is, the population must believe that its institutions and its ruling coalition are the most appropriate.[22] Legitimacy denotes the relationship between the political order and the citizens because no political regime is indifferent to the prevailing opinion among the majority of the population.

Legitimacy depends to a great extent on a regime's capacity to resolve the population's principal demands, find solutions to the issues that seriously have divided society, and satisfy the interests of the different power groups and elites that form the governing coalition. This requires the regime to act efficiently while discharging its governmental responsibilities.[23] The legitimacy of a political system generally is based on three different modes: historical or traditional legitimacy, which proceeds from the country's development; rational-legal or constitutional legitimacy, which is a product of judicial ordinance promulgated by the regime in accordance with a specific formal procedure; and forward-looking, performance-oriented legitimacy, which is sustained by policies that try to satisfy the citizen's most urgent needs.[24]

Performance legitimacy is intertwined deeply with the effectiveness of the political system, and is at the hub of the complex, delicate relationship between the economy and politics. The economy is based on politics, and the latter cannot be separated from the economy because all political systems are concerned with attending to the socioeconomic needs of the population.

Citizens evaluate the economic performance of a regime not by cold economic figures, but by the way in which the population actually benefits from the regime's economic policies.[25]

New political regimes tend to adopt a strategy of mixed legitimacy, thereby activating all three different modes. Of these the most important is forward legitimacy; the regime's success alone will provide the justification for its existence by virtue of the regime's substantive improvement over the one it deposed. New regimes that succeed at this also will have a cohesive governing coalition and will be able to satisfy the demands and expectations of the different power groups of which it is composed. A highly efficient regime in turn will have a high rate of integration and social and political cohesion, which will considerably facilitate regime consolidation. Therefore, failure in terms of efficiency or performance will affect the substance of the strategy of regime legitimization.

THE AUTHORITARIAN REGIME IN CHILE

The authoritarian regime installed in Chile in September 1973 may be analyzed according to three constituent elements: the heterogeneity of the regime's governing coalition; the adoption of a strategy of mixed legitimacy, in which economic success constituted its backbone; and a low level of institutionalization and a high level of personalization of power.

The Heterogeneity of the Governing Coalition

The first peculiarity of the Chilean authoritarian regime lies in the heterogeneity of its governing coalition, which is constituted by technocrats, nationalists, *gremialistas* (members of private sector associations, particularly those representing small business people) from the old PN, independents, and military personnel.[26] Each power group or elite has a political apparatus through which the regime has been able to integrate an extensive, varied range of interests. In order to enable these groups to participate in the political process, the regime had to adopt the consociational or proportional strategy for conflict regulation. The arenas for political and administrative coordination are not institutional. For example, the head of state, Pinochet—whose direct, immediate work is carried out by the presidential secretary, who is an army general—and not the cabinet plays the role of mediator or arbiter in the tensions and conflicts between the different power groups. Pinochet simultaneously implements government policies. These dual roles put him in a key personal and institutional position. Pinochet functions as an integrator in his daily role as coordinator of a governing coalition that comprises civilian and military groups.

TABLE 4.2
Military Participation in the Chilean Cabinet, September 1973–April 1986

Portfolios	Total Ministers	Total Armed Forces	Number of Ministers from Army	Navy	Air Force	Carabineros
Interior	6	3	2		1	
Foreign affairs	6	2		2		
Economy, development and reconstruction	13	4	3	1		
Mining	7	3	1	1		1
Finance	8	1		1		
Education	11	4		4		
Justice	7	1				1
National defense	6	6	5	1		
Public works	4	3	2		1	
Transport and Telecommunications	5	4	1		3	
Agriculture	6	3				3
Housing and urban matters	8	4	2	1	1	
Land and colonization	4	4				4
Labor (employment) and social security	10	2			1	1
Public health	7	6	6			
Government secretary general	10	6	6			
Total	118	56	28	11	7	10

It is important to emphasize that military personnel constantly have occupied senior positions of authority and power. Approximately one-half the ministers have been members of the armed forces (see Table 4.2). All regional superintendents and governors of Chile's fifty provinces are military officers in active service with direct command of troops. Governorships occupied by army officers outnumber those occupied by officers of other

TABLE 4.3
Provincial Governors and Their Distribution by Branch of the Armed Forces, Winter 1983

Branches of the Armed Forces	Governors	%
Army	33	66
Carabineros	12	24
Navy	4	8
Air Force	1	2
Total	50	100

branches of the armed forces (see Table 4.3). University rectors and delegates by and large have been members of the armed forces; at the University of Chile and the University of Santiago the rector-delegate has been a general in active service. Senior executives of a number of state enterprises are members of the armed forces. This differs substantially from the structure of the governing coalition in other authoritarian regimes, such as Argentina and Brazil, in which military participation has been considerably less (see Table 4.4). As commander in chief of the army, Pinochet has direct power and authority over civilian and military personnel in the governing coalition.[27]

This high level of military participation in the Chilean authoritarian regime contradicts Juan Linz's generalization on the gradual decline of military participation in government in favor of civilians.

> In regimes emerging from a military action, the army may enjoy a privileged position and hold on to key positions, but it soon co-opts politicians, civil servants and technicians who increasingly make most decisions. The more a regime becomes consolidated, the fewer purely military men staff the government, except when there are not alternative sources of elites. In this sense it may be misleading to speak of a military dictatorship, even when the head of state is an army man. In fact he is likely to carry out a careful policy of depoliticization of the army, while he maintains close ties with the offier corps to hold its loyalty.[28]

An interesting aspect of this highly constant political participation by the military is that it has not politicized the military institutions nor has it weakened their professionalism. This participation gives the regime and the head of state enormous political power, as shown during the *protestas* and the *apertura*. The lack of politicization among miliary institutions bodes

TABLE 4.4
Composition of the Cabinet in Argentina (1966-1973 and 1976-1983) and Brazil (1964-1983)

Argentina			Brazil		
	Total Ministers	Military Ministers		Total Ministers	Military Ministers
Interior	11	6	Interior	5	-
Foreign affairs	10	3	Justice	6	-
Justice	11	1	Foreign affairs	5	-
Economy	6	-	Army	7	7
Labor (Employment)	8	4	Navy	6	6
Agriculture	2	-	Air force	7	7
Finance	9	-	Finance	5	-
Industry and trade	4	-	Transport and public works	5	3
Energy and mines	3	-	Agriculture	5	-
Transport	2	1	Education	7	1
Defense	8	3	Labor and social security	6	-
Social security	13	5	Information	1	-
Education	11	1	Health	5	-
Planning	3	1	Planning and economic coordination	5	-
Health and environment	3	1	Communications	4	1
Housing	3	1	Administrative reform	1	-
Information	2	1			
Total	109	28		80	25

Source: Keesings' Contemporary Archives, corresponding years.

well for the future of democracy in Chile because a politicized armed forces leads to discord and a spiral of coups and countercoups. These, in turn, make it impossible to stabilize democratic order, as has been demonstrated in Argentina during recent decades.[29]

The Strategy of Mixed Legitimation and the "Chicago Model"

The new regime adopted a strategy of legitimation that was based on a backward historical legitimation that rejected the government of the Unidad Popular (Popular Unity) as well as the political and democratic advances of previous decades. The coup, therefore, was not only against one specific government but more fundamentally against the Chilean democratic tradition. The regime used historical legitimation to present a comprehensive political project tied to future goals. In turn, the backward legitimation also was useful for establishing the forward legitimation of the regime.

Forward legitimation posed the need for a new socioeconomic and political system in which the principal wants of individuals would be satisfied. The regime assumed power at a time when the country's economy was facing a serious crisis—hyperinflation, an enormous balance-of-payments deficit, and disarticulation of the productive apparatus. Thus, economic objectives and the economy in general received priority attention. In 1975 the new government enthusiastically put the conduct of economic matters in the hands of monetarist economists—the "Chicago boys"—who believed that the economy of the country might attain an spectacular development within the next few years.

The "boys" took advantage of a high rate of international liquidity, caused by increases in the price of petroleum, to give enormous advantages to foreign banks and thereby attract a massive inflow of foreign exchange. This was allocated primarily to consumer and speculative activities, to the detriment of productive activities. Borrowing created an image of economic success during the "boom" years of 1979–1981, a triumphant phase that carried the regime to its most ambitious policies. The social and political principles implicit in the economic model were applied to society in order to implement "seven modernizations," which included health, social security, education, and even voluntary associations and town planning. The government presented a proposal for reconstructing relations among the economy, society, and the state in order to create a socioeconomic system that was sufficiently solid to resist future alternation of government and regime changes. It was a plan, therefore, of revolutionary proportions.[30] However, the economic and political bases of the plan were extraordinarily simplistic and could not support such revolutionary aspirations. In fact, the regime handed over the allocation of resources to the financial market, confident that these would be distributed appropriately. It fragmented the trade union movement by means of the Plan Laboral (Employment Plan) and created intolerable economic conditions for the workers. The dismantling of the state health system obliged them to bear the costs of this service. The privatization of social security was another blow for the workers, who thus witnessed the dismantling of the bases of the welfare state in Chile, which had been created in the 1920s.

In a highly competitive international market only a modern system of industrial relations will ensure social peace and lead to economic success. However, that was not part of the Plan Laboral, which atomized the workers' organizations, thereby leaving the workers in a weak position vis-à-vis their employers and the business organizations.[31] Spanish employers found themselves in similar circumstances during the Franco era when they recognized the Comisiones Obreras (Workers' Commissions), which were illegal and dominated by the Communist party.[32] This was also the case in Brazil during the *abertura*.[33] The Plan Laboral did not assume a persuasive integration of the working class, and therefore it must be considered according to a precapitalist, rather than capitalist, rationale.

The strategy of legitimation by performance was the backbone of the regime's policy of consolidation and integral to the transition to democracy. Economic success would afford the regime cohesion and a strong legitimacy and would create solid bases for the establishment of the "democratic order" inspired by the 1980 constitution. The climate of economic success created during the boom perceptibly assisted the mobilization of support for the government, thus giving it a decided advantage in the 1980 plebiscite. Inflation had dropped sharply from 1,000 to 30 percent; Gross Domestic Product (GDP) was growing consistently at rates in excess of 8 percent per annum, an unprecedented level for Chile; and the balance of payments showed a healthy surplus as a result of nontraditional export earnings and the flow of external credits.[34] But the model was not a total success. Unemployment, including the Programa de Empleo Mínimo (Minimum Work Program, or PEM), exceeded 15 percent of the work force for six years. Real wages between 1976 and 1980 averaged less than 80 percent of their 1970 value and even in 1981 still had not recovered that of eleven years before.[35]

The close linkage between backward and forward legitimation was detectable in numerous dimensions, including the governing coalition. In actual fact, the coalition also included prominent personalities from the democratic era, including former presidents Gabriel González Videla (1946–1952) and Jorge Alessandri (1958–1964), who were members of the Council of State. Alessandri presided over the council until after approval of the constitution in the 1980 plebiscite. There were also former ministers, undersecretaries, and other senior officials of the Alessandri government occupying similar political positions in the Pinochet government. However, because this was a forward-looking regime, the top leadership was composed primarily of independent personalities who had not occupied public posts during the democratic era.

Legal Legitimation and Regime Institutionalization

The third mode of legitimation was a legal one. Its fundamental objective was the establishment of a new constitutional order. A few weeks after the September 11, 1973, coup, the government designated a commission to draw up a new constitution; the commission was presided over by the minister of justice in Alessandri's government, Enrique Ortúzar Escobar. Constitutionalists of various persuasions were integrated into this commission. However, those members who did not agree with the government's political proposals withdrew from the commission, and in this way it took on a single hue.

The 1980 constitution established two constitutional orders: one that will come into play after a period of transition and one that will prevail during the transition. The 1980 constitutional order took on the character of a "protected democracy," which establishes various mechanisms for defending the order from the "totalitarian threat" by excluding the parties that promote it (Article 8) and also from "demagogy" and the "tyranny of parties." The constitution affirms in Article 18 that the electoral system "will always guarantee complete equality between independents and political party members, both in the presentation of candidates and in their participation in the appointment processes." Article 18, therefore, expresses the political tenets of *gremialismo* and of the followers of Alessandri[36] and adopts a long held tradition of the Chilean Right—rejecting political parties—that dates back to Jorge Prat and the magazine *Estanquero* at the end of the 1940s.[37]

The period of transition was fixed at eight years and presented the constitutional plebiscite as a noncompetitive presidential election. This extended the sources of legitimation of Pinochet's power, thus enabling him to court and receive direct popular support. The government was able to mobilize the whole of the governing coalition and generate popular support through an intensive use of radio and television that trumpeted the economic achievements of the boom years. The opposition was denied access to media, was limited in its presentation of the negative alternative, and was unable to mobilize supporters, except to bring about ten thousand people to the Caupolicán theater to listen to former president Eduardo Frei. The government received 67 percent of the valid votes in the plebiscite.

It is worth noting that there was not a consensus within the governing coalition on the constitutional text submitted to the plebiscite. The text issued by the Council of State, which was prepared by the Ortúzar

Commission and firmly supported by Alessandri, established a period of transition of only five years, during which General Pinochet would remain in the presidency. There would be a Congress with representatives named by the junta and senators by Pinochet, and presidential and parliamentary elections would be held simultaneously ninety days before the expiration of the transition period, that is, at the end of 1984. Pinochet modified the regulation of the transition not only in terms of its duration but also with regard to the mechanisms constraining the use of political authority.[38]

Weak Institutionalization and Strong Personalism

The third feature of the Chilean authoritarian regime is a low level of institutionalization and a high personalization of power. It is difficult for authoritarian regimes to adopt institutional formulas because the options are either a one-party regime, as in Mexico, which presents problems for the politicization of society and requires an extensive number of activists, or a corporative formula, which runs the danger of being rejected as fascist. Pinochet rejected the two formulas and chose to maintain an "authoritarian situation" through an institutional network of territorial and functional bodies; a dominant presidential structure in which he himself wields the legal and historical powers that the office of the president had in the past; and a junta that exercises legislative power.[39] The armed forces and the security apparatus formally assumed a great political responsibility. The junta is autonomous, and differences of opinion are not unusual. For example, Admiral José Toribio Merino and General Pinochet disagreed on a bill that established the minimum membership required for legal recognition of a political party (Pinochet wanted a minimum of 150,000 members).

A low level of institutionalization did not favor the political participation of the different groups of the governing coalition that are highly dependent on Pinochet's decisions. Thus, no single power group has a specific area of state power under its control. The only exception was the Chicago boys who controlled economic policies of the government until the collapse of the "boom." Nevertheless, the importance of General Pinochet's strong personal power cannot be exaggerated because it operates in a complex, differentiated political system. This system has a fairly significant institutional sector as represented by the participation of the armed forces (see Tables 4.2 and 4.3). What is important to bear in mind is that Pinochet, unlike Franco, directly controls the state and the government in contemporary Chile. This entails an extremely heavy administrative and political burden; Franco delegated this responsibility to Admiral Luis Carrero Blanco, who exercised leadership with the assistance of the presidency and a modern state bureaucracy. General Pinochet's assumption of these functions and tasks implies a disproportionate concentration of the political and administrative work, thereby creating problems for the efficiency of the system.

The mix of low institutionalization and high personalization was criticized by sectors within the governing coalition during the drawing up of the present constitution. For example, Alessandri's formula proposed strong institutionalization at the expense of personalization and a limited term of office for Pinochet. This alternative proposal was compatible with the regime's basic criteria that there would not be any deadlines to meet, only goals to attain. The transition articles added to the constitution therefore were not directed primarily against the opposition but at the governing coalition itself in order to cement its cohesion behind Pinochet. This is why a noncompetitive election of the head of state was proposed—namely, to respond to strong criticism of the basis of his authority that had been surfacing within the governing coalition.

REGIME STABILIZATION AND THE POLITICS OF SYNCHRONIZATION

Juan Linz's model of an authoritarian regime was based on limited pluralism, which differentiates such a regime from totalitarianism and democracy.[40] Linz pointed out that the authoritarian regime may be analyzed in terms of its differences with totalitarianism and may be considered a limited monism. Where totalitarianism is determined through a comprehensive synchronization (*Gleichschaltung*) of the political, cultural, and social structures of a new state under a single party, the authoritarian formula prescribes a limited form of synchronization.[41] The Pinochet government closed Parliament and prohibited party activity but did not organize a mass party; it prohibited large trade union federations but permitted trade unionism; it intervened in the universities but did not synchronize their faculty and students with an official ideology and apparatus of party control; and it permitted large institutional spaces for the Catholic Church, including its lay organizations. All these give the Chilean authoritarian regime great complexity and heterogeneity.

The complexity and long democratic tradition of a country such as Chile did not permit a total synchronization. This would have required considerably more extensive, harsher repression at the inauguration of the regime and a successful struggle against a sophisticated democratic tradition with particularly strong social and cultural bases and a powerful Catholic Church. Thus, it is absurd to call the Chilean regime fascist or totalitarian.[42] In Nazi Germany, by contrast, there were fewer Catholics and many Protestant lay preachers found totalitarian appeals intensely appealing.

In Chile limited synchronization allowed for the survival of institutions of the democratic political system. A network of political party activities existed that was spread through family contacts. The Catholic Church provided arenas of freedom and pluralism, from which it was possible to develop a defense of human rights through the Comité de Paz (Peace Committee) and, later, when this was dissolved, through the Vicaría de la Solidaridad (Vicariate for Solidarity). The Catholic Church also created the Academia de Humanismo Cristiano (Academy of Christian Humanism) to protect academic pluralism, which had been stifled by government intervention of the universities. That intervention created a sectarian climate that sought to exclude ideologies other than the official one.[43]

The political system in Chile is not a *Monokratie* but a crypto *Polykratie* where the opposition has great problems of survival. However, it has more political resources than the oppositions of other authoritarian regimes, such as the Argentina of the *Proceso* (1976–1983) or Franco's Spain.[44] Initially, opposition activities were minimal and often were confined to social and professional activities. However, this opposition symbolically kept the democratic flame alight. Starting from this base, the opposition progressively expanded its activities when permitted or tolerated by the regime, voluntarily or involuntarily. Two events provided a strong impetus for opposition activity: the plebiscites in 1978 and in 1980, which were presented by the regime as General Pinochet's noncompetitive elections. The opposition made a brief gesture in rejecting the corresponding official formula and was able to present a relatively cohesive alternative through the leadership of ex-president Eduardo Frei, who acted as the polarizing alternative in both plebiscites.[45]

APOTHEOSIS AND POLITICAL FRAGILITY

In 1980 the regime reached its highest level of political and economic success, and it seized the opportunity to ratify the 1980 constitution by means of a plebiscite. Overwhelming confidence in the economy heralded a promising future, and regime officials were convinced that the transition to a "protected democracy" would be initiated immediately. Prominent right-wing figures were mobilized in support of the YES campaign, which obtained a very large majority. The press, radio, and television supported the official discourse, thereby creating a climate of proregime sentiment, which was reinforced by the arrogant confidence of the regime's economic team. Some weeks after the plebiscite Interior Minister Sergio Fernández demonstrated the strength of the government by exiling the president of the Partido Demócrata Cristiano (Christian Democratic party, or PDC) Andrés Zaldívar. The regime had attained its highest level of legitimacy. It had a new constitution and was supported by politicians from the democratic era and by extensive sectors of the population. The economy was growing steadily. The future looked marvelous. Chile was on the threshold of becoming a modern, advanced society.

This edifice soon began to crumble, beginning with the economy—the regime's foundation. Initially, the fissures were small, but they grew relatively quickly because the strategy of legitimation by performance became couterproductive. On April 29, 1981, a few weeks after the introduction of the new constitution, the first cracks appeared as one of the country's largest firms declared bankruptcy. This exposed the excessive borrowing undertaken by many Chilean companies. In November 1981 the government had to intervene in eight financial institutions that were on the brink of bankruptcy and had been utilizing official credit. In 1981 the deficit in current account was $4.8 billion, of which only one-quarter was due to external factors—declining copper prices, increases in international rates of interest, and falling export prices.[46] This deficit was the result of excessive imports, interest payments on foreign credits, and a host of other factors, and any reduction by means of a new inflow of international credits looked extremely difficult. There was a bottleneck in the economic model precisely where its "success" had originated. These problems did not act as a sufficiently important warning for the economic authorities to change course and thus prevent a deeper crisis. On the contrary, the authorities continued to be blinded by their excessive confidence in the economy; they maintained their policy, certain that the rules of the game would operate successfully.

The emerging crisis was immediately reflected in a decline in economic activity and, consequently, in an increase in an already high level of unemployment. Estimates by the Economics Department of the University of Chile showed that the level of unemployment in September 1981 was 8.1 percent; by December it had reached 10.9 percent and three months later, 19.9 percent.[47] These high levels of unemployment were even greater in certain sectors of economic activity, such as the construction industry. The National Institute of Statistics found that the 22.1 percent unemployment rate of October–December 1981 jumped to 35 percent for January–March 1982 and reached 62.2 percent in July–September 1982. In the industrial sector as a whole these percentages were 10.9, 16.1 and 30.1 percent respectively.[48]

There was no increase in the official unemployment figures once the government introduced a plan for community employment through the PEM and the *Programa de Empleo para los Jefes de Hogar* (Employment Program for Heads of Households, or POJH). The level of unemployment, including PEM and POJH, was 29.8 percent in November 1982. The Santiago metropolitan region registered a spectacular increase in community employment: The 43,500 people registered in the PEM in August 1982 rose to 54,800 in September and reached 69,500 by December. Meanwhile, in the POJH, there were 15,600 people enrolled in October, 43,700 by December, and the number of people covered continued rising throughout the first half of 1983. In May 1983 there were 92,937 workers in the PEM (the national total was 396,277) and 96,252 in the POJH (the national total was 132,499). By July 1983, 15 percent of the economically active population in the Santiago metropolitan region was enrolled in the PEM or the POJH. In May 1983 there were 500,000 Chileans enrolled in the PEM and 132,449 in the POJH. Despite the deteriorating economic situation, the government was able to keep discontent under control through this policy of economic patronage.[49] The crisis also was held back by a fluctuating economic policy that precluded a total break with the neoliberal scheme that had been incubating such a crisis since 1975.

As cracks became more visible, their political implications also emerged. Initially, members of the governing coalition were concerned, but in time that concern grew into something larger when those elites realized that they, too, might be affected by the crisis. They realized that the independent economists were right about the illusion of living on loans. This concern shown by sectors of the governing coalition stimulated opposition activity, which began to achieve some organization and mobilization in the universities, particularly in spring 1982. The government attempted to restrain certain opposition activity by means of coercive actions by organized groups, such as those of the so-called Gurkas, who beat up some journalists in December 1982. However, it soon became obvious that the crisis went even deeper and that a pending political and social explosion could not be defused through coercion alone.

The economic crisis was officially acknowledged by the government on January 13, 1983, when it ordered the intervention of five banks, the liquidation of three others, and the direct supervision of two more. These ten institutions accounted for 45 percent of the financial system's capital and reserves–64 percent if the Banco del Estado (Chile's Central Bank) is excluded. The state was forced to make huge contributions to financial institutions in liquidation as well as provide urgent loans and overdrafts. Between May 1982 and March 1983 this bailout represented a total of 189,000 million pesos, that is, 15 percent of the Gross Domestic Product (GDP) for 1982.[50]

Suddenly the government came to possess immense economic power, which was unprecedented in Chile and did not even prevail during the years of the Unidad Popular. In fact, two large organizations Allende's government was unable to control, the newspaper *El Mercurio* and the Banco de Chile (Bank of Chile), were dragged down by the regime's financial calamity. *El Mercurio* had to reach an agreement with the Banco del Estado in order to resolve its difficult economic situation. Ironically, this situation was a result of mounting indebtedness, which had been recommended by the paper's economic adviser, Sergio de Castro, a former Pinochet minister and leading Chicago boy. The Banco de Chile was dragged into government intervention owing to the fall of the Vial Group by whom it was controlled.

TABLE 4.5
Comparison of Personal Situations in 1973 and 1983 (in percentage)[a]

	Average Total[b]	Upper Class	Middle Class	Lower Class	Men	Women
No change	16.8	17.6	20.6	13.4	18.0	15.4
Worse	65.8	72.9	66.4	63.0	65.6	68.4
Better	12.1	5.9	9.3	16.5	10.4	12.5
Did not give an opinion	5.2	3.5	3.7	7.1	6.0	3.7

[a]Question: "How is your standard of living today compared to that of 1973?"

[b]n=319

Source: TESTMERC Survey, September 1983.

The economic model that sought to legitimize the regime through success had failed, thereby unleashing an extremely serious political crisis whose dynamics soon altered the regime's future policy. Paradoxically, the Chicago boys had taken the country back to the very point where it had started: a state playing a very powerful role in the economy that would now use those extensive resources in a highly political fashion.

The economic crisis signified not only the failure of the forward strategy for legitimation; the crisis also seriously undercut the historical legitimation of the regime, in terms of how the population compared its standard of living with that of the final days of the Allende government. As a result of this comparison, many Chileans concluded that the situation in 1983 was worse than that of 1973, as illustrated by a public opinion survey made in the streets of Santiago (see Table 4.5).

The economic crisis affected all social levels, particularly the poor. The minimum wage was frozen in September 1981, thus provoking a drastic fall in real wages (see Table 4.6). The middle class, which hitherto had benefited from the economic model, suffered the fierce and unexpected impact of the crisis. That impact caused the rapid politicization and radicalization of this class, thus converting it into a new and very dynamic political actor.[51]

Protestas and the Expansion of the Political Arena

Suddenly, quite unpredictably, the political system was shaken by protests. Thousands of Chileans, particularly in Santiago, showed their rejection of the prevailing situation in the same way that the opposition to the government

TABLE 4.6
Legal Minimum Wage, 1981-1985

Date		In Chilean Pesos (of each year)	Index[a]	Index[b]
September	1981	5,185.71	100.0	100.0
September	1982	5,185.71	89.8	85.0
March	1983	5,185.71	78.7	74.9
June	1983	5,185.71	74.2	66.0
September	1983	5,445.00	78.2	64.3
December	1983	5,445.00	70.0	62.2
March	1984	5,445.00	68.4	61.5
June	1984	5,445.00	65.7	58.5
September	1984	5,445.00	63.1	51.2
October	1984	5,445.00	58.3	s.d.
December	1984	5,445.00	56.9	50.7
March	1985	6,667.00	64.4	55.8
May	1985	6,667.00	61.7	--

[a]Deflated by IPC (cost of living index)---official. September 1981=100.

[b]Deflated by IPC---Employment Economics Program, September 1981=100.

Source: The Employment Economics Program of the Academy of Christian Humanism according to National Statistics Institute data.

of the Unidad Popular had reacted ten years before—by banging pans, honking horns while driving, and holding district meetings. These *protestas* were considerably more intense in the more marginal settlements. This was to be expected in view of the dreadful situation in which poor people were living. What surprised the regime most was that middle-class people participated actively in the *protestas*.

The *protestas* unleashed an increasing politicization within society that reached extremely high levels. Politics ceased to be a small group, underground activity and became an activity that moved with lightning speed through all social levels, intermediate groups, and society as a whole. The political arena was expanded abruptly, thereby creating significant new spheres of freedom.[52] The expansion of the political arena affected all relevant political actors of the government and of the opposition. This expansion meant a profound change in the political system that has had and will continue to have a prolonged effect on Chilean politics and will affect the conditions of a future democratic transition.

The government found itself criticized by a press anxious to exercise its newly won freedom and to unveil all kinds of government weaknesses. In fact, the press, once a protective factor for the regime, became a mechanism for criticism and control.[53] The press acted against the opposition with a ferocity that was just as intense as that employed against the regime. The opposition, now engaged in mass politics, had to face the scrutiny of a liberalized press. The opposition had to act in front of thousands of Chileans, frequently without an adequate opportunity to prepare.

During this *apertura* politics was expanded from the elite level, the politics of notables, to mass politics in which thousands of Chileans and numerous organizations participated. Competitive politics was revived through a flurry of elections in many organizations. These elections provided an institutional base to a polarized political conflict that had high personal costs. The democratic opposition was able to show its political strength through its success in elections held by student federations and professional associations.

These contests diminished the number of parties that emerged or reemerged during the *apertura*, as these elections pressed the parties to demonstrate their continued political relevance.[54] Very few parties were able to meet this challenge, and those that could were primarily the large historical parties, with the exception of *gremialismo* and the Unión Nacional (National Union, or UN), which showed that they had substantial organizational capacity. Several parties were able to avoid these competitive politics through coalition strategies, such as the Alianza Democrática (AD) and the Movimiento Democrático Popular (Popular Democratic Movement, or MDP). The AD brought together the PDC, the Partido Radical (Radical party, or PR), the Partido Socialista (Socialist party, or PS) headed by Carlos Briones, the small Partido Derecha Republicana (Republican Right party, or PDR) and the Social Demócrata (Social Democrat, or SD), which recently had separated from the Radical party. The MDP comprises the Partido Comunista (Communist party, or PC), a sector of the PS led by Clodomiro Almeyda, and the Movimiento de Izquierda Revolucionaria (Movement of the Revolutionary Left, or MIR).

The dichotomy between a few large parties and very many small parties having equal influence constitutes a recurring phenomenon in democratic oppositions. Many of the problems encountered by the AD originated principally in the conflict between the large and the small parties. Large parties such as the PDC could not easily reconcile their policies to the preferences of the small without subjugating the coalition. In the small parties, such as the PR, personal antagonisms reverberated more directly throughout the coalition as a whole. In the socialist sector party fragmentation prevented the development of a consistent policy.

Reemergence of the Parties and Political Competition

Political competition took place between the parties or movements of the regime and of the opposition and within each bloc. The competition between government and opposition was dichotomous in nature. To be sure, the government and the opposition blocs were extraordinarily heterogeneous, but the bipolar nature of the conflict and its intensity forced both sides to hold their internal differences in abeyance.

This competition was fueled by the history of party and organizational participation in the Chilean political process. A long, intense, and traditional competition among the political parties enabled them to achieve an extensive social and territorial presence and to secure deep loyalties that the regime could not eradicate. Political loyalties were maintained and passed on through family ties and contacts. There were various spaces of freedom that permitted the survival of party nuclei, although their organization was very limited. Chile thus was a very politicized society; extensive sectors throughout the entire country and at all social levels participated in politics and supported the parties. Even the *gremialistas* established a party, the Unión Demócrata Independiente (Independent Democratic Union, or UDI). Given these historical roots, it comes as no surprise that during the *apertura*, the parties that had existed before 1973 were able to reemerge, create a party apparatus, recruit activists, and mobilize followers.[55]

Thus, the politics during the *apertura* was led by historical personalities who had attained a degree of political leadership before 1973. They had more practical experience in the art of politics than the new politicians and also had an extensive network of personal and organizational contacts that enabled them to engage in party politics. The leaders with experience before 1973 ranged from mature people, such as Sergio Onofre Jarpa and the leaders of the historical parties, to young people.

This pattern prevailed as well in voluntary organizations. For example, the head of the Engineering Students Center at the end of the 1960s, Patricio Basso, became the moving force and president of the influential Association of Academicians of the University of Chile. This pattern is fairly characteristic of most interest groups. The presidents of the Association of Engineers (Eduardo Arriagada), of the Confederation for Production and Trade (Jorge Fontaine), and of the Confederation of Retailers (Rafael Cumsille) were also presidents of their associations in 1973. The leader of the National Agricultural Society, Manuel Valdés, was president before 1973. This reinstitution of old leadership occurred because there was no civil war in Chile, as in Spain, which would have destroyed the political elite. This was less true of the trade union movement and the left wing parties because they were more drastically affected by repression and exile.

It is important to consider the impact of this historical continuity because it again has acquired enormous significance; past positive as well as negative behaviors (the ability to organize rapidly in the former instance and the continuation of pre-1973 prejudices and political differences in the latter) have been brought to the fore. These micropolitical factors can become important obstacles to cooperation among elites. An adequate degree of continuity and replacement of elite politicians constitutes one of the most complex problems in the politics of the transition and installation of democracy in Chile, as it has been before in other cases.[56]

The PDC is the principal opposition actor. The PDC was the largest party in 1973; it obtained 28 percent of the vote in the parliamentary elections of that year, notwithstanding the dichotomous structure of the political conflict at the close of the Allende government, and had an electoral base comprising different social classes, a network of members throughout the entire country, and a great leader in ex-president Eduardo Frei.[57] The PDC managed to survive during the most difficult years of the authoritarian regime. Although the PDC was not the most persecuted party, it was the victim of coercion by the regime—outstanding personalities such as Renán Fuentealba, Jaime Castillo, Claudio Huepe, and Andrés Zaldívar were exiled, and an extremely large proportion of PDC leaders were the victims of government abuse. A survey carried out by the author among members of the Junta Nacional (National Executive Board) of the PDC at the beginning of June 1985 showed that 36.7 percent had been detained, tortured, or exiled, 20.4 percent were exonerated, and 15.6 percent had received anonymous telephone threats. Only 27 percent had not been victims of repression.[58] This is an exceptionally high degree of coercion and explains the PDC's resolute political opposition to the regime.

The PDC has attained a leading position in the opposition after having overcome certain internal and external problems. The principal internal problem was the sudden death of Eduardo Frei in January 1982, which raised a succession problem that other parties have not been able to resolve satisfactorily. Frei was the prime mover in uniting the opposition and was the primary force among PDC leaders; Frei also had considerable political power that accrued to him as a former president. Frei's succession was resolved successfully by the leaders through a policy of consensus, which resulted in former foreign minister Gabriel Valdés occupying the presidency of the PDC. The PDC demonstrated its cohesion during an internal electoral process, which lasted a year, that reelected Valdés and culminated in a meeting of the Junta Nacional in June 1985.

Externally, the PDC is seeking compatibility between a policy of coalition with other parties and its own course as the largest political party. The

PDC was the founder of the AD, but the latter has not taken shape as a political force different from the PDC. The role of the AD is complicated by the fragmentation of its member parties, which gives the PDC a hegemonic position, a position that derives from the PDC's political strength as well as from the divisions within the opposition parties. This makes it difficult for the PDC to depart from its isolated policies in order to advance with the others and share the successes, the sacrifices, and the costs of political action when democracy is restored.

The other outstanding political actor during this period was the Left or, more exactly, the lefts. A democratic Left joined the AD and its policy of social mobilization. This was basically the PS led by Carlos Briones and by Ricardo Lagos. A maximalist Left constituted within the MDP and composed of a sector of the PS, the PC, and the MIR attempted to sabotage AD policies. The disruption of the PS-PC axis by the former threw the PC into extraordinary disorder because it had to act alone or seek shelter under a political coalition.[59] In addition the PC's adoption of maximalist policies, including the use of violence, represented an important departure from its historical roots.

Chilean labor has changed considerably since 1973 when the PC played a leading role. Social and occupational changes have altered the bases and organizational dimensions of trade unions. The PC has reacted by trying to get the support of people in marginal settlements with its violent policies. This policy has traumatized a communist subculture accustomed to peaceful, parliamentary action, has brought extremely high personal costs to many communist militants, and may have cost the PC much operating efficiency. Moreover, this policy has been unanimously rejected by the rest of the opposition parties.

Socialism faced this new development with difficulty. The PS was not unified, and the small political parties that left the PDC before 1973—the Movimiento de Acción Popular Unitario (Unitary Popular Action Movement, or MAPU) and the Izquierda Cristiana (Christian Left)—did not want to merge with the PS in order to constitute a "new" Left.[60] Personal differences, leadership aspirations, and harassment by the PC contributed to the fragmentation of the Socialists, which weakened the democratic opposition. The PS also made tactical errors within the AD, which moderated its discourse too much and thus lost adherents on two sides (these tactical moves may have been inspired by the experience of the Spanish Socialist Workers party). The PS yielded space on the left to the PC, and its turn toward the center helped to legitimize the PDC's position. In addition, some Socialists fell into an extremely anticommunist discourse that, although well founded on international grounds, sounded discordant in the political culture of the Chilean Left. In short, the Socialists within the AD found themselves facing bilateral competition and losing political space to the PC and the PDC.[61]

How the discourse and organization of the Socialist party will be reunited is one of the key questions for the future of the democracy. In effect, this reunification will determine whether there will be a Left dominated by the PC, as in Italy, or a two-party Left with a weak PS that can grow, as in France, or with a dominant PS, as in Spain. In the latter case, the Socialist Workers party initially competed with Spain's Communist party from a decidedly left-wing position and not from the center, as the PS had done during the *apertura*. The Spanish example may not be the most appropriate for Chilean Socialists because in Spain there was no popular historical center party comprising different social classes, such as the Chilean PDC, and the Unión de Centro Democrático (Union of the Democratic Center, or UCD) was created as an electoral coalition after the death of Franco. The competition between Socialists and Communists represents one of the key issues for the future of transition to democracy in Chile.

The Fragmentation and Paralysis of the Government

I have discussed the fragmentation of the opposition and its impact on political activity. There also was fragmentation of government political forces, which rendered the government incapable of uniting its supporters in a single party and which constitutes one of the leaders' obsessions. Several traditional and new rightist parties existed whose leaders were incapable of defining common policies. Their situation was not easy. They were not officially part of the government because the regime refused to be of the single-party type. They were not part of the opposition either, given their support for government policies and rejection of those pursued by the AD.

Interior Minister Sergio Onofre Jarpa formed a right-wing party, the UN. The UN was to be a new center-right party capable of integrating the historical Right traditions, gathering together the principal personalities of the PN, and merging them with the new groups that had emerged during the authoritarian period. Examples of the first category were former senators Pedro Ibáñez and Francisco Bulnes. An example of the second was the leadership granted to Andrés Allamand as president of the UN. Allamand had not occupied any posts in the regime. However, the UN did not attract all the leaders of the PN that it desired. People such as former senator Sergio Diez were not incorporated into the UN or into the PN, which was reorganized in 1983 under the leadership of former deputy (*diputado*) Carmen Sáenz. Jarpa did not run any real risks for the UN; he was limited by his ministerial post and by the conflicts his assumption of leadership aroused among the old liberals and conservatives of the PN.

With Jarpa's UN the different parties of the Right tried to band together in the Group of 8, including the PN. Three of the eight were excluded later, and the remaining five formed the Acuerdo Democrático Nacional (National Democratic Accord, or ADENA), which was unable to attain organized political representation. Conservatives wished to form a broad electoral coalition that would challenge the assumption of leadership from the AD. That is why ADENA included groups ranging from Talleres Socialistas (Socialist Workshops), to the Movimiento de Acción Nacional (National Action Movement, or MAN), the UN, the *gremialistas*, the Partido Social Cristiano (Social Christian party), and other small parties. However, neither the Group of 8 nor ADENA was able to face the interest group elections, although the *gremialistas*, the UN, and the nationalists participated. Defeats in the elections, in the Lawyers Association, and in the Federación de Estudiantes de la Universidad de Chile (Student Federation of the University of Chile, or FEUC) in April 1985 indicated right-wing deterioration.

Pinochet and the military welcomed the fragmentation of the opposition, but they could not permit fragmentation within their own governing coalition. They were dismayed to see their own political parties and leaders falling into the same divisive, individualistic pitfalls for which the opposition had been criticized. This fragmentation of the right wing was decisive in preventing the creation of the congress that was advocated by the Group of 8. ADENA was dissolved immediately after the lifting of the *estado de sitio* (state of siege) in June 1985 without having achieved any political success.

Several nuclei of the governing coalition were increasingly critical of the government; they abstained from giving it any resolute public support and opted to remain silent or offer only lukewarm support on condition that there would be a return to democracy in 1989. Some wanted to cross the Rubicon and join the opposition, but they did not. There were many problems, ranging from party financing to the articulation of political and ideological plans different from those offered by the opposition parties.[62]

According to Juan Linz, semiopposition groups are not "dominant nor represented in the governing group but are willing to participate in power without fundamentally challenging the regime."[63] In the Chilean case several sectors may be considered semiopposition, including the PN and the UN. The semiopposition has not made up its mind regarding regime change; instead, it presents alternative views with regard to the policies pursued by the government. What may happen is that as certain groups become more disillusioned, they might shift resolutely from the semiopposition to the opposition.

The *apertura* spilled over into the forces of the Right, which wasted an excellent opportunity to assume leadership. They remained adrift; they lost the elections in which they participated and gave the impression that on the whole they tolerated the regime rather than accepted it. Jarpa himself had to leave the cabinet in February 1985 after he lost support within the government, broke off with the opposition, and clashed with the archbishop of Santiago.[64]

The Limits of Opposition: The Democratic Alliance

What was the politics of the democratic opposition, that is, of the AD? The AD proposed an immediate transition to democracy when it requested Pinochet's resignation at the outset of the *protestas* and the *apertura*. This left the AD with the task of provoking a regime change, which was a precipitous decision. In fact, this position complicated the "dialogue" with the government that took place in Santiago in September 1983 (organized by the new archbishop of Santiago, Monsignor Juan Francisco Fresno) and in which Jarpa participated. How could the government take part in a dialogue with the opposition if the latter proposed beforehand that the head of state must go?

Later, the AD could not consolidate itself politically, and its discourse in favor of regime change lost credibility. The AD did not succeed in leading the *protestas*, which were later discredited by the maximalist policies of the MPD; the *protestas* were called by the Comando Nacional de Trabajadores (National Workers Command, or CNT). Nor was the AD able to project itself on the interest group elections, even with the help of the Communists; the opposition was united, and where it was not, the electoral coalition diverged from the AD because the Communists voted for the opposition.

The discourse and anticommunist policies of the regime had an effect on AD activity, given that the AD wished to distance itself from the PC. The regime launched a drive against the opposition in the social organizations. While the regime's position hardened, differences within the opposition remained on a secondary level. This was increasingly obvious when the regime's security apparatus began to lose its cohesion, and extremely bloody incidents of repressison occurred.

The AD presented itself as an alternative and departed from the assumption that a regime change was inevitable in the near future. The AD believed that a government overwhelmed by the *protestas*, facing a severe economic crisis, and backed by a governing coalition without cohesion and mystique would weaken Pinochet's authority sufficiently to allow for his removal. The AD also was assumed that social mobilization would be maintained constantly.

However, Pinochet, both personally and in his institutional role as president and army commander in chief, was not as affected by the crisis as the AD had expected. One of the features of Pinochet's style of leadership has been his exercise of the role of president over that of government head through an emphasis on mediation and arbitration. As he does not appear publicly to be involved directly in the management of government affairs, he was not harmed personally by the economic collapse. Actually, the fact that the management of the economy had been given to the Chicago boys meant that responsibility for the economic crisis devolved on them and not on Pinochet. This was facilitated by the actions of the opposition, which directed its criticism and political activity against monetarism and the Chicago boys. Thus, at the time of the *protestas* the public did not see the president as directly responsible for the economic crisis. Instead, the government in general and the Chicago boys in particular were blamed.

A survey conducted in Santiago during September 1983 demonstrated this point very clearly (see Table 4.7): Blame for the crisis was placed on the government (55 percent), the economic team (21.9 percent), government advisers (19 percent), Pinochet directly (4 percent), and the armed forces (2 percent). The AD requested the resignation of the man whom the people did not hold responsible for the crisis.

Furthermore, the opposition disregarded the elements in Pinochet's leadership style, which is based on the presidential and paternalistic traditions of the Chilean democratic system. In view of this continuity, Pinochet has utilized traditional political resources to strengthen his authority and power. This style of leadership obviously is strengthened by the solemnity and formality that surround Pinochet's position as army commander in chief, which not only carries influence within the military but also within the population. Nor was he isolated politically and socially, as the AD had thought. In fact, Pinochet enjoys support from institutions and organizations that provide him with direct links to different sectors of the population.

In summary, the opposition underestimated the basic sources of Pinochet's personal and institutional power. Unlike the Spanish opposition to Franco, which had to acknowledge the fundamental source of his authority and power, the opposition in Chile continues to ignore it. The final balance of the politics of *apertura* was not a negative one for the head of state.

THE ROLE OF THE ARMED FORCES IN THE POLITICS OF LIBERALIZATION

One of the features of the politics of *apertura* was the evident inconsistency between a liberalization prompted by the Ministry of the Interior and a severe military control of public order exercised through the then *intendente* (mayor) of the metropolitan region, General Roberto Guillard. Military control in the popular marginal settlements was extremely severe, particularly during the *protesta* of August 1983. According to the Vicariate for Solidarity, between May 1983 and October 1984 a total of 134 persons died as a result of government violence against demonstrators; hundreds of people were injured. The regime did not hesitate to incur the high costs of represssion

TABLE 4.7
Responsibility for the Economic Crisis in Chile (in percentage)[a]

	Average Total[b]	Upper Class	Middle Class	Lower Class	Men	Women
Economic team	21.9	27.7	28.0	15.0	23.0	22.0
World recession	20.1	15.3	15.9	25.2	17.5	22.0
The government in general	55.5	50.6	57.0	55.9	55.2	54.4
Government advisers	19.0	20.0	19.6	18.1	18.0	20.6
Pinochet directly	4.0	--	4.7	4.7	4.9	1.5
Armed forces, *carabineros*, and so on	1.8	--	1.9	2.4	1.1	2.2
People who give orders to Pinochet	0.5	--	0.9	0.7	0.5	0.7
The public in general	1.4	--	2.8	0.7	0.5	2.2
Assassins (murderers)	0.4	--	0.9	--	--	0.7
Politicians	0.3	--	--	0.7	--	0.7
Did not know/did not give an opinion	1.1	--	0.9	1.6	1.1	0.7

[a]Question: "A large number of people think that the situation in Chile is bad. Who do you believe are responsible?" Multiple answers were allowed.

[b]n=319.

Source: TESTMERC Survey, September 1983.

because the opposition offensive was threatening the stability of the regime. It was able to do this because the armed forces assumed responsibility for the high cost of this situation.[65]

This greater military presence in political activity altered the parameters of regime functioning. Hitherto these parameters were marked by a low institutionalization and a high personalization of authority in the person of General Pinochet. Greater assumption of leadership by the armed forces strengthened the institutional dimension of the regime, and there was a consequent decrease in the personal element. This greater military presence demonstrated to the civilian groups within the regime that the military element would be decisive and that it could create many difficulties for them. For the first time, it was evident to them that if the armed forces proposed the reelection of Pinochet as president, there would be a great politico-military base that would not allow them to stand aside. Pinochet's participation in the 1980 plebiscite had been based precisely on the understanding that democracy would be established fully at the end of the decade.

This greater institutionalization of the regime and the strong military presence in political activity placed the opposition forces in an impossible situation. Their proposal for a transition to democracy clashed directly with the intentions of the armed forces, which had reiterated their loyalty to the validity of the 1980 constitution and to President Pinochet from the beginning of the *protestas* and of the *apertura*. PDC president Gabriel Valdés found himself in an uncomfortable situation once he had announced that Pinochet's resignation would be a preliminary condition of opposition activity. But Pinochet's power and authority did not deteriorate. Subsequent opposition efforts to weaken Pinochet's power and authority did not have the desired effect either. Other efforts, such as the October 1984 letter of the AD to the commanders in chief of the three branches of the armed forces proposing an advance toward democracy, had no effect whatsoever.

A strong military presence provides the regime with great authority and power but decreases the regime's already limited flexibility, which is based on legal-constitutional legitimation.[66] This is not a medium-term solution. The 1980 constitution established a mechanism for political succession that could prove very troublesome in practice. This mechanism may cause a bottleneck in 1988 because the reelection of the president entails an enlarged political mobilization. But that hardly could match the mobilization of 1980 because the governing coalition has become fragmented and the economic situation has worsened. This is one of the most serious dilemmas for Chile's political future.

Liberalization and Economic Patronage

The government was surprised by the extent of the *protestas* and was put on the defensive for some months, but it never lost political control of the situation. It progresively recovered political initiative by means of a strategy that combined politico-military control and a skillful, opportune patronage of the economy. The government's purpose was to weaken the opposition and to increase the cohesion of civilian groups that supported the regime, especially business and independent interest groups.

The politics of economic patronage had three components: Punish hypermobilization in the marginal settlements through political control of the PEM and the POJH, thereby drastically reducing the number of persons covered by these programs; discourage medium and small business firms—primarily merchants and lorry owners—from participating in the *protestas*; and deal with the needs of the large business firms affected by economic crisis.

The policy of community employment was marked by an increase in political control and a gradual reduction of the PEM. In May 1983, the month of the first protest, there were 396,277 workers enrolled in the scheme. This figure was progressively reduced to 309,670, 263,763, and 175,790 by September, December, and February respectively.[67] This was real punishment.

This economic reprisal meant a dramatic increase in unemployment in the marginal settlements. This increase was not expressed politically throughout 1984 because the populations in these settlements did not want to or could not protest, given that they wished to obtain a minimum wage and there was a drastic policy of politico-military control in the marginal settlements. This confluence of patronage and coercion is the reason for the demobilization of the marginal settlements in 1984 and 1985. The victims of the protests, however, were mainly young people. According to the Vicariate for Solidarity, about 25 percent of those killed in the protests were between sixteen and twenty years of age; an additional 32 percent were between twenty-one and thirty.

The second effort was directed at demobilizing the owners of small and medium business firms; attention was paid to the requirements of two pressure groups, lorry owners and merchants, that had important political and social power. They had been active in the opposition to Allende's government and, for a number of years, were firm supporters of the new regime. Even the presidents of the respective *gremios*, León Vilarín of the Lorry Owner's Federation and Rafael Cumsille of the Retailers' Confederation, had these positions prior to September 11, 1973. In recent years the two groups had adopted a critical attitude toward the Chicago boys' economic policies. The effects of the enormous concentration of wealth resulting from those policies seriously affected them as well as other owners of small and medium business firms.[68] In the case of the lorry owners, the impact of the economic crisis was doubly felt. They were deeply indebted in dollars—a fixed exchange rate of 39 pesos to the dollar had jumped to more than twice that amount—and had to carry the burden of the high cost of fines imposed for overladen cargoes. In this way, by August 9, 1984, there had been seventy-five hundred fines imposed for overloading, which represented 260 million pesos during the period September 7, 1981, to March 4, 1984.

As for the merchants, they went through a difficult period because sales had been reduced drastically. At the same time, they faced an energetic fiscal taxation policy enforced by the Internal Taxation Service (SII) so as to collect resources for a state that was facing a difficult economic crisis. The merchants' dispute with the government was made more acute when the SII accused Cumsille of tax evasion in his business in San Fernando. The director of the SII, Felipe Lamarca, a Catholic University economist linked to the *gremialistas*, created a confrontation with this key interest group at a decisive moment for the regime by taking advantage of Cumsille's imprisonment. This matter became a test of strength for Jarpa because Lamarca was resolutely supported within the governing coalition by the *gremialistas* and the interior minister wanted a compromise with the organization.

After months of tension, Jarpa succeeded in asserting himself and Lamarca had to give up his post when Luis Escobar, a former minister from 1961–1963 and former PR militant, accepted the minister of finance portfolio and supported Jarpa in giving precedence to a policy of effectively facing the opposition offensive. Henceforth, the SII adopted a considerably more flexible attitude in its fiscal and judicial treatment of the merchants; thus, the SSI succeeded in separating the merchants from the dynamic force of the *protestas*. This conflict damaged Jarpa's reputation because he appeared to have little influence within the regime. A few months earlier, however, Jarpa had been at the peak of his power, openly negotiating with the leaders of the AD on the future of the country. Cumsille was acquitted by the courts in January 1986.

The policy toward the lorry owners was more effective because there was a unified government command directing this policy. The vice president of the Corporación de Fomento de la Producción (Development Corporation, or CORFO), who would be responsible for looking into the rescheduling of debts, and the minister of public works, who would be responsible for looking into the problems of overloading fines, were both military officers. CORFO's policy consisted of offering a rescheduling of debts through a preferential rate of exchange, a reduction in rates of interest, and longer terms for repayment of capital. The negotiations on both these matters were subjected to pressure by the opposition's call for protests; the government had to acquiesce in order to prevent the lorry owners and merchants from joining these protests. This happened with the work stoppages in March and October 1984, in which they did not participate. In June 1984 Vilarín, who was a member of PRODEN, an opposition organization, was replaced as president of the Lorry Owners' Confederation by Adolfo Quinteros. On July 31, 1984, the junta approved a bill that canceled the fines for overloading, thus benefiting 90 percent of the lorry owners. On October 28, 1984, two days before the nationwide strike, CORFO approved a plan for the renegotiation of the lorry owners' debts, which amounted to $140 million. As a result of this action, the lorry owners were removed from the opposition.

Third, the government implemented a rapid, efficient policy to attend to the extremely severe economic situation faced by the owners of large business firms. In this connection, the policy was much more complex because any concessions would challenge the parameters of the economic model, which was never declared inoperable. The minister of finance until March 1984 was Carlos Cáceres, an economist identified with the ideological and technical inclinations of the Chicago boys. The initiatives that were implemented by the government were of an emergency nature: renegotiation of debts, a rise in import duties to protect the firms most effected by the liberalization of trade, and the utilization of Chilean manufactured products by state firms. The owners of business firms made a direct appeal for help to Pinochet. With the resulting support of the head of state, these measures were well received by the owners of business firms and by business leaders. Angel Fantuzzi, president of the Association of Metal Working Industries (ASIMET), publicly voiced satisfaction with this kind of economic support through his regular column in the magazine *Estrategia* under the suggestive title *Thank You President.*[69]

In synthesis, an economic crisis will not necessarily cause the collapse of the government of an authoritarian regime. On the contrary, with dwindling resources, an economic crisis may lead to the attainment of considerably greater political support for a government. The Chilean government obtained precisely that support during the *abertura* by means of skillful politics, thus demonstrating that the economy and politics have very different connections, depending on how a government seeks to relate them.

THE NEW POLITICAL ARENA: ELITE AND MASS POLITICAL ACTION

The political changes during the *protestas* and the *apertura* resulted in important modifications to the present political system. The crisis of the strategy of legitimation by performance triggered numerous, important political changes, including some that were sought by the actors and others that were not anticipated by them. When evaluating such changes it is necessary to recognize changes that are sought as well as those the actors did intend to attain. The latter changes are harder to enumerate because their characteristics are not so evident.

The study of economic crisis as a precipitant factor of political change cannot rely solely on an economic explanation. On the contrary, my analysis starts from a political perspective based on Max Weber's views on the political, economic, and cultural sources of legitimacy. What would a change of the present authoritarian regime be comprised of? The political system has succeeded in establishing itself by accepting numerous, important spaces of freedom that normally are associated with democracy as well as by using the authoritarian elements proper. The *apertura* produced some institutional differentiation owing to the politicization of society begun in the autumn of 1983. This differentiation affected an enlarged, heterogenous network of political and social organizations and created a complex predemocratic framework, which under an imaginative and energetic leadership could build up sufficient pressure for the acquisition of greater spaces of freedom and could reduce the margins of influence of the authoritarian components of the Pinochet regime.[70]

Consequently, the political system is a dyarchy with dual sources of legitimation in a situation of latent conflict. As long as the two segments coexist without consolidation, we may speak of an institutional schizophrenia. This predemocratic framework has enabled the political arena to expand. Currently, there is a political arena with elite action and also collective action. The opposition can count on greater resources for its political activity.

However, this expansion of the political arena presents Chile's political leaders with enormous difficulties because these leaders now need the capacity and political resources to act at elites level in which negotiation and personal contacts are the operative tactics and, simultaneously, to act in a mass arena, which requires organizational and leadership capacities for mobilization. In other words, the political leaders have to act through pressure from below and through elite accommodation. The two dimensions are complementary, not mutually exclusive, in the process of transition to democracy.

Not a single democracy has been established as a result of the influence of only one of these dimensions. For example, for there to have been negotiation in post-Franco Spain it was necessary that the opposition previously should have developed strong pressure from below. In exerting those pressures from below, the opposition faces enormous organizational difficulties in preventing elements of the extreme Left or extreme Right from sabotaging the intended effect of such pressures, as occurred in the *protestas*. This will present a serious challenge to the leaders who will have to show that they can act opportunely and with different styles at more than one level of political action. Leadership and organizational capacity for elite politics only or for mass politics only are insufficient conditions for the opposition to realize its goals. It must have at its disposal leadership and organizational capacity to act in politics at both elite and mass level.

FROM SCHIZOPHRENIA TO DIARCHY AND POLYARCHY

What are the implications of the political changes resulting from the *protestas* and the *apertura*? The failure of the strategy of forward legitimation seriously weakens the backward legitimacy of the regime. Chileans see the present situation as equal to or worse than 1973, and they envisage a future of great uncertainty. Legal-constitutional legitimacy has remained unharmed and constitutes the principal basis of regime legitimacy at the present time. This does not mean that the regime lacks legitimacy; I maintain only that it possesses one source instead of three, as before. In other words, the regime has a deficit of legitimacy.

Is legal legitimacy sufficient for establishing a political system that has acquired an extremely strong degree of political differentiation and has passed through an intensive political conflict? I do not think so. The present regime demonstrated precisely this point when it sought a mixed kind of legitimacy.

The regime, sooner or later, must implement a mixed strategy of relegitimation: forward and backward. However, the possibilities for success are not encouraging because future conditions will not be the same as they were in the initial phase of the regime. Then the regime enjoyed extensive political support that enabled it to offer the population great expectations for the future. Moreover, the regime itself has had its hands tied by the 1980 constitution, which established a deadline for the completion of the transition period—approaching at a rapid pace—and which has a mechanism for renewing the presidential mandate that will be difficult to fulfill in the light of the complex institutional framework attained by the opposition. At the present time the governing coalition does not possess the same degree of mystique and cohesion as it enjoyed hitherto; significant sectors have adopted either a passive attitude and suspicion of the government or have become a semiopposition, which probably will turn to full-fledged opposition when they have to decide on the question of the presidential mandate.

The only groups that continue clearly to support the regime are the hardline nationalists, *gremialistas*, and certain business sectors. However, the latter have no option but to give this support because of their economic dependence vis-à-vis the political authorities. This does not mean that the government is isolated socially. It has at its disposal an extensive, complex institutional and informal network to maintain links with the society. However, political resources are insufficient except when they are part of a decidedly political strategy to stimulate public adherence, and this can only be achieved through a new strategy of mixed legitimation that again emphasizes economic success as a priority goal. Is this possible?

There is nothing to prevent it if the government continues to count on the support of the business sector. But this new strategy of legitimation would have to be different from its predecessor (the neoliberal economic model) in order to succeed. It would have to represent a decided change, such as Franco initiated in 1953 when he set aside the autarchic era and adopted a policy of liberalization and development, which led a few years later to a spectacular economic boom and provided the regime with significant legitimacy until the Caudillo's death. Franco was able to accomplish this, among other things, because he could count on all the elites to support the model and because he had the people to implement it—technocrats, under the skillful leadership of Laureano López Rodó. Franco also counted on the support of the United States (given the military treaties between the two nations) and on the boom in the European economy after World War II, which absorbed Spain's unemployed workforce and helped facilitate the spectacular development of tourism and a burgeoning foreign exchange.

Can the regime count on a cohesive elite to provide it with that new economic policy? Even if this proved to be the case, the regime cannot count on as favorable international economic and political conditions as Franco had. We only have to remember that Chile's huge external debt—$20 billion—represents a formidable limitation on any model of development. If the success of the Spanish economy in the 1960s was for the benefit of the Spaniards, then the hypothetical economic success of a possible second stage of the regime in Chile must be assigned to the payment of interest on the external debt!

This stumbling block does not mean that the regime is in the midst of a grave crisis and that its fall is imminent or that it inevitably will be defeated in the noncompetitive election that will take place in 1989. In terms of a genetic analysis, the regime has a deficit of legitimacy, faces problems, and will have difficulty mobilizing its followers in a society that has been politicized for some years. Herein lies the problem: How will the regime be able to coexist with a society that has recovered its politico-institutional differentiation and is repoliticized?

Much will depend on the organizational capacity and political imagination of the opposition and of the semiopposition and on whether they can increase the scope of activity in the prevailing spaces of freedom. This situation will be determined by the opposition's capacity for effective and imaginative leadership in the many social organizations it has at its disposal; this will not be easy either. The opposition has had to undertake politico-administrative tasks in numerous pressure groups and voluntary associations that present enormous challenges and can divide it and erode its unity. Since the *apertura* political activity based on critical discourse has not been enough; now the opposition will have to show concrete results, provide positive answers, and present an effective and imaginative leadership.

In addition, the government will have to implement new policies, and the opposition will not be able to continue using the same policies, the same style, and the same language which it used during the *protestas*. It will have to present policies for a Chile no longer in the midst of the *protestas* and the *apertura*, a change that will be reflected in activity at both elite and mass level.

CONCLUSIONS

This analysis of policies during the *protestas* and the *apertura* leads to certain conclusions and some speculation about the future. First, the political regime remains the same but is different because it has experienced considerable institutional differentiation legitimated through competitive elections. Union organizations, student federations, and professional and academic associations constitute new political actors; these have emerged during a highly polarized period of political mobilization, the human cost of which was extremely high. The political parties also have contributed to this hypermobilization. Institutional differentiation now makes politics highly heterogeneous and complex and extends much further than the judicial and constitutional parameters of the regime. The political system has both democratic and authoritarian institutional spaces that coexist and interweave; thus, I speak of a political system with institutional schizophrenia. I assume that the coexistence of democratic spaces and authoritarian spaces generates a latent conflict, which sooner or later will become manifest.

During the period of the *protestas* and the *apertura* Chilean politics resembled the model of transition described by Dankwart Rustow.[71] There was an intense conflict with negotiations at the elite level and a mass political arena that required leadership by large organizations. Chilean politics was transformed from an underground affair centered exclusively on negotiations at the elite level to mass politics. This expansion of the political arena presents new and difficult changes for leaders who, having performed the role of a noninstitutional opposition for some years, advanced abruptly to occupy powerful roles they must exercise efficiently. The opposition will have to change its discourse and activity in accordance with the new reality of being the "government" in various interest associations.

The government also faces new and difficult changes: a deficit of legitimacy in a context of mass politics and of an increasingly politicized society, which cannot be controlled by means of political engineering or coercion, except at a very high cost. The efficiency of the policies to contain the opposition has caused an extremely high centralization of decisionmaking in the head of state. This high degree of centralization has caused a concentration of input in one single structure and in the hands of General Pinochet and the presidential secretariat; this contration is incongruent with the institutional differentiation going on at other levels of the political system. Centralization may be useful for decisionmaking during a crisis, but it is inefficient when reequilibration has been produced and can lead to paralysis. This occurs when a congestion of demands is produced, owing to an inefficient decisionmaking system for processing the demands and converting them into policies.

In addition, paralysis is produced when different groups and political actors wish to distance themselves from the government for fear that if they become involved in it, they might lose credibility. This complicates the recruitment and circulation of governing elites required to provide minimum credibility to government claims of representativeness.

The delays in designing a new economic policy to confront legitimation by performance and the extraordinary sluggishness of the decisions to change the incumbents of key public posts, such as rectors in regional universities and mayors in the Santiago metropolitan region indicates that the degree of decisionmaking paralysis is significant. What is now occurring in government led, in the case of Brazil, to

> the enormous centralization of power in the hands of a small circle of military officers and high-ranking technocrats [that] began to generate a black hole effect, that is, a loss of flexibility, rationality and efficiency because of the absence of proper channels of support and feedback.[72]

The future of politics in Chile lies in the establishment of democracy, and this will tend to resemble the Brazilian case more than any other. The Chilean case also has a strong electoral component that, with great pressure from below, will culminate in the noncompetitive elections prescribed by the 1980 constitution. In terms of the kind of transition to democracy, the Chilean case will tend to be one of *reforma*, instead of *ruptura*, in which the armed forces may be able to return to their barracks with dignity to resume their professional work. Thus, the evolution of politics in Chile could well be from the present schizophrenia of the political system to a diarchy in the near future and from the latter to a polyarchy in 1989.

NOTES

I wish to thank the Volkswagen Foundation for its generous support, which enabled me to gather data utilized in this chapter.

1. Some of the more interesting contributions not cited elsewhere in this volume include the special issue, "The New Mediterranean Democracies: Regime Transition in Spain, Greece and Portugal," *West European Politics* 7, no. 2 (1984); John H.

Herz (ed.), *From Dictatorship to Democracy* (Westport, Conn.: Greenwood Press, 1982); Samuel P. Huntington, "Will More Countries Become Democratic?" *Political Science Quarterly* 99, no. 2 (1984): 193–218; DESCO, *Democracia y Movimiento Popular* (Lima: Centro de Estudios y Promociones del Desarollo, 1981); D. Ruschemeyer, "Über Sozialökonomische Entwicklung und Demokratie," in G. Hischier et al., *Weltgesellschaft und Sozialstruktur* (Diessenhofen: Verlag Ruegger, 1980); and Dieter Nohlen, "El cambio de régimen político en América Latina: En torno a la democratización de los regímenes autoritarios," *Estudios Internacionales*, no. 68 (1984): 548–575.

2. For Argentina and Uruguay see Chapters 5, 7, and 8 in this book.

3. Juan J. Linz (ed.), *Crisis, Breakdown, and Reequilibration* (Baltimore, Md.: John Hopkins University Press, 1978).

4. For Portugal see Lawrence S. Graham and Harry M. Makler (eds.), *Contemporary Portugal: The Revolution and Its Antecedents* (Austin: University of Texas Press, 1979); and Philippe Schmitter, "Liberation by *Golpe*: Retrospective Thoughts on the Demise of Authoritarian Rule in Portugal," *Armed Forces and Society* 2, no. 1 (1975): 5–33.

5. See Chapter 3 and the sources cited therein.

6. Bolivar Lamounier, "Opening Through Elections: Will the Brazilian Case Become a Paradigm?" *Government and Opposition* 19, no. 2 (1984): 167–177. Also see Candido Mendes, "The Post-1964 Brazilian Regime: Outward Redemocratization and Inner Institutionalization," *Government and Opposition* 15, no. 1 (1980): 48–74; David V. Fleischer, "Da 'Distensão' a 'Abertura': A Evolução Socio-política do Brasil na Década de 80" and Bolivar Lamounier, "Dos Anos 70 aos 80: Estructura Social, Eleiçoies e Mudança Política no Brasil," both in Enrique Baloyra-Herp and Rafael López-Pintor (eds.), *Iberoamérica en los Años 80* (Madrid: Centro de Investigaciones Sociológicas, 1982), pp. 47–61 and 63–73 respectively. Also see Chapter 6 in this book and the sources cited therein.

7. Rainer M. Lepsius, "Machtübernahme und Machtübergabe: Zur Strategie des Regimewechsels," in H. Albert (ed.), *Sozialtheorie und Soziale Praxis* (Meisenheim: Anton Hahn Verlag, 1971).

8. For a comprehensive discussion on Pinochet's Chile, see Manuel Antonio Garretón, *El Proceso Político Chileno* (Santiago: FLACSO, 1983); and Carlos Huneeus, "La política de la apertura y sus implicancias para la inauguración de la democracia en Chile," *Revista de Ciencia Política* 7, no. 1, (1985): 25–84.

9. French priest Andre Jarlan was shot by a *carabinero* (policeman) while he read the Bible after having attended to dozens of people injured in the marginal settlement of La Victoria, a popular district of Santiago, during a *protesta* that was repressed very severely. See Patricia Verdugo, *Andre de la Victoria* (Santiago: Editorial Aconcagua, 1985).

10. I follow Juan Linz's model of authoritarianism. See his two works, "An Authoritarian Regime: Spain," in Erik Allardt and Yrjo Littunen (eds.), *Cleavages, Ideologies and Party Systems* (Helsinki: Westmarck Society, 1964), pp. 251–381; and "Opposition to and Under an Authoritarian Regime: The Case of Spain," in Robert A. Dahl (ed.), *Regimes and Oppositions* (New Haven, Conn.: Yale University Press, 1973), pp. 171–259.

11. The distinction between the functionalist and the genetic approach is from Dankward Rustow, "Transitions to Democracy," *Comparative Politics* 2, no. 3 (1970): 337–363.

12. Ralf Dahrendorf, "Pfade aus Utopia: Zu einer Neuorientierung der soziologischen Analyse," in *Pfade aus Utopia* (München: Piper, Verlag, 1967). Also see Dahrendorf's important book *Class and Class Conflict in Industrial Society* (London: Allen & Unwin, 1959); and Lewis Coser, *The Functions of Social Conflict* (New York: Glencoe Press, 1956).

13. Bolivar Lamounier and Eduardo Faria (eds.), *O Futuro da Abertura: Um Debate* (São Paulo: Cortez Editora, 1981).

14. More on this can be found in Carlos Huneeus, "Elecciones no competitivas en las dictaduras burocrático-administrativas en América Latina," *Revista Española de Investigaciones Sociológicas,* 13 (March 1981): 101–138.

15. For more detail see Gerhard Lehmbruch, *Proporzdemokratie, politisches System und politische Kultur in der Schweiz und in Österreich* (Tubingen: J. C. B. Mohr, 1967); and Gerhard Lembruch, *Parteienwettbewerg im Bundesstaat* (Stuttgart: Verlag W. Kohlhammer, 1976); and Arend Lijphart, *Democracy in Plural Societies* (New Haven, Conn.: Yale University Press, 1977). For the wider implications of the model of consociational democracy, see Reiner Lepsius "Paerteiensystem, Wählerbewegung und sozialer Wandel in Westeuropa," in O. Busch (ed.), *Wahlerbewegung in der Europäischen Geschichte* (Berlin: Colloquium Verlag, 1980). Also see Arend Lijphart, *The Politics of Accommodation: Pluralism and Democracy in the Netherlands* (Berkeley: University of California Press, 1968). Following the Lehmbruch criteria I have analyzed the case of Spain in "La Transición a la democracia en España, Dimensiones de una política consociacional," in Julián Santamaría (ed.), *Transición a la Democracia en el Sur de Europa y América Latina* (Madrid: Centro de Investigaciones Sociológicas, 1982), pp. 243–286 and in my book, *La Unión de Centro Democrático y la Transición a la Democracia en España* (Madrid: Centro de Investigaciones Sociológicas, 1985). Alberto van Klaveren has applied Arend Lijphart's version of the consociational scheme to postauthoritarian Chile in his article "Instituciones consociativas: ¿Alternativas para la estabilidad democrática en Chile?" *Alternativas,* 2 (January-April 1984): 24–55.

16. Lehmbruch, "Parteienwettbewerg," *op. cit.,* Chapter 1.

17. Klaus von Beyme, *Vom Faschismus zur Entwicklungsdiktatur: Machtelite und Opposition in Spanien* (München: R. Piper, Verlag, 1971).

18. For an emphasis on institutional elements, see Juan J. Linz, "The Future of an Authoritarian Situation or the Institutionalization of an Authoritarian Regime: The Case of Brazil," in Alfred Stepan (ed.), *Authoritarian Brazil* (New Haven, Conn.: Yale University Press, 1973), pp. 233–254.

19. Susan Kaufman Purcell and John H. Purcell, "State and Society in Mexico: Must a Stable Polity Be Institutionalized?" *World Politic,* 32 (1980): 194–227.

20. Dieter Nohlen and Carlos Huneeus, "Elitenwettbewerb in der Spätphase des Franco-Regimes, Der Kampf um die politische Reform," in Peter Waldmann, Walther L. Bernecker and Francisco López-Casero (eds.), *Sozialer Wandel und Herrschaft im Spanien Francos* (Paderborn: Ferdinand Schoningh, 1984).

21. See Klaus Hildebrand, "Monokratie oder Polykratie? Hitlers Herrschaft und das Dritte Reich," in Gerhard Hirschfeld and Lothar Kettenacker (eds.), *Der Führestaat: Mythos und Realitat* (Stuttgart: Klett-Cotta, 1981).

22. Seymour Martin Lipset, *Political Man* (London: Heinemann, 1960), p. 77.

23. Usage of legitimacy follows Linz in "Crisis, Breakdown," pp, 16–27.

24. Giuseppe di Palma, "Founding Coalitions in Southern Europe," *Government and Opposition* 15, no. 2 (Spring 1980): 162–189. Also see Max Weber's classic, "Die drei reinen Typen der legitimen Herrschaft," in *Soziologie: Weltgeschichliche Analysen Politik* (Stuttgart: Alfred Kroner Verlag, 1968), pp. 151–156.

25. Klaus von Beyme, "Authoritarian Regimes—Developing Open Societies?" in Dante Germino and Klaus von Beyme (eds.), *The Open Society in Theory and Practice* (The Hague: Martinus Nijhoff, 1974).

26. Carlos Huneeus, "Elecciones no competitivas." For an analysis of authoritarian regimes according to their governing coalitions, see Leonardo Morlino, *Dalla Democrazia all' Autoritarismo* (Bologna: Il Moulino, 1981); and Chapter 2 in this book.

27. The distinction between power and authority has been stressed by Dahrendorff, *op. cit.*, p. 166; and was taken from Max Weber, *Wirtschaft und Gesselschaft* (Tubingen: J. C. B. Mohr & Paul Siebeck, 1956).

28. Linz, "An Authoritarian Regime," p. 268.

29. Alain Rouquié, *Poder Militar y Sociedad Política en la Argentina* (Buenos Aires: Emece, 1981); and Robert Potash, *El Ejército y la Política en la Argentina, 1928–1962*, 2 vols. (Buenos Aires: Editorial Sudamericana, 1981).

30. Pilar Vergara, *Auge y Caída del Neoliberalismo en Chile* (Santiago: FLACSO, 1985).

31. Guillermo Campero and José Valenzuela, *El Movimiento Sindical en el Régimen Militar Chileno, 1973–1982* (Santiago: ILET, 1984). For the integration of the working class, see Gunther Roth, *Social Democrats in Imperial Germany: A Study in Working-class Isolation and Negative Integration* (Totowa, N.J.: Bedminster Press, 1964); Reinhard Bendix, *Work and Authority in Industry* (Berkeley: University of California Press, 1956).

32. José María Maravall, *Dictadura y Disentimiento Político: Obreros y Estudiantes Bajo el Franquismo* (Madrid: Ediciones Alfaquera, 1978).

33. Eli Diniz, "Empresariado e Transição Política no Brasil: Problemas e Perspectivas," IUPERJ, *Série Estudos*, no. 22 (1984).

34. José Pablo Arellano and René Cortázar, "Del milagro a la crisis: Algunas reflexiones sobre el momento económico," *Estudios Cieplan*, no. 8 (1982): 43–69; Ricardo French-Davis, "El experimento monetario en Chile," *Estudios Cieplan*, no. 9 (1982): 5–40, José Pablo Arellano, "De la liberación a la intervención: El mercado de capitales en Chile: 1974–1983," *Estudios Cieplan*, no 11 (1983): 5–50; and José Pablo Arellano, "La difícil salida al problema del endeudamiento interno," *Estudios Cieplan*, no. 13 (1984): 5–26.

35. Arellano and Cortázar, *op. cit.*, p. 44.

36. See Jaime Guzmán, "El camino político," *Realidad*, no. 7 (1982): 13–23.

37. I analyzed this in Carlos Huneeus, *Der Zusammenbruch der Demokratie in Chile* (Heidelberg: Esprint Verlag, 1981).

38. Compare the texts published by Instituto de Estudios Generales in *Textos Comparados de la Constitución Política* (Santiago: Editorial Universitaria, 1980).

39. On Chilean presidentialism, see Jorge Tapia-Videla, "The Chilean Presidency in a Development Perspective," *Journal of Interamerican Studies and World Affairs* 19, no. 4 (November 1977): 451–481.

40. Linz, "An Authoritarin Regime."

41. See Karl Bracher et al., *Die nationalsozialistische Machtergreifung* (Koln: Westdeustscher Verlag, 1962).

42. See Alvaro Briones and Orlando Caputo, "América Latina: Nuevas modalidades de acumulación y fascismo dependiente," in ILDIS, *El Control Político en el Cono Sur* (Mexico: Siglo XXI Editores, 1978). For a critique of Briones and Caputo, see Alberto van Klaveren, "Enfoques alternativos para el estudio del autoritarismo en América Latina," in Francisco Orrego (ed.), *Transición a la Democracia en América Latina* (Buenos Aires: Grupo Editor Latinoamericano, 1985).

43. For more on this, see Brian Smith, *The Church and Politics in Chile* (Princeton, N.J.: Princeton University Press, 1982).

44. For opposition to authoritarian rule, see Linz, "Opposition."

45. See Huneeus, "Elecciones no-competitivas."

46. Arellano, "De la liberalización," p. 48.

47. Programa de Economía del Trabajo, Academia de Humanismo Cristiano, *Chile: Coyuntura Económica*, nos. 8-9 (1983): 41, Table 2.9.

48. *Ibid.*, Table 2.11.

49. Program de Economía del Trabajo, *Serie de Indicadores Económicos y Sociales*, various issues (1982–1983). On PEM, see Jaime Ruiz Tagle and Roberto Urmeneta, *Los Trabajadores del Programa del Empleo Mínimo* (Santiago: Programa de Economía del Trabajo, Academia de Humanismo Cristiano, 1984).

50. Arellano, "De la liberalización," p. 49.

51. On the radicalization of the middle class see Lipset, *op. cit.*, Chapter 3. For a critique see H. Winkler, "Extremismus der Mitte?" *Vierteljahresheft für Zeitgeschichte*, no. 20 (1972): 175–191; and H. Winkler, *Mittelstand, Demokratie und Nationalsozialismus* (Koln: Kieperheur, 1972).

52. I analyzed this pehnomenon in "Unión de Centro Democrático."

53. For the role of the press during the transition, see Kenneth Maxwell (ed.), *The Press and the Rebirth of Iberian Democracy* (Westport, Conn.: Greenwood Press, 1983).

54. The relevance of parties is discussed by Giovanni Sartori, *Parties and Party Systems: A Framework for Analysis* (Cambridge: Cambridge University Press, 1976), p. 121.

55. For the continuity of parties, see Seymour M. Lipset and Stein Rokkan, "Cleavage Structures, Party Systems and Voter Alignments: An Introduction," in Seymour M. Lipset and Stein Rokkan (eds.), *Party Systems and Voter Alignments: Cross-National Perspectives* (New York: Free Press, 1967), pp. 1–64. For a critique of their model, see Robert Alford and Roger Friedland, "Nations, Parties, and Participation: A Critique of Sociology," *Theory and Society*, no. 1 (1974): 271–306.

56. On elite continuity and regime change, see Juan J. Linz, "Continuidad y discontinuidad en la élite política española: De la restauración al régimen actual,"

in Libro Homenaje al Profesor Carlos Ollero, *Estudios de Ciencia Política y Sociología* (Madrid: Gráficas Carlavilla, 1973), pp. 361–423.

57. Carlos Huneeus, "Los partidos políticos y la transición a la democracia en Chile hoy," *Estudios Públicos*, no. 15 (1984): 57–88.

58. Data are from a survey conducted by the author at CERC in cooperation with the European Elections Study project.

59. More on this can be found in Ricardo Lagos, *Democracia para Chile: Proposiciones de un Socialista* (Santiago: Pehuén Editores, 1985).

60. For the origin of MAPU and Izquierda Cristiana, see Carlos Huneeus, *Movimiento Estudiantil y Generación de Elites Dirigentes* (Santiago: Corporación de Promoción Universitaria, 1973).

61. For a contrast with socialist-communist competition in Spain, see José María Maravall, "Spain, Eurocommunism and Socialism," *Political Studies*, 27 (1979): 218–235.

62. See "¿Qué se hizo de la derecha?" *Qué Pasa*, no. 743 (July 1985).

63. Linz, "Opposition," pp. 191–202.

64. See "Documento: El plan oculto," *Qué Pasa*, no. 727 (March 1985): 34–39.

65. Robert A. Dahl, *Polyarchy: Participation and Opposition* (New Haven, Conn.: Yale University Press, 1971), p. 15, argued that the prospect for democracy increases when the costs of suppression are higher than the costs of tolerance.

66. For information on the military and the political system, see "Los hombres del presidente," *Qué Pasa*, no. 718 (January 1985); "La economía con uniforme," *Qué Pasa*, no. 722 (March 1985); "Los hombres del presidente," *El Mercurio*, July 6, 1980; and "El equipo militar," *El Mercurio*, May 2, 1982.

67. Programa de Economía del Trabajo, *Serie de Indicadores Económicos y Sociales*, various issues (1983–1984).

68. For this negative effect of economic policy, see Fernando Dahse, *Mapa de Extrema Riqueza* (Santiago: Aconcagua, 1978).

69. See *Estrategia*, March 25, 1984.

70. For a more detailed discussion, consult Guillermo O'Donnell's *Modernization and Bureaucratic-Authoritarianism* (Berkeley: University of California Press, 1973); Guillermo O'Donnell, "Reflections on the Patterns of Change in the Bureaucratic-Authoritarian State," *Latin American Research Review* 13, no. 1 (1978): 3–38; and Guillermo O'Donnell, *El Estado Burocrático-Autoritario: Triunfo, Derrota y Crisis* (Buenos Aires: Editorial Belgrano, 1982). Also see Karen L. Remmer and Gilbert W. Merkx, "Bureaucratic-Authoritarianism Revisited," *Latin American Research Review* 17, no. 2 (1982): 3–40.

71. Rustow, *op. cit.*

72. Lamounier, "Opening through Elections," p. 172.

5
DILEMMAS OF THE CONSOLIDATION OF DEMOCRACY IN ARGENTINA

Carlos Alberto Floria

The literature on the transition to democracy in Argentina has become fairly extensive, but studies on the problems of consolidation are still sparse. My intention in this chapter is to dwell on the lessons of transitions that have taken place in modern Argentina and that may be particularly relevant at present. I will review and critique some fairly current interpretations in the literature of events that took place during the "blind years" preceding the elections of October 30, 1983, which gave way to the constitutional government of President Raúl Alfonsín. At the same time, I shall address some issues regarding the Argentine transition that I consider to have been settled a bit prematurely. If the reflections put forward seem polemical, they are intended to be so in the interest of a sober examination of issues raised by the Argentine transition that could be concealed by certain "uncomfortable verifications."

THE COLLAPSE OF THE MILITARY REGIME

Some colleagues and I have written about the existence of a "secret Argentina."[1] This concept implies the existence of a society that has changed or is changing its structures, its basic beliefs, and the relative weight of the major political forces competing for power. We emphasized the importance of taking fully into account the effects of societal changes on the political process. This was overlooked in 1943, when some profound social change took place without being noticed by the political leaders of the time. The country had lost its most prominent leaders—Marcelo de Alvear, Agustín Justo, and Roberto Ortiz—at a time when the society was changing as a result of industrialization, internal migration, and the emergence of new political forces. It was in the midest of these circumstances that Peronism appeared on stage and would later become hegemonic.

Forty years later something similar has occurred. Juan Domingo Perón, the *caudillo justicialista* (Justicialist or Peronist party caudillo), and Ricardo Balbín, the stalwart of the Unión Cívica Radical (Radical Civic Union, or UCR), had died, just when labor relations, culture, and the economy again were undergoing profound changes. Therefore, it is tempting to draw some analogies. In 1946 Perón, a new leader with a military background, organized his own political movement, the Partido Justicialista (commonly known as Peronista party), and received 52.4 percent of the vote. In 1983 Raúl Alfonsín, long a UCR militant, standing as the presidential candidate of his party won 52 percent of the vote. To understand these watershed events we also should consider some of the important political, social, and economic transformations that took place between these changes of the guard.

Analysis of the relationship between politics and society in Argentina becomes clouded even without taking into account the aftereffects of the Peronist regime of 1946–1955. There was an extended period of anarchy, which was interrupted by the constitutional interval of 1955–1966, and military domination since 1966. It may seem superfluous to remember this sequence of political events, but it would be impossible to attempt an explanation of today's Argentina without any reference to that period. In 1966, for example, a coalition was built that included the military, sectors of the trade unions, and some significant economic groups that anchored the military autocracy. In 1973 President Héctor Cámpora, by contrast, headed a difficult Neoperonist alliance dominated by leftist radicals. The old alliance was reborn after the forceful removal of Cámpora and reincorporated some elements of the recognized opposition, labor, the military, and economic groups.

My reading of Argentine politics during those years vindicates the internal logic of politics and clarifies what might have seemed irrational to many observers. Often in political and economic life we call irrational what is just a rationality different from our own. Often, too, those who play public roles interpret reality erroneously and thereby attempt to evade a reality that they dislike. These attitudes usually lead to an incorrect diagnosis and subsequently to inadequate decisions. The development and the crisis of the military regime in power from 1976 to 1983 will not be analyzed here. Nevertheless, we should consider comparatively how the military takeover of 1976 and the recent return to democracy have been justified by their protagonists. The first paragraphs of the "proclamation" of the coup in 1976 are revealing in this respect.

> All constitutional measures having been exhausted, all possibilities of rectification through institutional means having been exceeded, and with the

> demonstration in irrefutable form of the impossibility of restoring the government process through its natural paths, a situation resulted which oppressed the nation and compromised its future. Our people have suffered another frustration. Faced with a tremendous vacuum of power, capable of overwhelming us with dissolution and anarchy, with the lack of capability for dialogue that the national government has demonstrated, with the reiterated and successive contradictions evidenced in the adoption of measures of all types, with the lack of an overall strategy which, led by political authority, could confront subversion, with the lack of solution for basic problems of the nation the result of which has been permanent increase of all extremisms, with the total absence of ethical and moral examples by those who have the leadership of the state, with the manifest irresponsibility in the management of the economy which has brought about the demolition of the productive apparatus, with the speculation and general corruption, all the forces which translate into an irreparable loss of the feeling of grandeur and faith, the armed forces, in the fulfillment of an unrenounceable obligation, have assumed the leadership of the state.[2]

One cannot fail to be impressed by the fact that in light of a similar diagnosis (whose only modification might be on the subject of subversion) the civilians and a large section of the military establishment as well have sanctioned the failure of the experience of the regime inaugurated in March 1976. To this we must add the isolation of the military rulers at the end of their "experiment" in 1983. There were no longer any coalitions that could support them, as in 1966, when they inaugurated a corporatist regime or, in 1976, when they came to power with the promise to reorganize society. In 1983 the moral power, the trade unions, the economic groups, and the political parties all had left the military government alone. In fact, that government had no authority because authority can only be rooted in society. These circumstances were quite different from those of the transition to democracy in Spain, which is cited sometimes as analogous. However, the two could not have been more different. In Argentina, just to point to one major difference, the military regime collapsed and had to surrender; this precipitated a transition conducted with a bare minimum of governing ability left to the regime. But the military regime as such had collapsed long before with the defeat in the Malvinas War. If anything, the point of departure of the Argentine transition could not have been more unfavorable to a democratic outcome.[3] It therefore is necessary to keep in mind the context of the beginning of the constitutional government.

THE OCTOBER 30 NATIONAL ELECTION: INTERPRETATIVE NOTES

This context made the national election of October 30, 1983, a crucial one. This election had a profound impact on the behavior of government officials and on the social forces and may be compared only to two other Argentine elections: the election of 1916, when the Unión Cívica Radical won the presidency with Hipólito Yrigoyen, and the 1946 election, when the Peronist victory produced the second change of direction in contemporary Argentine political history. The 1983 election marks the third political watershed of this century.

This part of my analysis is inevitably selective, and it focuses on the facts most useful in understanding the present and in considering what might happen in the near future. The 1983 election gave a boost to the ethical dimension of politics, which was a result of the historical style of the Radical party, the nature of Alfonsín's discourse, and the behavior of certain lesser leaders of Peronism, who were rejected by a substantial segment of the electorate. Before the election the UCR was only a "power aspirant." Its real chances depended on the behavior of the Peronist party, whose internal crisis was manifest. This partly explains the resulting polarization, which worked in favor of the Radicals. They easily doubled their historical average since 1956, which, in the best of cases, hovered around 25 percent of the national vote. In 1983 the UCR won a majority of the vote in the more developed provinces—the Federal Capital, Buenos Aires, Córdoba, and Mendoza—and matched the Peronist tally in Santa Fe. At first glance, this suggests that the Radicals attracted the votes of the younger generations and totally captured the conservative vote, which amounted to around 20 percent in 1973; part of the Left; and a portion of the floating vote that favored Peronism in 1973.

The opposite was true of Peronism. Perón was always mindful of the middle-class vote. In 1983 the Peronists lost it. Their 40 percent of the vote came primarily from underprivileged sectors in the prosperous districts and from the less developed provinces. The 1983 election, then, established a two-party system at the national level.

The first effect of the election victory was a strengthening of presidential power. One would have to go back to Hipólito Yrigoyen to find a civilian president elected by a majority of the citizens in a regime with democratic legitimacy. In this sense, a more robust presidential office would have benefited the country in its international negotiations and would have facilitated the subordination of societal forces to the authority of political institutions.

However, and unlike what happened in the 1946, 1958, and 1973 elections, the victorious party did not monopolize all power positions. Between them, Radicals and Peronists got almost 90 percent of the 1983 vote. It is possible that this marked a polarization of the vote will not occur again, but it is probable that the weight of this "hegemonic bipartidism," born of the elections of 1983, will hinder the future realignment of Argentina's political forces. This realignment may take place because the structure of the party system in Argentine is not necessarily bipartisan; rather it is moderately multipartisan (including Conservatives and Socialists). But it is one thing to appear as a "power contender" and quite another to be a mere "alternative of protest." In the first case, the Radicals and the Peronists will dominate. The Conservatives and the Socialists must still work hard to play a role other than that of an organized protest group.

Given the lessons of the past, it was vital for the stability of the new regime that Peronism be engaged in the democratic game and that it remain a viable power contender in order to prevent a new chasm between civil society and a hegemonic party. We must keep in mind that Alfonsín is not a new Perón and that the electorate chose neither a civilian dictator nor an absolute sovereign. Hundreds of other office holders also have been elected. As established in Article 1 of the national constitution, the president is the first magistrate but not the only one. In fact, Radicals and Peronists are co-governing. In the 1983 election, the UCR won the presidency, a majority in the lower House, and almost one-half the Senate. But the Peronists control twelve provinces as compared to the seven that went to the Radicals. Therefore, there is not, strictly speaking, one party in the government and another one in the opposition. The roles are intertwined at different levels.

In addition, the federal power structure has been achieved precisely through this mingling of roles and through the disproportionate influence of the marginal provinces. The Peronist majority in the Senate was based on the support of a little more than 23 percent of the electorate, with the marginal provinces being overrepresented. This overblown Peronist representation compounded an inability on the part of the Radicals to build legislative and political coalitions in Congress and in the provinces. This translated into a number of early UCR defeats in Congress, which in turn had a negative influence on the manageability of the state and on the expectations of the public. Is this a serious drawback?

CORPORATISM AND THE POLITICAL PROCESS

Political power may be defined as the capacity to make decisions that commit the entire community. No decision taken by any other actor in society can affect, or commit, the society as a whole. Should that be the case, that actor or sector whose decision has produced this effect is actually a power contender. This is exactly how one would describe the position of the military and labor in the "power constellation" of the Argentine political universe.

Institutional Political Power

In Argentina institutional political power converges on presidential leadership and on the party system, within the configuration suggested in the last paragraph. Presidential leadership evokes a ruler who must achieve a mixture of charisma, rationality, principles, and timing. President Alfonsín enjoys more popularity than his party does, and he is capable of communicating directly with people. These elements are part of his charisma. Ethics is an undeniable dimension of his rule, and this is part of the historical style of the Radicals and the personal style of the president. But his ethics reflect the requirements of politics and therefore are never absolute. Alfonsín tends to be a "political player," a risktaker who takes decisive gambles that can be disconcerting to the citizenry, his followers, and his opponents. Needless to say, the kind of leader that President Raúl Alfonsín may become is crucial to both the present situation and to future developments.

To be sure, these elements weighed very heavily on many of the early crucial decisions undertaken by the president. Paramount among these were his decision to hold a referendum on the conflict with Chile about the Beagle Channel, which resulted in an important victory for the government; his decision to prosecute the military commanders of the juntas of 1976–1983; and his Austral Plan for economic stabilization. The process of making these decisions revealed a president capable of leading the nation, even through what some qualified observers termed "monarchical raptures," and of evoking a responsive chord in Argentine society.

The president faces the dilemma of his role and its projections on his party and on the entire system. In theory an Argentine president—any president in a situation of transition—may play three different roles: leader of his or her party, head of the administration, and founder of the political system. The first is a partisan role, which is not always compatible with the other two. The second is mandated by the constitution. The third may be indispensable in a process of transition to democracy and especially in a society such as Argentina, which does not have a deeply rooted democratic tradition. Necessity forced President Alfonsín into the first role; partisan considerations and sectoral demands will make it very difficult for him not to cast himself in that role frequently. The nation's welfare needs a stable political system and demands an administration capable of governing. In addition, that administration has taken upon itself to create that structurally complex system that we call a democracy. The president has to meet these two demands as ruler and founder. This dilemma is not yet resolved, and the tension between party leader and the other two roles remains. This is part of the context in which a very popular president finds himself.

An analysis of the fragile and weakly structured party system of contemporary Argentina has to depart from an examination of the tensions within the dominant parties, the UCR and the Peronist party. Then we may look at the prospects and expectations of the so-called center-right, now represented by the Unión de Centro Democrático (Union of the Democratic Center, or UCD) in the capital, and of the leftist-socialists, represented by the Partido Intransigente (Intransigent party, or PI).

Tensions within the UCR are coming into the open because the party is in power. These tensions are a result of friction between the old "historical radicals" and the ideological neoradicals. In both factions some moderate trends coexist with others: the National Line and the Movement for Renovation and Change, associated with the former, and the "historical movement" and the Coordinadora (Coordinating) group, associated with the latter. Altogether both factions offer a very heterogeneous picture.

Three basic strategies are at play in the area of relations with the Peronists. For the time being only the first two seem plausible. The first entails conciliation and negotiation with the Peronists at all levels to make the system more viable and to avoid polarization. The second is to challenge the Peronists on their own historical "turf" in order to reshape the social coalition that led to the Radical victory in October 1983. This would imply sacrificing votes among the center-rightist electorate that supported Alfonsín in exchange for a more solid footing among traditional Peronist supporters. The third and less likely strategy for now would be to keep the October 30, 1983, coalition together; move the Radical party to the center of the political spectrum; leave the Peronists behind; and cement the loyalties of the newfound middle-class radicals. The first two strategies are consistent with the present style and policies of the Alfonsín government; the third one opens up new possibilities that are compatible with a productive economy.

Peronism is going through the most severe crisis in its history, a result of the death of its undisputed leader and the end of the movement's expansive cycle. Peronism now must become a real political party, a challenge made more difficult by the ideological vacuum that always has existed in Peronism. In addition, there is the ideological vacuum that Peronism has always had. The Peronist crisis does not bode well for the stability of the new regime. The gap between the "political class" and the labor leadership is compounded by internal cleavages within Peronism itself: urban versus rural, politicians versus trade unionists, "historical" versus new, and so on. Labor can no longer serve as the spinal column of the party. Actually, the party is invertebrate. The 1983 electoral defeat, the "patch-up" nature of Isabel Perón's attempts to keep the party together, and the party's indecision on whether to offer qualified support to President Alfonsín are all indicators of this internal crisis. Given the importance of the Justicialist party, this crisis affects the entire Argentine society. This situation, however, is certainly preferable to having Peronism in power where it can transmit and reproduce its internal crises and project these onto the state and society. Finally, the fracture that has separated the "promovement" faction from those who would prefer a "regeneration of Peronism" is another alarming expression of this crisis.[4] Given the Peronist overrepresentation in the Senate, these fracture lines can undermine the whole system.

The conservative UCD has adopted a strategy that tries to take advantage of this configuration. The UCD sees clearly the fissure through which it might reach importance in its role as opponent, gain strength through pacts and negotiation, and become politically relevant as an opposition party. The same strategy is used by the Intransigent party, in its search for sectors more inclined to favor leftist protest. These two political forces must overcome different obstacles. The UCD must overcome the "conservative issue," born of the clear inability of the conservative Right in Argentina to build an organic natural force during the last sixty years and to structure a political project that can offer a type of society and not just an economic model.[5] The Intransigents must somehow cope with the nonideological character of Argentine society, which leads it to oppose doctrinary or ideological "cleavages" that are too rationalist, as in the case of the local brands of Marxism.

The Military

The political role of the military is still an issue, not just a problem. Everyone is aware of the weight of the military in contemporary Argentina, but this subject lends itself to oversimplification. The military question is an issue because it involves an old tradition, born in the last century, when the military—just as the Catholic Church—preceded the founding of the nation state; a more recent tradition, which begins before the 1930s and includes the relevant influence of different versions of antiliberal nationalism; and the militaristic experiences of the last twenty years, when the political intervention of the armed forces adopted an institutional form never seen before the 1960s.[6] The different versions of the nationalist tradition—fascist, Hispanicist, and Maurrasean—must be factored into any explanation of Argentine politics since 1920. Nationalism has been a more potent, sustained influence than republicanism during this period.[7]

The present analysis is not the place to investigate all these features in full, but some attention must be devoted to them in order to underline the political and ideological complexities of the military question. The military question remains an issue for a host of well-known reasons: First, the intervention of 1976 ended in a political and professional fiasco; second, the internal crisis of the military endangers its cohesion and jeopardizes its reinsertion in a constitutional regime; third, the gap recent experiences have created between the military and the civilians must be bridged; and, finally, a military class that has become aloof and distant from society is a problem in itself.

President Alfonsín is well aware of this grave situation. The reform of the military code of justice has been the centerpiece of his legislative approach to the problem. The president and his party have received the support of the UCD and the relative cooperation of the Peronists. Despite frequent obstacles raised by Intransigent and Christian Democratic congressmen, the government has been able to evolve a prudent and realistic military policy. For the time being, the military appears willing to subordinate military to political power. But the full integration of the army into the allegiance system required by a strong constitutional democracy is hindered by the aftermath of the antiterrorist war; the siege laid by antiestablishment opponents trying to outflank the government and Congress from the Left; and the prosecution of military officers of varying ranks because of their behavior in the fight against the guerrillas. The fundamental question is how to shape a military community thar remains different, but not distant, and is imbued with values compatible with those of civil society. This question concerns politicians, civilians, and the military alike. It is, therefore, a national issue, and not only a civilian or military problem. A comparative analysis of similar cases could teach us quite interesting lessons, which Argentine society has yet to learn.

The Trade Unions

The relationship between the government and the unions is one of the most significant aspects of the present political process. As in all preceding cases, there is a history behind this subject and a "corporatist biography" to be developed. I will only examine some relevant stages.

During his first months in office President Alfonsín adopted a confrontational style against labor and rallied around his secretary of labor an "antibureaucratic" labor front comprised of dissident "Alfonsinists," Socialists, Communists, Marxists, anarchists, orthodox Peronists, and dissident Peronists. This heterogeneous coalition was assembled in an attempt to take over the traditional stronghold of Peronism. The traditional union leadership reacted to this by rallying around the unified Confederación General de Trabajadores (General Workers Confederation, or CGT) and by using labor's representation in Congress rather successfully. Toward the end of June 1984, the CGT obtained approval of an electoral code that allowed the control of the polls in union elections by existing labor commissions and the suspension of one article of the Law of Professional Associations, which forbids the unions to manage their organizational funds. The CGT also was able to prevent the secretary of labor from constituting temporary commissions and from placing certain trade unions under government control. This was the context in which the law regulating trade unions was repealed—partly as a result of the UCR's lack of parliamentary skill and partly as a result of the disingenuousness of union leaders. One hundred days after taking office, the president found a unified CGT, around which the opposition organized its protest. Subsequently, the traditional Peronist trade union movement has recovered its position of power, something unimaginable the day after the Radical victory on October 30.

The president was faced with the dilemma of fighting the traditional union movement or else counting on the support of other, more vulnerable labor sectors occasionally committed to official policy and therefore transitory allies. Faced with this dilemma, which emerged in the midst of a severe economic crisis, the president altered his cabinet significantly. Then, the situation evolved from imminent confrontation to an atmosphere of negotiation and from a militant attitude by the unions, leading to a general strike, to a strategy of sectoral strikes. Meanwhile, the crucial problems of social welfare organizations affiliated with different unions and their financial resources resurfaced once again. Even though the steps taken by a new secretary of labor diminished tensions between the unions and the government somewhat, these steps did not produce similar results on purely economic matters; neither did they dissipate the suspicion of the Peronist unions, which remained reserved and distrustful. In fact, the new secretary had the covert intention of dividing the unified CGT command, represented by Jorge Triacca and Saúl Ubaldini, and of avoiding the consolidation of their opposition. This tussle between Radicals and Peronists also involved the private sector and the Catholic Church.

The attitude of negotiation during 1985 appears to have been a truce rather than an institutional agreement, such as the Pacts of Moncloa in Spain or any other pacts made by a regime during a political transition. For the government as well as the unions the change of labor secretaries did not modify the main objective of official labor policy—that is, to fracture the Peronist hegemony of labor, to conquer by dividing. In any case, negotiation and dialogue did not prevent further conflict. In early 1986 the CGT came out very aggressively against the Austral Plan and became the government's principal opponent while the Peronist party itself was undergoing a process of renovation. In addition, the traditional Peronist labor leadership achieved a substantial political reconstruction. The Peronist labor leadership has shown a will to regain the advantages lost or threatened after October 30, and it has employed its representatives in Congress well. The repealed statute on labor elections and proliferation of labor conflicts show that the efficacy of the strategy of the "antibureaucratic front" is questionable.

Basically, the traditional leadership of the CGT approached negotiations with the government by yielding on some of its demands but without enunciating its basic policy. Initially, it said "not yet" to a general strike but "yes" to cumulative sectoral conflicts. However, labor has resorted to general strikes with alarming frequency. This strategy resembles a pendular movement, which swings from conditional negotiations to outright battles, while the Peronist unions refuse to give up their decisive political role within Peronism.

Ideological Cleavages

The Catholic Church is one of the main centers of moral power in Argentina, from which many spiritually grounded ethical considerations spring. Classical ideological disputes between nationalists and liberals, neo-capitalists and neosocialists, traditionalists and moderates, fill in the secular aspect of the ethical dimension of Argentine politics. Moral power is so heterogeneous and interspersed with old ideologies that each political party and each "star" in the constellation have to be carefully examined. For, in a nonideological or an aideological society such as Argentina, the political and social forces are not easily classified on a right-left continuum as might be the case in certain European societies. In Argentina the strains are much more variegated and amalgamated.

For example, every political party has been affected by the nationalist phenomenon during the last fifty years. Although the mainstream version of Argentine nationalism is antiliberal and authoritarian, there are other shades ranging from right-wing to Marxist and from elitist to corporatist. Peronism contains strong currents of authoritarian and corporatist nationalism that are rooted in traditional Catholicism but also in certain versions of European and local fascism. Argentines are accustomed to a statist, industrial nationalism and from this ideological mixture emerge the different postures found in each situation or process. The Radicals are politically liberal and want to be Social Democrats in economics, although it is doubtful that they have given much thought to the complex meaning of modern social democracy. Radicalism also includes a statist current, which would find approval among only a fraction of present radical supporters. The traditional statism of the Radicals was sorely tested by the Austral Plan of June 14, 1985, and by a series of messages on economic modernization issued by President Alfonsín ever since. Two powerful members of the cabinet, economics minister Juan Sourrouville and foreign minister Dante Caputo, have joined the president in challenging the traditional economic beliefs of radicalism.

The so-called "center" parties espouse economic neoliberalism, cultural pluralism, and the constitutional republic, but the notorious failure of the liberal Right to become an alternative of power has led its natural followers to support conspiracies or to choose the lesser evil. On the left, the

Communist and Intransigent parties hesitate between frontmaking strategies and opposition protest. These parties may increase their following due to the possible weaknesses of the governing party or the main opposition. But increasing their appeal falls short of articulating political options that could become alternatives for the society as a whole.

It is possible to define each ideological sector according to its current ideologies, the authoritarian or democratic mentalities, and the internal logic of the social forces. For example, the mention of constitutional democracy as a political system that bestows self-esteem on the Argentine people is, from an objective standpoint, significantly absent from all Catholic Church documents of the last forty years. But the Catholic Church in general, despite its traditional preference for a complex combination of leftist, humanist, and corporatist formulas, is showing signs of change since the Vatican II Council took place. In Argentina the same is happening since the return to democracy, which was supported openly by the episcopal conference, and references to democracy have become more frequent in Church documents since late 1982.[8]

Nevertheless, the Catholic Church still keeps a pontifical role for itself: the role of a "bridge" between society and the political community. The power of the Church to mobilize support is open to debate, but its power of veto is significant. The Church's fundamental concerns are education and family life as well as domestic and international peace, and these have a political, economic, social, and cultural impact.

The intellectuals are in search of a new alignment. Important changes in thinking have occurred among intellectuals in the last ten years. The culture and worship of violence severely wounded the intellectual world, whose share of responsibility in the emergence and perpetuation of that culture has not been negligible. But the most notorious change in thought has been a shift from a concern with ultimate ends to an agreement on the importance of the practical means. Democracy as a system has been revindicated by the Church and by a vast majority of intellectuals, even those whose conversion to democratic ideology is very recent.

The Near Future

Argentina is going through a difficult period of discontinuous transition, precipitated by the collapse of the military regime without a previous liberalization. Strong presidential leadership is a mixed blessing for the capacity of the government to handle today's conflicts. The president is overloaded with demands in a crucial process dominated by the issue of "governability." The consolidation of the system will depend on the government's ability to secure the political support of influential sectors, such as business and the military. On the other hand, organized labor is likely to remain a hub of opposition. Finally, the political process from 1984 to 1989 will be shaped by the mood of the electorate, by the reconstruction of social and political alliances, by the strength of the currency, and by the president's ability to prove that he is capable of governing while remaining popular. As in any democracy, electoral considerations will continue to influence the calculus of future decisionmaking. All of these impinge on the question of governability, the most crucial aspect of Argentine politics.

TRANSITION WITHOUT CONVICTION?

The first dilemma the Argentina transition poses for the intellectual dedicated to political analysis is existential. This stems from the depth of the emotions aroused by the subject among the participants in and the more dedicated observers of the most recent processes of transition in Argentina, particularly most recent one, which put an end to the "process of national reorganization" initiated in 1976. I shall mention four occasions on which, individually or with others, I tried to argue the case for a democratic transition in Argentina; the formats were somewhat dissimilar but expressive of our existential dilemma. They all shared a substantive preoccupation with the need to implement "with conviction" a deliberate, continual transition. Unfortunately, these appeals fell on deaf ears.

In 1968, during the course of the military regime of 1966–1973, at the moment in which General Juan Carlos Onganía was convinced that he enjoyed complete control of state and society in Argentina, the magazine *Criterio* (of whose editorial board I was and continue to be a member) published an editorial. The editorial set forth a clear strategy for transition based on a rational consensus on some substantive aspects that subsequently would become topics of the political science literature on Argentina. For example, the editorial argued that in the previous forty years, no stable political regime had existed in the country. Following this obvious and irrefutable fact, the editorial perceived the emergence of a new consensus arising from support for the rights and guarantees described by the national constitution; for the rule of law in a democratic republic; for the benefits and restraints of industrial society; and, consequently, for the relationship between economic growth and political democracy. These elements of consensus and a political analysis of Argentine styles and traditions inspired the idea of institutional reconstruction, which was meant to ratify the authoritarian regime as intrinsically transitional. Our proposition is of anecdotal interest but nonetheless not to be disdained.[9]

The second occasion came in two installments, one immediately before the military coup in 1976 and the other thereafter and "in solitude," as the Spaniards say. The editorial in the March 11, 1976, issue of *Criterio* included an analysis of the chaotic and violent political situation prevailing at the time. It repudiated the validity of an imminent military coup, which appeared to be a foregone conclusion to many, including important sectors of the Peronist government.[10] We even explained why this military solution, despite its appeal to many people, was a false "flight forward." In fact, the coup materialized a few weeks later, and to our knowledge that editorial was the only opposition expressed in print.

After the military coup, between August 29 and September 3, 1977, the Di Tella Institute organized a conference on the future of Argentine politics. My paper dealt with "The Transitional Regime and The Party System." The generous critique of the discussant and the discussion of the paper were unable to dispel the feeling that the subject was premature and, for many of those present, somewhat irrelevant.[11]

This feeling was confirmed by subsequent events, which brought about the third occasion to argue the case for a genuine democratic transition. In 1979 the military junta released a publication entitled "The Political Bases of the Armed Forces for the National Reorganization Process." *Bases* is a word that evoked, as did the designation of the military process, the work of Juan Bautista Alberdi and the post-Rosas political undertaking of organizing the Argentine republic—in short, the successful, deliberate transition of 1853–1910. Read without any reference to ongoing events the document could have been taken as a genuine blueprint for transition. The military sought to legitimize the origins of the "process" in a necessary struggle against subversion, while intimating a "national reorganization." But the corruption of the means dictated a different course, and transition, the deliberate change toward constitutional democracy, was once again stillborn.

The fourth and last occasion to which I will refer pertains to the final chapter of the military regime. Almost one year after the Malvinas War, in June 1983, a group of political leaders met at the University of Belgrano with members of the academic community to discuss the problems and questions surrounding the forthcoming political change. The deterioration of the authoritarian regime had been accelerated by military defeat in war. Leaders who now occupy positions of power in the government, in Congress, and in the court system were present. When the subject of voluntary transition, of "agreement on the rules" required to prevent greater turbulence, came up my feeling again was that this topic was inconsequential to a majority of the political participants. The members of the armed forces had never believed in the transition, and the civilians did not appear to be at all convinced of its necessity.[12] There are reasonable explanations for this attitude, but it would be worthwhile for a good diagnosis of the Argentine political process to discuss whether this apparent feeling of irrelevance was in accordance with reality. Subsequent events would indicate that it was.

Before delving into the dilemmas of transition to and the consolidation of democracy in Argentina, I believe it necessary to comment on the relevance of the theme of genuine transition for the participants, past and present. But there is a duality implied by our existential dilemma that arises from the extent to which the concept of transition as deliberate change was deeply rooted among Argentines. We have "preached" about transition. We have compared ours to other experiences. We have tried to ensure that transition, as a rational and voluntary political undertaking, will be taken seriously by the leaders of Argentine society. In interpreting events, we have attempted to view them against a background of other democratic transitions. But what happens when the historian's perspective encroaches upon that of the political scientist? To the historian, the differences between the Argentine case and comparable experiences are very marked. The main differences are not between contrasting styles and contexts, but between transitions that have been "pursued" and those that have been "precipitated;" between "continuous" and "discontinuous" transitions; and between those carried out with conviction and others resulting from defeat. Without intending to sermonize, I believe that precipitation, discontinuity, and defeat are the traits that best describe the transition of 1982–1983 in Argentina. The character of this transition gives rise to other dilemmas, which concern not only the installation of the constitutional government but the consolidation of democracy as well.

FACTIONALISM AND WAR

There are some verifications of reality that make the intellectual and even the politician uneasy. One of these, and not the least important, is the fact that war has been present, together with violence and "crime in its full glory," in all the transfers of power in Argentina during the 1970s and the 1980s. Strange as it may seem, war does not emerge as a privileged factor in most of the recent social science analyses of the Argentine case. Internal war is treated as a relevant factor in the political change that took place in the period between the military regime of 1966–1973 and the installation of the last Peronist government. International war is a decisive factor in the political change that occurred in 1983. Military defeat in that war added to the impossibility, given the human rights issue, of legitimizing the authoritarian regime internationally. It was the decisive factor that set in motion the process of political change, the collapse of the military regime, and the call to elections on October 30, 1983.

This "precipitate" transition gave rise to a series of dilemmas that the constitutional government has not yet been able to resolve, neutralize, or mitigate. The behavior of the government and the conduct, habits, and behavior of Argentine society played a part in preventing this precipate transition from becoming a deliberate one. A study of recent Argentine history demonstrates the persistence of authoritarian attitudes, corporative styles, and a tendency toward centrifugal factionalism. This not only runs through the military community but also the political community. The focus on the sad military experience of the years 1976 through 1983 has obscured the extent to which language and behavior in civil society—and in what I call the "militant community"—have been militarized.[13] Can Argentina democratize without restoring a liberal discourse and a civilized mode of political behavior?

THE BLIND YEARS

The blind years primarily comprise all the 1970s and possibly a few earlier and later years. The roots of the disaster of the blind years lie in the violent ideologization of some segments of Argentine society. During those years ideological discourse led to a polarization of political action pitting a violent, revolutionary, and narcissistic leftism against a violent military response. On the Left, this discourse sprang from a critical but not necessarily lucid Marxist analysis that postulated the necessity of a coup in order to deepen the contradictions between the armed forces and society for the benefit of the revolutionary elite.[14] On the Right this violent ideologization evoked totalitarian mentalities among alienated militants. Among the armed forces this discourse may have been the progeny of war hypotheses, some of which were offshoots of the doctrines of "national security" and "counterinsurgency." By those separate and concurrent ways, Argentina became trapped in a struggle between violent elites and a civilian population weakened by the cult of unrestrained violence. The objectives sought were vitiated by the corrupt measures taken to achieve them, and this corruption eventually contaminated Tyrians and Trojans alike.

Today a scrutiny of militant magazines—from the extreme right to the extreme left—and of the messages of old and new leaders that alienated so many young militants during the 1970s will highlight the extent to which the topic of the return to a legal, constitutional form of government has become relevant to even those sectors of the ideological spectrum responsible more directly for the blind years. That topic resounded as a vibrant theme for all Argentines who for decades have witnessed the national constitution being treated as bourgeois and decadent. Suddenly, the inbred common sense of politics, despised so much by the military forces, militiamen, and militants, has rediscovered the old constitution as if it were a beloved tradition, a touchstone for reconciliation within the law. But Argentina's "constituent process" cannot be similar to that of Spain or those employed in other comparable situations. Ours must be a "reconstituent" process strengthened by a "liberalization" from below that was left behind by a precipitate transition already in the stage of "democratization." The experience of the blind years must not be in vain. Argentine voters repudiated that experience in October 1983. But the blind years left the constitutional regime with unresolved questions and controversies, and the new government inherited them before the wounds had healed.

THE CONCRETE DILEMMAS

The Argentine political class, barely a year after the Malvinas War, was faced with the text of Electoral Law 22838, dated June 23, 1983. This political class had lived with the altered Argentina of the past thirty years (that is, since the installation of the second Peronist government in 1951).[15] But to what extent can an entire political class survive without competitive training or stable governments during more than a generation? Argentina had known national elections in 1916, 1922, 1928, 1931, 1937, 1946, 1958, and 1963, and then in 1973. But "free and open" voting, without fraud or proscriptions, had not taken place since 1973 and in turbulent circumstances at that, and prior to that date not since 1946. For almost forty years Peronism had been the dominant movement, a hegemonic party, a political force unchallenged by any other real power.

In those forty years, but especially in the last fifteen, Argentine society had changed political potentialities and social coalitions. It was possible to conjecture the existence of a "secret Argentina," one not easily scrutinized by opinion surveys and campaign strategies, that could make its sudden appearance as soon as certain conditions were met. This secret, untapped Argentina may have produced the power alternative that became evident on October 30, 1983.[16] Basically, that secret Argentine may have broken the spell of Peronist hegemony by responding to the proposal for reconciliation within the law presented by the Radicals.

In the current political process there are three different types of policy issues. I believe that if a discrimination is made among these, however debatable the denominations may appear to be, this might help explain the Argentine situation. For example, some policy issues are really *dilemmas* because they involve conflicts that may have no resolution—the conflict of legitimacy is one of these. Other policy issues involve *questions,* that is, broad subjects of disagreement and conflicts that should be identified in order that state and community be governable—the question of the disappeared may be one of these. Finally, there are policy issues that may loom very large as *problems* of political, economic, and social life—the problem of the foreign debt comes to mind here. In every society and, primarily, when qualitative political changes are involved, concrete dilemmas and questions are few even though the problems may be many. One attempts to identify these problems to clarify the diagnosis of a crisis or conflictive situation, to reach a consensus on its treatment, and to promote intelligent agreements among the political and the social leadership. But if no distinction is made between questions and problems, the resources of power and energy may be applied erratically, dispersed, or weakened without benefit for the ruler or the ruled. If dilemmas are not foreseen, nonexistent consensus may be presumed, and the cost may be onerous.

There are problems in abundance, and no contemporary government exists with the ability to deal effectively with all of them. I propose to reflect briefly on a number of concrete dilemmas connected with Argentine society.

The first dilemma may be stated as follows: Argentines believe there is a general consensus regarding a democratic political formula, but there may not be enough democrats around willing and able to live by it. A vast majority would agree with the political formula depicted by the constitutional, republican, and democratic regime. This belief probably could be upheld successfully, but I would not say that it is prudent to trust in it. There are representatives of the extreme Right and others of the extreme Left for whom the desirable political formula is not affected by constitutional democracy but by rather dissimilar justifications for dictatorships or autocracies. Second, there are authoritarian mentalities at work in important segments of the power constellations of Argentina, and these mentalities reappear in public opinion polls with eloquent regularity. Third, in organized sectors of the economy as well as within the military and in segments of the cultural world corporative behaviors and styles persist.

It may be true that "the social agreement" among the Argentine people favors equality, but Argentine exploitation of the state should not be overlooked. Constitutional democracy is not, after all, deeply rooted in Argentine traditions. It is an ideal, a horizon, and consequently is before the nation, not behind it in some sufficiently lengthy portion of the past.[17] This dilemma springs from a fragmented political culture and makes the consolidation of democracy a more difficult task.

If there is a fracture that may be expressed in the banner of "democracy versus authoritarianism," so aptly utilized by the Radicals in their 1983 campaign, there are also important ambiguities in the understanding of constitutional and, let us add, pluralistic democracy. Borrowing from the classics, there are constitutional democrats and "Jacobin" democrats, and although I will not try to prove the point, Jacobinism has dire consequences for real democratic life. If Jacobinism is at work in the present trend toward factionalism in Argentina, then we must debate the adequacy of extant interpretations of the political formula. But even in the intellectual world this debate seems shrouded in fear and distortion. The debate also hinges on the kind of democracy toward which Argentina is headed and even on the suspicion that what for some is a cherished objective is merely tactics for others.

The second dilemma is how to reconcile the type of society that most Argentines seem to prefer to the economic formula that such a society may require. In Argentina economics has been a topic of privileged discussion for quite a long time. However, it is no longer possible to find a common diagnosis of the characteristics and content of our long economic crisis among economists. In addition the consolidation of democracy is associated with increased production, with an economic system that dovetails with the political system. But there is no agreement about the appropriate role for the state in the economy. To what extent does the persistence of old public vices conspire against the consolidation of democracy? Is it accepted that the economic issue is not necessarily a decisive one for the establishment of constitutional democracy? Is it agreed that it is decisive, on the other hand, for democratic consolidation? These questions do not yet have legitimate answers.

External indebtedness hangs over the fragile Argentine constitutional democracy. But that democracy also is threatened by the priority assigned to the economy by those in command and by the kind of society evoked by such economic formula. The Austral Plan was not merely an economic policy; it had to address political and cultural issues as well. That is what made its implementation crucial and what enabled it to move interest groups and the society. The ultimate outcome of the plan will not change its implications. "Total planning," on the other hand, has been renounced for ignoring the role of the market. But discussion regarding the diagnosis of the crisis is open.

For a few decades it has not been clear who directs the Argentine economy or whether its relative autonomy is recognized. There are subtle differences between market and socialist economics, but these are not clear, nor are they distinguishable from each other. There are some who maintain that Argentine radicalism has never shown any effective interest in the economy, which it has unjustifiably subordinated to politics without granting it a space of its own, and that such a lack of interest characterizes the UCR leadership.[18] But despite doubts and ambiguities, the dilemma surrounding the political formula is sophisticated and seems to be resolving in favor of a constitutional democracy. However, the dilemma surrounding the kind of society conjured up by economists evokes confusion, technical ignorance, and clashing points of view, which are never fully exposed with complete sincerity. If Argentina "has no currency" today, it is because of this dilemma, which has been resolved only in part by the Austral economic package of June 13, 1985.

The third concrete dilemma concerns the cultural formula and may be defined as the perennial disynchronization between cultural and political pluralism in Argentina. It may be stated without exaggeration that the dilemmas of the Argentine transition toward democracy are, at bottom, cultural. A most pessimistic commentary on this may have been expressed in a sentence Jorge Sábato put in the mouth of "un amigo del cafe" (drinking pal): "I am beginning to think it is not that the deck has been badly shuffled but that the cards are no good." The deck is obviously Argentine society, where a fragmented political culture expresses its factionalisms in the controversies among civil society, the military, and the militant community. This could explain the difficulties that Argentines have in recognizing the wealth and the boundaries of pluralism to the extent that they are effectively in place in their society.

In civil society private and public matters are discussed endlessly. The degradation of this "interpreted reality" leads to a gradual elimination of distinctions between private and public categories. In totalitarianism, authoritarianism, or Jacobinism, civil society is absorbed eventually by the state and identified with it, even in the name of liberty or of the secular salvation of man by the state. From this point of view Julien Freund was able to say that Hitler was the "Jacobin of Germany."[19] Reviewers of the work of Alexis de Tocqueville have discovered in his work a contradiction between democracy and revolution and between democratic and revolutionary culture. His work is, in fact, an extended discourse on democratic political culture.[20]

Argentine society is plural. Is that why it is pluralistic? The first is a sociological fact; the second is a psychological fact, typical of collective conduct and behavior. Without absolute acceptance of dissent, of controversy, could there be real pluralism? Does the existence of different spiritual families necessarily imply pluralism? This dilemma is not new in Argentine society, but in the process of consolidating democratic political change the subject assumes paramount relevance. If political, economic, and cultural pluralism do not live in reciprocal association, civil harmony becomes difficult, the reconciliation of democracy with production problematical, and creative debate impossible.

Rafael Braun has pointed out that in Argentina all significant political groups have passed through the government on one or more occasions and that all have endured the constant and general imposition of martial law, proscription, and censorship.[21] Meanwhile, each group has had an opportunity to propose the "pure market model" in the political order insofar as ideological supply is concerned, while this pure market model was strongly attacked in the economic field by the majority of the political forces.

The lack of sufficient debate with respect to the consistency that pluralism requires and the limits that should be cautiously outlined for its salvation explains some of the dilemmas of the democratic transition at a time when this transition has retrieved some space of liberty for civil society. If any political value had existed that was recovered explicitly and implicitly in the 1983 national elections, it was precisely the value of liberty—political, cultural, and, but not necessarily or clearly so, economic.

It seems to me, therefore, that the gradation of "dilemmas" I am proposing for reflection may be useful for a deeper, freer analysis regarding the obstacles that the Argentine political process encounters in the consolidation of a pluralist constitutional democracy. To begin with, this gradation leads to a discussion that does not start with specific policy problems but rather with issues. But as these issues depend upon styles, traditions, and social habits, both the interpretation of history and the interpretation of society are matters for prior and special pronouncement. The meaning of transition itself and of the "conflict of legitimacies"—political, economic, and cultural—merit attention and place certain specific issues of the transition in proper perspective.

THE SPECIFIC QUESTIONS

The specific questions that must be identified in the current democratic process may be better explained within the context of a conflict of legitimacies that has caused Argentine life to be polemic during many lustrums. Politically, there are three questions: the party system, the military, and governability. This identification conceals, in effect, not only "the concrete dilemmas" mentioned earlier but also derivative issues.

Many years of authoritarianism without deliberate transition began to exhaust the political class and to disarticulate the party system. The dominant position of Peronism was transformed into a hegemonic position, and the Peronist-antiperonist cleavage shattered Argentine political culture for many years. Time partially healed this fracture, but it did not disappear altogether. In an impressionistic sense, it could be said that the 1983 election results and President Alfonsín's victory demonstrate the alignment of a nonperonist sentiment behind the current undisputable leader of the Unión Cívica Radical.

The electoral convergence of 1983, which aggregated 52 percent of the votes for the Radical candidate, conceals a heterogeneous and therefore potentially unstable social coalition. For the moment this presumed volatility does not necessarily imply spectacular defeats for the national government and for the Radical party in the forthcoming elections. There is a deep crisis within Peronism and the constitutionalist Right and Left would have to surmount too many difficulties to challenge the relative predominance of the Radicals at the polls.

The near exhaustion of the government under extremely difficult initial conditions brought tension among the different factions of radicalism to the surface. At the same time events demonstrated the absence of a valid spokesperson within the constitutional opposition. A party victorious at the national level cannot free the president from party duties without increasing the intensity of internal conflicts. But neither had it been able to generate the "agreement on essentials" or the pact of regime that could solidify the bases of loyalty required for the consolidation of democracy. The lack of an articulated, solid party system produces a negative effect on the consolidation process and so far has prevented the *aggiornamento* (coming together) of the Argentine political class. Undoubtedly, time is essential to understand the question fully, but the question persists and will continue to do so if the current opportunity is misused.

In this context the military question remains open. It did not arise, as we have seen, as a result of political change. As in the case of the Peronist crisis and the economic disputes, the military issue preceded change. To understand the military question in the Argentine case one must resort to a vast literature. Having considered this literature, one must acknowledge the reality of a military besieged by failures as government leaders and as professionals. War, once more, intrudes as a seriously discordant factor. The peace achieved by the constitutional government, with widespread popular support, in the serious conflict with Chile regarding the Beagle question sets a disturbing precedent. More specifically, "the stab in the back" theme stirred up by anticonstitutional nationalists with regard to the Beagle question is reminiscent of the "ambush tactics" endured by the Weimar Republic.

Whether because of a long tradition, which is well known and has been investigated thoroughly, or because the subject is complex, the military question is one of the keys to the consolidation of democracy. In functional terms the question seems to be relatively clear. Analysts describe the question in different ways, but these are substantially the same in content. In any complex society, military institutions are driven by what Samuel Huntington calls the functional imperative, which is to provide security for the society, and by the social imperative that springs from the play among the society's dominant forces, ideologies, values, and institutions. When Alexis de Tocqueville wrote more than a century ago that "the remedy for an army's defects are not to be found in the army itself, but in the country," he clarified the symbiotic nature of the question.

Acceptance of this proposition requires that neither civil society nor the military should close its eyes to dissimilar realities; both should practice self-criticism. We recently wrote that for Argentines "the first and most important ethical-social duty is to create a legitimate political system."[22] The military question is one of the dilemmas of the constitutional process because it should be resolved, on the one hand, by incorporating the armed forces into the loyalty system that sustains the democratic constitutional regime and, on the other, by punishing the culprits and stimulating critical self-examination within the military. Armed forces, alienated and remote, with frayed nerves and lacking intrinsic loyalty to the national constitution and to a political system reinstated on this basis represent a danger for society. Today, the military question is, in many respects, qualitatively different from the entire history of the Argentine people up to the mid-1960s. Civil society still is awaiting a pending introspection and self-criticism by the armed forces. If the "armed arrogance" of the guerrillas already was convicted by Argentine public opinion, what is still pending is evidence from the armed forces that they have conquered corporative arrogance, examined their doctrine, confronted their professional reform, and defined the question of security and defense in terms of constitutional security and not of security as an ambiguous or absolute symbol. The public trial of the principal military commanders constitutes a demonstration of the conditions and intensity of the military question and of the pressure it brings to bear on a relatively fragile process of democratic consolidation. President Alfonsín was criticized for establishing specific criteria for judging military responsibilities in the context of internal and external warfare, "excesses," and "dirty war." In my opinion, the president endeavored to advance in the right direction knowing that he would be hounded by hawks, executioners, and *justicieros* (revenge seekers). If the dilemma persists, it is partly because in extreme circumstances decisions constraining extreme mentalities and attitudes are difficult to make.

Nevertheless, I believe that the critics could not guarantee, with spiritual freedom and intellectual honesty, that the desired results of the alternatives they proposed or demanded would be preferable to those deriving from the criteria established by the president. The study of comparative history, particularly of Western Europe and the United States, contains sufficient ethical and political lessons to prevent us from feigning ignorance when judging or appraising the conduct of governors encouraged not only by the ethics of conviction but also of responsibility.

Finally, I would refer to the much debated question of governability, which subsumes the concrete dilemmas and the decisive issues enunciated in the preceding paragraphs. Argentina, for the first time in many years, lives in a state of legality, of government by law, with spaces of liberty and of participation. But the absence of a tested, experienced political class; the underlying conflicts of legitimacy, which reveal themselves in contradictory statements and behavior regarding the internal logic of a democratic republic; the lack of an economic diagnosis with sufficiently wide acceptance; and the influence of ancient, powerful customs that have turned Argentina into a laboratory of public and private vices that only can be altered or eradicated by persistent political and cultural resocialization, in line with those values favored by the constitution.

The domestic and external conditions affecting the economy, the military issue, and a psychology of decadence that longs for physical or psychological escape reflect the dilemmas of precipitate transition that must be revived in times that are becoming increasingly more difficult. This is happening to a society that achieved its modernity through, among other things, immigration and an ability to respond to the challenges of each period. To contemplate the transition, to be aware of the political system and of the inextricable relationship between democracy and production, to consolidate a democratic and patriotic culture, and to face reality in all its complexity appear to be indispensable if civil society is to recover from so many years of an inefficient, ungovernable state. It follows that the state is, after a fashion, one other "question" omitted from the list in order to abbreviate this chapter but that is, as I suggested, concealed in the subject of governability.

But what state is this for what kind of society? There is the society obstructed by a sinecurist, perverse state, and there is a state, huge but shapeless, besieged by an unruly society, which is particularly rebellious in the interior of the country against Buenos Aires, and by the middle sectors.

Democratic consolidation in Argentina should be an undertaking in need of people who think and intellectuals who act. The schism between thought and action often leads to irresponsibility, to "no reply" to the challenges of reality. That is what de Musset had in mind when he said, "When walking in times of crisis we can never be sure whether we tread on seed or stubble."

I have proposed a reading of contemporary Argentine political history that unearths the graves of failed transitions. The crisis of the blind years tested the capacity of the Argentines to reverse their national decline, to overcome authoritarian temptations, and to restore government under the law. Although the transition envisioned by Alberdi has been realized, the transition to a mass democracy envisioned by Roque Sáenz Peña has yet to be fulfilled.

In moments of decisive change, if intellectuals wish to contribute to the consolidation of treasured values, they should clear the field of stubble so that the seed may grow. They are laborers, not seekers of power, and, all of a sudden, the moralists of their time.

NOTES

1. "La Argentina secreta," *Criterio*, no. 1824 (November 22, 1978). Also see Rafael Braun and Natalio Botana (eds.), *El Régimen Militar* (Buenos Aires: La Bastilla, 1973); and Ricardo del Barco et al. (eds.), *1943–1982: Historia Política Argentina* (Buenos Aires: Editorial de Belgrano, 1983).

2. "Proclamation on Coup," *Foreign Broadcast Information Service, Latin American, Daily Report Annex* 6, no. 58 (March 24, 1976): B1–B2.

3. More on this can be found in Carlos A. Floria, "Quien quiere el fin quiere los medios," *La Nación*, July 28, 1983.

4. Guido di Tella, "La regeneración peronista," *Criterio,* no. 1918 (March 8, 1984): 45–50. For a comprehensive discussion of Peronism as an electoral force, see Manuel Mora y Araujo and Ignacio Llorente (eds.), *El Voto Peronista, Ensayos de Sociología Electoral Argentina* (Buenos Aires: Editorial Sudamericana, 1980). Also see Carlos Fayt, *La Naturaleza del Peronismo* (Buenos Aires: Ediciones Redacción, 1957).

5. Oscar Cornblit, "La opción conservadora en la política argentina," *Desarrollo Económico* 14, no. 56 (1975).

6. I have dealt with some of these issues of Carlos A. Floria, "El régimen militar y la Argentina corporativa (1966–1973)," in del Barco, *op cit.*, pp. 75–103. For a more thorough discussion of the political role of the Argentine military, see Robert A. Potash, *Ejército y Política en la Argentina,* 2 vols. (Buenos Aires: Editorial Sudamericana, 1970 and 1981).

7. For a comprehensive treatment of this topic, see Enrique Zuleta Alvarez, *El Nacionalismo Argentino,* 2 vols. (Buenos Aires: La Bastilla, 1975).

8. For illustration, see the texts of two statements, issued at the conclusion of the Forty-sixth and the Forty-seventh Plenary Assemblies of the Argentine Episcopal Conference: "En la hora actual del país," *Criterio,* no. 1901 (May 12, 1983): 195–196; and "Ante la nueva etapa del país," *Criterio,* no. 1914 (November 24, 1983): 662–663. Also see the April 1984 document entitled "Democracia, responsibilidad y esperanza," *Criterio,* no. 1921 (April 26, 1984): 162–165.

9. I have been referring to "Del gobierno revolucionario al orden constitucional," *Criterio,* no. 1549 (June 13, 1968): 371–375. Robert A. Dahl retrieved this editorial to include in his *Polyarchy: Participation and Opposition* (New Haven, Conn.: Yale University Press, 1971), p. 221, as part his discussion on strategies of change. It seems unnecessary to state that this editorial was of greater interest to North American intellectuals than to members of the Argentine armed forces and even to a part of the intellectual world more attracted to technocracy than to the changes of political regime.

10. The editorial has been reprinted in del Barco, *op. cit.*, pp. 138–147.

11. The proceedings have been published as *El Futuro de la Argentina Política* (Buenos Aires: Editorial del Instituto, 1978).

12. They may have felt that the perverse involutional cycle of the last forty years was leaving behind an authoritarian stage and that there was little that could be done except to use the government to prolong the new democratic stage as long as possible. For a discussion of this dilemma and of the mentalities at work, see Félix Luna, *Golpes Militares y Salidas Electorales* (Buenos Aires: Editorial Sudamericana, 1983). One notable exception was Raúl Alfonsín, the only professional politician to address the necessity of a transition with conviction at that time.

13. A political and ethical analysis undertaken with sufficient spiritual and intellectual liberty must necessarily include Pablo Giussani, *Montoneros, La Soberbia Armada* (Buenos Aires: Sudamericana-Planeta, 1984). The theme of ideology and militant activity has been developed further in contemporary history publications aimed at explaining the events and individual and collective behavior during the period of "Argentina's blind years."

14. See Claudia Hilb and Daniel Lutzky, *La Nueva Izquierda Argentina, 1960–1980: Política y Violencia* (Buenos Aires: Centro Editor de América Latina, 1984).

15. The expression "different Argentina" could be prudently applied to an earlier period, beginning in 1930.

16. Carlos A. Floria, "La Argentina secreta: Probablemente un país diferente," *La Nación*, October 23, 1983, restated what was advanced in a *Criterio* editorial fifteen years before. See note 1.

17. See Carlos A. Floria, "Una idea nueva: La democracia," *La Nación*, October 26, 1967; *¿En nombre de qué? Reflexiones para el Pensamiento Democrático* (Buenos Aires: 1977); and Carlos A. Floria, *Guía para una Lectura de la Argentina Política* (Buenos Aires: Editorial Atec, 1982).

18. See for example, Guido di Tella, *Perón-Perón, 1973–1976* (Buenos Aires: Editorial Sudamericana, 1983), pp. 61–66. Also see his chapter, "La Argentina económica, (1943–1982)," in del Barco *op. cit.*, particularly pp. 188–195.

19. Julien Freund, *Qu'est-ce que la Politique?* (Paris: Editions du Seuil, 1967); Giovanni Sartori, *Democratic Theory* (Westport, Conn.: Greenwood Press, 1962); and Alfred Grosser, *L'Explication Politique: Une Introduction à l'Analyse Comparative* (Paris: Armand Colin, 1972).

20. I have made this point before in "La transición hacia la democracia pluralista," in Jorge Aceiro et al., *Hacia una Argentina Posible* (Buenos Aires: Fundación Bolsa de Comercio de Buenos Aires, 1984), pp. 148–150.

21. Rafael Braun, "Los límites del pluralismo," in Carlos A. Floria and Marcelo Montserrat (eds.), *Pensar la República* (Buenos Aires: Persona a Persona, 1976).

22. "La ética política," *Criterio*, no. 1938 (January 24, 1985): 3.

6
THE POLITICAL TRANSITION IN BRAZIL: FROM AUTHORITARIAN LIBERALIZATION AND ELITE CONCILIATION TO DEMOCRATIZATION

William C. Smith

On March 15, 1985, Brazil returned to civilian government for the first time since President João Goulart was overthrown twenty-one years earlier in March 1964. The military's "return to the barracks" was applauded by virtually all Brazilians. However, this justifiable celebration of national civic pride was much subdued by seventy-four-year-old president-elect Tancredo Neves' sudden illness on the eve of assuming office. Tancredo's death on April 21st, after seven unsuccessful abdominal operations, sent the entire nation into collective trauma and cast a pall over Brazil's incipient democracy. Tancredo's illness led to the inauguration of José Sarney, his vice presidential running mate. Sarney, a recent convert to the democratic cause after a long record of loyality to the outgoing authoritarian regime, thus assumed command of Brazil's fragile democratic transition.

The high expectations generated by the restoration of political democracy were tempered by the harsh reality of Brazil's worst social and economic crisis since the 1930s. Many of the development gains of the "economic miracle" of the early 1970s had evaporated in the first years of the 1980s in the face of deep economic recession, an annual inflation rate of more than 200 percent, and the burden of servicing the Third World's largest external debt of more than $108 billion. In 1985 and 1986 external pressures together with the explosion of long-contained demands from the middle and especially the "popular classes" confronted the Nova República, as the new civilian regime has been christened, with the challenge of going beyond self-congratulation to address fundamental issues of social justice and balanced economic growth in an extremely stratified society.

The consolidation of Brazil's fragile democratic institutions is inextricably related to the challenge of modernizing and transforming the country's particularly perverse pattern of development, a pattern frequently referred to as "savaga capitalism." Perhaps as the leading "emerging power" on the semiperiphery of the global economy, boasting the world's eight largest market economy, Brazil all too frequently has been viewed by its own political elites and dominant classes and powerful international actors as a veritable "no-man's land waiting to be conquered and transformed into a profitable business." Brazilian capitalism in effect has expanded blindly without simultaneously developing either incorporative institutions or a strong, well-articulated civil society with the self-consciousness required to attenuate the sociopolitical tensions generated by an extremely unequal distribution of income, wealth, and life chances.[1]

Since 1950 Brazil's population has grown from 52 million to nearly 140 million, an expansion of almost 170 percent. As Table 6.1 demonstrates, Brazilian society has undergone extremely rapid urbanization and wholesale transformation of the social structure. Many aspects of Brazil's agrarian heritage still are visible in the economy, class structure, culture, and politics. By the 1970s, however, the dynamic core of productive activities was centered firmly in urban industry, with durable consumer goods and capital goods rapidly displacing simpler forms of manufacturing. Brazil's mode of insertion into the world economy also has changed significantly. By 1980 the export of industrial products, which was negligible thirty years earlier, accounted for nearly 60 percent of the total.[2]

The Brazilian state has played a primordial role in promoting these social transformations and in achieving an average annual growth rate of 7 percent in the postwar period. Since the 1950s, and especially under the auspices of the post-1964 military regime, the state also has played a strategic political role in the articulation of an ensemble of entrepreneurial interests—the so-called *tripé*. This "triple alliance" includes official banks, giant state and parastatal enterprises active in public services and directly productive activities, the largest and most dynamic domestic firms, and transnational industrial capital. This alliance is presided over by a power cadre of technobureaucratic state managers working with the armed forces; a pervasive privatization of the state has taken place hand in hand with the more visible "statization" and transnationalization of the economy.[3]

The socially perverse consequences of this Brazilian model of development are evident in the sharp polarities between mass poverty and concentrations of wealth. The large majority of the urban and rural popular classes has not benefited in any substantial way from the tripling of per capita income since the 1950s. As many as two-thirds of all Brazilians fail to attain minimally

TABLE 6.1
Indicators of Structural Transformation in Brazilian Society, 1950-1980

Indicator	Year Circa 1950	 Circa 1980
Structure of production		
Agriculture as % of GDP	24.9	13.2
Manufacturing as % of GDP	20.2	26.3
Industrial output		
% Nondurable consumer goods	72.8	34.4
% Durable consumer goods	2.5	13.5
% Capital goods	4.3	14.7
Exports		
% Coffee	60.0	13.4
% Industrialized	----	56.5
Economically active population		
% Primary	59.9	29.3
% Secondary	14.8	24.4
% Tertiary	25.3	46.3
Occupational structure		
% Agriculture and mining	57.8	31.1[a]
% Industry and construction	12.6	20.0[a]
% Technical and administrative	10.3	20.7[a]
Urbanization		
% In cities larger than 2,000	21.5	45.7
% In urban areas (according to census criteria)	36.2	67.7

[a]1979 data do not include rural areas in northern Brazil.

Source: Vilmar Faria, "Desenvolvimiento, Urbanização e Mudanças na Estrutura do Emprego: A Experiência Brasileira dos Últimos Trinta Anos," in Bernardo Sorj and Maria Hermida Tavares de Almeida, (eds.), Sociedade e Política no Brasil Pós-64 (São Paulo: Editora Brasiliense, 1983), Table 1, p.120.

decent standards of living; a woefully inadequate and inequitable educational system severely limits the possibility of social mobility through individual success in the marketplace. Malnutrition and substandard housing constitute massive public health problems, not only in the Northeast but also in the most highly developed areas, such as the state of São Paulo, which has a per capita income of more than $4,000 and is responsible for more than

TABLE 6.2
Income Distribution in Brazil, 1960-1984

Economically Active Population (Income shares by %)	1960	1970	1972	1976	1980	1984
Poorest 20%	3.9	3.4	2.2	3.2	2.8	2.8
Poorest 50%	17.4	14.9	11.3	13.5	12.6	13.6
Richest 10%	39.6	46.7	52.6	50.4	50.9	46.2
Richest 5%	28.3	34.1	39.8	37.9	37.9	33.0
Richest 1%	11.9	14.7	19.1	17.4	16.9	13.3

Source: Luiz Carlos Bresser Pereira, "Auge e Declínio nos Anos 70," Revista de Economia Política 3, 2 (1983), Table 8, p. 127 and Helio Jaguarike et al., Brasil, 2,000: Para un Novo Pacto Social (Rio de Janeiro: Paz e Terra, 1986), Table 2.12, p. 63.

40 percent of Brazil's net domestic product and 60 percent of total industrial value added. A rough idea of the massive social and economic inequalities associated with this pattern of forced-draft capital accumulation can be gleaned from Table 6.2

Income concentration reached a point of maximum inequality from 1967 to 1973; this so-called economic miracle combined the apogee of political repression with annual growth rates of 10–13 percent. Equity improved only marginally in subsequent years, with the overall pattern remaining remarkably stable. The deepening economic crisis and mounting distributional conflicts of the early 1980s sharply eroded the already precarious situation of the urban and rural poor and undermined the newly won status of large sectors of the hitherto privileged middle classes. Growing public awareness of these glaring disparities challenged the military's attempt to institutionalize authoritarian rule and, subsequently, sharply limited its ability to control the tempo of the process of regime transition toward civilian rule.

The success of the current political transition will in large measure hinge on the Nova República's wisdom, courage, and tenacity in strengthening and broadening the institutions of democratic rule. Success also will depend on effective reforms of the huge state sector of the economy, thus making it more responsible and accountable to popular control, and on the transformation of Brazil's "savage" model of economic growth in order to redress disparities and mitigate sharp class, sectoral, and regional conflicts. The findings of a special commission appointed by President Sarney to study Brazil's development options during the next decade indicate an awareness of this challenge. The commission characterized Brazil's economy as a "system of production adverse to the incorporation of the masses" and warned that if major reforms are not forthcoming soon, massive social and political unrest may be inevitable.[4]

This chapter will address some of the issues related to democratization of the Brazilian polity, society, and economy. First, I will advance some propositions about the transition process in order to introduce a more narrative discussion of the crisis of authoritarian rule and the process of liberalization from 1974 to 1985. Then I will analyze the new civilian regime's management of the democratic agenda during 1985 and 1986 and offer some tentative reflections on the prospects for future democratization.

THE BRAZILIAN TRANSITION

Several excellent comparative studies of recent transitions to democracy have identified three patterns of regime change. These are "transition after collapse," "transition through extrication," and "transition from above."[5] The fall of Portuguese authoritarianism and the demise of the Greek colonels illustrate the first pattern; the second is exemplified by the retreat of Argentina's generals in the aftermath of the Malvinas War. Spain and Brazil are prototypical of the third pattern. According to this approach, in transitions from above authoritarian elites stage manage their exit from power in a process of regime evolution initiated and largely controlled by the authoritarian elites themselves. Popular mobilization and democratic opposition rooted in civil society are secondary factors. Once the transition is underway, however, there may emerge a process of "transaction," or negotiation, bargaining, and compromises between authoritarian elites and their opponents. This process may lead to a series of implicit "pacts" or understandings regarding the tempo and general parameters of political and economic change.[6]

This comparative typology clearly has considerable analytical power in delineating broad patterns of democratic transition in Mediterranean Europe and the Southern Cone. Nevertheless, I believe that the notion of transition from above or transition through transaction does not capture fully the complexities of the Brazilian experience, which is characterized by the "permanent tension between continuity and change." Nor do these typologies capture the transition's "extreme gradualism, its almost experimental character, based as it is on an extremely diffuse agenda, and consequently by a permanent uncertainty regarding its very continuity."[7]

The ubiquity of change, contradiction, and constant experimentation evokes an imagery that seems too elusive to fit comfortably in any of the foregoing categories. It is exactly this indeterminacy that suggests an alternative visualization of regime transitions as "underdetermined social change." In this view, the outcomes of regime transition are shaped not only by elite calculations but also are influenced decisively by the resistance and opposition of subaltern groups in a "resurrection of civil society."[8]

This more nuanced view of the dialectical relationship between state and civil society and between elite initiatives and opposition resistance suggests that transitions should be understood as discrete historical configurations with their own specific internal causation. Priority should be given to the timing and sequence of events, to the internal logic, and to the inherent contradictions of the process of political opening. Analysis should proceed cautiously, employing general theoretical notions sparingly. This posture should not be construed as a rejection or as an alternative to comparative analysis, but as a prudent basis for the specification of the interaction between clusters of general causal factors within particular sociohistorical contexts.[9]

The perspective I propose is based broadly on an emergent consensus among Brazilian analysts that the political opening initiated in 1974 was *not* based on a well-thought-out, comprehensive plan. Rather, liberalization process was the result of "two basic convergent dynamics. A dynamic of negotiation and conciliation directed by the elites and a dynamic of pressures and demands triggered by the society [and] articulated by social movements and translated by political organizations."[10]

According to this view, *distensão* (decompression) and *abertura* (opening) were the crystallization of the complex, contradictory interplay between initiatives designed to maintain the position of incumbent elites and the resistance to authoritarian rule by a variety of groups in civil society. In manifesting their opposition to the regime, these groups underwent a complex process of "self-construction" during which they simultaneously constituted themselves as autonomous social forces and political actors in ideological and organizational terms while espousing political alternatives that envisioned a more rapid, more extensive democratization of state and civil society.

The interaction between state initiatives and civil society's resistance to them, and vice versa, points to the necessity of making an analytical distinction between an "opening process" and an "opening project."[11] The regime's strategy can be interpreted as a series of ad hoc modifications enacted by the authoritarian elites, which were obliged to accept changes that extended substantially beyond the original opening project of institutionalization and legitimation of military rule. President Ernesto Geisel (1974–1979) conceived *distensão* primarily as a gradual exit of the military from direct responsibility for executive power. This exit was to be achieved by forging an alliance among conservative politicians, civilian technocrats, and entrepreneurial elites; the alliance was to be substantiated by a cautious liberalization in deliberately circumscribed arenas: increased individual rights, eased press censorship, curbed physical coercion, and limited electoral competition.

Originally, the ensuing alternation of advances and retreats responded primarily to a logic of state power. Gradually this process acquired a dynamic of its own, which gave rise to an increasingly powerful societal logic of democratic expansion and freedom from state control. The resulting opening process, which was marked by the emergence of new opposition forces and the revitalization of existing ones, contributed to the progressive disaggregation of state power vis-à-vis civil society as well as to the regime's loss of control of the agenda and timetable of the transition. This loss of control contributed to an accelerating economic downturn and to a deepening sense of malaise and drift in the final years of military rule.

The transition from the original opening project to the opening process was punctuated by constant shifts in the balance of forces within the state, a progressive narrowing of the regime's base of social support, and the expansion of antiauthoritarian opposition groups. During the Geisel years the strategic political initiative still belonged to the regime, although it responded to pressures from society at critical moments. In contrast, during the administration of President João Figueiredo (1979–1985), the regime's ability to dictate the tempo of events was undermined precipitously by eroding elite and popular support and by increasingly confident, aggressive opposition. In 1983 and 1984 this erosion was manifested in the state's progressive loss of autonomy and a rapidly declining capacity to control the transition process. Interaction between this specifically political dynamic and the deterioration of the economy further accelerated the activation of civil society. The emergence of opposition forces with mass appeal soon exceeded the hopes of the opposition and the fears of the regime, as "slow, gradual, and sure" liberalization was transformed unexpectedly into a demand for democratization *tout court*.

The foregoing arguments may be recast as propositions that specify the interplay between liberalization under authoritarian auspices and genuine democratization in Brazil.

1. *Distensão* and *abertura* signify different phases of political transition. These two phases constituted an evolution from the more repressive authoritarianism of the late 1960s and early 1970s to a seemingly more institutionalized (but perhaps equally fluid and unstable) form of political domination characterized by the military's extrication from direct control of the executive branch of the state. For authoritarian elites, particularly for those in uniform, the essential condition for the continuation of the process was the preservation of the "security of the state" and the military's retention of control of the transition.

2. *Distensão* and *abertura* are not synonomous with liberalization and democratization respectively, nor can they be understood as different moments

in a linear process of deepening liberalization (although with advances and retreats) that finally ends in democracy. Liberalization is a matter of degree and refers primarily to the curtailment of state repression and the reestablishment of basic civil and political rights at the individual and group levels. Liberalization does not necessarily imply democratization, although substantial liberalization certainly increases the probability for successful democratization. Democratization without liberalization may foster either a return to authoritarian rule or a revolutionary rupture.

3. In the Brazilian case, liberalization was carried out through illiberal measures, including growing concentration of power in a nonaccountable executive and the infamous *casuísmos* (casuistry, or constant manipulation of the rules of the game) designed to preserve a nonrepresentative electoral arena. Even more significantly, the continuation of the liberalization process itself was made dependent on the concomitant strengthening of dictatorial safeguards, thus generating a specifically political contradiction within the *distensão/abertura* process.

4. The accentuation of certain dictatorial aspects of authoritarian rule during *distensão/abertura* provoked a further politicization of civil society. This politicization gathered momentum as each increment of liberalization activated a "multiplier effect," which resulted in a reduction of the cost of opposition for democratic forces and, conversely, an elevation in the costs of repression.

5. This politicization of civil society in Brazil (although certainly less extensive than in Argentina and Uruguay during their transitions) contributed to a significant erosion of the regime's political legitimacy as opposition sentiment began to articulate itself in specific demands by the various sectors of the population: the urban working class, the Catholic church, middle-class professionals, entrepreneurs, and various grass-roots social movements. Although patterns varied widely from group to group, these politicized demands tended to be directed primarily against key governmental figures and specific state policies, which gave rise to a "crisis of legitimation" or crisis of a specific group of incumbent elites. Only later would criticism be directed against the general structure of political rule, thereby producing a "crisis of the regime." Finally, only the most militant and radical opposition groups (the combative unions, some of the new social movements, and the militant Left) directed their criticism to the larger "pact of domination": Brazil's system of power, privilege, and wealth as crystallized in the state, the class structure, and the political economy. This potential "crisis of hegemony" never erupted (and the crisis of the regime was attenuated) because moderate elites, including dissident liberals affiliated with the military regime, successfully asserted their leadership over the democratic opposition and marginalized more radical leaders and social forces.

6. In the *distensão/abertura* process the politicization of demands in civil society found unexpected channels of expression in the limited public spaces

generated in the dialectic between state and society: in the mass media, through interest groups, in professional organizations, and in the electoral arena. Electoral competition and vehicles for legitimate representation in class and professional organizations as well as in the established or new political parties led to the gradual coalescence of a broad majoritarian opposition front.

7. The authoritarian regime's loss of legitimacy was not sufficient, by itself, to force further liberalization or democratization or both. The emergent majority opposition front performed a key role as the catalyst responsible for politicizing (in the sense of "making public") the regime's delegitimation by presenting a believable alternative program of government. The opposition front thereby was crucial in forcing the regime's opening project to become a genuine opening process that exceeded the military's original intention of limited liberalization and limited recognition of individual rights.

8. The final phases of *abertura*, which culminated in the inauguration of a civilian president, brought the transition process, in a strict sense, to a conclusion. In an important sense, however, democratization really began at this point by expanding the political agenda of the transition to include, for the first time, a crucial qualitative advance beyond liberalization toward a potential rupture with authoritarian practices.

9. The transition process resulted in the deinstitutionalization of authoritarianism and the emergence of an informal, transitional institutionality in which previous political structures and the legal system remained in force but were no longer accepted by crucial social and political forces as completely authoritative.

10. Genuine democratization—the task of the postauthoritarian regime—includes the establishment of institutional arrangements that make possible the implementation of meaningful associational freedoms for all groups: universal adult suffrage in secret balloting; regular competitive elections with alternation in power; and executive accountability. By the same token, genuine democratization almost certainly will generate additional pressures to go beyond the politico-institutional sphere to explore the extension of the "logic of the majority" to civil society and the economy—that is, to the spheres of culture, consumption, and production.

GEISEL AND *DISTENSÃO*: FROM OPENING PROJECT TO OPENING PROCESS

The System

The political logic of authoritarian capitalism under military rule was set into place by Generals Humberto Castello Branco (1964–1967) and Artur da Costa e Silva (1967–1969) in a consecration of the marriage of the Brazilian model of rapid capital accumulation and the doctrine of national security. General Emílio Garrastazú Médici (1969–1974) presided over the consolidation of political power of the military-technocratic elite and the aggrandizement of the executive branch.

The *Sistema* (plainly, the system) ruled on the basis of a "culture of fear" promoted by the repressive and autonomous intelligence agencies, the so-called *comunidade de informações.* Although certainly less savage than elsewhere in the Southern Cone, repression created an atmosphere of popular passivity, depoliticization, and withdrawal from politics that was reinforced by state censorship of the mass media and by heavy-handed publicity campaigns extolling annual growth rates of 10–13 percent. These "triumphs of the revolution" were woven together in an ideological discourse propagating such jingoistic slogans as *Pra Frente Brasil!* (Onward, Brazil!), *Ninquem Sequra Este País!* (No One Holds Back This Country!), and, of course, *Brasil: Ame-O ou Deixe-O!* (Brazil: Love It or Leave It!).

Regime strategists worked to erect a facade of political legitimacy by maintaining the trappings of regular electoral contests to assure comfortable majorities for the progovernment party, the Aliança de Renovação Nacional (National Renovating Alliance, or ARENA), over the officially tolerated opposition party, the Movimento Democrático Brasileiro (Brazilian Democratic Movement, or MDB). Belying its frequent promises of an eventual return to democracy, the regime emasculated virtually all representative institutions, from labor unions to municipal councils to state governments. Congress was closed by executive fiat from 1969 to 1971 and was opened only briefly in November 1969 to rubber stamp General Médici's assumption of the presidency following the incapacity and death of General Costa e Silva. One recent analysis observed that "never before, as in these years, was the country so close to the ideal image of it held by the extreme right."[12]

The "Opening" Decision and Military Factionalism

The 1973–1974 presidential succession was handled as a highly secretive, strictly internal military affair. General Ernesto Geisel, then the head of Petrobrás, the powerful state petroleum monopoly, known for his Prussian austerity and autocratic inclination, became Médici's successor in a complex political maneuver orchestrated by General Orlando Geisel, the army minister and Ernesto's brother, and retired general Golbery do Couto e Silva, the *éminence grise* of the post-1964 regime. The entire process amply demonstrated ARENA's total marginality as well as the imporence of civil society. The Electoral College overwhelmingly "elected" Geisel as the next president, notwithstanding the courageous campaign of Ulysses Guimarães, the MDB's "anticandidate."[13]

The *castelistas*, as the Geisel-Golbery group was commonly labeled, had come into prominence in the 1950s and 1960s as the intellectuals through their association with the Escola Superior de Guerra (Superior War College, or ESG) and their key role in the 1964 coup and the Castello Branco government. The *castelistas* had been relegated to the periphery of power under Costa e Silva and Médici, but they returned to center stage during the Geisel and Figueiredo years.

The liquidation of radical opposition, the weakness of the working-class movement, and the MDB's demoralization, plus the mood of national "grandeur" associated with the economic miracle, all made the succession a singularly propitious moment to effect midcourse changes in the regime's evolution. These factors are necessary but not sufficient to account for the military's decision to "open" the system. There is an ongoing dispute about the motives behind Geisel's and Golbery's shift in strategy.[14] What really motivated the *castelistas* to take a chance on liberalization? According to one widely held view, democratic beliefs were the prime causes, and the opening decision was an autonomous decision on the part of the "liberal authoritarians." Although psychological, ideological, and moral factors certainly should not be ignored, factors specific to the armed forces probably played the fundamental role in the decision to initiate the *distensão/abertura* process.

The heightened sense of professionalism of the Brazilian armed forces in the post-1964 period proved to be a double-edged sword. The armed forces' embrace of a particularly extreme variant of "savage capitalism" gave rise to an opaque power structure and a politico-administrative coordination with a distinctly militaristic imprint to the preexisting, in fact thriving, "parallel administration" in place since the 1950s. The consolidation of this new process of sociopolitical articulation was mediated by the military and its technocratic and entrepreneurial allies, thus effectively transforming politics and policymaking into an affair largely limited to the state bureaucracy. The transformation of the "armed corporation" into the regime's principal basis of support almost inevitably transformed the military into something akin to a "military party." Hard-won internal cohesion was threatened constantly by this development. The military-as-regime had to meet the challenge of formulating and implementing complex and controversial policies, with obvious negative consequences for the maintenance of professional norms.

The post-1964 politicization of the officer corps was refracted through factions based on services, branches, generational differences, and personal loyalties as well as on long-standing differences with regard to military doctrine and political ideology. The rise of a semiautonomous repressive apparatus during the apogee of authoritarian rule, although certainly not the only source of military factionalism, was probably at the root of the central cleavage in evidence at the time Geisel ascended to the presidency in March 1974. The *comunidade de informações*, which expanded dramatically following the 1964 coup and particularly during the war of repression against the clandestine opposition, was centered around the system of political control headed by the Serviço Nacional de Informações (National Intelligence Service, or SNI), a combination CIA and FBI, and allied agencies in the army, navy, and air force as well as the federal and state police. Estimates place the total number of full- or part-time salaried members of this "community," which Golbery, its founder, once referred to as a "monster," at 250,000, with perhaps another 750,000 collaborators.[15]

The expansion of the SNI and other coercive agencies within the state constituted a threat to the rest of the armed forces. The threat stemmed primarily from the emergence of a parallel career structure with its own ladder for promotion; an entirely separate communications system rivaling those of the regular branches; and an omnipresent ability to infiltrate all civilian ministries, state enterprises, autonomous parastatal entities, the universities, and even the military itself. This extensive network of intelligence gathering and surveillance gave the security agencies enormous power and autonomy in both domestic and foreign policymaking.

> For the first time in its history, the Brazilian armed forces incorporated a sector [the security agencies] not subject to the [regular] chain-of-command, with the freedom to organize itself autonomously from other sectors of society, whose acts are not judged according to [normal military] disciplinary regulations and whose activities are financed by generous budgets not subject to routine external administrative controls. The new military segment had rights that the conventional segment did not have in terms of professional access and [fringe benefits].[16]

Institutional rivalries concerning this "unconventional segment" were exacerbated by the decision to transfer existing intelligence courses to the newly created Escola Nacional de Intelligência (National Intelligence School, or ESNI). The creation of the ESNI also made the *comunidade de informações* into the principal guardians and interpreters of the doctrine of national security. This was bound to cause resentment among neutral, nonaligned members of the officer corps and certainly antagonized Geisel, Golbery, and the other *castelistas* because it significantly downgraded the power and preeminance of the ESG and those active-duty and retired officers (and many civilian alumni) associated with it.[17]

For Geisel and Golbery, the placing of curbs on the autonomy and impunity of the *duros*, or "hardliners," within the repressive apparatus was a prerequisite to the consolidation of their own position within the state and the advancement of their preferred social and economic policies. In addition, Geisel and Golbery believed that control of arbitrary repression would strengthen the regime's political legitimacy vis-à-vis elite groups while helping to refurbish Brazil's international image, which had been tarnished by publicity about human rights violations.

Transformism and Authoritarian Liberalization

Geisel and Golbery deliberately encouraged expectations of a softening of Médici's hardline policies. Their slogan of "continuity without immobilism" was reiterated constantly in references to "relative democracy" and "strong democracy." These recurrent ambiguities and contradictions were inherent in the variant of military "transformism."[18]

The long-range direction of Geisel's thinking was revealed on March 1974 during the first cabinet meeting of the new government. Geisel expressed an interest in engaging society in a "honest and mutually respectful dialogue," but he stressed that potential interlocutors had to accept the regime's principal objective: the "full institutionalization of the principles of the Revolution of 1964." Ignoring public demands for the abolition of the executive's extraordinary powers, Geisel defended the regime's use of its "exceptional instruments" as necessary to maintain an "atmosphere of security and order fundamental for the economic and social development of the country." He limited himself to expressing the "hope" that henceforth these measures would not be relied upon as a "lasting and frequent" exercise, although they would be maintained should more "energetic containment" of antiregime forces prove necessary.[19]

Geisel also repeatedly called upon the military and opposition elites to exercise "creative political imagination" as regime political strategists put into motion a politico-ideological operation geared to long-term transformations of the state's modus operandi in dealing with civil society. The existing corpus of dictatorial legislation would not be abolished but simply would be allowed to fall into gradual disuse. Simultaneously, "efficacious safeguards," performing the same functions of sociopolitical control, would be incorporated into the legal system.

Geisel's discourse and the regime's political practice hinged on the notion of the state's "potential for repressive action." This potential was to be manifested selectively as a necessary pedagogical tool for the resocialization of civil society in general and the political class in particular. Geisel promised nothing and refused to commit the regime to any timetable for decompression. Moreover, he made the entire enterprise explicitly contingent on the opposition's "sincere, effective collaboration" and its acceptance of the parameters of acceptable political behavior as defined by the regime.[20]

The scope of this transformist project was underscored by the reactions it evoked from both the opposition and from the *duros* within the regime, who were identified by Geisel as "radical but sincere" opponents of *distensão*. Geisel and Golbery made overtures toward a rapprochement with the most vocal critics of the regime's human rights record. In parallel fashion, they encouraged speculation about the lifting of censorship of the mass media. Some minor changes in economic policy and a series of programs also were enacted with the announced goal of implementing a "social opening" to workers and the poor. Many in the opposition were caught off guard and reacted with a mixture of skepticism and cautious optimism.

The security forces, which opposed anything smacking of complicity with the opposition, wasted no time in registering their disapproval. Conflicts within the regime, which pitted Geisel and Golbery against the *duros*, resulted in a series of crackdowns against the print media. Journalists were prosecuted in military courts under the National Security Law, and entire editions of the more outspoken magazines were confiscated, which resulted in heavy financial losses that frequently led to the closure of these magazines.

Throughout his rule Geisel was obliged to make periodic tactical revisions in his overall strategy. These revisions came in response both to the oppositions' testing of the limits of *distensão* as well as in response to occasional flare-ups of ever-present tensions within the regime itself. In August 1974, for example, Geisel employed the intriguing notion of "useless violence" to issue an obvious warning to the opposition that "undue pressures or demands" for "premature changes in the national political structure" would bring *distensão* to a halt. At a more subtle level, Geisel also was warning the repressive apparatus to exercise greater restraint or face reprisals. What Geisel left unsaid was particularly ominous: Some violence was "useful," and the regime would not hesitate to use it.

The Pandora's Box of Electoral Politics

The first key test of the strategy of "controlled opening" came in the congressional and state assembly elections of November 1974. Regime strategists were confident that ARENA again would score comfortable majorities. But there was a catch. If the 1974 elections were to extract genuine popular support for *distensão*, they could not be tainted by the pervasive censorship, harassment, and intimidation of opposition candidates and voters which had marked previous contests. An ARENA victory was crucial, but for legitimacy purposes it also was essential that the official MDB-led opposition participate actively in the electoral process rather than sit out the election in protest.

The MDB accepted the electoral challenge, and opposition candidates served an intensive apprenticeship by taking advantage of the comparatively free access to television and radio, although existing legislation entitled the ARENA to more than two-thirds of free air time based on the number of elected representatives. The MDB managed to break the imposed silence of earlier campaigns and effectively focused public debate on such fundamental

TABLE 6.3
Congressional Elections, 1966-1978

Federal Senate

Year	Total Votes (1,000s)	% ARENA	% MDB	% Null and Void Votes
1966	17,260	44.7	34.2	21.2
1970	23,493	43.7	28.6	27.7
1974	28,981	34.7	50.0	15.1
1978	37,775	35.0	46.4	18.6

Federal Chamber of Deputies

Year	Total Votes (1,000s)	% ARENA	% MDB	% Null and Void Votes
1966	17,286	50.5	28.4	21.0
1970	22,436	48.4	21.3	30.3
1974	28,981	40.9	37.8	21.3
1978	37,629	40.0	39.3	20.7

Source: Calculated from Bolivar Lamounier and Rachel Meneguello, Partidos Políticos e Consolidação Democrática: O Caso Brasileiro (São Paulo: Editora Brasiliense, 1986), Table 3, p. 123.

issues as violations of civil and human rights, the excesses of the National Security Law, and the sharp decline in real wages. These diverse issues were articulated in a comprehensive critique of the post-1964 economic model, which was blamed for exacerbating inequalities of wealth and for the rapid denationalization of strategic sectors of the economy.

As the results presented in Table 6.3 reveal, opening the Pandora's box of electoral competition placed the government in a surprising position as the victim of its own strategy. The senatorial vote, the most accurate indicator of national opinion, revealed a sharp reversal of the 1970 outcome: The MDB received 14.5 million votes in contrast to ARENA's 10.1 million, thus capturing 50 percent of the total votes to the ARENA's 34.7 percent and sweeping sixteen of the twenty-two disputed seats.

Even in the vote for federal deputies, a contest notoriously susceptible to the *voto de cabresto* (clientelistic "herd voting") the MDB's electoral support grew substantially, and the opposition party sharply increased its representation in the lower chamber. More significantly, the MDB's campaign turned the 1974 elections into a virtual plebiscite on the regime's popularity. This can be seen in the number of blank and null votes (a typical expression of antiregime sentiment where voting is obligatory) channelled back into the party system, as invalid votes declined significantly compared to the 1970 elections.[21]

The 1974 elections demonstrated that one of the basic premises of Geisel's and Golbery's strategy of "slow, gradual and sure" normalization of the regime—widening of the regime's political legitimacy and support basis via elections—had been seriously miscalculated. The risks were immense for a regime whose tenuous legitimacy rested on its economic performance (threatened by the 1973 petroleum price shocks) and its promise to reestablish a "state of law." Before Geisel's term was out, the regime would have to confront two further contests with the opposition in 1976 and 1978. The 1978 congressional elections were particularly significant because a good showing by the MDB threatened to give the opposition virtual veto power in Congress over government initiatives requiring constitutional revisions.

This future risk was compounded by another unforeseen consequence of the government's setback in 1974. The MDB's victory in state legislative elections had given the opposition majority control in several states, including the four key states of São Paulo, Rio de Janeiro, Rio Grande do Sul, and Paraná. As matters stood, the opposition would be able to select several of the state governors scheduled to assume power in 1979. This prospect presented Geisel with a serious dilemma. If MDB politicians were allowed to assume executive power in important states, the federal government would lose some control of the reins of executive power. The other alternative was perhaps even more unpalatable: *fechamento* (authoritarian closure via repression) which would reinforce the power of the *duros* within the armed forces.

Elite Surrogates and Civil Society's Activation

Elections had to be held for reasons of legitimacy, but as Geisel repeatedly had made clear, the regime never contemplated the possibility of a real transfer of power to the opposition. How could the regime maintain *distensão* in this new atmosphere? What could be done? To analyze Geisel's response we must consider the significant changes taking place in the nature of the opposition in the mid-1970s.

Chief among the unintended consequences of political decompression was the impetus given to the search for new channels of opposition apart from the limited electoral arena. This led to the gradual activation of civil society and to the unfolding of an antiauthoritarian societal logic manifested through a variety of collective actors. The tempo of each actor's political mobilization and emergence as an autonomous social force varied considerably. The urban and rural poor were not in the vanguard of the first phase of the reactivation of civil society. In fact, during the first years of the Geisel regime, elite opposition was more significant in questioning the regime's legitimacy.

In the early 1970s elite opinion became somewhat more critical of the regime's economic orientation, and some sectors gradually began to express cautious support for land reform, income redistribution, and protection for national companies threatened by the penetration of transnational firms. Survey data reveal that these elites increasingly resented the rulers' "sustained intrusions into their own spheres of privilege and influence" and were drawn into opposition out of "a sense that the regime had plunged the country into a deepening reign of terror and arbitrary lawlessness from which the elites themselves were not safe."[22] The hierarchy of the Catholic Church and dissident sectors of the middle class, especially liberal professionals, assumed the leadership in catalyzing and channeling elite disaffection and in openly criticizing the regime's policies.

Riding the wave of confidence generated by the MDB's showing in the 1974 elections, the Conferência Nacional dos Bispos do Brasil (National Conference of Brazilian Bishops, or CNBB), the Ordem dos Advogados Brasileiros (Brazilian Bar Association, or OAB), and the Associação Brasileira de Imprensa (Brazilian Press Association, or ABI) stepped up their long-standing opposition to the regime's excesses. In their persistence in raising such sensitive issues as censorship, human rights, freedom for political prisoners, political amnesty, and protection of the Indian population, these organizations in effect were serving as "surrogates" for the rest of civil society.

During the Geisel years, the 350-member CNBB (the second largest in the world) moved beyond the denunciation of repression and human rights abuses to assume an increasingly active leadership role in organizing opposition to the Brazilian model. Particularly important was the establishment of a series of pastoral commissions that brought the Church hierarchy into close contact with priests, religious laypersons, and others in a concerted effort to foment grass-roots social movements. This pastoral work was instrumental in mobilizing support throughout society for the needs of specific social groups, such as the *boiás frias* (landless rural workers); urban slum dwellers; urban industrial workers; abandoned children; blacks and indigenous peoples; and the victims of human rights violations. In parallel fashion the CNBB also supported the expansion of *comunidades eclesiais de base* (Christian base communities, or CEBs) as an integral part of a spirit of social reform in consonance with the Church's "preferential option for the poor" and the tenets of liberation theology, then rapidly making inroads among Brazilian Catholics.[23]

The Catholic Church's social and political activism had several important consequences. First, as the Church strove to become "the voice for those without a voice," it extended its institutional prestige and protection to the subordinate sectors of society without their own legitimate channels of expression. Some 80,000 CEBs were founded, with a membership of approximately 2 million. The CEBs, according to their intellectual mentors, functioned as "seedbeds of participatory democracy" for social groups long accustomed to a political culture of class subordination and social deference. Second, the Church's protagonistic role and the high visibility of such prelates as Dom Paulo Evaristo Arns, archbishop and cardinal of São Paulo, made opposition to authoritarian rule more legitimate. The Church's role was particularly significant for the middle class. Large sectors of this heterogeneous class had reaped considerable benefits from authoritarian rule, but many, including conservatives, were repelled by the regime's violation of human rights and anxious for opportunities for political expression.[24]

The Bar Association and the Press Association played similar roles by taking full advantage of the limited space created by *distensão*. Beginning in 1974 the OAB initiated a series of offensives against the regime and the doctrine of national security in defense of political prisoners and human rights, using its prestige to delegitimate the authoritarian regime's tenuous claim to legality. Simultaneously, the Press Association stepped up its criticism of the state's strict vigilance over all forms of mass communications, including the press, book publishing, music, TV, radio, theater and film—all considered potential vehicles of psychological warfare—that had been codified in the National Security Law and the Press Law. Beginning in 1975 the press assumed an increasingly important role in expanding liberalization beyond the limited reforms envisioned by the regime, thereby making an important contribution to the breakdown of the "culture of fear."[25]

In short, by acting as elite surrogates for the popular sectors and the middle class in a civil society still lacking in autonomous political organizations, the civil rights and organizational successes achieved by the Conference of Bishops, the Bar Association and the Press Association had far-reaching consequences that were not clearly foreseen by the groups involved and certainly not by the regime. Each partial victory had its own specific multiplier effect and raised the costs of repression for the regime and lowered the costs of organization and activities for other groups.

The Hardline Responds

The hardliners were perhaps most clairvoyant in perceiving the implications of *distensão*. The repressive apparatus wasted little time in responding immediately to the first signs of civil society's reactivation. Charges that the opposition's 1974 victory was the work of Communists infiltrated into the MDB leadership resulted in a series of police raids in São Paulo in 1975, directed against the illegal, but well-organized pro-Moscow Partido Comunista do Brasil (Communist Party of Brazil, of PCB).

In response to this rearticulation of right-wing opposition within the regime, Geisel was forced to use his "potential for repressive action" to decree numerous *cassações* (suspensions of individual civil and political rights) suspending the mandates and political rights of judges, opposition figures, and even ARENA politicians accused of corruption. Geisel once again was obliged to issue stern warnings against opposition efforts to "artificially accelerate the process of political development." In a significant hardening of his rhetoric, Geisel referred to democracy as an "outmoded formula inadequate to Brazilian reality." If the electoral route presented difficulties because of opposition recalcitrance, Geisel intimated that legitimation could be sought by other means. *Distensão,* he declared "ought not to be only political or even predominately political. What we seek is integrated and humanistic development." In fact, government social programs directed to the poor and to certain regional constituencies were implemented to provide an alternative method of social integration.[26]

But even this scaled-down version of *distensão* was dealt a serious blow with the death, in October 1975, of Vladimir Herzog, a well-known Jewish television journalist in São Paulo. Accused of communist connections, Herzog died while being tortured by operatives of the Divisão de Operações Internas-Centro de Operações de Defensa Interna (Division of Internal Operations–Center for Internal Defense Operations, or DOI-CODI) acting under the protection of Second Army Intelligence. The official claim of Herzog's "suicide" voiced by the commander of the Second Army provoked a massive wave of public outrage marked by strikes by university students, protests by the Bar Association and the Press Association, and a well-attended public ecumenical mass presided over by São Paulo's archbishop Evaristo Arns.[27]

Geisel's failure to act immediately against such hardline impunity further emboldened the right-wing opposition within the regime. Geigel preferred to bide his time preparing his counterattack. In January 1976, when union activist Manoel Fiel Filho died under torture at the hands of the São Paulo DOI-CODI, the Planalto palace retaliated decisively. Without consulting the army's High Command, Geisel immediately dismissed the Second Army's commander, General Eduardo d'Avila, replacing him with General Dilermando Gomes Monteiro, a personal friend and a political moderate. Violence unauthorized by the presidency was "useless" and counterproductive and would not be tolerated. The *duros* were put on the defensive.

Geisel's successful assertion of his authority came at a high price. To placate the *linha-dura* and to contain the threat of the opposition, the president was obliged to assume a much tougher stance with the opposition. A significant manifestation of this new posture was a new law, the Lei

Falcão (named after the minister of justice), decreed in June 1976. This arbitrary measure was designed to undercut the MDB's electoral prospects by severely curtailing opposition access to the mass media, permitting only the candidate's name, electoral number, a brief biography, and a photograph (in the case of television). No mention of party platforms or criticism of government policies was allowed. Meanwhile, ARENA's candidates were promoted shamelessly by the regime's supposedly nonpartisan use of the media.

Even such draconian measures proved incapable of undermining the opposition's popularity, as the MDB scored another impressive showing in the 1976 municipal elections. Nor did Geisel's tougher posture dissuade the *linha-dura* from launching another wave of right-wing terrorism. These acts, carried out in the name of the Brazilian Anti-Communist Alliance, included firebombings against the Brazilian Press Association headquarters, the kidnaping of a prominent bishop, and threats against progressives in the Catholic hierarchy. All told, some two thousand arrests were made during the 1975–1976 wave of repression.[28]

The Pacote de Abril: The Illiberal Face of Liberalization

Hopes for a resumption of *distensão* also received a near fatal blow from Geisel himself. By early 1977 Geisel and Golbery increasingly were concerned with the upcoming 1978 congressional elections and the very real possibility that the MDB would win majorities in both the Senate and the Chamber of Deputies. As observers aptly noted, the regime acted upon Machiavelli's advice to the prince to "do 'good' in gradual doses, and 'bad' in one massive dose." Geisel seized upon a dispute about a proposed bill to reform the judicial system to order Congress closed and cynically justified this action by charging that the MDB had constituted itself as a "minority dictatorship." Geisel took advantage of Congress's closure to assume all legislative prerogatives (as permitted by the regime's arbitrary legislation) to decree a series of constitutional changes known as the Pacote de Abril, or "April Package."[29]

The Pacote was the crowning illiberal measure required to guarantee the continuity of Geisel's project of authoritarian liberalization. In addition to incorporating a series of so-called judicial "safeguards" into the military-approved constitution of 1967, the Pacote reduced the two-thirds majority required for constitutional amendments to a simple majority, thereby reducing the risk that a future MDB victory in Congress might tie the government's hands. Other feats of "electoral engineering" also were decreed, including measures designed to skew significantly the electoral system to ARENA's advantage by reducing the representation in Congress and in the Electoral College of the more populous, urban, and industrialized states of the South and Center-South, while overrepresenting ARENA strongholds in the North and Northeast. Other innovations included the indirect election of state governors and the indirect election of one senator from each state—promptly christened "bionic" senators—to guarantee a governmental majority in the upper chamber. Finally, the presidential mandate was extended from five to six years for Geisel's successor.

The Pacote de Abril provided the legal fig leaf Geisel required to control the future evolution of the regime, and he was quite clear about his motives for these acts, proudly referring to the Pacote as his government's "most outstanding achievement."

Succession Struggles Within the Military

Even as these authoritarian measures to prevent genuine liberalization were being enacted, Geisel's and Golbery's drive to consolidate their power provoked redoubled resistance from within the armed forces. The upcoming presidential succession exacerbated long-standing institutional and personal rivalries, but Ernesto Geisel, in contrast to Médici, was a consummate practioner of the art of military politics and took steps to transform the presidential succession into what the rich Brazilian political lexicon identifies as *uma ação entre amigos*, "a private affair among friends."

Geisel won an important first victory in his struggle with the *linha-dura* in the ouster of General Ednardo d'Avila in January 1976. A second battle was fought during 1977 and also ended with a decisive victory. Geisel, together with Golbery, carefully embarked upon a campaign to install General João Baptista Figueiredo in the Planalto presidential palace in March 1979. Figueiredo's credentials were solid. He had participated in the 1964 military-entrepreneurial coup as a colonel under Golbery's command and subsequently became head of the military household and secretary general of the powerful National Security Council under Médici. In 1974 Geisel named Figueiredo to head the SNI. Figueiredo thus had strong ties with both the Médici *duros* and the *castelista* factions within the army, although his ultimate loyalty always had been to the latter group and, especially, to Golbery. He therefore made an ideal middleman in the Byzantine world of military politics.[30]

Two serious rivals emerged from the top echelons of the army, General Sylvio Frota, minister of the army, and General Hugo Abreu, chief of the presidential military staff. Neither Frota nor Abreu was originally considered a *duro*, but both were forced by political exigencies to become the hardliners' candidates in the struggle against Geisel and Golbery. Frota's and Abreu's military and civilian supporters attacked on three fronts. First, they charged that Geisel's and Golbery's support for Figueiredo was a deliberate violation of the established tradition of consultation with the military hierarchy. They also played upon resentments occasioned by the fact that as Figueiredo was only a three-star general, to become president he would have to be favored with a *carona*, or "free ride," in order to be promoted to four-star status over generals with more seniority. Second, their supporters charged that liberalization was tantamount to "softness on communism." The "subversion" issue and the threat of inquiries into human rights violations were expected to gain the support of the "colonels of the repression" of the late 1960s and early 1970s, many of whom were soon to be promoted to the rank of general. Third, they accused Geisel, Golbery, Figueiredo, and their business allies of heading a "corrupt establishment group" representing "an oligarchy committed to the hidden interest of multinational groups."

Geisel first eliminated Frota's challenge to his authority. In early October 1977, following elaborate preparations, Geisel summoned Frota to the Planalto palace to inform him that he was dismissed from his post. In a telling twist upon the tradition that army ministers dismissed presidents, not vice versa, Frota's attempt to mount a countercoup proved a total failure. General Abreu then picked up the gauntlet. However, when he failed to block Figueiredo's candidacy, Abreu resigned in noisy protest in early 1978. Geisel then immediately announced to journalists what everyone had long known: Figueiredo was indeed his candidate. Almost as an afterthought, ARENA's leadership was informed of Geisel's decision a day later.

The Classes and the Masses Enter the Scene

Figueiredo's nomination as ARENA's standardbearer confirmed Geisel's virtually absolute sway within the armed forces. However, 1978 was not to be a mere rerun of 1973. The limited liberalization permitted by *distensão* and the electoral victories of 1974 and 1976, plus the evident division within the armed forces, prompted the opposition to mount an aggressive challenge to the regime's candidate. The MDB leadership reasoned that even in the rigged Electoral College an opposition candidate might have an outside chance if he could attract the support of ARENA dissidents.

The MDB decided to confront Figueiredo with its own military candidate. In something of a paradox, the selection of a military candidate was defended most ardently not by the conciliatory moderates but by the MDB's more progressive *autêntico* (authentic) wing. In mid-1978 retired General Euler Bentes Monteiro, the ex-superintendent of the development agency for the Northeast and a respected nationalist, was chosen as the MDB's presidential nominee.

The MDB's military candidate proved to be a surprisingly effective campaigner. General Bentes Monteiro appealed to all opposition forces by running as the candidate of the Frente Único pela Redemocratização (United Front for Redemocratization) and calling for immediate revocation of all the regime's "exceptional" laws and the convocation of a constitutional convention; a generous amnesty for political prisoners; reduction of the presidential mandate from six to four years and the return to direct presidential elections in 1982; and labor union autonomy from state control and the right to strike. Bentes Monteiro also alerted his active-duty comrades to the Planalto's manipulation of their "respect for discipline and hierarchy." The maneuver to impose an unpopular candidate, he warned, would "transform the Armed Forces into a political party," thereby undermining professionalism and promoting dangerous factionalism within the officers corps.

The MDB's 1978 campaign had an impact that far transcended Ulysses Guimarães' symbolic "anticandidacy" five years earlier. This greater impact was largely due to the fact that civil society itself had begun to organize. The earlier efforts undertaken by the Church, the OAB, and the ABI began to show demonstrable results, and antiregime forces expanded to include sectors beyond the MDB. The Church, led by the CNBB, stepped up its level of opposition in 1977 and 1978 and issued Christian Demands for a New Order, a passionate demand for deep reforms in Brazilian capitalism and a return to democratic rule. The CEBs and the other grass-roots organizations linked to the church's pastoral network joined with secular grass-roots groups, many under leftist leadership, to form mass-based social movements.[31]

The most influential of these new grass-roots social movements included the Movimento Custo de Vida (Cost of Living Movement), which emerged as a popular protest against inflation and the scarcity of such basic foodstuffs as beans, rice and corn; the movement of university students, which organized to protest the regime's educational policies and to rebuild the organizations that had been dismantled after 1964; and the amnesty movement, which catalyzed a broad spectrum of middle-class opinion to press for amnesty for political prisoners and exiles. These movements succeeded in mobilizing thousands of people during the 1978 presidential campaign and played an important role in civil society's reactivation, thereby further undermining the regime's legitimacy.

In the midst of the 1978 electoral campaign another new social force made its startling debut upon the political scene: militant labor unions associated with the *sindicalismo novo* movement.[32] The roots of the "new unionism" can be traced back to earlier efforts to organize truly independent unions. The military regime's modernization of the corporatist labor code dating back to the late 1930s was the primary obstacle to an autonomous workers movement. Although state action against unions, including direct intervention and removal of leaders, cancellation of elections, or dissolution by decree, declined significantly during the Geisel years, the working class continued to suffer severe limitations on its capacity to organize.

The rapid pace of economic growth led to a doubling of the number of unionized workers from 1965 to 1978, which reached almost 4.3 million in the latter year. Still, in relative terms, union membership remained virtually stagnant, reaching only 14.1 percent of the economically active population in urban areas in 1978. Even in industry and commerce, only one-fifth to one-quarter of employed workers was unionized. Labor apparently had been brought under effective state control, and the continued docility of the working class seemed guaranteed.

In 1977 the economic authorities were forced to admit the falsification of official inflation statistics for 1973 and 1974. This manipulation resulted in a sharp fall in real wages. This admission was the catalyst to an unprecedented mobilization under the leadership of the metalworkers of São Bernardo do Campo, an industrial suburb of the city of São Paulo. The resulting "34.1 percent campaign" highlighted workers' grievances against the policy of *arrocho salarial* (wage controls tied to rises in the cost of living index) and the pliant *pelegos* (government-controlled labor bureaucrats) who dominated the official union structure.

The first significant strikes in a decade erupted without warning in May 1978 in the important auto industry (1 million vehicles produced in 1978). The strike soon spread to nine cities in São Paulo's industrial belt, with 250,000 workers laying down their tools. By the end of 1978 more than 500,000 workers had struck. Although perhaps two-thirds of the strikers were skilled and unskilled blue-collar workers, significant numbers of white-collar professionals in education, medicine, and banking also participated. Many striking unions obtained significant wage increases that were 10–30 percent greater than the official indexes, including a 59 percent raise won by some São Paulo metalworkers. Not surprisingly, union membership in the auto industry increased 10–27 percent by the end of 1978.[33]

The emergence of the *novo sindicalismo* movement had far-reaching consequences. The strikes in 1978 and subsequent years demonstrated the ability of the working class to paralyze the modern nucleus of Brazil's industrial park. This in turn opened the way for significant changes in the triangular relationship among labor, employers, and the state. In this system, the state had long acted as the mediator of struggles between capital and labor, systematically favoring the former in the name of capital accumulation. Concomitantly, the militancy manifested in the 1978 strikes was a significant affirmation of a new collective identity on the part of workers in the most dynamic sectors of the Brazilian economy. This identity had been forged in the workers' awareness of their exploitation and lack of effective citizenship in a model of economic concentration and promotion of opulent consumerism in a highly stratified society. Many university professors, doctors, and other professionals, whose status and income had been eroded seriously by the regime's economic policies, also were affected by the new militancy and began to construct their own specific identities. New sectors of the population, both workers and members of the middle class, thus began to raise their voices and contribute their political will to demands for social and economic reforms and an end to dictatorial rule.[34]

Nor did the dominant classes remain untouched by the political tremors shaking civil society. Brazil's largest industrial, commercial, and financial interests, comprising the domestic private sector member of the *tripé*, certainly had benefited tremendously during the economic miracle. In contrast, their relatively secondary role in post-1964 politics seemed to confirm the view, still common among many social scientists, that Brazil's entrepreneurial class had neither a "vocation for hegemony" nor a true "national project." This ignored the fact that the dominant sectors of Brazilian capitalism always had "played their own game" independently of, and even in conflict with, their military and technocratic partners. This was certainly the case during the Geisel years.

Open conflict emerged in 1975 and 1976, provoked by the regime's response to the petroleum shocks and the quadrupling of Brazil's import bill. The regime's strategy of adjustment to the new international situation called for accelerated import substitution and massive state investments in capital goods and infrastructure. Domestic industry, particularly capital goods producers, at first responded very positively to the new opportunities created by the strategy of "forced march" industrialization. But when inflationary pressures and a scarcity of foreign exchange forced the government to retreat somewhat from its extremely ambitious plans, many of the largest and most dynamic firms found themselves in dire straits, with sharply declining profits and mounting indebtedness.[35]

In the ensuing *estatização* (statization) controversy, private sector ideologues became increasingly critical of the public enterprises and the parastatal companies that spearheaded the state's deepening involvement in directly productive activities in competition with private capital. The subsequent "entrepreneurial rebellion," which was led by the capital goods sector, involved others as well and was directed initially at the Geisel regime's economic policies, with only muted criticism of the authoritarian regime itself.

The gradual politicization of key sectors of the entrepreneurial class in opposition to the authoritarian Leviathan led to the articulation of an ideological discourse centered on the demand for greater liberalization. At first, liberalization was understood to pertain almost exclusively to the economic sphere and certainly did not entail major social change or the immediate return to competitive politics. By 1978, however, entrepreneurial calls for "democracy without adjectives" were fueled by growing dissatisfaction with the extreme centralization and technocratic closure of decisionmaking. Many in business charged that technocratic insulation from the "producing classes" had deprived private capital of its status as the privileged interlocutor of state power. Some activists in the "free enterprise movement" even went so far as to warn of an impending threat to market capitalism itself.

Domestic capital's opposition gradually acquired an implicit democratic content, notwithstanding the deeply conservative, even authoritarian tendencies of the Brazilian entrepreneurial class. By the time of the struggle over the 1978 presidential succession, many businesspeople began to distance themselves, albeit very cautiously and tentatively, from the military's authoritarian excesses. But there was no unanimity among businesspeople. In fact, there was considerable political and ideological diversity within Brazil's capitalist class. On the right, many sectors continued to adhere to strongly proregime positions. While strongly attacking statism in the economy, these conservatives also warned the president about the "communist threat" and the dangers of allowing political liberalization to go too far.

More "progressive" businesspeople, most of whom were members of São Paulo's powerful Federação das Indústrias do Estado de São Paulo (Federation of Industries of the State of São Paulo, or FIESP), called for an acceleration of political liberalization. They issued an important manifesto, sometimes called the Manifesto of the Democratic Bourgeoisie, signed by eight of Brazil's most distinguished businessmen, that publicly expressed support for the modernization of Brazilian capitalism with greater concern for "social justice," freer collective bargaining, and greater attention to the health, education, and welfare needs of the poor. The manifesto concluded with the declaration that "there is only one regime capable of promoting the full explicitation of interests and absorbing tensions without transforming them into an undesirable conflict of classes—the democratic regime."[36]

This "progressive" entrepreneurial discourse, notwithstanding its many ambiguities, clearly went beyond the "free enterprisers'" narrow defense of business's own corporate interests.

> The defense of liberalism à la Locke by entrepreneurs, the return to the idea of the indivisibility of the "two liberties," the economic and the political—an image used and abused between 1974 and 1977 in speeches, interviews, roundtables, etc.—can only have been seen as a kind of codified language that prudently employs the arguments of economic liberalism as a way to make explicit demands for other liberties.[37]

This rupture of the authoritarian political pact often has been exaggerated, but even the partial withdrawal of the dominant classes' enthusiasm for military rule did have important political consequences. Some sectors of the "classes" now began to join, albeit belatedly, with the "masses" in a broad, frequently contradictory, multiclass opposition to the continuation of authoritarian rule.

A Paradoxical Victory

The broadening of antiregime sentiment and shifts in the balance of forces implied by civil society's gradual activation were important but were not capable of immediately altering the outcome of the 1978 presidential succession. The regime's political engineering proved quite effective: General Figueiredo received 355 votes to General Euler's 266 votes in the Electoral College. Even the Pacote de Abril, however, could not reverse the erosion of the regime's electoral base. The growth of opposition votes continued in the November 1978 congressional elections (see Table 6.3). However, the subterfuge of the "bionic" senators did assure ARENA control of the Senate in spite of the fact that MDB candidates garnered 46.4 percent of the total votes to 35.0 percent for ARENA. Similarly, in the lower chamber, ARENA's razor-thin victory—40.0 percent to 39.3 percent—was transformed artificially by the 1977 "reforms" into a more comfortable majority, with 231 seats (or 55 percent) given to ARENA, while the MDB was awarded only 189 seats (or 45 percent).[38]

President Geisel still had some unfinished business before turning command over to General Figueiredo. In the last months of his mandate Geisel scaled down some aspects of the regime's "potential for repressive action," thus partially redeeming his promises made five years earlier. Although strongly criticized by the opposition for not going far enough, Geisel did relinquish the president's power to close Congress, to cancel congressional mandates, and to strip citizens of their political rights. Habeas corpus was reinstituted for those accused of political crimes, and prior censorship was lifted from the electronic media. Concomitantly, however, the president received significant grants of new authority, including the power to declare a limited "state of emergency" without prior congressional approval.

Geisel also imposed some modifications in the National Security Law. Despite its apparent softening of existing legislation, this reform was opposed by the Bar Association, by most human rights organizations, and by a majority of the MDB. In an additional overture to placate rising demands from the amnesty movement, Geisel also lifted banishment orders affecting more than 120 political exiles who had left Brazil during the height of the armed struggle.

The paradox of *distensão* during the Geisel years is that these positive aspects of liberalization were achieved through profoundly undemocratic means. Congress was still virtually powerless on important questions, such as budget appropriations. The bloated, autonomous security apparatus remained intact, ready to act when necessary. The deeply illiberal bent of the *distensão* project made future prospects for democratic transition dangerously dependent on the political skills and idiosyncrasies of a very small, and increasingly isolated, group of men of profoundly authoritarian vision and temperament.

ABERTURA UNDER FIGUEIREDO: REGIME EROSION AND LOSS OF CONTROL

General João Figueiredo assumed power in March 1979 with a solemn promise to "make Brazil a democracy." This pledge was designed to offset statements during the campaign in which he affirmed his disdain for "classical liberal democracy" and declared that he was determined to pursue the regime's policy of gradual political opening even if he had to "arrest and break" his opponents. An ardent soccer fan, Figueiredo also had announced that he alone would be the "owner of the ball." He warned that "if the politicians play by the [regime's] rules, that's fine. If they don't, I'll pick up the ball and leave the field. The game will be over."[39]

Figueiredo's six year effort to "make Brazil a democracy" occurred in three broad phases. During the first phase, which closed in August 1981, the regime attempted an ambitious, but ultimately unsuccessful, strategic political offensive to consolidate its hold of *abertura*. The second phase concluded with major advances for the opposition in the November 1982 elections. The third phase witnessed the regime's progressive, irreversible loss of control of its own decade-long project of political opening.

Escaping the "Black Hole"

General Golbery continued to dominate the Planalto as Figueiredo's chief political strategist. In May 1980 Golbery gave a major speech at the Escola Superior de Guerra (Superior War College, or ESG) reviewing the Figueiredo administration's plans for advancing *abertura*.[40] In a revealing exposition of the logic of liberalization, Golbery warned the largely uniformed audience that the military had no alternative except to support *abertura*: Fifteen years of "growing compression" had turned Brazil into an "enormous pressure cooker" ready to explode. Candidly criticizing the regime's "maximum centralization combined with maximum inefficiency," Golbery likened the military's dilemma to the "phenomenon of 'black holes' discovered by modern astronomy, in which even a star's own light cannot escape growing gravitational pressures."

In order to escape the black hole effect, Golbery proposed even greater concentration of political power at the apex of the state to prepare the transfer of power to reliable civilians susceptible to military influence. The principal obstacle to this project, in Golbery's view, was the "formation of a single opposition front" pushing for rapid democratization. To circumvent this obstacle, he called for the dismantling of the artificial two-party monopoly the military itself had imposed in 1965.

Golbery's plan called for incumbent elites to play upon civil society's weakness and "innate heterogeneity" through a policy of cooptation of moderate elites and social forces. In a second step toward the "immediate disarticulation of the opposition system," the state would administer "pedagogical" lessons at "irregular intervals" to isolate and destroy, one by one, militant unions, clandestine parties, the CEBs, and other "dissociative tendencies." Political stability thus could be established in a liberalized polity with a weak multiparty system dominated by a strong progovernment coalition. The difference between liberalization and democratization was clear for Golbery: If implemented properly, careful doses of liberalization could substitute for genuine democratization, thereby maintaining the political exclusion of subaltern groups and preempting meaningful demands for real reform of the economic model.

This blueprint was impressive but fallible. Society's growing demand for political amnesty was one of the new administration's first challenges. Figueiredo and Golbery deftly vented the "pressure cooker" on this issue with the approval of a compromise amnesty bill in August 1979. Strong criticism from the *duros* prevented acceptance of the "full, total and unrestricted amnesty" demanded by the opposition, but the final version did allow the return of political exiles, the reinstatement of most public employees purged after 1964, and the eventual release of all political prisoners. The *duros* won two significant victories: the extension of an across-the-board amnesty to military and police personnel implicated in repression and torture and the veto of a return to active duty of officers and enlisted men ousted since 1964 for political reasons. The return from exile of Leonel Brizola, ex-governor of Rio Grande do Sul; Luís Carlos Prestes, general secretary of the Brazilian Communist party; Miguel Arraes, ex-governor of Pernambuco; as well as other well-known figures provoked the ire of conservative civilians and military hardliners. But for regime strategists this was a necessary evil that facilitated their larger goal: implosion of the MDB-led opposition front.

The Figueiredo administration was less successful in managing the economy and containing labor unrest, both of which were crucial to controlling the direction and tempo of *abertura*. Figueiredo assumed the presidency in the midst of another wave of strikes and mass mobilizations in São Paulo's satellite industrial communities—the ABC region. The 1979 strikes were more widespread than those of the previous year and posed a more immediate threat. Previously, strikes and mobilizations had been directed primarily against employers. Beginning in 1979 strikes and labor mobilizations were more politicized and went beyond traditional demands for higher wages and better working conditions to challenge the state's corporatist system of control.[41]

The regime initially resorted to harsh repressive measures to confront an alleged "threat to national security." Soon, however, Planalto strategists realized that intransigence only served to further politicize the workers and to generate support for their cause among other sectors of society, thus isolating the government and undermining the *abertura* project. Consequently, in a startling about-face, a wage reform package was approved in September 1979 that granted semiannual, instead of yearly, salary increases. Moreover, the new package included a so-called "cascade" feature promoting limited income redistribution. Lower-paid workers and employees (those receiving between two and five times the minimum wage) were favored, but the overall functional distribution of income between capital and the workers and the salaried middle class remained highly skewed.

At the same time the regime was making these concessions on the wage front, the second round of petroleum price hikes in 1979 exacerbated the economic difficulties afflicting Brazil since 1974, thereby feeding inflationary pressures and further eroding the already precarious balance-of-payments situation. Figueiredo's economic team was deeply split, pitting the so-called "realists," led by planning minister Mário Henrique Simonsen and finance minister Karlos Rischbeiter, both holdovers from the Geisel administration, against the "developmentalists," headed by Antônio Delfim Neto, ex-minister of planning under Médici and minister of agriculture in Figueiredo's first cabinet.

Delfim Neto argued that significant idle capacity permitted growth without slashing wages or cutting investments. In contrast, the fiscal orthodoxy defended by the "realists" prescribed the bitter pill of recession to cool off the economy and meet Brazil's debt obligations. With strong entrepreneurial backing, the "developmentalists" triumphed, and Delfim replaced Simonsen in the planning ministry, thereby recovering his former role as the regime's "great planner."

Ironically, it fell to Delfim Neto, the supertechnocrat to whom moral and social concerns always had been secondary if not entirely meaningless, to argue that "sound" economic policy (at least as defined by conservative orthodoxy) now had to be subordinated to the larger political exigencies of *abertura*; political liberalization was impossible without social peace. Delfim's loose monetary and expansive fiscal policies fostered a brief spurt of renewed growth, but a second "miracle" was not in the cards.[42]

In 1979 Gross Domestic Product (GDP) expanded at a rapid rate of 6.4 percent; GDP grew at an even faster 7.2 percent clip in 1980, but the bubble burst in 1981. Delfim's pump-priming policies, coupled with the delayed effects of the doubling of petroleum prices, led to a contraction of -3.2 percent in GDP, or -5.6 percent on a per capita basis. Simultaneously, inflation increased dramatically from 40.8 percent in 1978 to 80 percent in 1979 and then stabilized at 100 percent from 1980 to 1982.

Faced with troubles on the economic front, Figueiredo and Golbery increasingly became concerned with the upcoming 1982 elections, in which voters would directly elect governors for the first time since 1965; an Electoral College also would be chosen to select the next president in 1985. Particularly disturbing was the decline of ARENA's support in the South and Center-South, which made the government dangerously reliant on the rural North and Northeast. Consequently, a party reform bill effectively abolishing the two-party system was forced through Congress in December 1979 to implement Golbery's dictum to splinter the opposition front.

Six parties emerged from the reform.[43] Progovernment forces dropped the discredited ARENA label and regrouped in the Partido Democrático Social (Social Democratic party, or PDS). The MDB became the Partido do Movimento Democrático Brasileiro (Party of the Brazilian Democratic Movement, or PMDB), thereby conserving its makeup as a heterogeneous opposition front but with a much smaller congressional delegation. The more conservative opposition formed the Partido Popular (Popular party, or PP). Led by luminaries like Tancredo Neves and bolstered by strong support from industrialists and financiers, this so-called "banker's party" saw the possibility of playing a key role in a transitional government through a power-sharing arrangement with the military.

The pre-1964 Partido Trabalhista Brasileiro (Brazilian Workers party, or PTB) was resurrected with behind-the-scenes support from Golbery. The PTB sought to bring the most traditional sectors of the old labor bureaucracy together with remnants of the old conservative populist machines in São Paulo and Rio de Janeiro for the purpose of supporting the PDS in Congress in exchange for government patronage. The Partido Democrático Trabalhista (Democratic Workers party, or PDT), was less a genuine offshoot of pre-1964 trade unionism than a personal political machine designed to further the electoral ambitions of Leonel Brizola, the party's charismatic leader. The PDT's *socialismo moreno*—brown socialism—represented an amalgamation of traditional populism, leftist rhetoric, a vaguely social democratic program, and clientelistic patronage designed to appeal primarily to the urban poor as well as to intellectuals and the middle class.

The sixth party, the Partido dos Trabalhadores (Workers party, or PT) definitely was not envisioned in Golbery's master plan. The PT was a vehicle for the militant unionism created by the strikes of 1978, 1979, and 1980. Led by Luís Inácio da Silva, popularly known as Lula, the PT prided itself on being the only party in Brazil organized from the "bottom up," in contrast to the elitist character of the other parties. The PT's radical democratic platform for the empowerment of the disenfranchised and the autonomous organization of the working class found supporters among the more politicized industrial and rural workers, leftist intellectuals, the Christian base communities, and the new grass-roots social movements.

Golbery's Fall and the 1982 Elections

Throughout 1980 the fragmented opposition seemed to act out the script written by Golbery. By 1981, however, it became clear that the vitality and flexibility of the democratic forces had been underestimated by regime strategists. They likewise miscalculated the challenges to *abertura* from the hardliners and the *comunidade de informações*. Acts of right-wing terrorism actually declined considerably after 1975 (only ten reported bombings in 1976, six in 1977, and fifteen in 1978) as military *duros* were forced to assume more clandestine forms, such as the paramilitary Aliança Anti-Comunista do Brasil (Anti-Communist Alliance of Brazil). Approval of the amnesty fueled right-wing fears, which led to a sharp upsurge in violent activity, with forty-six bombings in 1980, many directed at the leftist media.[44]

Right-wing terrorism escalated further in late 1980 and early 1981, including the kidnapping of priests and Catholic activists, and a respected jurist; the mailing of a letter bomb to the president of the Bar Association in Rio de Janeiro, which killed his secretary; the bombing of the chambers of the Rio de Janeiro municipal government; and the bombing of the house of an outspoken PMDB congressman. This wave of terror was designed to intimidate the opposition, but the real target was *abertura* itself. Figueiredo recognized the threat, vowing that "four, twenty, or a thousand bombs exploding over our heads" could not force the regime to abandon controlled liberalization.[45]

Right-wing violence climaxed in a bungled terrorist attack on April 30, 1981, directed against a musical event promoted by a coalition of progressive groups, which was underway with a crowd of some twenty thousand at the Riocentro convention center in Rio de Janeiro. Two bombs exploded, one of which did no damage; the other went off in a nearby car, killing an army sergeant and severely wounding a captain. Both were on undercover assignments for Rio's DOI-CODI under the orders of the commander of the First Army. Despite an abundance of incriminating evidence, the military's investigation was more of a damage-control operation than an impartial inquiry. A military tribunal issued an acrimonious split decision and failed to return any indictments. Serious dissension within the armed forces was amplified by unanimous condemnation from the mass media and every sector of society.[46]

The Riocentro episode and ensuing cover-up directly implicated the chain of command of the *comunidade de informações* in acts of terrorism designed to sabotage the regime's *abertura* policy. Military cohesion was undermined by sharp divisions between those formerly or presently involved in repression, who opposed liberalization, and those concerned with the institution's professionalism and hence anxious to proceed with *abertura*. Golbery strongly urged Figueiredo to punish those responsible, including high-ranking generals. Instead, Figueiredo vacillated and, under pressure from the *duros*, forced Golbery's resignation in August. Brazil was stunned by the fall of the man whom many erstwhile opponents now eulogized as possessing a "total vision of the revolutionary process." Golbery's dismissal was a tacit admission of the regime's disorientation and marked the "end of *abertura* as a relatiely planned and controlled process of political change."[47]

Golbery was replaced as head of the Planalto political staff by João Leitão de Abreu, a civililan jurist linked to the Médici administration, who during the next three years never attained his predecessor's power and status. Planning minister Delfim Neto and SNI chief General Octávio Medeiros, both of whom had been in constant conflict with Golbery, took advantage of the partial vacuum at the top and successfully expanded their influence on the regime's political strategy. Figueiredo's leadership suffered accordingly.

The new pact between Figueiredo and the High Command was sealed in a private bargain: The Riocentro incident would be "absorbed," and in exchange the right-wing apparatus within the military and police would be placed on a short leash, with the understanding that any similar future episodes would bring swift reprisal. Several generals were eased into retirement, but Figueiredo replaced them with equally hardline officers. In effect, Figueiredo agreed to make the pace of *abertura* subject to the whims of powerful antiliberal forces within the miliary. But Figueiredo's combination of tact, personalism, and face saving seemed to work where Golbery's more ingenious stratagem failed to resolve the crisis. By carefully fostering a network of loyal officers, Figueiredo managed to defuse all but the most recalcitrant opposition while extracting grudging approval for the military's withdrawal from power.

The Riocentro episode and Golbery's ouster were followed in September 1979 by the first of Figueiredo's bouts with serious coronary problems. Aureliano Chaves, the civilian vice president, assumed the presidency thereby creating an air of intrigue and uncertainty. When Figueiredo reassumed the presidency in November after a six-week convalescence, General Medeiros and the SNI were issuing alarming forecasts of major losses for the PDS in the 1982 elections.

The government, in an attempt to reassert its control and to shore up the PDS's eroding electoral base, forced yet another electoral *pacote* through Congress in November 1981, which prohibited party coalitions and imposed a "straight ticket" ballot. This latest manipulation backfired when the Partido Popular decided to merge with the PMDB, thereby partially resurrecting the broad opposition front. To minimize the impending disaster, additional safeguards were imposed in mid-1982 and thereby restored the required majority for constitutional amendments to two-thirds (the Pacote de Abril had reduced it to a simple majority) and altered the formula for determining the composition of the Electoral College.[48]

TABLE 6.4
1982 Election Results
(Percentage of Total Valid Votes)

Party	Chamber of Deputies	Senate	State Governments	Electoral College
PMDB	43.0	43.7	44.0	39.5
PDT	5.8	5.9	6.1	2.0
PTB	4.4	4.6	4.7	4.3
PT	3.6	3.7	3.7	1.3
Opposition Subtotal	56.8	57.9	58.5	47.1
PDS	43.2	42.1	41.5	52.9
Total Number Valid Votes	48,455,879	48,746,803	48,188,956	695 delegates

Source: Luiz Carlos Bresser Pereira, *Pactos Políticos: Do Populismo à Redemocratização* (São Paulo: Brasiliense, 1985), Table 1, p. 127

The 1982 electoral results, presented in Table 6.4, were sufficiently ambiguous to provide both the government and the opposition with cause for celebration. The PDS retained its two-thirds majority in the Senate but lost its majority in the Chamber of Deputies, thus forcing it to rely on a fragile coalition with the PTB. As in past elections, the PDS's strong showing was primarily the fruit of the government's casuistry: The PDS received 43.1 percent of the valid votes but was awarded 49.1 percent of the seats, while the combined opposition won 57.8 percent of the vote but garnered only 50.9 percent of the seats.[49]

The opposition's most impressive showing came in the contests for state governors. The PDS won twelve governorships, but the opposition increased its control from one to ten statehouses. The PDS was rejected overwhelmingly in most of the more developed regions, winning only 17 of the 100 largest cities to the opposition's 83 (including 75 by the PMDB). The states won by the opposition boasted almost 62 percent of the national electorate, 58 percent of the nation's population, and generated 75 percent of Brazil's GDP. Tancredo Neves, elected governor of Minas Gerais for the PMDB, put it well when he remarked acidly that "the PDS had become the party of northeasterners" and could only win the "*grotões*" (rural backwaters or hick towns) of modern Brazil.[50]

On balance, the 1982 elections revealed that in defiance of Golbery's strategem to fragment the opposition, the PMDB continued to represent a broad prodemocratic coalition led by pragmatic, moderate politicians. Moreover, the opposition gained important institutional control in key states, including the big three of São Paulo, Rio de Janeiro, and Minas Gerais. Intensive press coverage and lively public debate on key issues such as inflation, the debt, and human rights gave the opposition an even more solid base of legitimacy than before. Finally, electoral competition stimulated considerable mobilization and autonomous organization of subordinate groups in civil society and established more complex ties between the political party system and the labor unions, peasant organizations, and grass-roots neighborhood movements.

The regime could find some solace in the fact that the PDS had managed to eke out a thirty-six-vote majority in the Electoral College that would select Figueiredo's successor in November 1984. This slender margin seemed a sufficient guarantee of control of the *abertura* process. But could it be sustained?

Diretas Já! Regime Crisis and Loss of Control

The economic crisis reached its apex in 1983. Between 1980 and 1983 gross domestic production, measured in current dollars, fell by 16.6 percent, and per capita income dropped by 23.4 percent levels. The utilization of installed capacity in manufacturing averaged only 72–74 percent. With the onset of the recession industrial employment declined sharply, falling by 25 percent in São Paulo by mid-1984. The combined impact of the crisis meant that real GDP in 1983 was nearly 20 percent (or $52.2 billion) less than it would have been at "full employment." Price increases took a further step toward hyperinflation and rose more than 230 percent.[51]

The recession was caused largely by contradictory government responses to the debt crisis that hit with full force in 1982, leaving Brazil tottering on the brink of default. Negotiations with the International Monetary Fund (IMF), which had been kept secret until after the 1982 elections, led in February 1983 to the first of many stand-by agreements (none fully implemented) with the IMF and over more than seven hundred private international banks to roll over debt payments. The quid pro quo exacted by the international financial community was Brazil's agreement to draconian austerity measures ranging from a 30 percent maxi-devaluation of the cruzeiro to wage cuts and a sharp reduction of the gargantuan public deficit.

One of the most contentious issues centered on the IMF's insistence on major modifications in the 1979 wage law granting semiannual wage increases. A dizzying parade of five different government-proposed wage bills in 1983 chronicled the regime's declining legitimacy, which was marked by an erosion in government control of the PDS, difficulties in working the administration's will in Congress, and government failure to convince key elites and the general public that familiar technocratic practices would suffice to "administer" the crisis.[52]

The opposition, backed by strong labor pressure, aggressively criticized Delfim Neto's "economic dictatorship" and the subordination of domestic recovery to the humiliation of constant "monitoring" by IMF economists. The regime's growing isolation was evidenced in September when the Congress, for the first time since 1964, rejected an executive decree designed to limit wage increases; the united opposition (241 of 244 deputies) was joined by 11 PDS deputies in voting down the government's bill. A substitute wage decree subsequently was withdrawn before it even went into effect, and another substitute also went down to defeat in Congress. Divisions within the government's top echelons deepened when the president of the Central Bank, Carlos Langoni, a Chicago-trained economist, resigned to protest the adoption of IMF proposals; he soon was followed by the social welfare minister, Hélio Beltrão, long a regime stalwart, who charged that the social costs of austerity on the poor were unacceptable.

In October 1983 the government, with the support of PTB deputies, finally secured approval of compromise legislation. But even passage of this watered-down bill came only at the price of a state of emergency declaration in Brasília that suspended civil liberties, stepped up media censorship, and employed massive army troops to create a climate of intimidation. This law substantially reduced the purchasing power of wage and salary earners. According to the calculation of the National Confederation of Industry (whose president was a PDS senator), from 1981 through the first semester of 1984 purchasing power declined an average of 38 percent. Middle-class protest was so strong that many large firms, including state enterprises, openly violated the law by granting higher-than-permitted wage increases. Mounting public disaffection registered by pollsters and outbreaks of mass violence (900 food riots and supermarket sackings in the first three-quarters of 1983), combined with a progressive loss of control of the PDS, hardly could have been a less propitious context for the government to select its candidate for the January 1985 indirect presidential election.

By late 1983 four candidates were vying for the PDS's nomination: Paulo Maluf, federal deputy and ex-governor of São Paulo; Mário Andreazza, retired army colonel, former minister under Médici, and Figueiredo's interior minister; Aureliano Chaves, Figueiredo's vice president and ex-governor of Minas Gerais; and Marco Maciel, senator from Pernambuco. The regime's kingmakers were divided in their loyalties. The three service chiefs and ex-president Geisel were reported to back Chaves. Military and civilian hardliners, led by General Octávio Medeiros, chief of the SNI, and justice minister Abi Ackel supported Maluf's candidacy; Golbery, in a surprise move, also placed his not inconsiderable talents at Maluf's disposal. Andreazza, who could trade on the patronage generated by the billions of cruzeiros spent by his ministry, was widely believed to be Figueiredo's *in pectore* candidate. Maciel was a dark-horse candidate in the event of a deadlock. Aureliano Chaves enjoyed strong support from the powerful São Paulo business community, and national surveys showed he was the public's clear favorite.[53]

Divisions within the PDS and the growing estrangement between the party and the president reached crisis proportions in early 1984. In frustration, Figueiredo announced his decision to abandon the "coordination" of the PDS's presidential campaign. Figueiredo's abdication strengthened Maluf's standing within the party, but elite and mass opposition was galvanized by the prospect of an official candidate widely repudiated for his record of corruption and repression while governor of São Paulo, as well as his arrogant, authoritarian style. This rejection went beyond the person of Maluf to question the legitimacy of the process of indirect elections, which increasingly were unacceptable to the population at large.

From January to April 1984 Brazil experienced a wave of popular mobilization with hundreds of marches and massive demonstrations behind the rallying cry of *Diretas Já!* (Direct Elections Now!). All the principal opposition figures, including Ulysses Guimarães and Tancredo Neves of the PMDB, Leonel Brizola of the PDT, and Lula of the PT, along with dozens of the Brazil's most popular entertainers, embarked on a marathon tour throughout the country. Vigorous mobilization efforts by labor unions, peasant movements, the women's movement, human rights groups, and neighborhood organizations assured an enormous popular turnout.

A number of prominent PDS politicians, with vice president Chaves leading the way, ignored their party's position and came out in favor of direct elections. Media coverage and astute political marketing techniques projected an image of the entire nation waving yellow banners (from the national flag) while sporting T-shirts with slogans such as *Eu Quero Votar para Presidente* (I Want to Vote for President). The campaign ended in mid-April with huge demonstrations of 1 million or more persons in Rio de Janeiro and São Paulo.

The *Diretas Já!* campaign reached its climax on April 25th, when the opposition's amendment for the approval of direct elections (and abolition of the Electoral College) faced a key vote in the Chamber of Deputies. The regime and the PDS were deeply split. Liberals within the PDS, led by Chaves and Maciel and supported by Leitão de Abreu and the chiefs of the air force and navy, called for negotiations and compromise. They argued that even if the direct elections amendment were defeated, the next president would be unable to govern due to popular opposition. Maluf and

Andreazza, SNI chief Medeiros, and *duros* within the army adamantly rejected any concessions and advocated riding out the storm.

The *duros* carried the day. Figueiredo staged a massive display of military force in Brasília to prevent planned demonstrations and to dissuade wavering PDS deputies from defecting. These intimidation tactics prevailed one last time. Although the amendment received 298 votes (62 percent), including 55 from the PDS, this fell 22 votes short of the required 320 votes. The last minute change in the rules requiring a two-thirds majority once again frustrated the popular will.

The regime had won the battle but was rapidly losing the war. In the past, *abertura* had held out the promise of eventual democratization, but a deep change in public opinion was taking place, and Planalto strategists found themselves in the untenable position of defending unpopular candidates whose only chance for victory hinged on transparently antidemocratic procedures. This was no longer convincing, not only to the vast majority of ordinary Brazilians, but also to many of the regime's members and allies. Opinion polls found that more than 80 percent of the public was in favor of direct elections. Conversely, Figueiredo's past popularity as the champion of *abertura* had evaporated, and his support plunged precipitously along with the rating of his government's handling of the economic crisis.[54]

The opposition's campaign had convincingly placed responsibility for the economic crisis and the political impasse squarely on Brazil's authoritarian political system. There seemed to be but one alternative. The *Diretas Já!* campaign symbolized popular acceptance of the opposition's central thesis: Rapid return to democracy was the only solution to economic crisis and political impasse.

All but the most recalcitrant authoritarians sensed the shift in the prevailing political winds as two parallel movements began to converge in favor of an opposition victory. First, the moderate sectors of the PMDB, directed by Tancredo Neves' consummate skillfullness at the politics of *conchavos* and *conciliação* (back room deals and compromise), convinced the party's Left to pursue the presidency within the Electoral College system. The fundamental objective, Tancredo's supporters argued, was to guarantee the transition to civilian rule; the broadest possible coalition was necessary to prevent the victory of the authoritarians.

Simultaneously, a second shift occurred within the PDS itself. In June 1984 PDS liberals made a last ditch effort to prevent Maluf or Andreazza from winning their party's nomination with a proposal for a party primary to select the most popular candidate, most probably Aureliano Chaves. Figueiredo initially agreed, but under strong pressure from the Maluf and Andreazza forces, he reversed himself. Vice President Aureliano Chaves and Senator Maciel then withdrew their candidacies and, joined by José Sarney, who resigned as president of the PDS, organized PDS dissidents in a new party, the Partido da Frente Liberal (Liberal Front party, or PFL). Claiming more than sixty votes in the Electoral College, the PFL entered into prolonged negotiations with the PMDB that led to the creation of an opposition electoral coalition, the Aliança Democrática (Democratic Alliance).

The scene was set. On August 11th, Maluf defeated Andreazza for the PDS nomination in a three-day convention at which $10 million reportedly were spent in vote-buying activities. The following day Tancredo Neves was ratified as the nominee of the Aliança Democrática, with José Sarney of the PFL named as his vice presidential running mate.

Sectors within the armed forces were extremely concerned. In July the *duros* briefly discussed a "military solution" to the crisis, but a secret meeting of the army High Command vetoed plans for overt military intervention. During the next several months Figueiredo and the three service chiefs issued frequent public warnings of the "dangers of radicalization" of the political process and criticized some PFL leaders as "ungrateful traitors." The head of the Joint General Staff issued a statement openly urging the president to employ "the civilian ministries and their structures, at all levels, in the effort to achieve the final objective," namely, the election of the official candidate. Less public efforts by the SNI and army intelligence kept up the drumbeat with even more inflammatory denunciations of "communist subversion" within the Aliança Democrática.[55]

Tancredo Neves and the Aliança took these threats extremely seriously, especially during the "100 days of fear" from mid-August to mid-November. A sophisticated *dispositivo militar* (military task force), staffed by active-duty and reserve officers, including ex-president Geisel, was personally directed by Tancredo. The purpose of the *dispositivo* was to establish direct contact with the three service chiefs as well as with influential generals, brigadiers, and admirals to assure them of Tancredo's good faith and moderation and especially to offer guarantees that if elected his government would not countenance *revanchismo*, the military's code-phrase for Argentine-style investigations into past human rights abuses or crimes of corruption.[56]

Tancredo's strategy worked. Maluf desperately engaged in a number of heavy-handed attempts to influence the naming of the delegates of the state assemblies to the Electoral College. He also tried unsuccessfully to change the rules for voting in the Electoral College to prevent PDS defectors from voting for Tancredo. Despite the expenditure of enormous sums, these maneuvers backfired and actually cost Maluf votes, as many waverers went over to the Tancredo camp. In early November Maluf's situation was virtually hopeless, which led him to make ironic statements charging that Tancredo was the "status-quo candidate" while he was the "real" opponent of the military regime.

Recognizing the impossibility of military intervention so late in the game, the group of thirteen four-star generals comprising the army's High Command made a major decision in late November, signalling its acceptance of the impending opposition victory: They removed General Newton Araújo de Oliveira e Cruz from the key Planalto Command. General Cruz, one of the most aggressively reactionary generals, was widely believed to favor military intervention to prevent the victory of the Aliança Democrática candidate. A statement issued by General Ivan de Souza Mendes (later to be named head of the SNI under civililan rule), expressed the reasoning behind this display of political pragmatism: "The Army has no candidate but it cannot lose the elections, it cannot be defeated. And what is the best way not to lose the election? The Army should withdraw from the political process [and] assume a professional posture, accepting the victory of the opposition candidate."[57]

Several nervous weeks later the Electoral College met in Brasília on January 5, 1985, and overwhelmingly chose Tancredo Neves as the president-elect by giving him 480 votes to 180 for Maluf. Tancredo received 271 votes from the PMDB, 113 votes from the PFL, 38 votes from the PDT and the PTB, 3 votes from PT delegates disobeying their party's official position, and 55 votes from PDS defectors.

THE NOVA REPÚBLICA AND THE DEMOCRATIC AGENDA

The Birth of the "New Republic"

Tancredo Neves spoke eloquently after his victory of founding a Nova República based on civilian rule, national reconciliation, and social justice. His tragic death cut short his struggle to fulfill this ambitious project. In his place, José Sarney, ex-president of the PDS, assumed the presidency on March 15, 1985. Tancredo's inaugural address to the nation set the tone for the Nova República by reiterating the plea for "reconciliation without revenge." Tancredo's inaugural address, delivered by Sarney, boldly if somewhat misleadingly asserted that Brazil's progress toward democracy "owes much more to the force of contestation of the common man than to the conscience of the elites."[58]

The installation of the Nova República marked the end of the phase of authoritarian liberalization under the aegis of military rule. With the trappings of representative government soon in place, Brazil, by conventional standards, became a political democracy. However, from a different point of view, one more demanding in terms of the content and quality of the political institutions being created, Brazil's transition from authoritarianism was really only entering a new and in some ways more complex phase in which genuine democratization could unfold.

Many participants in the struggle for democracy have expressed frustration with the Sarney government's conservative view of popular participation, its reliance on old-style clientelistic practices, and its lethargy in addressing the enormous social and economic disparities in Brazilian society. Raymundo Faoro, former president of the Bar Association and one of Brazil's leading intellectuals, for example, has compared the present situation to the dictatorial rule of Getúlio Vargas in the late 1930s and early 1940s by labeling the new civilian regime the "Estado Novo [New State] of the PMDB." Leonel Brizola, PDT opposition leader and governor of Rio de Janeiro, claims that his administration is the victim of political persecution and that Figueiredo was better than Sarney. The PT charges the Sarney government with alleged "dirty tricks" designed to undercut the popular appeal of the PT's radical demands for an overhaul of Brazilian society and economy and full citizenship for all Brazilians.[59]

Are these criticisms justified, or are they just the normal rough and tumble of a still-fragile democracy? Will continuity or rupture with the military's authoritarian legacy prevail in the Nova República? To pretend any definitive answers would be foolhardy in the extreme. Rather I will address these complex questions by first briefly reviewing the conflict regarding the nature of the new democratic institutions and then by examining the relationship between the state and the subordinate sectors of Brazilian society. I follow this with a brief description of the management of the economy and conclude with a discussion of parties and electoral competition and the role of the military in the new regime's consolidation.

Consolidation of New Democratic Institutions

The first and in many ways the most crucial problem facing all postauthoritarian regimes is the construction of new democratic institutions. The *remoção do entulho autoritário* (removal of the authoritarian debris), as Tancredo so aptly put it, was carried out with surprising rapidity. During the brief period from mid-March to mid-May 1985, a period that PMDB president Ulysses Guimarães termed "democratic ungovernability," Congress eliminated many of the most egregious aspects of authoritarian rule. The reforms voted by Congress included direct election for all executive posts, including the presidency; legalization of the various communist parties; legalization of national labor confederations; extension of suffrage to illiterates; and abolition or relaxation of many restrictions on political parties.

Removing this type of "debris" was relatively easy, but the implementation of promises of a constitutional convention proved far more problematic. Sarney and virtually the entire Aliança Democrática rejected demands for direct presidential elections in 1986, thus leaving the duration of Sarney's mandate, whether four or six years, to be decided as part of a revision of the military-promulgated constitution of 1967. On a related issue, the government also defeated proposals by PMDB reformists and the Left for an "autonomous" convention with full constitutional power. To the dismay of the Bar Association, noted constitutional scholars, and progressive politicians, Sarney appointd a preconvention study commission of "notables" led by eighty-four-year-old conservative jurist Afonso Arinos de Mello Franco. In late 1985 Congress approved a formula favored by the conservative forces whereby the Congress to be elected in November 1986 would sit simultaneously as the long-awaited Constituinte (Constituent Assembly).[60]

So far, those sectors favoring the limitation of popular participation in the process of constitutional reform remain in control, and although they are being actively contested by reformist forces determined to forge more open, democratic institutions, conservatives are likely to dominate the Constituent Assembly slated to open deliberations in 1987.

The State and the Working Class

The working class is one of the principal actors pushing for an expansion of popular participation and the enactment of political reforms with wider social and economic implications. Real wages for many occupational categories have fallen dramatically since 1980. Consequently, the Sarney government has confronted consistent pressure from organized labor to make democracy a reality for the working class. Although without the drama of earlier strikes, labor mobilization has increased to levels greater than those reached during the last years of military rule. More than 6 million workers went out on strike at some point during 1985. Strikes in São Paulo and other major urban centers by metalworkers, employees, doctors, nurses, and postal workers occurred in 1985 and 1986. The country's entire financial system was paralyzed briefly in September 1985 by strikes involving more than 700,000 bank employees. Efforts by bank employees to repeat this feat in 1986 failed, however. The coming of democracy also witnessed an event without precedent: A major strike took place in 1985 in São Paulo's richest agricultural zone where the boiás frias layed down their tools during the sugar, orange, and coffee harvests. Similar rural protests occurred again in 1986.

The Sarney government has reacted to labor's challenge in a schizophrenic fashion. Led by labor minister Almir Pazzianotto, an ex-labor lawyer on good terms with many of Brazil's most combative unions, reformist forces within the PMDB spoke out frequently in 1985 in favor of the idea of a "social pact" between labor, capital, and the state. Despite numerous discussions with both major confederations, the Central Única dos Trabalhadores (United Workers Central, or CUT) and the Confederação Geral dos Trabalhadores (General Confederation of Workers, or CGT), the idea of the social pact foundered in 1986 due to a lack of government interest in advancing concrete proposals.[61]

Pazzianotto, the reformist wing of the PMDB, and the PT also proposed major reforms of existing labor legislation to recognize the legality of strikes and to free unions from onerous state controls. From March to October 1985 Pazzianotto sent no less than ten labor reform bills for the president's approval. Only in July 1986, however, did Pazzianotto finally succeed in submitting a redrafted and much watered-down bill to Congress. This proposed reform fell far short of the wide-ranging revision of existing labor legislation promised by Sarney in 1985; it seemed intended to combine some modest concessions with an attempt to curtail the influence of the PT and the power of the more militant unions and their umbrella organization, the CUT.

In addition to adamant opposition from powerful entrepreneurial interests, one of the primary reasons for the regime's impasse with organized labor has been the armed forces' resistance to the modernization of Brazil's corporatist labor legislation. SNI chief General Ivan de Souza Mendes has vied actively with Pazzianotto for leadership in coordinating the governmental response to labor mobilizations and has pressed for the use of the draconian antistrike law to "guarantee the maintenance of public order and social peace." Pressures have on occasion been so strong that the climate within the SNI has been likened to a "state of quasi-hysteria." Pazzianotto's firm defense of a conciliatory approach has so far prevented the Sarney government from resorting to outright repression. Concern with the negative consequences repression could engender at election time also has been decisive in the government's restraint; major confrontations in 1987 are a distinct possibility.

The State, Peasants, and Agrarian Reform

An armed struggle is taking place today in Brazil. This is not a guerrilla war, but a war waged by landowners against the landless. According to official figures, 567 people died in rural violence between 1980 and 1985, with 155 people killed in 1985. Unofficial figures place the body count at more than 370 dead during 1985, with another 120 dead in the first five months of 1986. Most of the dead have been peasants killed by *jagunços* (gunslingers) hired by large landowners, but several priests and lay activists also have been numbered among the victims. Dom Luciano Mendes de Almeida, general secretary of the Conference of Bishops, has blamed the killings on the "selfishness and evil" of the landowners. Meanwhile, peasant resistance and casualties, including displaced families, continue to mount; at least forty-two separate groups of landless peasant families comprising some 60,000 individuals were living in impoverished tent encampments in eleven states in early 1986.[62]

Concentration of land ownership, tremendous income inequality, and rural violence have deep roots in Brazilian history, but they were exacerbated in the 1970s and early 1980s by the emergence of a modern agroindustrial complex, a growing orientation to export crops, and the rapid expansion of the agricultural frontier. Consequently, agrarian reform became one of the principal symbols of the Nova República's commitment to the poor. Not surprisingly, the increase in rural violence in 1985 and 1986 has been influenced by Sarney's public promises of land reform. Peasants and landless rural workers, feeling encouraged and legitimate, have accelerated their efforts to acquire land and occasionally have resorted to illegal takeovers.

In response, the ministry of agrarian reform and the Instituto Nacional de Colonização e Reforma Agrária (National Institute of Colonization and Agrarian Reform, or INCRA) proposed a major effort calling for the distribution of 100 million acres (430 million square kilometers) to 1.4 million landless families. This proposal, which enjoyed the strong backing of the Catholic hierarchy and activist priests, was blocked by an extremely aggressive campaign by *fazendeiros* (large landowners) and their allies in Congress and the administration. A much weakened bill was approved by Congress in October 1985, which prompted INCRA's president to resign in protest.[63]

The bill languished in the Planalto until May 1986, when Sarney weakened the plan even further. A major political crisis ensued. Peasant organizations protested vehemently the government's "betrayal." *Fazendeiros* and major landowner organizations, in a revealing contrast, expressed strong satisfaction. Their victory notwithstanding, large landowners, supported by old-line, right-wing extremist groups like Tradição, Família, e Propriedade (Tradition, Family, and Property) and a new political action group called the União Democrática Ruralista (Democratic Rural Union) actively began to recruit private paramilitary militias.[64]

In consternation, the Catholic hierarchy initiated an acrimonious public confrontation with the Sarney government. Dom Ivo Lorscheider, president of the Conference of Bishops, publicly denounced the government's failure to enact an "agrarian reform that merits the name, an authentic revision of the country's structure of land tenure." Dante de Oliveira, a left-wing PMDB deputy and sponsor of the ill-fated *Diretas Já!* amendment, was named to replace Nelson Ribeiro, who had been forced to resign from the post of minister of agrarian reform. In response to church and peasant criticism, the new minister charged that opposition to oppose agrarian reform plans "conceived within the capitalist system to promote the rational utilization of rural property was unpatriotic." Proponents of more far-reaching changes began to question the government's sincerity and its ability to stand up to landowner interests. The failure of Sarney's highly publicized visit to the Vatican in July 1986 to enlist the pope's help in curbing the

Catholic hierarchy's support for more rapid, extensive land reform did little to ease tensions in the countryside, although public criticism by church officials was muted somewhat.[65]

Agrarian reform encompasses both colonization programs (*assentamentos*) and expropriation of underutilized land for more equitable, productive redistribution. To date, expropriations have been virtually paralyzed. Land distribution through colonization has not fared much better. Indeed, landowner resistance and opposition within the government meant that only 3,000 families had been resettled by mid-1986, as against the target of 150,000 families for 1986 (there were 800,000 beneficiaries during Figueiredo's six years), and that only 69 rural properties, corresponding to 273,000 hectares, in fact had been expropriated by late 1986. Although Sarney hardly can afford to abandon this politically popular issue, it is unlikely that any major reform actions will be taken in the short run. The SNI and the CIEX meanwhile have been directed by Sarney to investigate the ideological leanings of peasant leaders and all governmental personnel involved in agrarian reform issues. In essence, no end is in sight to this undeclared war in the countryside.[66]

The Cruzado Plan: The Politics of Economic Management

The Sarney government faced a daunting economic agenda upon assuming power. Challenges abounded on all fronts: management of the Third World's largest foreign debt; a severe state fiscal crisis; triple digit inflation; rampant financial speculation; falling investment in productive activities; unrest fueled by high expectations among workers and the middle class; and the list goes on. Some of the more critical indicators are presented in Table 6.5.

Brazil's capacity for sustained capital accumulation has been constrained in recent years by the need to generate annual trade surpluses of $12–$13 billion in order to service the foreign debt. This has meant transferring 4–5 percent of GDP or 30 percent of net domestic savings overseas. How can economic expansion be placed on a sound, noninflationary footing in this difficult context?

The government's internal divisions, lack of clear direction, and plain mismanagement during its first six months transformed Sarney into a symbol of indecision for the many Brazilians who expected more from the civilian regime. By mid-1985 an economic recovery was underway, but runaway monthly inflation rates of more than 10 percent threatened renewed recession. Finally, fearing an imminent loss of political support and facing mounting calls for early presidential elections, Sarney acted in August 1985 to put the government's economic house in order. The president named São Paulo industrialist Dilson Funaro to replace Tancredo's nephew Francisco Dornelles in the key post of finance minister, thus making the first important shift in the cabinet inherited from Tancredo.

TABLE 6.5
Principal Economic Indicators, 1981-1985

Economic Indicator	1981	1982	1983	1984	1985
Production, inflation, public sector finances	Annual growth rates (%)				
Gross domestic product (GDP)	-1.6	0.9	3.2	4.5	8.3
Industrial production	-5.5	0.6	-6.8	6.0	9.0
GDP per capita	-4.0	-1.5	-5.6	2.1	5.9
General price index	95.2	99.7	211.0	223.8	235.1
Expansion of money supply	87.2	65.0	95.0	203.5	312.1
Federal budget deficit	7.1	6.2	3.0	1.6	3.2
Wages and employment	1980 = 100				
Minimum wage	99.0	100.0	88.0	83.0	86.0
Industrial wages	102.9	109.8	92.0	106.8	141.1
Industrial employment	92.6	87.7	80.3	80.1	87.5
Balance of Payments	Billions of US dollars				
Current account balance	-11.8	-15.4	-6.8	0.1	-0.1
Merchandise balance	1.2	0.7	6.5	13.1	12.5
Exports	23.3	19.0	21.9	27.1	25.6
Imports	22.1	18.3	15.4	13.9	13.2
Net services	-13.2	-16.1	-13.4	-13.2	-13.3
Capital account (net)	12.8	-10.8	5.5	5.0	1.0
Disbursed foreign debt	71.9	83.2	91.6	99.8	99.7
Debt service ratio (Interest/Exports in %)	40.2	60.5	43.4	39.5	41.9

Source: Data on production, inflation, money supply, and wages calculated from Central Bank, Conjuntura Econômica and Boletim, various numbers. Balance of payments data from Inter-American Bank, Economic and Social Progress in Latin America: 1986 Report (Washington, D.C.: IDB, 1986).

Dilson Funaro's pedigree is impeccable. He is one of Brazil's leading entrepreneurs (named "businessman of the year" in 1984 by one journal), and his democratic credentials are vouchsafed by his participation in the *Diretas Já!* campaign. Analysts of varying persuasions echoed the view that his appointment as finance minister meant that "for the first time in several decades a representative of the industrial bourgeoisie—the private sector—is in charge of the economy."[67]

Funaro, João Sayad, the planning minister, and a team of young opposition economists affiliated with the PMDB took immediate steps to reorient economic policy. They began by pursuing a "tough" posture in negotiations with the IMF and the international financial community. "We will only pay what we can. If some creditor does not agree, he can send back the check," Funaro announced in June 1986.[68] Brazil rejected IMF monitoring of its economic policy and began negotiating directly with its creditor banks. By late 1986 aggressive use of Brazil's considerable bargaining power had proven a considerable success.

The Funaro team's strategy for a return to sustained economic expansion had to take into consideration the large shifts in income and wealth since the late 1970s. Wages and salaries had declined precipitously, falling from 51.8 percent of national income in 1981 to 46.7 percent in 1984. This large shift in favor of capital had been very unequally distributed: In 1978 the portion of capital's share of national income appropriated by interests was only 36.4 percent, but booming financial speculation during the Figueiredo years boosted this figure dramatically to 59.3 percent in 1980 and 80.8 percent in 1984. Concomitantly, fixed capital investment, which had been approximately 26 percent of GD in the 1970s, declined to only 16 percent of GD by 1984–1985. To address this situation, Congress reluctantly approved Funaro's plan for an overhaul of the tax system to cut the fiscal deficit, assure greater equity, and redirect savings to productive investment.[69]

Growth in 1985 was a very strong 8 percent, particularly in São Paulo, which was responsible for 40 percent of total GDP. *Paulista* industry expanded at an 11 percent clip, the total wage fund jumped 25 percent in real terms, and manufacturing employment increased by 6 percent. Nevertheless, the economy was in deep trouble in 1985 as inflation approached the 230 percent mark. Inflation skyrocketed 16.2 percent in January 1986, and projections indicated that the annual rate could reach 400 percent or even more.

The alarming prospect of an Argentine-style hyperflation galvanized Funaro's advisers into furious completion of a secret antiinflation plan. President Sarney announced the new monetary reform and economic stabilization plan, referred to as the Zero Inflation Plan or the Cruzado Plan, in a dramatic TV address on February 28, 1986. Sarney presented the plan in populist terms as a "program to defend the purchasing power of wage earners." Stressing price freezes, Sarney told Brazilians, "You are appointed by the president to be a price inspector in every corner of Brazil."[70]

The Cruzado Plan (named after the new monetary unit that replaced the cruzeiro), like the Austral Plan implemented earlier in Argentina, was premised on a radical attack on "inertial inflation" by means of a swift deindexation of the economy—the so-called "heterodox shock" treatment. The key instruments were simultaneous freezes of prices and wages (which were first increased 8 percent), the imposition of strict fiscal and monetary restraint, and the abandonment of daily minidevaluations in favor of a fixed (but flexible) exchange rate. In contrast to the Austral Plan, which was implemented following years of severe economic contraction, the Cruzado

Plan was inaugurated in the midst of a strong cyclical expansion following the 1981–1983 recession.[71]

The Cruzado Plan's immediate impact was little short of miraculous: Inflation fell sharply to a monthly rate of about 1 percent; inflation for the March–October period was less than 10 percent. These results seemed to validate Funaro's promise of "Swiss inflation with Japanese growth." By mid-1986 the plan was working up to expectations, but there were troubling clouds on the horizon, including the proliferation of black markets, long lines, illegal price gouging (*ágio*), and shortages of milk, meat, and other consumer items. Also, many government ministries and state enterprises strongly resisted the new diet of budgetary austerity. Moreover, contrary to expectations, the price freeze unleashed a veritable binge of consumer spending that ran the risk of overheating an already feverish economy. Many businesspeople complained that price freezes had reduced profit margins, and many entrepreneurs were reluctant to increase investment to meet rising consumer demand, even though the economy was approaching full utilization of installed capacity.

The Funaro team reacted to these disquieting signs in two stages. First, new measures were announced in late July 1986 to buttress the Cruzado Plan, including a new public investment program of approximately $10 billion to be raised through an unpopular compulsory levy on income, gasoline, and purchases of automobiles and luxury items. This program was supposed to guarantee 6.8 percent annual growth rates through the end of the decade. According to Sarney's grandiose description, the long-range objective was "a Brazil with a standard of living for all the population equal to that of Mediterranean Europe." Immediately following the November 15, 1986, elections the government implemented a second package of economic adjustments—quickly dubbed the Cruzado II—to correct growing distortions and to rein in the superheated economy. The principal instruments to force a reduction in middle-class consumption included a return to daily currency minidevaluations and price increases in the 30–100 percent range on items such as automobiles, gasoline and alcohol fuel, electricity, telephone and postal services, and liquor and cigarettes. In addition to restraining demand these measures also were designed to alleviate public sector debt by augmenting government revenues by $11.5 billion (more than the July increases).[72]

Elections and Party Competition

From March 1985 to February 1986 José Sarney was constrained by the fragile political pact negotiated by Tancredo Neves during the final months of the military regime. True to its heterogeneous composition, the Aliança Democrática proved far more suited to the exigencies of guaranteeing the transition and the military's exit than to the stable exercise of state power.

The difficult cohabitation of the PMDB and the PFL in Sarney's cabinet was aggravated by the PMDB's occasional "irresponsibility" in Congress, the fruit of its long years in the opposition and hesitancy in asserting its role as the dominant coalition partner. The resulting acrimony was exacerbated periodically by conservative campaigns against PMDB "radicals" and frequent warnings of danger of "too many leftists in the government."

The Aliança Democrática's fragility became clear to all in the November 1985 municipal elections.[73] These elections in all state capitals and most important cities, including 179 municipalities previously designated as "national security zones," accelerated the unraveling of the PMDB-PFL alliance. The PMDB remained the largest party, winning 110 of 201 municipal contests and capturing 19 state capitals while losing in only 4 (São Paulo, Rio de Janeiro, Recife, and Fortaleza). The PMDB won 33.9 percent of the popular vote nationwide. The PDS was the biggest loser and all but disappeared in the larger cities in southern Brazil, while the PFL emerged as the leading conservative party, although it failed to win control in any state capital. The combined vote for the PFL, the PDS, and the PTB was 28.2 percent, indicating the continuing decline of electoral support for the conservative parties.

Significant political and ideological polarization of the electorate (especially in the South and Center-South regions) translated into a modest advance for the Left. The combined popular vote for the PDT, and PT, and the newly created Partido Socialista do Brasil (Socialist Party of Brazil, of PSB) was 26.5 percent. This tilt to the left came at the expense of the PMDB, which became more of a centrist party, thus leading to predictions of the PMDB's "domestication."

Notwithstanding the conservative parties' poor showing nationally, the Right scored a very significant victory in the crucial São Paulo mayorality race. The breakdown of the Aliança Democrática, plus a strong swing to the left, permitted ex-president Jânio Quadros to win with 37.5 percent of the vote as the PTB candidate supported by the PFL. Senator Fernando Henrique Cardoso of the PMDB received 34.3 percent of the vote, and 19.8 percent went to Deputy Eduardo Matarazzo Suplicy, the PT candidate. Underlying these results is the fact that political campaigning in the Nova República is enormously expensive. Approximately $80 million was spent nationwide in the extensive use of political consultants, opinion polls, and electoral propaganda in the mass media.

Jânio Quadros' victory in São Paulo was followed three months later by a ministerial shake-up that gave the Sarney government a decidedly conservative complexion. The new cabinet included twelve ministers who, like Sarney himself, had opposed the direct presidential elections in April 1984. Six of the new ministers had been governors for the PDS or ARENA. The fifteen PMDB-controlled ministries included finance and planning along with agriculture, justice, labor, and health, but the five PFL ministries—mines and energy, communications, education, civil cabinet, and foreign relations—controlled budgets two-and-a-half times as large. Marco Maciel left the Education Ministry to head Sarney's political staff in the Planalto. Maciel immediately moved to establish himself as the government's "superminister" by centralizing and concentrating power to an extent not seen since Golbery's resignation in 1981. In parallel fashion, entrepreneurs in industry, finance, commerce, and agriculture simultaneously began to organize themselves politically, attempting to set aside sectoral conflicts, in order to enhance business influence in the government and to maximize business clout in upcoming electoral contests.[74]

The new cabinet's make-up led to jubilation in the PFL and among conservatives. Ex-minister Delfim Neto, who had supported Jânio Quadros, applauded, saying that "the new ministry is excellent." Conversely, despair reigned in the PMDB as party leaders briefly considered breaking with Sarney and leaving the government coalition. The PMDB leader in the lower chamber, Pimenta da Veiga, asked how he could "explain from now on that Sarney [the party's honorary president] belongs to the PMDB?" Senator Fernando Henrique Cardoso resigned his post as government spokesperson in the Congress, saying that the "New Republic is the same as the Old Republic" under the military: "Ruling Brazil today are the moderate wing of the army and the liberal wing of the former government, plus a group of the president's friends." Raymundo Faoro charged that the government had "taken off its mask" and declared that "there had not been any transition [from the military regime]. The removal of the authoritarian debris was just a slogan."[75]

The fanfare of the Cruzado Plan, coming soon after these conservative advances, once again demonstrated the new regime's contradictory impulses. Leaving aside facile ideological interpretations, Sarney's rightward shift at the cabinet level combined with the strengthening of the PMDB's moderates in control of the Cruzado Plan can best be seen as a pragmatic attempt by the government to regain control of the economy while searching for greater maneuvering room in preparation for the November 1986 elections and future debates on constitutional reforms. In the long run, such maneuvers may be shrewd moves by Sarney to free himself from the PMDB's reformist leadership and the party's left wing in order to strengthen his own electoral support, perhaps in the form of a new moderate, center-right party or coalition that brings together the PFL, the anti-Maluf wing of the PDS, PMDB moderates, and unaffiliated conservatives.

Sarney's gamble has paid handsome short-run dividends. In March and April 1986 many Brazilians sporting green and yellow buttons identifying their wearers as *Fiscais do Sarney* (Sarney's price inspectors), demanded that supermarkets, drugstores, and hamburger stands roll back prices to officially approved levels. A poll of middle-class respondents verified a sharp reversal in expectations following the plan's announcement: In March fully 80 percent of the respondents affirmed that their income situation had improved significantly, although this figure fell to 44 percent by the end of August. Approval of Sarney among businesspeople soared: According to one survey, the president's performance was rated "excellent" by 82 percent, compared to 48 percent in January before the unveiling of the Cruzado Plan.[76]

The plan's favorable political impact began to taper off by September. Resistance to wage and price freezes soon emerged from organized labor, and strike activity actually increased compared with the same period in 1985. Industrialists, middle-class professionals, agricultural producers, and merchants also voiced discontent with one or another aspect of the new economic controls. Support for the Cruzado Plan remained firmest among the poor. Still, the Cruzado Plan's popularity outweighed all other issues in the generally nonideological campaign leading up to the November elections. Centrist PMDB candidates won twenty-two out of twenty-three state governorships, including the key states of São Paulo, Rio de Janeiro, Minas Gerais, and Rio Grande do Sul. PMDB moderates and conservatives will have a majority in both the Chamber of Deputies and the Federal Senate. The PFL emerged as Brazil's second party. The Left parties fared poorly, receiving a smaller share of the popular vote than in the 1985 municipal elections.

Yet the PMDB's sweeping victory did not assure continued mass support for the Sarney government. The announcement of the Cruzado II package a week after the elections made manifest the contingent nature of the government's popular support in the form of unexpected outbursts of collective protest, including a demonstration by some five thousand protesters in Brasília, which was repressed by troops employing tear gas. The potential for discontent was further registered by the brief general strike in mid-December 1986. With public opinion strongly opposed to the new economic package, Sarney's popularity experienced a sudden, sharp drop, particularly among the middle class (in Rio de Janeiro and São Paulo the president's approval rating fell from 72 percent in September to only 34 percent in early December).[77]

In 1987 inevitable adjustments to the Cruzado Plan and the certainty of renewed inflationary pressures may exacerbate distributional conflicts. These prospects and the likelihood of further erosion of support for the Sarney government will provide the backdrop for the Constituent Assembly's efforts to write a new constitution and also will increase pressures for a realignment of the party system. Many of the thirty legal parties surely will disappear, and even the larger parties, including the PMDB, may experience major transformations in the next several years.

The Democratization of the Military?

There is little likelihood, baring unforeseen economic disaster and major social unrest, that the armed forces will resort to direct political intervention prior to the next presidential succession. Nevertheless, the extent of the military's own democratization will influence profoundly the consolidation and future direction of the new institutions of civilian rule. On this score, there is cause for considerable concern. The repressive apparatus remains intact, the armed forces' underlying interventionist posture is largely unchanged, and the military presence in the state has not been affected by civilian rule.

The National Security Council, the SNI, and the security apparatus of the army, navy, and air force remain unscathed by the democratic reforms implemented since March 1985. In fact, the *comunidade de informações* has not only continued its traditional practice of ideological control, but has acquired new functions in the mediation of bureaucratic conflicts within the government. The *comunidade* is extensively involved in coordinating Sarney's contacts with state governments, entrepreneurs, and other influential groups.

The interventionist thrust of the doctrine of national security has not been modified under the Nova República. The armed forces have opposed successfully any significant modification of the National Security Law. A government-proposed substitute, the Law for the Defense of the Democratic State, has been criticized by many jurists for not going far enough in repealing the state's arbitrary powers. The military aggressively has opposed investigation of past scandals involving high-ranking officers and has blocked any constitutional changes limiting its role as the guardian of "internal security."[78]

General Euclydes Figueiredo, the ex-president's brother and the commander of the Superior War College before his retirement in late 1985, openly criticized the legalization of the Communist party, warning that "we should not accept the communist parties because they are not democratic. We are going to pay dearly. The enemy is the enemy." Similarly, army minister General Leônidas Pires Gonçalves, expressing the predominant view among high-ranking officers, has peremptorily warned Congress and candidates for election to the Constitutional Convention that "the duties of the armed forces are a tradition that need not be changed."[79]

Post-1964 militarization of the Brazilian has given the armed forces a considerable presence in civilian administrative agencies, which has led to the emergence of a veritable military-bureaucratic complex. According to one study, nearly 30 percent of 360 key decisionmaking posts in the federal government during the Figueiredo government were entrusted to military officers. This penetration included a far-flung network of military technocrats, including twenty to forty thousand retired officers, extending outward into the state governments as well as into the private sector. There is no evidence that this impressive degree of militarization has changed substantially since March 1985.[80]

The emergence of a thriving arms industry complements these mechanisms of formal and informal penetration. After only fifteen years of intensive development, Brazil now meets about 80 percent of its needs for war matèriel through local production; Brazil now is the world's fifth largest weapons exporter, with annual sales of some $3 billion. The Brazilian military-industrial complex comprises approximately 350 firms and 200,000 employees and reportedly is responsible for as much as 4–5 percent of GDP. There is considerable debate about the meaning of these figures. Some argue that the military-industrial complex—and the lessons of Argentina's humiliating defeat in the Malvinas War—has been instrumental in forging a new awareness among the officer corps of the armed forces' vital "external mission" and therefore may be a force for democratization. Others affirm exactly the opposite. In any case, this vast amount of power under substantial military control confers tremendous influence on issues related to national security policy, foreign trade and international economic policy, protectionism and industrial promotion, labor matters, and so on.[81]

One close observer of the Brazilian military concluded that "the political system—and with it, the armed forces—has not taken the relevant steps to seriously reexamine the basis premises of military interventionism."[82] The military's capacity to limit the tempo and the extent of social, economic, and political transformations in Brazilian society remains basically untouched by the Nova República. Given the appropriate concatenation of economic crisis, social upheaval, and perceived weakness by civilian elites, direct military intervention certainly cannot be discounted. But for the foreseeable future the armed forces most likely will seek to shape national politics by means of discrete pressures applied in conjunction with their civilian allies plus occasional, more overt warnings to civilian politicians.

DEMOCRACY AND ELITE CONCILIATION: SOME CONCLUDING SPECULATIONS

Judgments of the outcome of the Geisel-Figueiredo *distensão/abertura* project must yield a mixed verdict. From the point of view of the outgoing military regime, authoritarian liberalization succeeded in protecting the military from reprisal and preserved the military's institutional power and capacity to exercise influence in the new civilian regime. By the same token, however, even the military regime's manipulation of a deliberately nonrepresentative elctoral arena failed to produce a transfer of state power to reliable civilians openly loyal to the "revolution of 1964." The best efforts of the authoritarian liberals could not halt the plebiscitary advance of the opposition, a broad front led successively by the MDB, and PMDB, and, in the final phase, by the Aliança Democrática.

This chapter has argued that the limited pluralism permitted by the *distensão/abertura* process led to the resurgence of mass-based politics in the electoral arena and that this allowed moderate political elites to consolidate control of the democratic opposition. Similarly, the analysis of the Geisel and Figueiredo years noted that the reactivation of civil society was crucial in eroding regime legitimacy and in strengthening moderate opposition leaders. The gradual shift in the correlation of forces in society under Geisel and Figueiredo eventually overwhelmed the original "opening project," thereby leading to an "opening process" in which the original logic of state power was defeated by an increasingly challenging and resilient logic of democratic opposition.

The overview of the Sarney government's handling of the democratic agenda reveals that the return to civilian rule did not put an abrupt end to the opening process. On the contrary, the interplay between the social and political forces expressed through the logic of state power and the logic of democratic expansion continues under the Nova República. It is precisely this interplay of the two logics that currently confronts the Nova República with the challenge of establishing and consolidating a new democratic institutionality and simultaneously meeting its daunting social and economic responsibilities.

The current democratic regime faces a choice between two alternative national projects. Both projects profess democratic values, and both are clearly compatible with a market economy, but there are fundamental differences between them. Many Brazilians refer to the first project as *conciliação pelo alto*, or "elite conciliation from above." This project would be "liberal," but its democratic potential, particularly regarding fundamental social and economic questions, would be limited sharply by the implicit consensus among the dominant classes and leading elites to preserve the fundamentally authoritarian and exclusionary traits of Brazil's "savage capitalism."

The second alternative may be labeled "fundamental democratization" and intends to evoke a much broader project for the extension of citizenship for the subaltern classes.[83] Such a project (which of necessity will take several decades) could facilitate the toleration of "predictable uncertainties" and speed the institutionalization of "democratic class struggle" through the electoral and party systems. Successful modernization of the political economy, which would bring Brazilian capitalism into the twentieth century, certainly would be a tremendous accomplishment but hardly would be unique in historical terms. On the contrary, although varying considerably with regard to specific features, this outcome would be broadly similar to the route followed by Western democracies. In these societies, political democracy is less the product of an underlying "consensus on fundamental values" than a "second best" solution to the multiple conflicts inherent in contemporary market economies.[84]

The principal social forces in the conciliation from above scenario include, at a structural level, the more traditionalist wing of large productive and financial capital and rural landowners. The conservative sectors of the urban middle class and those technobureaucratic sectors linked to the "pharaonic" development projects initiated under military rule also would be strongly attached to such a project. Rural populations in the *grotões* presumably could be mobilized electorally as a support class through clientelistic means.

This alliance of classes and sectors supports orthodox, monetarist economic policies, close alignment with U.S. foreign policy, and strict adherence to the rules of the international financial community. Its hegemonic groups also would favor an antistatist thrust toward the privatization of public enterprises. Conversely, this alliance would generally oppose income redistribution schemes, modernization of existing labor legislation, extensive agrarian reform, and constitutional changes conducive to expanded popular participation. At the political level, this "liberal bourgeois pact" would find its principal exponents in the PFL, the PDS, the PTB, and the conservative, antireformist wing of the PMDB.

The second, more "progressive" or change-oriented project potentially encompasses a more contradictory ensemble of classes and sectors. In structural terms, this alliance would include those entrepreneurs, both large and small, who would benefit from an expansion of the domestic market, the curbing of financial speculation, and new export opportunities. It also would attract the more liberal sectors of the urban middle class and public employees, especially the new technobureaucratic groups now in charge of economic policy. In addition, urban workers favored by rising real wages and the expansion of employment and rural workers and peasants whose hopes depend on agrarian reform could find much to support in this project.

This heterogenous alliance would tend to support economic policies of the sort contained in the Cruzado Plan, although the more reformist sectors could be expected to push for more rapid income redistribution, more ambitious labor reform legislation, more rapid agrarian reform, and broader expansion of citizenship rights for subordinate classes. At the political level, the centrist and reformist wings of the PMDB would constitute the principal congressional and electoral base of this "popular democratic pact." Although the parties to the PMDB's left—the PDT, the PSB, the various communist parties, and especially the PT—have their own, more ambitious democratic projects, they could provide crucial votes on specific issues in a loose parliamentary coalition with the PMDB reformers. The left parties, for reasons of political survival, ideological identity, and personal ambitions (e.g., Brizola of the PDT) generally would be reluctant to join permanent electoral alliances.

The outcome of the impending constitutional revision, the possible realignment of the party system, and decisions regarding the length of Sarney's mandate and the choice of his successor will be crucial in deciding whether Brazil will embark upon deepening democratic reforms or whether the current transition will be limited to a game of *conciliação pelo alto* with only minor changes in the social and economic orders. The enormous weight of Brazil's firmly entrenched conservative forces clearly militates in favor of elite conciliation from above. Progressive forces probably are weaker than they may appear. The PMDB party machine—the sine qua non of any more progressive political option—currently is dominated by moderates and conservatives. The 1986 congressional and gubernatorial elections confirmed this conservative domination of the PMDB and the conservative cast of Brazil's present party system. Local contests such as the 1985 municipal elections tend to overrepresent modern, urban Brazil. Conversely, statewide and national elections, which are decisive factors in shaping national politics, tend to overrepresent the regions and social forces most resistant to fundamental social change, thus undercutting the impetus for more rapid democratization. The existence of this relationship was confirmed by the results of the November 1986 elections, and the same logic no doubt will apply in future presidential elections to select Sarney's successor.

In short, I believe the most likely scenario for at least the next several years will be quite conservative. If the forces favoring elite rule and *conciliação pelo alto* are able to strengthen further their social and political hegemony, the effort to consolidate a liberal political regime will be successful. Coming after twenty years of military authoritarianism, such an outcome would be hailed by many as a significant achievement, and they would be correct. The concern is that consolidation of liberal democracy with strong elitist and exclusionary tendencies may come at a very high cost—namely, the postponement of the basic redistribution of power and the fundamental transformations needed to institutionalize a more participatory politics and ensure a more just and equitable social order.

Yet elite conciliation from above is not a foregone conclusion. The direction of the democratic transition is still being contested hotly. Fortunately, not all social and political actors need be convinced democrats for a democratic consolidation to occur. Moreover, much recent scholarship on transitions to democracy suggests that the *aggiornamento* of traditional elites and dominant social classes and the establishment of democratic rule usually occur as the culmination of a prolonged process of social and political transformations. The military, the dominant classes, and conservative political elites may come to embrace, albeit reluctantly, the wisdom of accommodation to exigencies of a more legitimate and inclusionary system of mass politics. Contemporary Brazil has an extensively industrialized market economy with strong state participation and its highly diversified social structure is articulated by a complex ensemble of dynamic social movements and sophisticated political actors. The question of democracy will necessarily stand at the top of the political agenda in such a society. Indeed, democracy may be the only solution for the current crisis and the best hope for Brazil's future.

NOTES

1. Régis de Castro Andrade, "Brasil: A Economia do Capitalismo Selvagem," *Revista de Cultura e Política*, 4 (1981): 7–30.

2. Vilmar Faria, "Desenvolvimento, Urbanização e Mudanças na Estrutura do Emprego: A Experiência Brasileira dos Últimos Trinta Anos," in Bernardo Sorj and Maria Herminia Tavares de Almeida (eds.), *Sociedade e Política no Brasil Pós-64* (São Paulo: Editora Brasiliense, 1983), pp. 118–163.

3. Peter Evans, *Dependent Development: The Alliance of Multinational, State, and National Capital in Brazil* (Princeton, N.J.: Princeton University Press, 1979); Luciano Martins, *Estado Capitalista e Burocracia no Brasil Pós-64* (Rio de Janeiro: Paz e Terra, 1985); and William C. Smith and René A. Dreyfuss, "Reflexões Sobre a Articulação da Elite Orgánica em Escala Mundial: Novas Formas de Intervenção Política Entre o Estado Nacional e o Capital Transnacional," *Estudos PECLA* 2, no. 1 (1983).

4. Paul Singer, *Repartição da Renda: Pobres e Ricos sob o Regime Militar* (Rio de Janeiro: Jorge Zahar, 1985); and Sérgio Henrique Abranches, *Os Despossuídos: Crescimento e Pobreza no País do Milagre* (Rio de Janeiro: Jorge Zahar, 1985). On the findings of the presidential commission, see Hélio Jaguaribe et al., *Brasil, 2.000: Para um Novo Pacto Social* (Rio de Janeiro: Paz e Terra, 1986).

5. Eduardo Viola and Scott Mainwaring, "Transitions to Democracy: Brazil and Argentina in the 1980s," *Journal of International Affairs* 38, no. 2 (1985): 193–219; and Donald Share and Scott Mainwaring, "Transitions Through Transaction: Democratization in Brazil and Spain," in Wayne A. Selcher (ed.), *Political Liberalization in Brazil: Dynamics, Dilemmas, and Future Prospects* (Boulder, Colo.: Westview Press, 1986), pp. 175–216.

6. *Ibid.*

7. Eli Diniz, "A Transição Política no Brasil: A Uma Reavaliação da Dinámica da Abertura," *Dados* 28, no. 3 (1985): 329–346; and Bolivar Lamounier, "Apontamentos Sobre a Questão Democrática Brasileira," in Alain Roquié, Bolivar Lamounier, and Jorge Schvarzer (eds.), *Como Renascem as Democracias* (São Paulo: Editora Brasiliense, 1985), pp. 104–140.

8. For this position see Guillermo O'Donnell and Philippe Schmitter, *Political Life After Authoritarian Rule: Tentative Conclusions About Uncertain Transitions* (Baltimore, Md.: Johns Hopkins University Press, 1986).

9. For a provocative discussion of "lumper" and "spliter" approaches to comparative analysis, see J. H. Hexter, *On Historians* (Cambridge: Cambridge University Press, 1979), pp. 241–243.

10. Diniz, "A Transição Política no Brazil," p. 333.

11. Wanderley Guilherme dos Santos, "Autoritárismo e Após: Convergências e Divergências Entre Brasil e Chile," *Dados* 25, no. 2 (1982); and Celso Lafer, "The Brazilian Political System: Trends and Perspectives," *Government and Opposition* 19, no. 2 (1984): 179–187.

12. Sebastião C. Velasco e Cruz and Carlos Estevam Martins, "De Castello a Figueiredo: Uma Uncursão na Pre-Histoória da Abertura," in Sorj and Tavares de Almeida, *Sociedade e Política*, p. 43.

13. Carlos Chagas, *A Guerra das Estrelas (1964/1984): Os Bastidores das Sucessões Presidenciais* (Porto Alegre: L & PM Editores, 1985), pp. 199–221.

14. Marcus Maria Figueiredo and Antônio Borges Cheibub, "A Abertura Política de 1973 a 1981: Um Inventório de um Debate," *Boletim Informativo e Bibliográfico de Ciências Sociais*, no. 14 (1982): 29–61; and Fernando Henrique Cardoso, "Regime Político e Mundança Social," *Revista de Cultura e Política*, no. 3 (1981): 7–26.

15. See Ana Lagoa, *SNI, Como Nasceu, Como Funciona* (São Paulo: Editora Brasiliense, 1983); and Archdiocesis of São Paulo, *Brasil: Nunca Mais* (Petrópolis: Vozes, 1985), Chapter 2.

16. . Walter de Góes, "Sobre a Gênese da Abertura Política" (Sixth ANPOCS conference, Nova Friburgo, Brazil, October 1982), p. 4.

17. See Alfred Stepan, "O que Estão Pensando os Militares," *Novos Estudos CEBRAP* 2, no. 2 (1983): 2–7.

18. Transformism differs from democratic reformism in its rejection of changes in political regime and in the social and economic bases of political domination. See Antonio Gramsci, *Selections from the Prison Notebooks* (New York: International Publishers, 1971), pp. 58, 97, 128, 227.

19. Cited in Bernardo Kucinski, *Abertura, A História de uma Crise* (São Paulo: Editoral Brasil Debates, 1982), p. 20.

20. Cited in Edgar Pontes de Magalhães, "Mobilization and Liberalization: University Professors Organize in Brazil" (Ph.D. diss. in progress: Stanford University), p. 14.

21. Bolivar Lamounier and Fernando Henrique Cardoso (eds.), *Os Partidos e as Eleições no Brasil* (Rio de Janeiro: Editora Paz e Terra, 1976).

22. Peter McDonough, *Power and Ideology in Brazil* (Princeton, N.J.: Princeton University Press, 1981), pp. 125, 232.

23. See Scott Mainwaring, *The Catholic Church and Politics in Brazil, 1916–1985* (Stanford, Calif.: Stanford University Press, 1986), for an excellent discussion.

24. Maria Elena Moreira Alves, *Estado e Oposição no Brasil (1964–1984)* (Petrópolis: Editora Vozes, 1984), pp. 200–208, 230–236; and Scott Mainwaring, "Grass Roots Popular Movements and the Struggle for Democracy: Nova Iguaçú, 1974–1985," in Alfred Stepan (ed.), *Democratizing Brazil* (New York: Oxford University Press, forthcoming).

25. *Ibid.*, pp. 209–217.

26. On social policies and legitimation, see Régis de Castro Andrade, "Política Social e Normalização Institucional no Brasil," in Luis Maira et al, *América Latina: Novas Estratégias de Dominação* (Petrópolis: Editora Vozes, 1980), p. 87–114; and Barry Ames, *Political Survival: Spending and Policy in Latin America* (Berkeley: University of California Press, forthcoming), Chapter 5.

27. Fernando Jordão, *Dossie Herzog—Prisão, Tortura e Morte no Brasil* (São Paulo: Editora Global, 1979).

28. On the 1976 elections, see Fabio W. Reis (ed.), *Os Partidos e o Regime: A Lógica do Processo Eleitoral Brasileiro* (São Paulo: Símbolo, 1978). On repression, see Moreira Alves, *Estado e Oposição no Brasil*, pp. 209–217.

29. David V. Fleischer, "Constitutional and Electoral Engineering in Brazil: A Double-Edged Sword (1964–1982)," *Inter-American Economic Affairs* 37, no. 4 (1984): 3–36.

30. Chagas, *A Guerra das Estrelas*, Chapter 6; Hugo Abreu, *O Outro Lado do Poder* (Rio de Janeiro: Nova Fronteira, 1979); and Walter de Góes, *O Brasil do General Geisel* (Rio de Janeiro: Nova Fronteira, 1978).

31. Ruth Cardoso, "Movimentos Sociais Urbanos: Um Balanco Crítico," in Sorj and Tavares de Almeida, *Sociedad e Política*, pp. 215–239; and Renato Boschi (ed.) *Movimentos Coletivos no Brasil Urbano* (Rio de Janeiro: Zahar, 1983).

32. Maria Herminia Tavares de Almeida, "O Sindacalismo Brasileiro Entre a Conservação e a Mudança," in Sorj and Tavares de Almeida, *ibid.*, Tables 1, 2, 3, pp. 193–194.

33. John Humphrey, *Capitalist Control and Workers' Struggle in the Brazilian Auto Industry* (Princeton, N.J.: Princeton University Press, 1982), Chapter 6.

34. *Ibid.*, Chapter 9; José Álvaro Moisés, "A Estratégia do Novo Sindicalismo," *Revista de Cultura e Política*, no. 5/6 (1981); and Margaret Keck, "The New Unionism in the Brazilian Transition," in Stepan, *Democratizing Brazil*. On professionals, see Pontes de Magalhães, "Liberalization and Mobilization."

35. Carlos Lessa, *A Estratégia de Desenvolvimento 1974–1975—Sonho e Fracasso* (Thesis for Full Professor, Federal University of Rio de Janeiro, 1978); Antônio Barros de Castro and Francisco Eduardo Pires de Souza, *A Economia Brasiliera em Marcha Forçada* (Rio de Janeiro: Paz e Terra, 1985); and Sebastião C. Velasco e Cruz, "A Indústria de Bens de Capital e o Governo Geisel," *Série Estudos* (IUPERJ), no. 48 (June 1986). Also see Eli Diniz and Olavo Brasil de Lima, "Modernização Autoritária: O Empresariado e a Intervenção do Estado na Economia," *Série Estudos* (IUPERJ), no. 47 (May 1986), for an excellent survey of entrepreneurs in Brazilian politics.

36. See Fernando Henrique Cardoso, "O Papel dos Empresários no Processo de Transição: O Caso Brasiliero," *Dados* 26, no. 1 (1983): 9–27 for these events.

37. *Ibid.*, p. 14.

38. Bolivar Lamounier (ed.), *Voto de Desconfiança—Eleições e Mudança Política no Brasil, 1970–1979* (Petrópolis: Editora Vozes, 1978).

39. Carlos Wagner Morais (ed.), *O Livro dos Pensamentos do General Figueiredo* (São Paulo: Editora Brasiliense, 1978), pp. 53, 83, 98.

40. Golbery do Couto e Silva, *Conjuntura Política Nacional: O Poder Executivo e Geopolítica no Brasil* (Rio de Janeiro: Livraria José Olimpio, 1981), p. 3–35.

41. Humphrey, *Capitalist Control and Workers' Struggle*, Chapter 7.

42. Maria da Conceição Tavares and José Carlos de Assis, *O Grande Salto para o Caos* (Rio de Janeiro: Zahar Editores, 1985), p. 18.

43. Olavo Brasil de Lima Junior, "Continuity and Change: Parties and Elections in Contemporary Brazil" (Paper presented at a conference on Opportunities and

Constraints in Peripheral Industrial Society: The Case of Brazil, Stanford-Berkeley Joint Center for Latin American Studies, January 30–February 2, 1984).

44. Pontes de Magalhães, "Liberalization and Mobilization," Chapter 2.

45. Cited by Enrique A. Baloyra, "From Moment to Moment: The Political Transition in Brazil," in Selcher, *Political Liberalization*, p. 45.

46. See the *Folha de S. Paulo* during May–July, 1981.

47. Walter de Góes and Aspásia Camargo, *O Drama da Sucessão e a Crise do Regime* (Rio de Janeiro: Nova Fronteira, 1984), p. 190.

48. Glaucio Ary Dillon Soares, *Colégio Eleitoral, Convenções Partidárias e Eleições Diretas* (Petrópolis: Editora Vozes, 1984), pp. 25–48.

49. David V. Fleischer, "Brazil at the Crossroads: The Elections of 1982 and 1985," and Gluacio Ary Dillon Soares, "Elections and Democratization in Brazil," both in Paul W. Drake and Eduardo Silva (eds.), *Elections and Democratization in Latin America, 1980–1985* (San Diego, Calif.: Center for Iberian and Latin American Studies, 1986), pp. 273–298, 299–327.

50. *Folha de S. Paulo*, November 27, 1982; *Jornal do Brasil*, December 6, 1982; and *Folha de S. Paulo*, March 13, 1983.

51. William Tyler, "Stabilization, External Adjustment, and Recession in Brazil: Perspectives on the Mid-1980s" (Paper presented at the conference on the Brazilian Crisis, University of Florida, November 15–16, 1984), pp. 23–28.

52. Barry Ames, *Political Survival*, Chapter 5.

53. For public opinion data, see *Estado de Minas*, November 5, 1983; *Jornal do Brasil*, May 29, 1983; and *Veja*, September 28, 1983. On the campaign, see Gilbert Dimenstein et al., *O Complot que Eleqeu Tancredo* (Rio de Janeiro: Editora Jornal do Brasil, 1985); and "Os Segredos da Vítoria da Oposição," *Veja*, January 16, 1985, pp. 22–55.

54. For survey data, see Soares, *Colégio Eleitoral, Convenções Partidárias*, p. 60; and *Veja*, March 14, 1984.

55. See Dimenstein et al., *O Complot que Eleqeu Tancredo*, pp. 228–235, for the texts of numerous military comuniqués issued during this period.

56. *Ibid.*, 164–181; and "Os Segredos da Vítoria da Oposição," pp. 40–45. In May 1986, Senator Fernando Henrique Cardoso revealed the existence of secret agreements between Tancredo and the military to guarantee the transition. See *Senhor*, May 27, 1986, p. 22.

57. Cited in "Os Segredos da Vítoria da Oposição," p. 43.

58. For the events surrounding Tancredo's death, see Antônio Britto with Luis Claudio Cunha, *Assim Morreu Tancredo* (Porto Alegre: L & PM, 1985).

59. Raymundo Faoro, "O Estado Novo do PMDB," *Senhor*, December 31, 1985, p. 12; *Veja*, May 21, 1986, pp. 25–26; and the interview with Lula in *Senhor*, August 19, 1986, p. 28–29. Also see Florestan Fernandes, *Nova República?* (Rio de Janeiro: Zahar, 1985).

60. Emir Sader (ed.), *Constituinte e Democracia no Brasil Hoje* (São Paulo: Editora Brasiliense, 1985); and Renato Lessa, "Dilemmas da Institucionalização Brasileira: Os Primeiros Passos Rumo à Constituinte," *Série Estudos* (IUPERJ), no. 46 (April 1986).

61. Ulysses Guimarães, PMDB leader and president of the Chamber of Deputies, observed that "a pact can be reached only in the first 100 days of government,

when confidence is high," *Latin American Regional Reports: Brazil*, May 31, 1985, p. 1.

62. *Veja*, May 21, 1986, pp. 28–33; and May 28, 1986, pp. 20–23.

63. See the interview with the ex-president of INCRA in *Senhor*, February 11, 1986, pp. 5–10.

64. See the study of UDR and alleged official involvement by IBASE, *Políticas Governamentais* (July 1986).

65. *Senhor*, May 13, 1986, pp. 52–53; May 27, 1986, pp. 13–14; June 3, 1986, pp. 22–31; June 10, 1986, p. 26–29; and July 22, 1986, pp. 26–35.

66. *Ibid.*, May 13, 1986, p. 53; and IBASE, *Políticas Governamentais* (October 1986).

67. IBASE research group cited by *Latin America Regional Report; Brazil*, October 18, 1985, p. 4–5. Also see *Senhor*, September 15, 1985, pp. 46–47.

68. *Miami Herald*, June 12, 1986, p. 17A.

69. *Senhor*, September 18, 1985, table on p. 50; November 6, 1985, p. 38–41; and December 11, 1985, pp. 38–41.

70. *New York Times*, March 2, 1986, p. 11. Also see *Senhor*, February 2, 1986, pp. 26–29; and March 4, 1986, pp. 28–30.

71. See the interviews with key architects of the Cruzado Plan in *Senhor*, March 25, 1986, pp. 5–12. Also see Francisco Lopes, *O Choque Heterodoxo: Combate à Inflação e Reforma Monetária* (Rio de Janeiro: Campos, 1986).

72. For details, see *Senhor*, July 29, 1986, pp. 24–31. For scathing critiques by a prominent North American conservative economist and a leading Brazilian leftist economist, see Paul Craig Roberts, "Brazil Takes Hocus-Pocus Economic Show on the Road," *Wall Street Journal*, September 5, 1986, p. 9; and Paul Singer, "O Plano Cruzado e Suas Três Inflações," *Folha de S. Paulo*, September 6, 1986, p. 22. On the Cruzado II, see *Wall Street Journal*, November 24, 1986, p. 11; and *Veja*, November 26, 1986, pp. 36–45.

73. For analyses, see IUPERJ, "Eleições Municipais de 85 e a Conjuntura Política," *Cadernos de Conjuntura*, no 3 (December 1985). Also see the coverage in *Senhor*, December 11, 1985, pp. 34–37; December 18, 1985, pp. 94–97; and December 31, 1985, pp. 42–47.

74. *Veja*, February 19, 1986, p. 20–26; *Senhor*, February 25, 1986, pp. 24–25, 28–34; May 13, 1986, pp. 26–30; and March 4, 1986, pp. 49–51. Also see Eli Diniz, "O Empresariado e o Momento Político: Entre a Nostalgia e o Temor do Futuro, *Cadernos de Conjuntura*, no. 1 (October 1985).

75. *New York Times*, March 2, 1986, p. 11; *Senhor*, March 3, 1986, pp. 5–11; and *Veja*, February 19, 1986, p. 26.

76. *Senhor*, March 11, 1986, pp. 26–28; and April 29, 1986, pp. 36–38; and *Latin American Regional Reports: Brazil*, August 14, 1986, p. 8.

77. *Veja*, November 26, 1986, pp. 36–41, 48–55; December 3, 1986, pp. 36–43; and December 10, 1986, pp. 42–43.

78. See the interview with a member of the commission that drafted the proposal for the new legislation in *Senhor*, February 18, 1986, pp. 5–13.

79. For these and similar statements, see *Senhor*, October 16, 1985, pp. 68–69.

80. Walter de Góes, "O Novo Regime Militar no Brasil," *Dados* 27, no. 3 (1984): 361–378.

81. Paulo Kramer, "Complexo Industrial Militar e Exportação de Armamento no Brasil," *Perspectivas Internacionais*, no. 4 (1984); and Walter de Góes, "Os Militares e a Transição Política," (Paper presented at the Tenth ANPOCS conference, Aguas de São Pedro, Brazil, October 1985).

82. *Ibid*., p. 17.

83. For an interesting, if very schematic, discussion of alternative political projects, see Luíz Carlos Presser Pereira, *Pactos Políticos: Do Populismo à Redemocratização* (São Paulo: Editora Brasiliense, 1985). On elite conciliation in Brazilian history, see Michel Debrun, *A Conciliação e Outras Estratêqias* (São Paulo: Editora Brasiliense, 1983). Also see Guillermo A. O'Donnell, "¿Y a mi qué me importa?: Notas sobre sociabilidad y política en Argentina y Brasil," *Estudios CEDES* (November 1984): and Scott Mainwaring, "Grass Roots Popular Movements, Identity, and Democratization in Brazil," *Comparative Political Studies*, forthcoming.

84. On the role of institutionalization of conflict and the reconciliation between political democracy and market capitalism, see Claus Offe, "Competitive Party Democracy and the Keynesian Welfare State" in his collection of essays *Contradictions of the Welfare State*, edited by John Keane (Cambridge, Mass.: MIT Press, 1984).

7
POLITICAL PARTIES AND ELECTIONS IN THE PROCESS OF TRANSITION IN URUGUAY

Juan Rial

On November 25, 1984, an election was held in Uruguay. The results of the election made possible the installation of a democratic regime, but that installation did not come as the last link in a single causal chain of events. During 1980–1984 three interrelated processes had been afoot in Uruguay: a process of "transition from above," through which the military tried to institutionalize a "restricted" democracy; an uncertain liberalization, which proceeded by fits and starts; and an electoral campaign, begun in 1980 as part of an attempt to secure a consensus for the military's political project, that enabled the traditional political parties to push the transition toward a democratic outcome with plenty of support "from below." It was not clear at the time whether the election was a "forward flight" or a necessary preamble to the inauguration of a democratic regime.

A democratic inauguration in Uruguay can lead either to a stable and strong regime or to a weak democracy prone to constant unmanageable pressures.[1] Political parties will play a determining role in this consolidation, but they must cope with some problems of their own. In 1973 the prolonged crisis of the traditional parties (TPs) of Uruguay—the Partido Colorado (Red) and the Partido Nacional Blanco (White)—and the disaffection and dubious loyalty to the democratic regime of some of their factions and of the Left, contributed to the climate that led to the military coup. The crisis of the traditional parties had its roots in the 1950s; beginning in that decade the principal factions of the TPs alternated in the presidency because neither party was able to achieve dominance. This led to a power vacuum in which no new political project was forthcoming, and the parties were unable to implement changes that would ensure the survival of the Uruguayan democratic regime. Thus, the parties fell back upon the maintenance of a liberal discourse in their programs and on reinforcing their clientelistic networks through "political clubs." As a result of these weaknesses, the parties proved unable to check the increasing autonomy of the armed forces.[2]

Have the parties profited from this experience? Have they taken into consideration the changes produced in society after eleven years of authoritarianism? Have the linkages between parties and civil society evolved in a manner that will help to consolidate the democratic regime?

POLITICAL PARTIES AND THE PROCESS OF TRANSITION TO DEMOCRACY

Restoration or Renovation?

The three main parties of Uruguay and their factions experienced different kinds of hardships under authoritarian domination. The TPs and those factions of the Left that had come together in the elections of 1971 under the Frente Amplio (Broad Front, or FA) and were considered neither Marxist-Leninist nor violent were "suspended" by the military.[3] In addition to the Colorado and Blanco parties, the suspension included the Partido Demócrata Cristiano (Christian Democratic party, or PDC) and some small groups such as Agrupación Pregón of Alba Roballo and the Lista 99 Por el Gobierno del Pueblo of Zelmar Michelini. Both the Pregón and the 99 were Colorado factions. Incredibly enough, the electoral front created by the Communist party of Uruguay, (the FIDEL) and some of its components, such as the Movimiento Popular Blanco y Progresista led by former senator Francisco Rodríguez Camusso of the Partido Nacional were not declared illegal. All these groups were under the same "freezing" as the TPs. However, their leaders and many of their affiliates (which were not included in the lists of candidates) were not authorized to act politically until 1991. The freeze was relaxed in 1982 and lifted in March 1985.

The parties that were defined ideologically as Marxist-Leninist, such as the Communist and the Socialist parties as well as some other small groups and legal organizations close to or representing violent movements, were declared illegal. A decree dated November 28, 1973, dissolved the Partido Comunista, the Partido Socialista (Socialist party), the Movimiento 26 de Marzo (March 26 Movement), Enrique Erro's Unión Popular (Popular Union), the Pro-Cuban MRO, the pro-Chinese Partido Comunista Revolucionario (Communist Revolutionary party) and Agrupaciones Rojas (Red Groups), the Grupos de Acción Unificada (Unified Action Groups, or GAU), and other small groups including FEUU, the Federation of University Students of Uruguay. Their cadre tried to keep them going, but after a short period of time, they had to leave the country.

Some Colorado factions that had supported the administration of Juan María Bordaberry from October 1972 onward supported the new authoritarian regime. This they did not as party factions but as a party of notables. A majority of the Unión Nacional Reeleccionista (Reelectionist National Union) from the Partido Colorado, a name adopted by the Unión Colorado Batllista in 1971 to support presidents Jorge Pacheco Areco and Juan María Bordaberry, supported the coup. Within the Partido Nacional, *herreristas* who had promoted the conservative candidacy of (retired) general Mario Aguerrondo in 1971 identified themselves with the coup. The military was not able to increase this relatively meager base of support among the TPs because it was unable to coopt additional TP factions. Perhaps the military's most notable success was Juan Carlos Paysée, who had served as private secretary to Senator Wilson Ferreira Aldunate; Paysée became an official of the military regime and was the last mayor of Montevideo under the dictatorship.

TP opposition to the military regime emerged from Blancos who supported Ferreira Aldunate and part of the *herreristas*. Among the Colorados, the *batllistas* of Unidad y Reforma (Unity and Reform) split with President Bordaberry after Jorge Batlle's imprisonment by the military in 1972. Minor Colorado factions led by Amílcar Vasconcellos and Flores Mora also opposed the regime from the first. Later on Colorados dissenting from Pacheco and other Blanco *herreristas* abandoned the regime and joined the opposition.

Frozen parties were in a better position to reconstruct the political community once the legal restrictions on them were relaxed. Despite proscription and their internal divisions into pro- and antiregime factions, the traditional parties survived. It does not seem that the military had intended to destroy the TPs. In 1976 President Bordaberry made a proposal to supress all parties and to reorganize the Uruguayan polity along corporatist lines. But the armed forces rejected the project, dismissed Bordaberry from the presidency, and dclared that leaders, not the parties themselves, had caused the crisis of democracy.[4] The project of the armed forces implied a restoration of the political community not a renovation of the type proposed by Bordaberry. This restoration made it possible for each party to preserve its traditional identity. But the military favored a project of renovation involving the state itself—that is, a *democradura*[5] legitimized by elections where old political parties would take part but under a new leadership adhering to this blueprint.

In essence, the opposition took up the restoration project of the military to defeat the refoundation aspects of the armed forces's plans. The TPs played on the emotional aspects of party identification. Blanco oppositionists rescued the old *saravista* discourse of the late nineteenth century and presented the party as the most passionate defender of public liberties, especially those related to political rights. Their Colorado counterparts replied with a *batllista* discourse that not only demanded democracy but yearned for a return of the "anticipatory" and "consensual" style of development that had characterized the traditional democratic regime.[6] Rhetorically this *batllismo* proffered a provident statism in marked contrast to the elitist neoliberalism practiced by the regime since 1974.

Within this framework, the TPs had to reenter the political arena by defining themselves in relation to the restoration plan of the armed forces. This produced a strong realignment of the most important constitutive factions of the parties, electorally called *sublemas*.[7]

The reorganization enacted to implement the restoration favored big *sublemas* and left small factions or those formed by smaller subunits, or *listas*, in a precarious position. Whereas partisans of the regime dispersed their strength in a large number of factions, especially in Montevideo, regime opponents within the TPs came together in a smaller number of factions. The party reorganization imposed by the military in 1982 led to alliances among different *listas* and to the impression that the TPs had become more coherent than was actually the case. What is even more interesting is that there were new factions on the left of both traditional parties that before the authoritarian situation would have been considered members of the Left. These included the Corriente Batllista Independiente (CBI) and the Corriente Popular Nacionalista (CPN), although the majority sector of the latter, called Por la Patria (For the Fatherland, or PLP), is even more to the left.

Freezing or Renovation of Leadership?

Renovation and restoration in the Partido Nacional affirmed the leadership of Ferreira Aldunate, already established in 1971, and led to the decline of party leaders close to the military regime. In the Partido Colorado the changes were broader in scope. Colorado officialists also were defeated, but, in this case, it meant a reversal of the fortunes of the factions. The leading faction of former president Pacheco Areco was punished as he suffered a humiliating defeat. Although his position as first man in the party was never very secure, it became unstable in 1980 despite all official efforts on his behalf. Neither did the other Colorado leader of 1971, Jorge Batlle, recover his position. His close relation to the Pacheco administration together with strong accusations of political corruption damaged his reputation. Following his proscription, there emerged new figures who, supported by the party machinery, soon came into their own. Julio María Sanguinetti became a leader in the Partido Colorado in his own right, which he was not in 1971, and not as a proxy for Jorge Batlle. In essence, there was a restoration of the leading Blancos of 1971, while there was a renovation of sorts among the Colorados.

In general, the Blanco restoration did not appear to favor the transition. Ferreira waged a hard personal battle against the armed forces for the right to be a candidate in 1984. His troubles and the military's veto of his candidacy evoke other famous cases involving similar confrontations: Víctor Raúl Haya de la Torre in Peru and Juan Domingo Perón in Argentina are probably the paradigmatic examples. The Blanco renovation, by contrast, helped avoid a similar conflict between Jorge Batlle and the armed forces.[8]

The outcome of the restoration-renovation dilemma within the different parties is not without irony, and it yields very interesting insights about processes of political transition. In general, parties frozen by an authoritarian regime tend to rally around their leaders, as if to preserve their best people for the aftermath of the regime's fall. The cases of Haya, Perón, Hernán Siles Suazo of Bolivia, Leonel Brizola of Brazil, Arnulfo Arias of Panama; and José María Velazco Ibarra of Ecuador come to mind in this regard. In the case of Uruguay, both Ferreira and Líber Seregni, the leader of the Frente Amplio in 1971, saw their positions ratified and their influence increased within their parties in 1984. But precisely because in 1971 the internal situation of the Partido Colorado favored leadership inclined to a "semiauthoritarian" solution, the Colorados found it indispensable to renew their leadership in 1984.

The military tried to discontinue party acronyms and symbols prohibiting the use of old numbers in the *hojas de votación* (ballots) utilized in the 1982 party primaries. But party elites devised new ways in which voters could identify them. For example, Amílcar Vasconcellos has suggested that the purpose of the "triumvirates" created to direct the Partido Colorado and the Partido Nacional during their total exclusion from party activity was to prevent them from disappearing altogether.[9]

The Persistence of Party-Society Links

The restoration of a party system based on the predominance of the TPs and the element of renovation within the restoration framework proposed by the military suggest that the link between traditional parties and Uruguayan society was stronger than anticipated. This challenges the contention that the TPs were about to disappear in 1971–1973.

Restoration seemed to occur indeed in 1976 as a result of a military decision to discard the diagnosis that forecast the death of the TPs. The ban on party activity enforced since 1973, the serious disruption of internal party life under the military, and the progressive disorganization of the parties since the 1950s seemed to support that contention. Party conventions had not met in many years. There were no permanent party bodies. Party members were working either as government officials or as part of the state bureaucracy. Party functionaries such as executive board members had little influence with their official counterparts. Only factions at the *sublema* level were important. Communication with party adherents was fluent only during electoral periods, when political clubs flourished. These formal communications disappeared later on and were replaced by private ones or by the reappearance of the clientele system. A party of notables was the essence of the party. Bordaberry understood all this and tried to suppress the TPs and replace them with "currents of opinion."[10] His proposal appeared inspired by the Francoist formula of reducing politics to "legitimate differences of opinion."

The armed forces did not reject Bordaberry's proposal outright. In a compromise between *duros* (hardliners) and *blandos* (softliners), the military decided to keep parties "frozen" but, at the same time, to purge their leadership. In 1976, therefore, an institutional act marked the transaction between those who wanted to destroy the existing system of parties and those who wanted it to continue. The TPs were allowed to survive, but their leaders were deprived of their political rights until 1981. This measure was even more severe for leftist parties because of the larger number of people affected by this prohibition. It was thought that there would be either a renovation of the TP leadership or that TP leaders would be coopted by the regime.

In 1980 the military submitted its constitutional blueprint for *democradura* to a referendum. The proposal was defeated soundly. Once the project was rejected, the military insisted its blueprint be part of the transition package it tried to sell to the traditional parties. All prohibitions on TP leaders began to disappear—except the one on Ferreira—and from 1981 onward the traditional leadership of the TPs began to reassert itself. The constraints on leftist leaders were relaxed more gradually. These were contradictory options, and one of the two had to prevail. Restoration won, and thus the project of a renewal of TP leaderships manipulated by the military collapsed.

From the moment the negative results of the 1980 plebiscite were in, the military sought to implement its blueprint through negotiations with the TPs. With the concurrence of party leaders the military prescribed a minimal legal structure for the parties. Bodies representing "adherents" were created.[11] During discussions to elaborate the basis for the by-laws, the TPs resisted the attempt of officialist groups to impose the affiliation of TP followers on those who wished to elect party representatives. Regime representatives argued that there was a danger of infiltration from the Left in the TPs. It was agreed that only those who wanted to hold representative positions in the party had to be formally affiliated with it.[12] However, Institutional Act no. 19 eliminated the affiliation requirements. TP executive committees were established both at national and departmental levels, and common criteria were adopted regulating the committees' public functioning.[13]

The military continued to push for renovation prohibiting the participation of several old leaders in the 1982 internal party elections for representative bodies. At the time of the internal elections there were about twenty TP leaders who could not take part, including Jorge Batlle, Amílcar Vasconcellos, Raumar Jude (the members of the triumvirate that led the Partido Colorado during the authoritarian period). In retribution for combative speeches during the electoral campaign, Carlos Rodríguez Labruna, Alberto Zumarán, and Terra Arocena of the Partido Nacional were imprisoned and lost their political rights. (Retired) Rear-Admiral Juan José Zorrilla of the Partido Colorado, who as chief of the navy opposed the insurrection of February 9, 1973, also lost his rights. But despite these proscriptions the military suffered a new defeat. Then, in November 1983, the military rehabilitated all party leaders with the sole exception of Ferreira Aldunate on the grounds that Military Justice wanted him for possible involvement in subversive activities.

Behind the resurgence of TPs there lies the link with a society that conceives of the future within a framework dictated by the past. The hope for a "better yesterday for tomorrow," expressed at the level of a party discourse asking for social justice, implied the return to a provident political style based on a paternal state.[14] Both traditional and nontraditional political parties expressed a collective hope for change that in real terms meant nothing but a "return to the past." This being the case, parties, when they did reappear, took on their old tribunal style and voiced the thinking of many citizens who cling to the old vision of "exemplary," happy Uruguay. Even sectors that doubt the viability of such a restorationist project and a sizable sector of the Left, whose goal is an alternative socioeconomic system, utilized this rhetoric in their campaign discourse.

Restoration of the TPs implies great weakness for both the political society and the democratic regime in the near future. The existing fragmentation is maintained. Intraparty pacts, supported by electoral legislation, are in force as a way of ensuring party hegemony. But in order to govern, to obtain legislative support, intraparty alliances are not enough, and it is necessary to resort to interparty coalitions.

The restored system gives more importance to factions than to parties. Its pillars are the *sublemas*, or factions that form a multiparty system of sorts, which are preserved and privileged by complex legislation. This system appears to adopt a bipartisan albeit fragmented configuration at election time, when the electorate is emotionally involved, in order to obtain a favorable result. After the election, factions regain their predominance, and the multiparty configuration reappears. But in order to lead the political community a hegemonic actor is required. Without that option, party cooperation to control public entities and positions in a never-dismantled welfare state, which is intertwined deeply with a sophisticated election machinery, is necessary, as are intra- and interparty agreements that lead to a "compulsory co-participation" of the TPs. This can hardly be avoided in the future.

Liberalization, Transition, and the Electoral Campaign

The starting point of the *apertura* (opening) was centered upon the behavior of the citizenry. The rejection of the project for an authoritarian constitution in 1980 and the acceptance of that rejection by the armed forces marked the start of the transition process, the liberalization, and the electoral campaign.

The liberalization process was hindered constantly by the military regime; thus, this process evolved more slowly but led finally to the Pacto del Club Naval (Pact of the Naval Club) of August 1984.[15] The action of political parties and of extraparty social movements turned into political agents was important in bringing about a liberalization opposed by the majority of the members of the regime.

The transition process presupposed a change of regime. While the armed forces looked for a reequilibration that would finally enable them to impose a *democradura*, the majority of party and extraparty political agents used the transition to push toward a democratic solution. Although military control of the transition suggested that a *salida* (way out) would be granted, the effective *salida* was put together in the negotiations that led to Institutional Act no. 19, which involved constitutional reforms.[16]

The electoral campaign started very slowly in 1980 and gained momentum once the 1982 internal party elections were confirmed. Parties as well as extraparty social movements representing the Left had influence as a result.

These three processes interfered with each other, given their contradictory aims. There was no linear progression from one to the others. The three took place simultaneously. The electoral campaign and the transition were particularly antagonistic as different interests attempted to regain their positions in the political arena of the future democratic regime. The electoral campaign required competition among the parties while actions to affirm liberalization, and thus to stress the transition toward democracy, required collaboration among the opposition factions of the TPs and strong support from a mobilized society. This type of collaboration involved extraparty organizations as well, including left-leaning ones, and was institutionalized through a coalition called the Multipartidaria, which gathered all political parties under its aegis; through the Intersocial, which did the same with social movements; and finally through the Concertación Nacional Programática (National Programmatic Agreement, or CONAPRO).[17]

The TPs felt relatively secure going about one of their traditional activities—namely, electoral mobilization, which presupposes conditions for competition and political stability. The difficulties they faced in this regard were imposed precisely by the mechanism at hand. They had to rely on a system of electoral rules evolved gradually since 1910 that was related intimately to the configuration of the contemporary system of parties. Students of the electoral rules in Uruguay speak of two different systems: a simple majority, winner-take-all system utilized to elect executives (president, vice-president, and departmental *intendentes*, or mayors) and a system of proportional representation for the election of collegial bodies. Both systems allow for the accumulation of votes, which introduces uncertainty and potential vote manipulation.[18]

These systems create and perpetuate the different TP factions' need to form electoral and government coalitions. But recent electoral campaign offered the spectacle of members of the same party working for diametrically opposed ends. There were Colorados and Nacionalistas working for and against the regime. This favored the electoral *salida*, given the diverse and contradictory interests at that level, and the uncertainty of the outcome appeared to soothe military apprehensions. But it did not necessarily favor the inauguration of a democratic regime.

TP Factions: Changes Within the Context of Continuity

There was neither change nor renovation in the party system as such, but there appears to have been some renewal in the parties and in their constituent factions. The antiregime TP factions gave unequivocal signs of renewal of their medium-level cadres, which included young as well as older people without previous militancy. The most obvious and relevant case involved a lawyer, Enrique Tarigo, who became leader of a Colorado faction called Libertad y Cambio (Liberty and Change) and who is now vice-president of Uruguay.

A sizable number of "new men" were victorious in the internal elections of 1982. For example, in Montevideo, the Adelante, con Fé! (Forward, with Faith! or ACF) list of the leading (Ferreira's) opposition faction of the Partido Nacional elected 163 convention members, 86 percent of whom were "new"; the same was true of 45 of the 90 delegates elected by the Unidad y Reforma list. In the CBI list this percentage was almost 100 percent. By contrast, only 15 percent of the most-voted list of the Pacheco sector of the Colorados was new.

It appears that a relegitimation of traditional party factions took place and caused people who hardly would have acted in politics in 1971 to do so in the early 1980s. This renovation, which occurred within the legal framework of the 1982 party by-laws, affirmed the restoration of the party system.

This renovation was fueled by the democratic discourse assumed by opposition TP factions. This highlighted the people's trust in democracy and in elections as efficacious instruments of democracy.[19] Therefore, there was something substantive underlying this renovation. The TPs were flexible enough to modernize their structures while keeping their historical identification, a heritage that ensures their place in the Uruguayan political universe. This suggests that they remained the best representatives of the citizenry and, consequently, the pillars of political society.

The TPs already have overcome a historical situation in which the Colorados assumed the main responsibility for building the state and in which a dangerous convergence led them to promote jointly a paternal, statist style of development. But now the TPs must assume a crisis administration under a democratic regime together with a leftist coalition that has just regained its position in the party system.

The failure of the authoritarian regime to implement a new development project favored the idea of a return to a style of development based on the welfare state. Despite protestations to the contrary (in favor of a new alternative; a social democracy [Partido Colorado]; a more libertarian practice [Partido Nacional]; or a true socialist future [Frente Amplio]), there seems to be a widespread, latent hope for a return to a hallowed past.[20]

The Left: A Search for Space in the Political Arena

For leftist parties, restoration meant regaining some space in the political arena. The military regime tried to remake the leftist opposition by limiting it to "protest" groups that were responsible or semiloyal but hardly dangerous. The strong repression suffered after 1973 by some members of the Frente Amplio forced some to seek shelter abroad, and they hardly had any activity in Uruguay. The Partido Comunista made new alliances during this period and got close to the sector of Wilson Ferreira, especially through his son Juan Raúl. The latter was the active agent of the Convergencia Democrática Uruguaya (Uruguayan Democratic Convergence, or CDU), a vehicle for denunciation and agitation abroad composed of members of the Frente Amplio and by some leftist elements of the Partido Nacional. But the CDU had little impact on local politics in Uruguay. The attempt to widen the alliance of the Left from abroad had few chances to crystallize if the blueprint for restoring the TPs as the key factor in political society was successful, and the crystallization attempt was abandoned in April 1984.

The Left rejoined political society in the negotiating process of the *salida* with great difficulty. Not all the parties included in the 1971 coalition had the same opportunity to act. The armed forces had clearly identified those they considered antisystem.[21] The reintegration and relegitimation of these proscribed leftists required the support of other members of political society.

At the outset, their reintegration came by proxy extraparty social forces that represented the Left, but also with the support of the opposition factions of the TPs, particularly those of the Colorados. The Colorados could not go it alone; the participation of the Left was necessary for the legitimation of the democratic regime.

This required the Left to assume the democratic discourse in full, which was a relatively easy step for intellectuals and party elites but not an entirely easy one for activists and cadre. The majority of leftist political leaders who could speak publicly before the elections stressed their loyalty to the democratic regime, even to a greater extent than did extraparty leaders. This suggested that they would defend the democratic regime in the future.

The effort toward a "negative integration" of the Left is closely linked to the democratic discourse. The image presented by the Left and its setting in the political spectrum stress moderation. The most moderate tone is found at the level of party politics and the most radical within extraparty political movements, especially militant unions. Students appear influenced by a nonpartisan, even depoliticized, radicalism. This is a harbinger that some leftist parties will be under strong pressure to be more radical from extraparty leaders who, given the proscription of their parties' leadership, became protagonists during the mobilization and the electoral campaign and have shown a more uncompromising leftist stance in recent times.

Elections as the End of the First Stage of Transition

Institutional Act no. 19 specified that an election would be held at the end of 1984, according to a schedule established previously by the armed forces. Negotiations had led to a *salida* that favored the triumph of moderate forces and a future government that would not depart very radically from the basic policy guidelines of the military regime.

Presupposing that only one TP participated in these negotiations and that most observers assumed the electorate would continue to favor the TPs, the bets for an orderly transition were on the triumph of the party that played the role of *blando* in the *salida*; the Left, which had been the political actor most affected by the dictatorship, was expected to legitimize the agreement and the process of transition with its participation. However, the outcome of the election was the only way to validate such a forecast. The experience of post-Franco Spain and, to a somewhat lesser degree, of post-Malvinas Argentina suggested that the moderate alternative could prevail.

Until the very end of the campaign the Partido Nacional maintained a very hardline stance, but this turned out to be at variance with the centrist tendency of the electorate. Although the Left adopted a moderate stance, this was perceived by the public as *duro*. By contrast, the stance of the Partido Colorado appeared to coincide more with the modal position adopted by the electorate.

ELECTIONS AND DEMOCRATIC INAUGURATIONS

Elections and Their Veils

Traditionally, Uruguayans have considered elections mechanisms of social integration that create legitimacies. These legitimacies may be challenged in a postelection period or rather in an interelection period, but they are considered substantial nonetheless.[22] Voting turnout was very high, particularly in Montevideo, for the general election of November 25, 1984, and reached 95.7 percent of the resident population.[23] Julio María Sanguinetti, of the Partido Colorado, was elected president. Sanguinetti was sworn in as president in March 1985. However, due to the peculiarities of the Uruguayan electoral system, the results are somewhat more complex because winners and losers finally have to collaborate in order for the government to function. One must take this into consideration in order to evaluate the outcome of the election, which requires an analysis at different levels of the system.

The Results at the *Lema* Level

According to electoral legislation, the main election is the one at the presidential level for it determines the possibilities of accumulation of votes among the different factions within the parties. The three competitors were the Colorado and the Blanco parties, and the Frente Amplio coalition under the *lema* Partido Demócrata Cristiano (Christian Democratic party, or PDC). The first two were the only ones with any chance to win the national election, whereas the Frente had a considerable opportunity to win the *intendencia* (municipality) of Montevideo, where one-half the population lives. Basically the 1971 scheme of two-and-one-half parties was repeated. But despite the basic outcome of TP restoration, the similarities with 1971 were more apparent than real. Time had introduced important changes.

The Partido Colorado won the election at the national level with 40.2 percent of the vote, practically the same percentage as in 1971 (40.96 percent); the Partido Nacional received 34.2 percent and the Frente, 21.2 percent. If the increase in the number of voters is taken into account, the Colorado victory was not entirely satisfactory. Although Colorado votes were 13 percent greater than in 1971, those of the Frente Amplio increased by 34 percent. The votes of the Partido Nacional decreased by 1.20 percent as the Blancos generally fared badly. They fell below their 40.1 percent of the vote in 1971. They had not polled less than 35 percent since 1954. The Frente Amplio had received 18.3 percent in 1971 (see Table 7.1).

Sanguinetti was elected with 29.3 percent of the presidential vote—the most decisive triumph for a president in recent years. Nevertheless, the

TABLE 7.1
Results of the General Election of November 25, 1984

Presidential Ticket	Senatorial Ticket	Listas	Uruguay	Montevideo	Rest of the Country
Sanguinetti-Tarigo	Sanguinetti (Cigluitti)				
	Tarigo	15+85	458,807	160,631	298,176
	Flores Silva	89	72,502	41,817	30,685
	Singer		31,296	11,486	19,810
	Vasconcellos		25,920	20,018	5,902
	Subtotal		588,525	233,952	348,671
Pacheco-Pirán	Jude		170,796	75,855	94,941
	Silveira	723	12,792	7,615	5,177
	Subtotal		183,588	83,470	100,118
	Totals for Colorado Party		772,113	317,422	448,789
Zumarán-Aguirre	Pereyra		428,776	176,460	252,316
	Lacalle		117,597	48,812	68,785
	Garat		14,121	1,448	12,673
	Subtotal		560,494	226,720	333,774
Ortiz-Paysée	Ortiz		76,014	5,278	70,736
	Paysée		21,903	6,549	15,354
	Subtotal		97,917	11,827	86,090
	Totals for National Party		658,411	238,547	419,864
Crottogini-D'Elia	Batalla	99	157,808	128,805	29,003
	Cardozo (P.S.)		61,278	41,417	19,861
	PS + 99		219,086	170,222	48,864
	Araujo (Democracia Avanzada	1001	113,116	83,491	29,625
	Young (Democracia Cristiana)	808	39,203	22,170	17,033
	Roballo (IDI)		26,783	21,341	5,442
	Totals for Frente Amplio		617,274	467,446	149,828

Sources: Reproduced from Juan Rial, Uruguay: Elecciones de 1984, Un Triunfo del Centro (Montevideo: Ediciones de la Banda Oriental, 1985), Anexo 2, pp. 65-66; from Uruguay, Corte Electoral.

president cannot count on the automatic support of his party's delegation in Congress, which got there with 41 percent of the parliamentary vote. In addition, the Partido Colorado would not have won the elections without the 183,000 votes received by former president Jorge Pacheco Areco, who was also a Colorado candidate for the presidency. Finally, some 23 percent of the Colorado votes came from the right wing of the party, which was identified strongly with the dictatorship.

The Partido Nacional had the same scheme as in 1971. Its present right wing fared very badly. Candidates Dardo Ortiz and Juan Carlos Paysée barely received 100,000 votes, whereas Wilson Ferreira, the "vicar" incarcerated during the election, had 530,000 votes. Alberto Zumarán obtained 83 percent of the total Blanco votes for president, a categorical majority that is much larger than the one obtained by Sanguinetti in his own party.

There were sizable internal changes in the Frente Amplio. It had to gain new voters because it assumed that many emigrants outside Uruguay were *frenteamplistas*. The result of the election showed that the Frente had some success. It registered a small (5.57 percent) increase in its 1984 vote compared to 1971.

In terms of parliamentary positions, the second election for senators and representatives, which took place at the same time, produced a situation dangerously similar to that of 1971. The Colorados won exactly the same number of senators (thirteen); the *frenteamplistas* won one more (six); and the Nationalists won one less (eleven). There are now forty-one Colorado representatives (same as in 1971); thirty-five Nationalists (there were forty in 1971); twenty-one *frenteamplistas* (versus eighteen in 1971); and two from the Unión Cívica, a small party with no representatives in 1971. These similarities in congressional representation mask some important changes in the internal composition of the parties.

The Results at the *Sublema* Level

The *sublema* is the legal name of a party faction but not the only recognized one. There are others at the level of *hojas de votación* (ballots) that are identified with a number or a letter; these sectors commonly are called *listas*. Each of these levels is taken into consideration in the accumulation process. In this analysis, I will aggregate the votes by *sublemas* according to the linkages between the *hojas de votación* and national leaders and voting groups. For example, Sanguinetti got 75 percent of the Colorado vote, but within the spectrum covered by that vote there were several alternatives that, starting from the center, were meant to catch voters from center-left and center-right. When we break this down in terms of parliamentary representation we see that Lista 15, which gave Sanguinetti its strongest support, had 44 percent of the party vote. A new sector, Lista 85, led by Enrique Tarigo, Sanguinetti's running mate, got 17 percent. The old Pacheco sector, which had twenty-eight representatives in 1971, got five with 24 percent of the party vote. A traditional clientelistic sector and a new sector of the left, the Corriente Batllista Independiente, got two representatives each. In the Senate six of the thirteen Colorados belong to Lista 15, three to the Tarigo sector, three to the Pacheco sector, and one to an old clientele leader.

Both the Manuel Flores Silva (CBI) and the Tarigo (Lista 85) *sublemas* are new in the party. They received votes from old sectors, especially from Lista 15 which in turn received votes from the Pacheco sector. In Lista 15 there was a dispute between Batlle and Sanguinetti, with the balance in favor of the latter. Sanguinetti tried to appear as the unifying force of all the Batllista sectors opposed to Pacheco. As a whole, the party also had a large number of votes from people who had voted from the Partido Nacional in 1971.

In the Partido Nacional, the 1971 tendency was confirmed overwhelmingly as the sector led by Wilson Ferreira had an absolute majority within the party. However, this overlooks the fact that the strong nucleus of the Wilsonista leadership, the Por la Patria sector has practically the same representation. In 1971 there were twenty-one, and one more representative was added after being elected by another sector. The right wing of the Partido Nacional apparently transferred some votes to the sector of Luis Alberto Lacalle of the Consejo Nacional Herrerista (National Herrerista Council), but many voters defected from the party, presumably to the Partido Colorado. In turn, the Movimiento de Rocha (Rocha Movement), the most moderate sector, won relatively more votes than the one led directly by Ferreira. The most left-wing sector of the party, the Corriente Popular Nacionalista (Popular Nationalist Current), which did not register its votes separately because it was included in the lista Por la Patria, had one representative. Changes seem to be less obvious here, but we must bear in mind the strong shifting of politicians from one sector to the other, the high attrition of leaders, and the strong internal renovation even in groups that seem to have a similar representation such as Por la Patria and Movimiento de Rocha, despite considerable internal renovation.

In the Frente Amplio, despite a parliamentary representation of similar magnitude to that of 1971, changes were obscured by overall results. The strong shift of the Frente toward the center is palpable, due especially to the vote of the group identified by *hoja de votación* number 99, Por el Gobierno del Pueblo, now led by Hugo Batalla, the successor of the murdered Zelmar Michelini. Batalla was the defense counsel for Líber Seregni during his imprisonment. This change came with a new electorate whereas old factions, such as the PDC, suffered a predictable disaster. The Partido Comunista had to present both allies and nonconfessed Communists and registered a slight percentage decrease in the election. In 1971 the FIDEL had 6.13 percent of the vote. In 1984 Democracia Avanzada (Advanced Democracy) had 5.70 percent, despite an increase of approximately 8 percent in the votes received. However, the most interesting aspect of the vote of the Frente is the persistence of its national distribution. In 1971 the Frente got some 33 percent of the vote in Montevideo and 32 percent in the rest of the country; in 1984 it got 27.7 percent in Montevideo and 29.6 percent in the rest of the country.

The Partido Socialista had a strong increase, but we must bear in mind that it had a small electorate in 1971. The PDC suffered a strong deterioration due to changes in the international Christian Democratic movement; its decline in Latin America; the fact that Uruguay is one of the few places where Christian Democrats are still allied with leftist forces (the other being Ecuador); and hesitation (the PDC left the Frente and reentered it in February 1984, thereby causing an internal division that led to the resignations of all the old leaders, led by Juan Pablo Terra). The Unión Cívica, and old Social Christian conservative group, had more votes than the Christian Democratic sector (Democracia Cristiana, or DC) of the Frente, which indicated a considerable change in the electorate of that sector. The few but firm votes of the new DC suggest the emergence of a new sector.

The "old current" identified with the radical anticommunist Left of 1968 and 1971 was divided. Some voted for the Izquierda Democrática Independiente (Independent Democratic Left, or IDI) but others voted for the Socialists and many more for Lista 99. With only 6.7 percent of the Frente vote, IDI had a very meager result suggesting a complete loss of the vote of the late Enrique Erro. The Por la Victoria del Pueblo (For the People's Victory, or PVP) and the GAU did not make much of an effort to improve the electoral fortunes of the Frente. Finally, the Lista 99 was the recipient, and a passive one at that, of the independent *frenteamplista* vote. This is more a current of opinion than a militant group, with a lovable although not charismatic leader—Hugo Batalla. The Lista 99 was the last option for those who had a moderate position and who wanted to reconstitute the system once again but without the verticalism of party machines. This was a vote similar to those of traditional parties where there are no highly disciplined cadres.

The Unión Cívica had two representatives. Its importance, however, is considerably larger because it is a pressure group rather than a party and a nucleus of high-level conservatives where Sanguinetti recruited collaborators for his own cabinet and for public entities.

A Centrist Vote

In analyzing the vote in Montevideo, a center of decisionmaking in a macrocephalic country, one detects a pattern of winners and losers favoring those who moved toward the center and punishing those who moved away from it. In aggregating the *hojas de votación* independently of their respective parties and taking into consideration the ideological and programmatic positions of the candidates, one finds that the majority of the electorate in Montevideo opted for the center (see Table 7.2). This result had been forecasted by preelection surveys that had explored the ideological leanings of the electorate.

In September 1984 Gallup Uruguay had estimated that some 16 percent of the electorate identified with the Right and 24 percent with the Left. Among those who liked the Partido Colorado, only 5 percent considered themselves leftists, whereas in the Partido Nacional they were 14 percent

TABLE 7.2
Ideological Leanings Among Montevideo Voters (according to the *hojas de votación*)

	Right			Center-Right			Center-Left			Left		
		Percentages			Percentages			Percentages			Percentages	
	Votes	(1)	(2)	Votes	(1)	(2)	Votes	(1)	(2)	Votes	(1)	(2)
Colorados	101.8	92.1	32.1	174.7	57.4	55.1	40.3	14.2	12.7	--	--	--
Blancos	8.8	7.9	3.8	129.6	42.6	56.2	92.1	32.5	39.9	--	--	--
Frenteamplistas	--	--	--		--	--	150.9	53.3	51.5	142.1	100.0	48.5
Total	110.6	100.0	13.1	304.3	100.0	36.2	283.3	100.0	33.7	142.1	100.0	16.9

Note: Votes in thousands. (1)= percent, position; (2)= percent, party.

Source: Uruguay, Corte Electoral, preliminary scrutiny.

and 69 percent in the Frente Amplio. Among those self-identified as Colorados, some 28 percent were rightists, compared to about 20 percent of their Nationalist counterparts. A majority of the 65 percent of the Colorados defined themselves as centrist, compared to 66 percent of the Blancos and 31 percent of the *frenteamplistas*. A EQUIPOS survey conducted two weeks before the election in Montevideo confirmed the centrist tendency of the electorate. Interviewees had to place themselves on a ten-point scale running from extreme Left (one) to extreme Right (ten). The results for the 308 valid cases in the analysis (76 persons refused to answer) showed about 25 percent of them on the Left (values between 1 and 3); 62 percent on the Center (values between 4 and 7); and 13 percent of the Right (8 and greater). The sample average reported in the study was 4.89, or slightly to the center-left. The study reported a relationship between years of formal education and ideological self-placement, with the averages for individuals with similar levels of education fluctuating as follows: 6.29 for those with less than the sixth grade; 4.64 for those with a secondary education; and 4.11 for those with more than thirteen years of formal education. In essence, the survey shows a center self-identification of the electorate in Montevideo, which presumably could not be very different in the rest of the country given the traditional tendency to the Right outside the capital.

My reading of this evidence is that from this moderate position citizens voted for "political goods" rather than for socioeconomic change. The election was a mechanism of legitimation of a social integration attained previously. In this case, integration presupposed an elite agreement, more specifically, the Pacto del Club Naval of August 1984, which allowed for a *salida* to the authoritarian crisis. Basically, the election of 1984 ratified this agreement between military and political moderates. The Pacto and the possibility of creating a transitional government were the initial topics of the political campaign. The majority faction of the Partido Nacional miscalculated very badly when as part of its electoral strategy it denounced the agreement.

The 1984 vote was a vote for moderation, pacification, and democracy, as exemplified by the Sanguinetti campaign slogan: "a change in peace." The voters also were motivated by fear: fear of recreating a disequilibrium that could make the new democracy ungovernable soon after its installation; fear from the bulk of an aging population longing to return to a "better yesterday" in a viable "tomorrow"; fear of returning to an arbitrary, repressive regime; and fear of fear, all of which led to a preference for centrist options. This preference expressed itself clearly in the election. Many of those who in 1973 had an extreme Left position supporting different types of radical actions now defended moderate positions. Many who had espoused an extreme Right view abandoned it for a centrist one. Very few dared to be marked by the stigma of defending the military regime. Many candidates who had taken part in the regime or who once favored it distanced themselves as much as possible, anticipating that failure to do so would be penalized by the voters.

The Center had two key connotations. The first one was substantive and palpable in the discourse of a large number of the members of the political class who resorted openly or subliminally to social-democratic metaphors. In his acceptance speech, Julio María Sanguinetti suggested that in Europe people call social democracy what in Uruguay is known as *Batllismo*. Wilson Ferreira was careful not to assume this position openly, but his program was clearly reformist, and he was fully in contact with international social democracy. In the Frente Amplio, the trend toward the right—that is, to the center of the political spectrum—was led by Líber Seregni from the very first day he came out of prison. Shortly before the election, a meeting of the Socialist International was held in Rio de Janeiro, where the three leaders of the parties were invited: Seregni for the Frente, Zumarán for the Partido Nacional, and Sanguinetti for the Partido Colorado. To a certain extent they all wanted to be Social Democrats.[24]

The second connotation was a pragmatic partisan attempt at sweeping votes starting from the Center. The most effective sweep was achieved by the winner, the Partido Colorado, which was anchored by a strong vote from the Center and then received votes from the Right; and many from the Left identified with the senatorial candidacy of Manuel Flores Silva. In the Partido Nacional the trend was more to the left, whereas the trend to the right in the Frente meant success for Hugo Batalla and his faction in Lista 99.

The EQUIPOS survey shows that a centrist self-identification predominated among Colorados and Nacionalistas and that it was very high in the Frente. Although identification with the Left predominated in the Frente, at the time of the election, however, the tendency was more to the center-left. Considering the age of those surveyed by EQUIPOS, the Center predominated in all cohorts as the prevalent tendency similar to the modal center-left. The frequency of a leftist self-identification decreased with age, except among those aged fifty to fifty-nine whose childhood was during World War II and whose adolescence was in the happy Uruguay of the 1950s.

Rational, *Pertenencia*, and Clientele Votes

Voting results at the national level and in the main department, Montevideo, show the strong stability of vote distribution compared to the situation prior to the 1971 coup. This suggests that party efforts at restoration were quite successful and that at the end of an authoritarian interlude the same party configurations tend to reappear.

Nevertheless, despite some changes, the electoral legislation in force is essentially the same. At the aggregate level this can obscure changes in the way parties are perceived. For example, the Uruguayan TPs, protected and encouraged by voting accumulation mechanisms, seek and accept extremely diverse currents; the Frente Amplio utilized this mechanism to become an electoral coalition. This was clearly recognized by the negotiators of the Pacto del Club Naval and previously in the by-laws of political parties. When these by-laws were approved in 1981, the rules that operated to benefit the TPs through the accumulation mechanisms were kept, despite an attempt to rationalize and reduce factions.

Fundamental Law no. 2, amended by Law no. 4 and by Institutional Act no. 18, reversed those changes, thereby making fragmentation possible once again. Nevertheless, it must be pointed out that the emergent post-authoritarian system of parties was notoriously less fragmented than its predecessor. This is verifiable first by the fewer number of *hojas de votación* presented finally and by voters avoiding fragmentation, especially in Montevideo, by supporting only a limited number of *hojas*. This also must be analyzed in relation to the clientele problem. The Frente Amplio in its turn negotiated under the condition that its legalization be within the normal legal framework and allow each political force of the coalition to count its votes separately. This was incorporated in Institutional Act no. 18. Consequently, electoral rules did have an influence on the transition and the liberalization even though they appeared to have been put in place during the campaign for ostensibly restorationist purposes.

Clientelism was minimized in the emerging configuration, at least the traditional and somewhat patrimonialist clientelism. The traditional boss who acted as intermediary between the state and the individual in exchange for the vote may have suffered a serious setback, at least in the capital. There was nothing much to offer in 1984 so it is safe to say that the more traditional forms of clientelism were in dire straits.[25] The impact of clientelism on electoral choices may be gauged indirectly by voting intention and by the influence of primary reference groups on voting intention.

A postelectoral survey made by Gallup shows that the majority of the electorate in Montevideo already had decided how to vote some time before the election. According to this survey, a full 75 percent of Montevideo voters had made up their minds "many months before the election"; while 16 percent did so "a couple of months before"; and only 6 and 2 percent made up their minds "during the last week" or "on election day" respectively. One percent of the sample did not answer this question.

Although the margin of error was relatively high in this survey—between 7.5 and 12.5 percent—the percentages still suggest that the electorate may have been guided primarily by traditional party loyalties that foster a sense of *pertenencia*—that is, of identification with the party. This would not preclude some voters changing or making up their minds at the last moment in favor of the Partido Colorado. According to the same Gallup survey, the outcome of the election in Montevideo was decided in this fashion because the difference between the Partido Colorado and the Frente Amplio was only 2.28 percentage points. Given the fact that the Frente was authorized to take part in the election in August—that is, only three months before—*pertenencia* appears like a more potent force behind the vote of this coalition. In sum, *pertenencia* has to be included as a significant factor among the determinants of the vote.

The impact of reference groups was gauged by a different battery of questions in the Gallup survey including: "Did you vote the same sector as your family?" (yes, 65 percent); "did you vote the same sector as the majority of your friends?" (yes, 49 percent; no, 39 percent; and 13 percent did not know); "did you vote the same sector as your workmates or fellow students?" (yes, 34 percent). These questions arise from the assumption that socialization in the family group or among peers, especially friends and mates, is important in determining voting intention. The survey confirmed a pattern of voting intention shaped not only by traditional electoral rules and by new clientele forms but by substantial ideological influences.[26]

Electoral Triumph and Political Uncertainty

The electoral campaign, the transition process, the liberalization process, and a dispute about real power in civil society overlapped and finally led to the triumph of the Partido Colorado. In Montevideo this party is supported mainly by old rather than by young people, by inactive rather than by active people, and by social sectors that adhere more strongly to a conservative ideology. Although this profile is somewhat exaggerated, it does contrast with that of the Frente Amplio, whose support comes from young and more educated people and industrial as well as salaried workers.

The overlapping processes favored a moderate *salida* from the dictatorship. Was this a solution? Were there really any winners? Is this the way to consolidate a democratic regime?

The fact that Sanguinetti won the election, even by a very high percentage (according to Uruguayan standards), does not hide the fact that he does not have a majority in Parliament. Moreover, parties continue to be fragmented, and the dispute about real power could lead to the return of forces that can veto each other and make government impossible. Also, a certain degree of "mass praetorianism" has reappeared, which is a result of constant conflicts in the labor sector.

What did the electorate intend? Evidently, Uruguayans did not vote exclusively for "political goods" on election day. The week before election day the same EQUIPOS survey asked, "Do you think that the next

TABLE 7.3
Policy Preferences of Montevideo Voters, November 1984 (in percentage)[a]

Policy Emphasis[b]	Colorados	Blancos	Frenteamplistas	All
Liberty and salaries	51.4	56.5	74.8	61.6
Salaries	42.1	37.0	17.8	31.3
Liberties	2.8	4.3	6.7	4.7
Does not know/no answer	3.7	2.2	0.7	2.4

[a]n= 380.

[b]Question: "Do you think that the next government should be more concerned with ensuring liberties and rights or with improving employment and salary levels?"

Source: EQUIPOS survey, Montevideo, November 1984.

government should be more concerned with ensuring liberties and rights or with improvement employment and salary levels?" The answers presented in Table 7.3 suggest that the bulk of the electorate opted for both "political" and "economic goods"—that is, for a democracy with both substantive and formal contents. Many Colorados and Blancos emphasized economic (substantive) democracy over a formal democracy. Although this does not bode well for governability, it does not necessarily translate into a threat against "formal" democracy, given the high level of support for the defense of political liberties.

To win an election under circumstances that previously did not ensure governability, but presently indicate that the possibility of blackmail by adversaries is high, in a notoriously complicated, conflictive political arena, underlines the caveat that one electoral triumph does not a democracy consolidate. But it is hard to imagine the recent democratic installation in Uruguay without the electoral campaign of 1980–1984.

RECAPITULATION

Although Uruguay is a country of long democratic tradition and a high degree of consensus, the 1973 coup could not be avoided. Is it possible to avoid the repetition of the conditions that favored an authoritarian regime? The possibilities are very few. The current international economic situation is not evolving so that Uruguay's share of the international markets on which it depends will be secure. It is not clear that a ruling class faction has a project for itself and for society that is consistent with the recently renovated and restored political community.

The most intriguing aspect of Uruguay's democratic crisis and restoration is that this is not a society where claims come from the need to enlarge citizenship. Political citizenship as a problem was resolved in the early 1900s. Social citizenship was extended an "anticipatory" and "consensual" type of development, so that in the postwar period, the majority of the social sectors took part in the redistribution of income, assistance, and state promotion services. There are no new sectors to be included, as in the majority of Latin American countries. However, there is a search for a restoration of social citizenship, so that the patterns of income distribution that ensure democratic stability can be regained.

Today, the political society and the parties face the need to reach consensus once again and to rebuild political legitimacy for a democratic regime under circumstances that surely can satisfy past social demands. Political restoration hardly can be successful unless there is a social restoration. The alternative could be an undesired repetition of the conflict of 1973 that led to dictatorship. The election of 1984 provided a *salida* for the transition process, but it cannot assure a consolidation.

NOTES

The author wishes to acknowledge the support of the Friedrich Ebert Stiftung, Federal Republic of Germany; the International Development Research Center, Canada; and the Swedish Agency for Research and Cooperation.

1. Installation is the conventional formal date of the starting point of a new regime. Inauguration is produced when decisions are reached in order to implement a new political, social, or economic model opposed to the existing one.

2. For a more detailed discussion of the crisis leading to the coup and of its possible interpretations, see Juan Rial, *Partidos Políticos, Democracia y Autoritarismo, II* (Montevideo: Ediciones de la Banda Oriental, 1984), pp. 7–47.

3. "Suspended" is used here in the ironic sense utilized by Charles Gillespie in "From Suspended Animation to Animated Suspension, Political Parties and the Reconstruction of Democracy in Uruguay," Centro de Informaciones y Estudios del Uruguay (CIESU), *Documento de Trabajo no. 94* (1985).

4. For some of the more relevant documents concerning the installation and inauguration of the military regime, see Uruguay, Junta de Comandantes en Jefe, *Las Fuerzas Armadas al Pueblo Oriental, I. La Subversión*, and *II. El Proceso Político* (Montevideo: 1978).

5. *Democradura* is literally a hard democracy. The term was introduced by Philippe C. Schmitter in "The Portugalization of Brazil?" in Alfred Stepan (ed.), *Authoritarian Brazil* (New Haven, Conn.: Yale University Press, 1973), pp. 185–186.

6. For a discussion of these styles of development, see Jeremy Richardson (ed.), *Policy Styles in Western Europe* (Winchester, Mass.: Allen and Unwin, 1982).

7. In Uruguay a *lema* is a party label—for example, the Colorado and Nacional (Blanco) labels of the traditional parties. *Sublemas* are party factions that under the traditional electoral statutes of Uruguay can present their own candidates for president. The Corriente Batllista Independiente, the Lista 15, and the Lista 85 emerged from the transition as the most important factions of the Colorados, while the Por la Patria, Movimiento de Rocha, and the Consejo Nacional Herrerista appeared the more robust of the Blancos after the 1984 elections; and the Lista 99 and the Democracia Avanzada fared best among the Frente Amplio factions in those elections. The interesting and complicating twist is that under the law voters can elect as president the most-voted *sublema* candidate of the most-voted *lema*. For more details, see Juan Rial, "Elecciones: Reglas de juego y tendencias," *Historia y Política*, Cuaderno no. 3 (November 1984): 13–26.

8. In 1972 Batlle had a confrontation with the military that compromised his chances as a transition candidate.

9. *El Día*, November 20, 1982, p. 8.

10. See Juan María Bordaberry, *Las opciones* (Montevideo: 1980).

11. "Adherents" is translated literally because Uruguayan political parties do not have affiliates. They are catch-all parties, with a very flexible framework for their electorate. Attempts to impose a more rigid organization upon them always have been rejected.

12. On April 4, 1984, there were only 25,658 party affiliates, or 1.17 percent of the citizenship. Some 14,471 belonged to the Partido Colorado; 9,957 to the Partido Nacional; and 1,230 to the Unión Cívica. *Búsqueda*, April 11, 1984.

13. I am referring to Estatutos de los Partidos Políticos, Ley Fundamental no. 2, passed on June 7, 1982; amended in April 1984; and amended by Institutional Act no. 18 in August 1984. In actual practice the statute had become obsolete before its formal derogation in 1985.

14. See Carina Perelli, "25 de Noviembre: Los programas partidarios: Análisis y comparación," *Historia y política*, Cuaderno no. 4 (November 1984).

15. This is the name given to the negotiated agreement between military commandants on behalf of the armed forces and the leaders of the Partido Colorado, the Frente Amplio (legalized during the negotiation), and the Unión Cívica. Following this negotiation the military issued Institutional Act no. 19, which appeared to set forth the implementation of the terms of the agreement.

16. These were, for the most part, provisions for military promotions and for exceptional powers to deal with actions by subversive groups. Article 6 of the act established that, beginning in March 1985 the constitution of 1967 would be in effect incorporating these changes as "transitional" amendments. See Juan Rial, "Las reglas del juego electoral en el Uruguay y sus implicancias," CIESU, *Documento de Trabajo*, no. 85 (1985), note 1, p. i.

17. The Multipartidaria stopped working with all its members during the negotiations leading to the Pacto del Club Naval because the Partido Nacional did not take part. I have examined the activities of these coalitions in more detail in Juan Rial, "Concertación y gubernabilidad: Proyecto, acuerdo político, y pacto social: La reciente experiencia uruguaya." CIESU, *Documento de Trabajo* (1985).

18. See Luis E. González, "Political Parties and Redemocratization in Uruguay," CIESU, *Documento de Trabajo*, no. 83 (1984); and Alberto Pérez Pérez, *La Ley de Lemas* (Montevideo: FCU, 1970).

19. In June 1983 the Instituto Uruguayo Gallup de Opinión Pública asked respondents in a national sample whether they thought that the elections of November 1984 would be a very important step toward democracy. About 76 percent said that they would be very important; an additional 11 percent described them as important. *Indice Gallup de Opinión Pública*, no 335, Table 12.

20. The Partido Colorado approved its Program of Principles on December 17, 1983, that reiterated the *batllista* model of 1925. The shorter declaration of principles of the Partido Nacional was approved on the same date. It coincides with the tenets of Colorado statism but emphasizes the defense of public liberties. However, the most *batllista* of all programs was that of the Frente Amplio. See Perelli, *op. cit.*; and also her "Transtextualidad e intertextualidad en los programas," CIESU, *Documento de Trabajo*, no. 119 (1985).

21. This designation included Marxist-Leninist parties such as the Communist party; and those considered maximalist or violent such as the Grupos de Acción Unificadora (GAU); Movimiento 26 de Marzo, legal spokesman for the *tupamaros* until 1973; or the recently created Partido por la Victoria del Pueblo (PVP).

22. More on this can be found in César Aguiar, *Uruguay, País de Emigración* (Montevideo: Ediciones de la Banda Oriental, 1982).

23. Juan Rial, *Uruguay: Elecciones de 1984, Un triunfo del Centro* (Montevideo: Ediciones de la Banda Oriental, 1985), p. 8.

24. See Carina Perelli and Juan Rial, "El discreto encanto de la socialdemocracia," *Nueva Sociedad* (Caracas), no. 77 (May-June 1985): 147–153.

25. This, to be sure, does not imply that other, more sophisticated forms of clientelism linked to the official bureaucracy and even to the armed forces, disappeared as well. Several retired officers formed or headed some of the lists in favor of Pacheco Areco in the 1984 election. See *Búsqueda*, December 12, 1984, p. 7.

26. Gallup data reported in *Búsqueda*, December 27, 1984, p. 27.

PART THREE

ON GOVERNABILITY

8
ARGENTINA: POLITICAL TRANSITION AND INSTITUTIONAL WEAKNESS IN COMPARATIVE PERSPECTIVE

Waldino C. Suárez

Political institutions in contemporary Argentina are notoriously fragile. The nation's success at political consolidation ranks among the lowest in Latin America. Argentina has experienced eleven regime breakdowns since 1930, and since World War II its political system has not been able to complete a full decade without undergoing a change of regime. This certainly defines a major component of the instability syndrome that has haunted Argentina for so long.

Unlike some recent, well-known examples of regime change in Latin America and Southern Europe, Argentina has been living in a state of transition for several decades. Such a distinction, it will be argued, is crucial for a proper evaluation of the current Argentine transition to democracy. The country's problems and resources are different from those affecting countries that replaced a consolidated regime with another that was able to assert itself as a new, established political order. This is not the case of Argentina. The recent return to democratic rule represents the sixth attempt at civilianizing the political system and the third time in the last fifty years this is done without resorting to a major proscription. Not surprisingly, everybody seems aware of this novelty: the public, politicians, and academics. Their interest in the subject recently has increased.

The issue of democratic consolidation has gained new political significance, as shown by the electoral campaign of 1983. Politicians are very inclined to stress the importance of putting a definite end to constitutional-military cycles; and quite a few academics have been concerned with examining some of the causes and consequences of this sequence of failed transitions. The existing body of research is growing and varied. Some scholars have favored a culturally oriented approach.[1] Several others have sought a contextual explanation of this phenomenon.[2] Everyone, I believe, shares the feeling that a comprehensive evaluation of Argentine politics is not possible unless one is also in a position to account for the causes and consequences of the absence of a consolidated regime.

Some recent historic events are responsible for this belated increase in the amount of research undertaken on this topic. First, few military regimes have come as close to consolidating an authoritarian political order as in the past two decades. The mean duration of these regimes has lengthened in inverse proportion to the life of constitutional regimes. Argentina moved from a predominantly, although interrupted, constitutional period between 1930 and 1966 to a predominantly authoritarian situation with one brief civilian spell since that date. The military nearly managed to devise a workable succession mechanism in the late 1970s, which could have prolonged its grip on the country considerably. This fell through in the end but certainly represented an "improvement" on previous experiences.

Second, the heritage of authoritarianism has never been so painfully clear before. Argentina is trying to leave behind a period of violence and socioeconomic crisis without precedent; one would have to go far back in the history of the country to find a situation as politically disruptive as today. In addition, contemporary authoritarian regimes have modified the socioeconomic profile of Argentina far more profoundly than did earlier military governments.[3]

Third, the regional dimension also has to be taken into account. The effects of international factors on institutional cycles of Argentine politics has never been perceived so widely. This has been triggered by sustained military rule in Argentina and by the very strong wave of authoritarianism that swept the region during the 1970s (which also is coming to an end in several other countries).[4] These events dramatize the dangers involved in not having consolidated the democratic regime in the country as well as the importance of securing it now. The result is a healthy renewal of interest in the study of political consolidation in general and the feasibility of democracy in particular among specialists in Argentine politics, at home and abroad.[5]

THE INSTITUTIONAL APPROACH

The state of the art is far less satisfactory than the size of the burgeoning literature would suggest. Major shortcomings in the way this subject matter has been approached have prevented research from advancing further and from offering practical information to decisionmakers on how best to proceed at the very outset of a democratic experience.

My first criticism is methodological. There is an insufficient amount of solid empirical work that tests the accuracy of currently held generalizations about Argentine politics. Some often are evaluated in the light of fragmented and clearly insufficient information. There is also a need for a more systematic utilization of the comparative method. There are many factors influencing a process of political transition, some of which can be observed only from a comparative perspective.[6]

My second criticism is substantive. The study of Argentine politics still suffers rather acutely from what R. Macridis described as "inputism" (nonpolitical explanations of politics) some time ago.[7] This is not a matter of underestimating the importance of contextual variables. I simply want to acknowledge the existence of some problems linked to a tradition that has systematically understated, even neglected, the relevance of political structures and institutional design.[8]

Both traditions reinforce each other rather strongly. The dearth of research on political institutions weakens the urgency for more systematic comparisons. The structure of complex organizations has provided one of the most fertile fields for comparative analyses since the mid-1970s. However, an excessive concentration of efforts on a reduced, unrepresentative, somewhat randomly chosen set of case studies is not very likely to provide enough incentives for the widening of the universe of analysis, over time and cross-nationally.[9]

In a sense, these two traits highlight the existence of a paradox that is not so easy to explain. The importance of creating the necessary conditions for the consolidation of a democratic order have been acknowledged repeatedly, but we have not treated systematically enough some of the core dimensions of this same problem. We lose sight of the fact that regime breakdowns are situations in which a country's leading institutions are incapable of coping with existing conflicts; these breakdowns posit extreme cases of "overload."[10]

To be sure, it is necessary to explore the origins and profiles of such conflicts, the internal and international environments that exacerbate them, and scores of other, related contextual variables. But it is equally important to have a satisfactory knowledge of the political mechanisms employed in order to cope with them in a given situation as well as to choose other alternative modes. Otherwise, it does not seem likely that we shall ever be in a position to identify the main causes of regime breakdown or the type of practices most likely to be valued in a particular political order.

This is exactly what happened in Argentina. For example, we have not studied systematically which party system is the most appropriate for the country or what the best way is of securing a fluid relationship between social structure and political organizations, let alone the case for constitutional reform. Yet these are all pressing problems that demand rather urgent solutions. This is quite unfortunate because it has left unattended numerous important constitutional traits that could be evaluated properly from a performance-oriented, functional perspective.

A possible explanation for this lack may be the relative dominance of approaches that have not placed institutions at the core of their discourse. But this lack also is a function of the inability of political scientists to take the initiative in an issue that, regardless of its substantive importance, has not been considered seriously by Argentine political practitioners. It is very striking to observe, for example, how little energy has been spent by politicians, their advisers, or opinionmakers to work out ways of updating the country's institutional framework in order to secure its viability during an extended period of time. The "resilience" of the Argentine constitution of 1853 is in open contrast to the chronic instability of the Argentine political system in other aspects.[11]

Politicians may have good reasons to pursue a long-term enforcement of a constitution that precludes the modification of much of its contents, especially in a coup-prone country such as Argentina. But the fact remains that this attitude also has prevented decisionmakers from discussing alternative ways of overcoming some serious institutional weaknesses, thereby reducing the prospects for democratic consolidation. Political science should contribute to a public debate on this and related issues, especially when it matters most: during the inaugural stages of a democratic process. Unfortunately, political scientists have failed utterly to do this, leaving the field to more classic constitutionalist scholars.[12]

Summing up, it is very important to undertake a more systematic analysis of the political and institutional factors that have contributed to make regime consolidation more difficult in Argentina and to do so within a comparative framework. Second, we also should evaluate more critically the political formula currently employed by Argentina in its drive to democratic rule. Third, we must place the prolonged transitional period in proper perspective.

The analysis to follow rests on some assumptions that may now be made explicit.

1. Argentina has had an atypical, extended transitional period during which neither authoritarian nor democratic regimes have been consolidated. This absence of an established political order differentiates Argentina from most other Latin American countries, which have had greater, although varying, success at regime consolidation. This is verified by the global comparison of Latin American countries undertaken in this chapter for the 1940–1980 period.

2. The absence of regime consolidation in recent decades has undermined the functional adequacy of the Argentine political system. This state of chronic transition seriously has disrupted the country's political leadership and has disorganized Argentina's leading governmental institutions.

3. The double, negative effect of chronic transitions on Argentina's political life is a function of the varying conceptions of political order intrinsic to the design of political regimes. On the one hand, these conceptions entice individuals into taking up politics on a more or less full-time basis. This has produced higher-than-average dropout rates among leaders, which thus decimates their ranks and muddles working conditions. On the other hand, these conceptions assign profoundly different responsibilities to each one of their governmental institutions, including those whose operations were rarely discontinued by a change of regime: the presidency and the cabinet. Thus, frequent regime changes compel political systems to underwrite costly internal rearrangements that often limit the capacity for action of those structures most affected. This is clearly the case in Argentina.

4. Regime type has a definite impact on political performance; in the short run regime type articulates different interests and affects patterns of governmental and societal stability. In the long run regime type affects a regime's degree of consolidation. Some types of regimes perform very poorly in the long run. This is true for both "classic presidentialism" and "classic militarism" in Latin America. Neither has produced consolidated situations as often as have other types of regimes.

5. The chronic inability of contemporary Argentina to secure a political order is related to the fact that the country is one of the few in Latin America that did break away from these two classic types.

6. The chances for consolidating the recently restored democracy would be enhanced greatly if the political leadership undertook a new institutional design whose objective would be to eliminate the main weaknesses of the current constitutional organization and minimize the legacy of the previous, extended transitional experience.

EXTENDED TRANSITION AND INSTITUTIONAL WEAKNESS

A process of political transition involves some profound changes in the "rules of the game" that regulate the political process. Such situations are referred to here as "change of regime." In such circumstances, a political system typically revises existing mechanisms whereby government officials are appointed, popular participation is regulated, and an institutional network is defined. This is true for military regimes, for parliamentary systems, and for the different types of presidentialism.[13]

To be sure, the choice of regime is a function of demands imposed on the political system by societal changes, the sort of sectoral interests to receive preferential treatment, and myriad related factors. Profound adjustments are costly. They only can be undertaken sporadically—that is, in order to facilitate the responsiveness of the political system to drastic change—and have to be completed fairly quickly. If these conditions are not met satisfactorily, the system will have its operative capabilities weakened and will find it difficult to perform effectively.

Transitions so defined imply the importance and difficulty of dealing with social change and political order simultaneously. Transitions need to adjust a given institutional design to societal changes, and they need to develop some accepted, feasible, easily identifiable bargaining rules and exchange patterns.[14] The dilemma is much more difficult to sort out when such adjustments cannot be undertaken incrementally. Therefore, the effectiveness of a transition process requires that a new political order be consolidated as quickly as possible. Its success is not assured simply by the breakdown of the previous regime.

This problem takes on a new dimension in modern times; it takes longer to get a contemporary institutional network and its officeholders into working shape than at any time in the past. The complexity of meeting societal demands, the cost of failing to do so, and the close relationship between the latter and the handling of political transitions are nowhere clearer than in the analysis of the relationship between political leadership and institutional design. There are other traits that could put the adequacy of a complex structure to the test, but these two are certainly among the most important.

In addition to the substantive elements already mentioned (modern decisionmaking and governmental performance), there are some analytic reasons that further justify the choice made. Sometimes we fail to consider the need for professionalization imposed on political practices by modernity.[15] In this context professionalization has nothing to do with any of the enlightened despotic syndromes so important in the political and ideological debate in Europe some centuries ago; nor does it necessarily vindicate elitist or technocratic conceptions of the political process. This is not an argument in favor of philosopher-kings. The point being made is simply that the division of labor typically associated with modern societies has had as much impact on politics as it has had on economics and other social activities. We must take this into account.

In the economy the units of production are larger, more differentiated internationally, and managed by a growing number of specialists of different sorts. Something similar happens to the role of intermediaries in the realm of politics. As the number and complexity of conflicts have grown, so has the demand for larger political organizations and a more numerous, professional, and fully differentiated political class.

A core proposition of this chapter is that institutions and politicians need the benefit of a stable set of rules during a minimum period of time—a decade or more. When this is not the case, institutions are subject to constant, costly rearrangements, and politicians are not allowed to develop into a well-structured group capable of mediating social conflicts.

POLITICAL TRANSITION AND GOVERNMENTAL INSTITUTIONS

It is not easy to consolidate a regime in Latin America. Typically, a Latin American country changes its regime once every 7.2 years. There have been 140 political regimes between 1940 and 1980. Half did not last forty-eight months; 25.9 failed to survive their first year. They operated uninterruptedly during an extended period (for ten years or more) in only 31 cases.[16] Latin American regimes behave quite differently regarding this aspect of instability. An analysis of these regional trends has a direct bearing on what has been said about Argentina. A change of regime triggers a chain of institutional rearrangements. Some organizations simply are dismantled (like parliaments under most classic military regimes) while others have their roles profoundly modified. The latter is typically the case of the presidency and the cabinet; they perform widely different functions in democratic and authoritarian settings. This forces them into adopting quite different organizational forms in order to operate in each of these circumstances.

Institutional disruptions, such as dismantling a congress, are too obvious to be ignored, but the costs involved in "adjusting" presidentialism to authoritarianism often are underestimated. This point is especially valid for countries such as Argentina, where the organizational effects of extended transitions have virtually devastated the inner organization of the executive branch.[17]

Explanation for this must be sought primarily in the ways various regimes have responded to the political and administrative components of the differentiation imposed by modernity on top governmental institutions. Growing complexity of governmental goals has administrative and political aspects. Each requires longer, more complicated processes of elaboration.[18] Accordingly, an administratively biased regime will tend to favor, ceteris paribus, smaller cabinets than do politically oriented ones. Continued alternation between regimes with administrative or political biases is very likely to produce more intense cyclical rearrangements than would be strictly warranted by more routine changes in public policies.

The main effects of regime breakdowns on pattern of government reorganization may be hypothesized as follows:

1. The procedural profile of a given institution is a function of gross level of differentiation and of the source of its complexity.
2. Administratively oriented differentiation favors verticalization.
3. Whatever the basic pattern of differentiation, its effects are felt more clearly at its inauguration—that is, before the imperatives of policy-making force the pattern to accommodate other sources of complexity.
4. In extended transitional periods regime biases are very likely to produce intense, cyclical government reorganizations that do not necessarily affect the secular, organizational evolution of the state apparatus. This is exactly what happens in Argentina as a result of the repeated alternation of military and constitutional regimes.

This is certainly not the place for a thorough test of these hypotheses. However, we can examine Latin America and Argentina to assess the extent to which governmental institutions are affected by regime breakdowns. By and large, available information tends to confirm my suspicions about the impact of consolidation on institutional development: Reiterated transitions account for a considerable percentage of cyclical governmental reorganization exercises in the twenty countries examined.

There are some interesting correlations between frequency of regime change and consolidation levels and ministerial rearrangement rates. The relationship is too strong to be dismissed as irrelevant. Between 1940 and 1980 a total of 612 ministerial units were affected by successive cabinet reorganizations in twenty Latin American countries (see Table 8.1). Such changes are equivalent to 31.9 times the mean cabinet size of the region, estimated at 12.3 portfolios. It seems as if not only ministerial tenures are short-lived (the average duration of a minister has been 19.4 months during this period) but that ministerial structures also are dismantled easily in Latin America.[19] Some of the tables that follow provide a general panorama of the problem at hand, its major cross-national differences, and the various techniques employed during the implementation of such rearrangements.

A complete explanation of why Latin American governments have spent so much time and energy redesigning their executive branches has to take into account many variables. The first is the expansion of state activities. It has compelled political systems to restructure their top executive offices. It is easy to notice that cabinets have been modified functionally in order to facilitate control of the decisionmaking processes in new policy areas.[20] Tables 8.2 and 8.3 show that quickly expanding policy areas have been rewarded with a faster-than-average increase in the numbers of portfolios. These involve administration, economic policy, and social welfare. In short, states have grown to adjust to the increasing societal complexity.

Second, there are important cross-national differences that are very difficult to explain solely in terms of public policy fluctuations. Otherwise some

TABLE 8.1
Modes and Frequency of Ministerial Reforms Between 1940 and 1980

	Creation		Partition		Expansion		Transfers		Transformation		Merger		Reduction		Elimination		Total	
	G[a]	N[b]	G	N	G	N	G	N	G	N	G	N	G	N	G	N	G	N
Argentina	29	14	7	0	1	0	1	0	0	0	5	0	1	0	30	0	74	14
Bolivia	23	10	2	1	5	1	0	0	1	0	1	0	0	0	17	1	49	13
Brazil	14	12	2	0	0	0	0	0	1	1	0	0	1	1	5	1	23	15
Chile	7	6	0	0	1	0	0	0	1	0	0	0	1	0	1	0	11	6
Colombia	6	4	0	0	0	0	0	0	0	0	0	0	1	1	2	0	9	5
Costa Rica	12	8	1	1	5	0	0	0	3	1	0	0	2	1	5	1	28	12
Cuba	30	16	2	1	0	0	0	0	4	0	0	0	0	0	21	0	57	17
Dom. Rep.	28	13	4	2	0	0	1	0	0	0	2	0	3	0	21	1	59	16
Ecuador	7	5	1	1	4	2	0	0	0	0	0	0	3	0	2	0	17	8
El Salvador	10	8	3	0	3	0	0	0	0	0	0	0	2	0	4	0	22	8
Guatemala	9	6	1	0	0	1	1	0	0	0	1	0	0	0	6	0	18	7
Haiti	17	9	3	1	6	2	15	4	0	0	2	0	9	4	12	2	64	22
Honduras	13	6	3	2	3	0	0	0	1	0	0	0	2	1	9	0	31	9
Mexico	18	12	0	0	0	0	1	0	0	0	2	0	2	0	6	1	29	13
Nicaragua	14	11	0	0	1	1	0	0	1	1	0	0	0	0	5	2	21	15
Panama	8	6	0	0	3	2	3	2	0	0	0	0	3	2	2	0	19	12
Paraguay	7	4	0	0	0	0	1	0	0	0	1	0	3	0	2	0	14	4
Peru	8	8	3	2	7	3	2	0	1	0	2	0	3	0	2	0	28	13
Uruguay	6	4	0	0	2	2	0	0	0	0	1	0	2	0	1	0	12	6
Venezuela	18	16	3	3	2	2	0	0	1	1	0	0	0	0	3	1	27	23
Latin America	284	178	35	14	43	16	25	6	14	4	17	0	38	10	156	10	612	238
Greater than gross total	62.68		40.00		37.21		24.00		28.57		0.00		26.30		6.41		38.88	
Greater than grand total	46.50		5.72		7.03		4.08		2.29		2.78		6.21		25.49			
			28.11															

[a]gross.
[b]net.
Source: Waldino Suárez, "El Gabinete en América Latina: Organización y cambio," *Contribuciones*, no. 1 (1985):50

TABLE 8.2
Interfield Distribution of Portfolios I

Area of Activity	Regional $\bar{x}$	National $\bar{x}$	% Greater than Total	Slope
Global	43.43	2.17	17.58	0.73
Political	53.50	2.67	21.64	0.12
Economic	91.43	4.57	37.03	1.24
Social	58.56	2.93	23.74	0.78

Source: Waldino Suárez, "El Gabinete en América Latina: Organización y Cambio," Contribuciones, no. 1 (1985): 51.

TABLE 8.3
Interfield Distribution of Portfolios II

Area of Activity	Size	Regional $\bar{x}$	National $\bar{x}$	% Greater than Total	Slope
Social welfare	very large	1.84	36.80	15.04	0.03
Finance and Commerce		1.41	28.20	11.53	0.01
Defense		1.25	25.00	10.22	0.00
Administrative	large	1.22	24.40	9.97	0.04
Public works		1.21	24.40	9.89	0.01
Primary sector		1.19	23.80	9.73	0.02
Education		0.99	19.80	8.09	0.01
Foreign affairs	average	0.94	18.80	7.69	0.00
Interior		0.94	18.80	7.69	0.00
Justice		0.50	10.00	4.09	0.01
Industry	small	0.36	7.20	2.94	0.01
Energy		0.26	5.20	2.12	0.01
Social Services		0.12	2.40	0.98	0.01

Source: Waldino Suárez, "El gabinete en América Latina: Organización y cambio," Contribuciones, no. 1 (1985): 51.

small, not very rapidly developing countries, such as Haiti, the Dominican Republic, and Bolivia, would appear to have imposed on their public sector a faster growing, functional load than have Brazil, Venezuela, and even Cuba. At best, this is not easy to demonstrate empirically.

Third, there is a very strong correlation between cabinet expansions (creation of ministerial units) and reduction rates. This is certainly the case in countries that have subjected their cabinets to the most intense reorganizations in the region. Such unstructured patterns rarely have followed the more linear evolution of public spending. Argentina is an extreme example of this; it has experienced the most intense cabinet reorganization in the region. It has created, modified, and dismantled seventy-four ministerial units. It enacted some of the most sweeping, drastic reductions in the number of portfolios. For example, in 1966, after a drastic overhaul by the incoming military regime, only five ministries were left. Thus, Argentina provides an excellent case study for analyzing this problem.[21]

Fourth, there is a very interesting inverse relationship between cyclical changes (gross changes minus net changes) and consolidation patterns (Pearson $r = -.665$), which does not hold when only net changes are considered.[22] This is typically the case of Argentina, where there is a clear relationship between public spending and cabinet size. The Argentine state and its top executive branch have grown at a similar rate. Public expenditure increased fourfold between 1945 and 1978 while the size of the cabinet and related offices (top administrators excluded) was roughly 4.4 times larger than in 1941 (see Tables 8.2 and 8.3). Although these figures do not establish a causal relationship, they do suggest the validity of intuitive assumptions concerning a strong interdependence between the degree of state activism and the size of peak government organization.[23] However, new policy areas hardly can be considered the only variable affecting such rearrangement rates. There are other factors that also affect the frequency and mode of cabinet changes. The evidence shows that consolidation patterns seem to be one of them.

A considerable amount of ministerial reorganizations have not affected seriously the extant sectoral distribution of portfolios. Only 38.9 percent of the 612 identified cases qualify clearly as net changes. A thorough explanation of why the remaining 374 changes have taken place at all seems to require the help of these additional factors. These data convey a double message: Political consolidation (or lack of it) has not interfered significantly with the secular expansion of cabinets. The public sector has expanded as a result of contextual factors and regardless of the resilience of political regimes in Latin America. But regime breakdowns do impose some additional cyclical rearrangements on the affected institutions.

In addition, "reshuffling scores" are significantly higher during the inaugural year of each regime. During their first year in existence new regimes undertook reorganizations that affected, on average, 25.4 percent of the units they found in place.[24] The reshuffling scores for subsequent years never come close to this average.[25] Indeed, there seems to be no political transition without some serious rethinking about how best to organize the state apparatus. This has palpable implications for the size of the cabinet and its inner composition.[26]

In Argentina Juan Perón introduced profound changes through the constitutional reform of 1949. That reform was the largest single reorganization of the executive branch since 1930. Arturo Frondizi was the first to employ "secretaries of state with ministerial rank" in his government. General Juan Carlos Onganía reduced the number of ministerial units to five (see Table 8.4). The frequency of governmental rearrangements has

TABLE 8.4
The Argentine Cabinet: Size and Hierarchical Design

Year	Ministries N	Ministries %	Secretariats of State N	Secretariats of State %	Undersecretariats N	Undersecretariats %	Total N
1930	8	44.4	1	5.6	9	50.0	18
1943	8	38.1	2	9.5	11	52.4	21
1944	8	30.8	4	15.4	14	53.9	26
1946	8	28.6	5	17.9	15	53.6	28
1949	20	41.7	5	10.4	23	48.0	48
1950	20	40.8	5	10.2	24	49.0	49
1951	20	39.2	5	9.8	26	51.0	51
1952	21	40.4	5	9.6	26	50.0	52
1954	20	44.4	5	11.1	20	44.4	45
1955	17	44.7	3	7.9	18	47.4	38
1956	13	39.4	5	15.2	15	45.5	33
1958	8	20.0	12	30.0	20	50.0	40
1961	8	19.5	12	29.3	21	51.2	41
1962	8	17.8	16	35.6	21	46.7	45
1963	8	17.0	18	38.3	21	44.7	47
1964	8	17.4	17	37.0	21	45.7	46
1965	8	17.8	14	31.1	23	51.1	45
1966	5	10.4	18	37.5	25	52.1	48
1967	5	9.3	21	38.9	28	51.9	54
1968	5	9.1	21	38.2	29	52.7	55
1969	8	14.3	21	37.5	27	48.2	56
1970	8	13.1	21	34.4	32	52.5	61
1971	12	23.5	4	7.8	35	68.6	51
1972	12	21.4	4	7.1	40	71.4	56
1973	8	10.7	24	32.0	43	57.3	75
1974	8	10.4	23	29.9	46	59.7	77
1975	8	9.8	23	28.0	51	62.2	82
1976	9	10.2	28	31.8	51	58.0	88
1977	9	11.0	22	26.8	51	62.2	82
1978	8	10.1	20	25.3	51	64.6	79
1981	13	20.3	0	00.0	51	79.7	64
1982	10	13.3	9	12.0	56	74.4	75

Source: Waldino Suárez et al., "Some Notes on Governmental Rearrangements in Argentina Since 1930," ECPR Occasional Paper (1982).

increased rather dramatically since the 1966 reform, and it has not stopped since.

The two types of regime observable in Argentina since the mid-1940s (classic presidentialism and classic militarism) have implemented rather markedly different criteria on this issue. The case of military regimes is very interesting for a number of reasons. These regimes often have tried unsuccessfully to check the secular expansion of the national executive. They tried this in 1955–57, in 1971, and more recently in 1981. The result has always been the same: a cycle. They ended up with cabinets that resembled very closely the ones they intended to replace. That is why

TABLE 8.5
Regime Duration and Cabinet Growth, 1930-1982

Regime	Total Duration	Year: expanding	Year: stable	Year: contracting	Yearly[a] Increase
Military	22[a]	9	5	8	-.035
Civilian	30	12	16	2	+4.75

[a]1931 excluded.
Source: Computed from data in Table 8.4

TABLE 8.6
Cabinet Size During Military Regimes

Regime	Average Size
1930-1932	18
1943-1946	24.33
1955-1958	34.66
1962	45
1966-1973	54.42
1976	82.28

Source: Computed from data in Table 8.4

military regimes split their tenures rather evenly between expanding and contracting years. Their mean yearly expansion rate is practically nil, and this score is in sharp contrast to civilian rates. The cabinet has grown at an average yearly rate of 4.8 during the thirty years controlled by civilians since 1930.

Military takeovers seem to be carried out within a strong rationalistic and bureaucratic framework, one strongly biased toward the administrative dimension of governmental performance, only to come to terms with the more political dimensions of the problem at a later date. Hence, the early restrictive efforts of these authoritarian experiments are offset largely by equally strongly expansive years within the very same regimes (see Tables 8.5 and 8.6). This explains why military rulers modify the organization of their cabinets much more profoundly than do civilian regimes during the noninaugural years of their existence. Their average reshuffling score is 16.7, versus 5.5 for the civilian regimes.[27]

To be sure, intermittent military rule might not have affected the secular evolution of Argentine cabinets, but it certainly has imposed extra burdens on the patterns of reorganization observed. It would be quite difficult to explain Argentina's institutional evolution, especially its short-lived cycles, by looking exclusively at changes in the substance of public policies pursued by the national government.[28]

The problem became more pronounced for recent military regimes as they lengthened their life span considerably. The military regimes of 1966–1972 and 1976–1983 are clear examples of this. Both undertook some of the major reshuffles since 1930, and they did so during the closing years of their existence. This very well may be the result of some acute problems of consensus, which forced these regimes into widening their governing coalitions with new groups. Having no parliament through which to express these changes institutionally, they resorted to profound reorganizations of the cabinet.[29]

This first legacy of extended transitions is very costly. In addition to spending a considerable amount of resources on a permanent redesigning of most of its leading structures, these extended transitions also make policymaking more difficult.[30] Internal communication networks become inefficient, the timing of substantive decisions is disrupted, and even the most important offices (the presidency and major ministries included) have their real, functional competence curtailed seriously. In short, repeated transitions impose an organizational style that enables chief executives to perform some of their leading activities effectively, such as coordinating governmental policies and presiding over their implementation.[31] This cost must be added to the critical time spent on such rearrangements.

POLITICAL TRANSITIONS AND LEADERSHIP DEVELOPMENT

An extended transition also wreaks havoc among the political class. This second dimension of the problem is very important in the modern world, but it has not been treated systematically enough. This might be due to the less-than-fluid relationship between the study of governmental performance and leadership analysis. Some promising breakthroughs have been achieved in the public policy field, although they clearly are insufficient.[32]

There is simply no standard criterion by which the functional adequacy of leadership may be identified. Political scientists seem unable to decide on which capabilities a country's top leadership needs in order to become a viable, major bargaining agent. The problem is, of course, exceedingly difficult, but the relationship between political transition and leadership consolidation must be examined. As a prelude I must make explicit some leading assumptions.

Assumption 1: A modern political system requires a growing number of specialists willing and able to operate political institutions on a more or less full-time basis. Without this, the society will find it very difficult to function. The need for professional leadership arises from the complex political process in contemporary societies, where a large number of individuals and an increasingly wide, varied set of interests are affected by such processes.

Assumption 2: Three specific conditions appear to be essential for the development of a viable political leadership:

1. Its component individuals must acquire enough expertise (political knowledge, not technical training) before being promoted to leading decisionmaking roles.
2. A standardized (i.e., recognized and accepted) set of rules is necessary whereby leaders can settle their individual and sectoral differences.
3. A communications system that allows the electorate to articulate their interests and the regime to influence them has to be established.[33]

Assumption 3: It is not very easy to meet these three requirements in countries where the careers of individuals are very short or a once-in-a-lifetime affair or both. Although there is no conclusive proof in support of this assumption, the intensity and profile of dominant governmental instability patterns in Latin America suggest that this statement is largely correct. It describes a situation in which it is quite difficult for a political class to flourish for three reasons:

1. It is very unlikely that a person will undergo strict training in order to acquire costly professional abilities if these abilities only will be put into practice briefly.
2. Even when politicians find a way of acquiring the necessary political expertise without holding governmental offices, job stability is still problematic because contested policy proposals are difficult to implement in a brief period.[34]
3. It is difficult to imagine why and how individual leaders run out of political resources so early in their tenure, as is the case in some Latin American countries. This should not be so common among top executive officers who get to government after having satisfied the three conditions discussed.[35]

The general panorama described in the next pages fits much more easily into an alternative picture of political disorder where there is no established political leadership and where it is easy to get into office but very difficult to hold on to it.

Government stability patterns have two important traits in Latin America. First, tenures are extremely brief. On the average, Latin American countries rotate about two-thirds (63.7 percent) of their cabinets every year. In the region a cabinet minister typically stays in office 19.4 months (see Table 8.7). The tenures of the 5,252 individuals who served as cabinet ministers

TABLE 8.7
Ministers and Mandates, 1940-1980

Country	Number of Ministers	Single Mandate Ministers	Multiple Mandate Ministers	% col. 3 over col. 1	% Multiple Mandates over Total Mandates
Argentina	527	465	62	11.76	23.01
Bolivia	467	366	101	21.63	39.03
Brazil	293	252	41	13.99	26.10
Chile	418	306	112	26.79	47.87
Colombia	323	235	88	27.24	48.24
Costa Rica	167	140	27	16.17	28.57
Cuba	296	227	69	23.31	43.39
Dom. Rep.	250	179	71	28.40	52.39
Ecuador	339	285	54	15.93	29.28
El Salvador	208	181	27	12.98	23.63
Guatemala	227	182	45	19.82	36.36
Haiti	177	147	30	16.95	31.94
Honduras	139	122	17	12.23	23.75
Mexico	179	166	13	7.26	13.99
Nicaragua	153	125	28	18.18	34.37
Panama	186	133	53	28.49	47.84
Paraguay	98	67	31	31.73	54.42
Peru	319	264	55	17.24	32.31
Uruguay	205	162	43	20.97	37.69
Venezuela	281	231	50	17.79	34.93
Latin America	5,252	4,235	1,017	19.36	36.36

Source: Computed from data in Table 8.1

in Latin American countries between 1940 and 1980 may be classified as short-lived, temporary, transitional, stable, or long-standing, depending on whether such tenures lasted less than twelve, twenty-six, forty, or seventy-two months, or more.[36] More than one-half of all appointees did not complete their first year in office, and only 20 percent lasted more than forty. Only in the latter case were appointees in office long enough to make their stay in government count.

Second, returning to office is quite an accomplishment in most Latin American countries. Reappointment practices highlight one of the most difficult, even conflictive, questions regarding government stability—namely, what is the value of having individual politicians occupy government office repeatedly? In a sense, this question cannot be fully settled unless returning rates are explicitly related to overall levels of ministerial tenure. For instance, high returning rates have a positive impact on government performance when they take place in largely unstable settings. The same is true of low returning rates in stable environments. In Latin America, the dominant analytical view emphasizes the dangers typically associated with long-standing tenures—excessive personalism.[37] But it is possible to view reappointment as a mechanism whereby a political system allows its leadership to regulate and administer acute societal conflicts. According to this view, reappointment facilitates the constant adjustment of governmental coalitions to many strong, overlapping political cleavages without seriously disrupting the leadership affected by such changes.

Latin America's average ministerial mandate is so short-lived that successive reappointments have allowed only a handful of individual officeholders to extend their total, disjointed stay in power beyond the upper limit of what could be considered a workable tenure (forty-eight months). Far more often successive reappointments have enabled Latin American leaders to suffer extremely conflictive circumstances without undergoing total disruption. In this sense, Latin American ministerial reappointment practices resemble more closely the cases of contemporary Italy, the Fourth French Republic, and Finland than those where a closely knit clique exercises tight control of governmental office for extended periods of time.

Indeed, multiple-tenure ministers are not very common in Latin America. Only 1,017 of the 5,252 ministers considered (19.4 percent) managed to secure a second or further appointment. This is only 36.4 percent of all incumbencies. The percentage is significantly smaller if mandate extensions are not considered, and it is also markedly lower than in other more stable regions of the world.

These empirical findings support my assumptions regarding Latin American governmental instability. Not only are most leaders unlikely to secure a workable mandate for themselves, but they also find it very difficult to come back to office. This certainly sets the region's dominant instability patterns apart from other, well-known examples of party systems that experience great difficulty in putting together workable winning coalitions.

In sum, the combination of short-lived tenures and a limited number of multiple incumbencies makes Latin America a region where the political career of a government official is strenuous, easily disrupted, and hardly compatible with modern policymaking requirements. Most other traits associated with reappointment point in the same direction. The mean tenure of noninaugural incumbencies of cabinet ministers is even shorter than the overall average (17.1 months). In addition, only seventy-six incumbents had long-standing tenure.

Such relationships should be examined cross-nationally, given the wide behavioral differences of Latin American countries. Such a comparison enables us to define cases according to reappointment practices that are negatively related to overall ministerial stability. In cases where they are not related we further distinguish between overrepresentation (long tenures coexisting with high returning rates) and underrepresentation (short tenures and a limited number of reappointments) of multiple incumbencies.

The twenty countries considered here may be clustered around three distinct groups that correspond neatly to the specifications just mentioned. This "fit" verifies the actual existence of patterns in which both dimensions of ministerial stability are consistent with the consolidation of a governmental elite. These cases show a marked tendency to favor fluid access by officeholders to the decisionmaking process, either allowing them to enjoy "workable" incumbencies or affording them access to multiple, shorter-lived tenures. The third type of situation produces either personalized governments—long-standing tenures and numerous reappointments—or serious disruptions in the working conditions of government leaders. This is very often a side effect of excessively brief governmental tenures imposed on leaders by short mandates and insufficient returns to office.

The neatness with which these twenty cases may be differentiated into these three clusters is striking. Balanced situations are represented by the middle group, where the difference between the two standardized scores is near zero. Group one comprises countries with a tendency to favor personalized governmental practices, and group three represents cases that have found it difficult to keep a government team in working condition. Argentina is markedly worse off than the rest of Latin America, and it ranks at the bottom of the third group.

The performance of Argentina is also poor regarding this second test of institutional strength. Its leadership combines one of the lowest ministerial duration rates in the region (15.55 months) with a very low proportion of reappointments (marginally greater than 10 percent). In addition, the few ministers who returned to office rarely found their working conditions improved as a result. These noninaugural incumbencies are too brief and are separated by very long periods of time.[38] This is not very common even by Latin American standards and hardly is limited to the executive branch. Not many Argentine congressmen, for example, have had their mandates renewed. In Argentina only 14.7 percent of all senators and 18.4 percent of the members of the lower house have managed to do so since 1930. This is also in open contrast to what happened elsewhere.[39] The pattern affects state governors with equal strength; they occupy their offices briefly (their mean stay has been estimated at 14.2 months) and only once (just 7.6 percent of them have been reappointed).[40]

We may distinguish twenty countries in Table 8.8 according to their consolidation patterns. The magnitude and sign of the ministerial stability scores depicted on Table 8.8 seem to vary with reappointment practices. This emerges more clearly in Table 8.9, which discriminates the region's political systems into consolidated, personalized, and transitional.[41] (The data are the same for both tables.)

The stability pattern typical of disrupted political leadership may be found only among political systems in transition. There is an almost perfect overlap between extended tenures and disrupted leadership, as shown by the negative coefficients clustered in this group. At the other extreme, consolidated regimes offer a more suitable relationship between leaders and

TABLE 8.8
Ministerial Stability and Reappointment Practices
(Z scores)

Country	Stability Score	Type of Practices
Paraguay	2.99791	personalized
Cuba	1.19559	
Dom. Rep.	1.10570	
Mexico	1.01094	
Nicaragua	0.79658	
Panama	0.69925	
Colombia	0.26309	
Costa Rica	0.03766	
Uruguay	0.02870	
Chile	-0.00405	
Guatemala	-0.02036	equilibrated
Venezuela	-0.14640	
Honduras	-0.15746	
Haiti	-0.36691	
Bolivia	-0.92888	
Peru	-0.93167	
El Salvador	-0.96711	
Brazil	-0.98241	unstable
Ecuador	-1.68370	
Argentina	-1.87608	

Source: Waldino Suárez, "Transición política y clase dirigente" (Buenos Aires: University of Belgrano, 1983), manuscript.

government decisionmaking. This set of countries boasts unstable cabinets and frequent reappointments (e.g., Chile) or stable governments and single-mandate ministers (e.g., Costa Rica). Finally, personalistic regimes have a near monopoly of ministerial personalism as shown by Paraguay, Cuba, the Dominican Republic, and, less obviously, Nicaragua.

This effect also is felt by most members of Parliament. The Argentine Congress has been staffed with freshmen after each military interruption. Reappointment rates increase quite strongly in successive renewals when the impact of continued practices is felt.[42]

This seems to constitute the second great difference between surviving a crisis and undergoing a regime breakdown. In the absence of breakdown government officials are not discarded so thoroughly, which facilitates the accommodation of leaders to frequent changes in coalitions.[43] The explanation must be sought in the political stimuli that various regimes offer to individuals. Different regimes recruit their officeholders from different strata. They utilize social and political personalities rather differently. Most frequently, aspiring leaders are not equally eager to participate in varying political models. This adds to obvious differences in sectoral interests fostered by institutional

TABLE 8.9
Leadership Development and Consolidation Patterns

Regime Type	Country	Coefficient
Consolidated	Mexico	1.01094
	Costa Rica	0.03766
	Colombia	0.26309
	Uruguay	0.02870
	Chile	-0.00405
	Venezuela	-0.14640
	Panama	0.69925
Stabilized	Nicaragua	0.79658
	Dom. Rep.	1.10570
	Haiti	-0.36691
	Paraguay	2.99791
	Cuba	1.19559
Transitional	Brazil	-0.98241
	Honduras	-0.15746
	El Salvador	-0.96711
	Bolivia	-0.92888
	Peru	-0.93167
	Ecuador	-1.68370
	Guatemala	-0.02036
	Argentina	-1.87608

Source: Waldino Suárez, "Transición política y clase dirigente" (Buenos Aires: University of Belgrano, 1983), manuscript.

designs of various sorts, which also explains why so few individuals have occupied governmental offices under several regimes. More than 70.8 percent of all reappointments to major political office in Latin America have taken place during the same regime.

In short, there is a very intimate relationship between patterns of weak consolidation and the frequency of institutional and leadership disruptions. The data allow only tentative conclusions but are quite consistent with the idea that a political system gets into full gear only after it has reached some minimal levels of consolidation. This is one of the central dilemmas facing Argentina in its current drive for democratic consolidation and socioeconomic recovery.

CLASSIC PRESIDENTIALISM, POLITICAL ORDER, AND THE ARGENTINE SYNDROME

The thrust of this chapter suggests that the democratic regime installed in Argentina in 1983 began to operate under some marked disadvantages. These affect government institutions and leadership, and they are attributable to the avatars of previous failed transitions. An early removal of such weaknesses would enhance the prospects for democratic consolidation very substantially; midwife the crystallization of a strong, autonomous political system; and provide a framework to resolve inherited socioeconomic problems.

The appropriateness of this or similar proposals concerning institutional change is intimately related to three questions.

- What factors best explain the extended transitional period initiated in Argentina five decades ago?
- What is the most appropriate way of avoiding these disruptive factors in the future?
- What short-term measures should be taken to minimize the negative effects of the weaknesses cited here during the early stages of the present democratic regime?

The first question deals with context and, specifically, with the social and economic evolution of the country. These aspects have been analyzed by many scholars.[44] However, even if politics always were treated as an inevitable "dependent variable," a satisfactory answer will not be forthcoming unless some politico-institutional factors are considered also. A proper analysis of the repeated breakdowns experienced by Argentina cannot avoid examining the "procedural formulas" employed by authoritarian and democratic regimes. This is very important because, as we shall see, the two political models that have dominated Argentine politics since the early 1940s were very fragile, and they easily broke down when put to the test in the majority of the countries where they have been tried.

A comparative analysis of contemporary Latin America rapidly confirms this thesis. Classic presidentialism and classic militarism have produced the shortest-lived governments and least-durable regimes since 1940. Such institutional designs seem destined to weaken the political system independent of contextual specificity. For example, classic presidentialism defines an institutional arrangement that rests on rigid presidential timetables. Classic militarism refers to governments controlled by armed forces without the adornment of any constitutional legitimation.[45] As Table 8.10 indicates, these governments are much shorter-lived than those set up by other types of military regimes and according to other models of presidentialism.

Table 8.10 shows the higher-than-average instability levels of chief executives appointed according to these two basic models, at least in relative terms. A comparison of the nine categories enumerated on the same table yields some interesting results. Some pertain to important variations within military categories and some to differences within presidentialist categories. A very striking difference between the duration of governments organized and ruled by institutionalized military domination and those that followed

TABLE 8.10
Presidential Tenures and Types of Regime

Types of Regimes	N	Tenure[a]	Regime Duration[a]
Patrimonial	3	59.31	135.69
Extreme presidential	15	49.06	100.20
Controlled	21	47.22	120.55
Institutional	24	47.37	135.26
Semipresidential	5	44.98	100.00
Revised presidential	3	44.65	143.94
Classic presidential	23	31.34	104.26
Revolutionary	8	22.46	100.00
Classic military	37	16.25	103.24
Overall	139	-	-

[a]Average duration (in months)

a classic military pattern is verified easily. The difference is just too large to be treated as a side-effect of some other macro socioeconomic function or dismissed as a happenstance.

The mean tenure of "institutionalized military" chief executives is nearly three times that of "classic military." The 47.4-month average duration of the former places it nearly within the boundaries of "workable" tenures, whereas the mean classic military chief executive fails to complete one-and-one-half years in office. This disparity in the mean tenure of both types of military rule is significant (P<.05) even after the test of difference of means has been controlled for levels of overt political conflict.[46]

A comparison of the five major presidentialist forms also produces some interesting findings. By and large, two conclusions stand as most relevant. First, controlled presidentialism outperforms other types of presidential regime in this respect, and classic presidentialism ranks lower among the latter. The performance of constitutional governments improved whenever their organizational formats did not follow the classic presidentialist design very closely. Second, classic forms of presidentialism also have a marked tendency to break down more easily; their consolidation rates are among the poorest of the region. Their difference with nonclassic alternatives is significant at .01 (see Table 8.11). If both groups are broken down into their specific types, this difference is further confirmed (see Table 8.12).

The type of regime existing in a given country, therefore, is not irrelevant to the regime's institutional performance in the short and long term. These preliminary findings open up a discussion that concerns one of the central dimensions of the political process. However, as my concern is with prospects for democracy in Argentina, some comments about the merits and weaknesses

TABLE 8.11
Classic and Nonclassic Regimes

Type of Regime	Duration Types (Months)				
	Short-Lived	Temporary	Transitional	Long-Standing	Total
	(12)	(13-48)	(49-120)	(120)	
Nonclassic	14	11	23	20	68
Classic	18	23	12	7	60
Overall	32	34	35	27	128

TABLE 8.12
Types of Regime and Consolidation Levels

Regime Type	Percentage of Consolidated Observations
Patrimonial	100.00
Semipresidentialist	40.00
Revised presidentialist	33.33
Controled presidentialist	33.33
Institutionalized military	29.17
Classic presidentialism	21.73
Extreme presidentialism	20.00
Revolutionary	12.50
Classic military	5.40

of strong and classic presidentialism are in order here. After all, they have been the only two competing designs employed by that country since the mid-1940s.

Presidentialism appears to be capable of producing "durable" governments and consolidated regimes in only two circumstances: when the original blueprint undergoes serious modifications or, less clearly, when presidential regimes have to operate in fairly simple contexts. The former is usually achieved by curtailing the freedom with which various groups can compete for office. Rigid constitutional cycles, the formation of broad but inflexible coalitions, unclear functional assignments to the presidential office, a vague executive-legislative relationship, and a disorganized party system are some of the structural weaknesses that reduce the prospects for regime survival. These and similar components are largely controlled/reduced in most nonclassic alternatives of the presidentialist model, which would explain most of the differences observed.

The second circumstance (simple contexts) accounts for the odd behavior of cases of extreme presidentialism regarding governmental stability. At first glance their placement in Table 8.10 challenges what has been said about presidentialism throughout; they have kept unmodified most of the defining traits of the formula under observation. But the puzzle is not very difficult to explain given that extreme presidentialism can be found only in simple, not very modern, small countries. Most of them are in Central America. This would seem to confirm the fact that presidentialism is at its best in traditional societies. It provides perhaps the most suitable formula for regulating political processes in social settings where the complexity of government is in no way as pronounced as in contemporary democracies. In simple contexts the need for a well-structured, autonomous party system is not so urgent, and the organization of a political leadership is a fairly simple task.

This is also a fair description of Central America, which is the region where extreme presidentialism is more frequent. Recent high levels of overt conflict should not cause us to overlook the fact that Central American countries are still quite simple societies, with a limited number of political actors, and a far-less-complicated government machinery.

The ineffectiveness of presidentialism becomes manifest in more modern contexts, and the countries affected have tried to overcome this by incorporating some parliamentary features into their constitutional designs. This is important for Argentina, which is the only case of a large Latin American country that has not tried to break away from its classic, even extreme, presidentialist mold. This is surprising, especially when Argentina's poor institutional performance is taken into account. It seems we have reached a point at which one misses the absence of a richer, institutionally oriented tradition among Argentine political analysts. The reason is clear: There is an uncomfortably close association between classic presidentialism and regime breakdowns. This surely has exacerbated the Argentine propensity to constitutional disruption, and there is no reason to believe this will not have the same effect in the future if the model is not modified.

It would be useful to examine thoroughly how other Latin American countries have worked on their presidentialist blueprints and to determine the impact of such reforms. This is not a matter of recommending the implementation of some risky, constitutional overhaul but of providing relevant information that may highlight some of the major dangers implicit in the existing constitutional setup.

Last but not least, the third question stated at the beginning of this section suggests that the success of Argentine democracy also depends on what is done to remedy the serious institutional disruption inherited from failed transitions. It is imperative to prevent future breakdowns, but it also is necessary to take care of the current disarray imposed by the recent past and to do so in a way that is compatible with the effective management of the present socioeconomic crisis. This certainly highlights a second feature of Argentine politics in recent times. Politicians and other decisionmakers have not felt compelled to negotiate and agree on a temporary political pact at the inauguration of a regime with the avowed purpose of ensuring its consolidation. Yet this seems to be indispensable for the consolidation of a democratic regime. Spain, Venezuela, Colombia, Costa Rica, Brazil, and many other historic examples tend to confirm this thesis.

Such a political contract deals with some fundamental questions of political practices, and its effects are much longer lasting than a mere negotiated agreement on a specific package of policies. It introduces some order into the typically confused landscape of a recently installed regime, and it broadly defines the systemic coalition without which institutions can hardly operate. In this sense, an *acuerdo de régimen* (regime agreement) defines a mechanism that helps politicians regroup, strengthen their institutional habitat, and legitimize democratic rule. An *acuerdo de régimen* emphasizes the fact that the survival of a regime is dependent not only on the success with which it tackles impending socioeconomic crisis at the beginning of its life span, but also on its ability to work out a viable, lasting political formula capable of dealing with future conflicts.

For this to happen major actors must agree on a set of procedures that maximizes the effectiveness with which political leaders may play their roles. Other things being equal, it is more difficult to work out a major package of policies without a prior agreement among those who will implement it or can prevent a successful implementation. An agreement of this sort quickens significantly the recovery of capabilities lost as a result of a string of regime breakdowns. The relevance of such an agreement is particularly great in countries such as Argentina, whose political system is trying to overcome a sequence of several failed transitions. Yet this hardly has been discussed.

There certainly have been several occasions in which parties have gotten together in order to work out some sort of agreement before (the Multipartidaria, a coalition of opposition parties) and after (the Carta Democrática, or Democratic Charter) the general elections of 1983. But they have focused largely on negotiating common policies (*concertación*), or they have dealt with institutionalization patterns only marginally and vaguely. The emphasis has been on substantive desiderata, not on the mechanism to bring them about. In short, the consolidation of democracy in Argentina will be enhanced greatly if a new impetus is given to the analysis of institutional engineering. Two of them, constitutional designs and *acuerdos de régimen*, have been briefly discussed here.

SOME CLOSING REMARKS

Although exploratory, this chapter has discussed traits of Argentine politics that deserve to be studied more systematically. The Argentine institutional network currently suffers from basic weaknesses that make it rather inappropriate for a modern society. Accordingly, political analysts and politicians should put more emphasis on a "depresidentialization" of the Argentine political system.

The change need not be abrupt, but the development of criteria for such modifications should not be delayed any longer. To make a positive contribution to this change, political scientists should revise some of their current conceptions of the value and functions of institutions. In this way, they would be contributing to the development of democracy by emphasizing the current institutional "decay" of Argentina. Political scientists also should stress the extent to which this decay has been caused by the weakness of consolidating regimes, the importance of rethinking the organization of the Argentine political system, and the urgency of doing it now, at an early stage in the democratization process.

Last but not least, this chapter has stressed the need to approach such problems from a more comparative perspective. The Argentine consolidation and the intensity of its effects may be atypical, but it begs improvement. My comparative analysis of a badly neglected dimension of Argentine politics is suggestive of where the relief might come from. This approach does not intend to diminish the relevance of economic, cultural, and historical factors. It has been contended that in the Argentine case the weight of these factors is simply too overwhelming for any institutional design to bear. The evidence reviewed here suggests that inadequate institutional arrangements have contributed to the disarray of contemporary Argentine politics.

NOTES

1. Argentina long has been regarded as culturally atypical. As is often the case with culture-oriented research, insufficient information makes most statements on this issue rather impressionistic and not very solid empirically. See David J. Elkins and Richard Simeon, "A Cause in Search of Its Effect, or What Does Political Culture Explain?" *Comparative Politics* 11, no. 2 (January 1979): 127–145.

2. The existing literature is very extensive, including C. A. Medina "Condicionamentos Socials e Ação Militar: O Golpe de Março de 1964 no Brasil," *Desarrollo Económico*, nos. 30-31 (1968); Guillermo A. O'Donnell, "Modernización y golpes militares," *Desarrollo Económico* 12, no. 47 (October-December 1972): 519–566; Leopoldo Allub, "Estado y sociedad civil en Argentina: Patrones de emergencia, desarrollo y estabilidad del estado argentino," *Revista Mexicana de Sociología* 37, no. 3 (July-September 1975): 655–696; D. Cochrane, "U.S. Policy Toward Recognition of Governments and Promotion of Democracy in Latin America Since 1963," *Journal of Latin American Studies* 4, no. 2 (1972): 275–291.

3. Benjamin A. Most, "Authoritarianism and the Growth of the State in Latin America: An Assessment of Their Impacts on Argentine Public Policy, 1930–70," *Comparative Political Studies* 13, no. 2 (July 1980), pp. 173–204.

4. Waldino C. Suárez, "On Military Regimes and Procedural Practices," *ECPR Occasional Paper* (1978).

5. "Sobre el sentido de la república," *Criterio*, no. 1857 (1981).

6. G. Bingham Powell Jr., "Party Systems and Political Performance: Participation, Stability, and Violence in Contemporary Democracies," *American Political Science Review* 75, no. 4 (December 1981); Francisco Cumplido Cereceda, "El sistema democrático en América Latina: Su eficacia, el régimen presidencialista y las posibilidades del régimen parlamentario," *Contribuciones*, no. 1 (January-March 1985): 15–30.

7. N. Johnson, "The Place of Institutions in the Study of Politics," *Political Studies* 23, no. 1 (1975).

8. F. F. Ridley, "Political Institutions: The Script Not the Play," *Political Studies* 22, nos. 2-3 (1974): 365; Waldino C. Suárez, "Diseño institucional y consolidación democrática," (Buenos Aires: Centro de Estudios Norteamericanos, University of Belgrano, 1984). Also see F. R. Loñ, "Constitución, estabilidad y sistema de partidos," *Criterio*, no. 1989 (1981).

9. Waldino C. Suárez, "Transición política y clase dirigente: Algunas reflexiones sobre la Argentina contemporánea" (Buenos Aires: University of Belgrano, 1983), mimeo.

10. It is very difficult to find articles based on solid empirical work that recommend which party system, congressional inner composition, and the like are most appropriate to such circumstances. See *ibid.*

11. Jacques Lambert, *América Latina* (Buenos Aires: Ariel, 1978). There has been only one thorough revision of the constitution in this century.

12. The problem of political order and democracy has been discussed very thoroughly in an anthology recently edited by Konrad Adenauer Stiftung E.V., *Democracia Representativa y Parlamentarismo* (Buenos Aires: CIEDLA, 1985).

13. The typology of regimes employed here has been elaborated in Waldino C. Suárez, "Political Regimes: A Taxonomic Scheme," *ECPR Occasional Paper* (Lancaster: 1981).

14. Waldino C. Suárez et al., "Some Notes on Governmental Rearrangements in Argentina Since 1930," *ECPR Occasional Paper* (Freiburg: 1982).

15. Suárez, "Congreso."

16. Suárez, "Diseño institucional," *op. cit.*

17. The analysis also should include public enterprises and the decentralized sector. The analysis of these complementary areas is very rewarding. See, for example, A. Bonifacio, E. Salas, and W. Suárez, *La Administración Descentralizada en el Sector Público Latinoamericano* (Buenos Aires: INCIP, 1980).

18. Suárez, "Some notes," p. 7.

19. In an earlier article, a distinction was made between net and gross changes. Net changes modify the functional profile of cabinets by either incorporating new fields of activities or eliminating existing ones. See Waldino C. Suárez, "El gabinete en América Latina: Organización y cambio," *Contribuciones*, no. 1 (January-March 1985): 31–55.

20. Suárez, "Some notes."

21. Suárez, "El gabinete."

22. Suárez, "Some notes."

23. *Ibid.*

24. This score computes the percentage of portfolios modified relative to the size of the cabinet.

25. This is largely due to the fact that some regimes undertook some serious ministerial overhaul only after some months in office.

26. Suárez, "Some notes."

27. *Ibid.*

28. *Ibid.*

29. *Ibid.*

30. Since 1941 Argentina has witnessed a massive reorganization of the cabinet every three years or so.

31. This aspect of Argentine presidentialism is badly neglected. This is unfortunate because the current design of the chief executive office hinders its effective control of some central, basic activities such as planning, budgeting and the civil service. In this sense, Argentine presidents are notoriously weak.

32. Lewis Edinger, "The Comparative Analysis of Political Leadership," *Comparative Politics* 7, no. 2 (January 1975): 253–269.

33. More on this can be found in Suárez, "Congreso."

34. Richard Rose (ed.), *Challenges to Government: Studies in Overloaded Politics* (Beverly Hills, Calif.: Sage, 1980).

35. One assumes that, other things being equal, politicians who work their way through to government after having satisfied these three conditions do so with a considerable amount of political standing. Thus, they have a chance of staying in office longer than someone who scores more poorly in such tests.

36. This has been dealt with in greater detail in Suárez, *Diseño institucional.*

37. Waldino C. Suárez, "El poder ejectivo en América Latina: Su capacidad operativa bajo regímenes presidencialistas de gobierno," *Revista de Estudios Políticos*, no. 29 (September-October 1982): 109–144.

38. V. Mate and W. Suárez, "Estabilidad ministerial en la Argentina," *Documento IAPP* (Buenos Aires: 1982).

39. See Burdett A. Loomis, "Congressional Careers and Party Leadership in the Contemporary House of Representatives," *American Journal of Political Science* 28, no. 1 (February 1984): 180–202.

40. E. A. Salas, "La inestabilidad de los poderes ejecutivos provinciales en la Argentina, 1930–1981," (La Plata: Universidad Católica de la Plata, IV), pp. 15–16.

41. Suárez, "Transición política."

42. This is being examined in an ongoing research on the Argentine Congress, University of Belgrano, 1984.

43. It is very interesting to observe how little attention has been paid to the relationship between coalition building and party systems in Latin America. This contrasts to what happens elsewhere.

44. The literature on development is very rich on this. See P. Meadow, "Development: Some Perspective Orientations," *International Journal of Comparative Sociology* 14, nos. 1-2 (1973): 19–34.

45. Suárez, "Diseño institucional."

46. A complex scale of conflict intensity has been developed with *World Handbook II* indicators. Such a scale has been employed as a covariable, and the covariance coefficient obtained is significant at .05.

9
CONCLUSION: TOWARD A FRAMEWORK FOR THE STUDY OF DEMOCRATIC CONSOLIDATION

Enrique A. Baloyra

Preliminary comparative efforts have advanced a modest inventory of propositions about the processes of transition in Latin America from 1975 to 1985. Most of these propositions call attention to observed regularities and simultaneities. First, there appears to be a somewhat paradoxical relationship between type of authoritarian regime and its likelihood of deterioration. For example, it was not anticipated that the "new" bureaucratic authoritarian (BA) regimes of South America would deteriorate and break down so soon.[1] Essentially, the BAs failed to live up to expectations and did not become a "one-thousand-year Reich." At the other end of the spectrum we find more "primitive" forms of authoritarian domination such as the classical personalistic dictatorships and oligarchic regimes of "reactionary despotism."[2] These are particularly resistant to change and have lasted much longer than bureaucratic authoritarianism. The cases contemplated in this book have dealt with the more advanced and, in hindsight, less stable forms of authoritarian domination.[3] One important lesson here is that even the most ferocious forms of authoritarianism deteriorate and break down. Where does the impulse for this decay come from?

Second, we know that most of this impulse is endogeneous and that the impact of exogenous variables has been relatively marginal in most cases. On paper, two of these variables appear to merit the status of direct causal factors: the role of the United States and the impact of international economic disequilibria on regime performance. U.S. participation in these processes has varied with geographic area and the traditional political role of the United States in it; with the probability of outcomes considered threatening by the United States; and with the size and external linkages of the country in question. Accordingly, the United States has been more involved in Central America and the Caribbean—in a very controversial, prominent way in Nicaragua and in El Salvador, and, previously, in a milder, much more effective manner in the Dominican Republic. With the exception of the Argentine case, one finds nothing in South America comparable to the U.S. role in the Philippine process of transition of 1984–1986 and in orchestrating the 1986 coup against Jean Claude Duvalier in Haiti. During the mid-1980s the United States adopted a more activist role in Paraguay and Chile. This was a welcome but hardly sufficient change to determine the eventual breakdown of those regimes. The emphasis in this book on southern Europe and South America enabled us to go beyond the simplistic demonology conjured up by the metaphors of Cuba and Vietnam that clouds the analysis and discussion of the Central American situation in the United States. Therefore, we could emphasize other, more relevant aspects of these transitions without having to address Manichean discussions about the role of the United States.

Third, we know that these processes have taken place against the grain—that is, in the middle of serious economic crises. This leads to two types of arguments about external economic determinants of transition. One is that authoritarian regimes are as vulnerable to economic deterioration and as capable of creating economic crises as their democratic counterparts are. This lesson is a major political and ideological defeat for those who argue that effective approaches to development are incompatible with democratic regimes.[4] The other argument is that the military extrication from power at the present time in South America represents a tactical decision to abandon the field to the civilians at the worst possible moment. Apparently, the military has recognized that this is a "democratic phase" in the convoluted cycle of Latin American political economy.[5] Whatever the merits of each argument, neither has established the preponderance of economic factors among the determinants of transition. Our analysis has shown that economic factors contributed to the deterioration of these regimes but did not predetermine their breakdown.

All in all, it appears that the impulse for the deterioration and breakdown of these regimes is not primarily external. In other words, these regimes do not have to be overthrown by an external adversary. However, the cases of Portugal and Argentina show that defeat at the hands of such an adversary may precipitate deterioration and even breakdown.

Fourth, we know that elections have served as efficacy tools for the resolution of processes of transition. As a matter of fact, free and competitive elections appear to be one of the indispensable requirements of a genuine democratic transition. Essentially, without elections there is no democratic transition. This is not necessarily a reflection of a sudden change of heart on anyone's part but of a lack of viable, peaceful alternatives. However, there is an obvious, painful overlap between efficacious elections of transition and the absence of violence on a large scale. On first impression, this would suggest that revolution is as viable an alternative as elections. If by revolution we understand a military movement similar to the April Spring of Portugal or to the military revolt against Ferdinand Marcos, the answer is probably yes. Elections are one of the acid tests of the authenticity of a transition. In addition, the cases of Brazil and Uruguay illustrate how, under certain circumstances, unanticipated electoral outcomes contribute to regime deterioration and to make the regime more vulnerable to breakdown as a result of its inability to manage a controlled liberalization.[6] Even under the dire and ominous conditions of El Salvador, where the context of the transition is a civil war, a series of elections may and in fact does have a positive impact.[7]

Fifth, we know that unlike the case of Spain, undoubtedly the one studied and cited most frequently as a relevant precedent, the recent South American transitions have not been predicated upon *reformas pactadas* (agreed-upon reforms) or *pactos de régimen* (regime agreements). Instead, what we have are very tentative understandings between the opposition and an official caretaker coalition trying to manage the transition from the authoritarian regime. At best there is a tacit agreement on some procedural—primarily electoral—ground rules for the transition, but only that. As a matter of fact, the absence of consociational formulas and the adoption of fully competitive, even adversarial relations seem to characterize these recent transitions. One could suggest here that these have been "transitions without reconciliation."

Sixth, except for Spain and including Portugal, all the cases discussed in this book implied a military extrication from power. These cases of transition witnessed a military government that managed the transition; presented the process in concessionary terms; refusing to account for or to allow inquiries into the behavior of previous military governments; sought to proscribe certain actors from the process; neutralized obstructionists attempts to derail the implementation of the transition; and eventually accepted the outcome of the electoral competitions.

The role of the military has been so significant in these processes that it would be possible, although hardly satisfactory, to approach these transitions as cases of conflict resolution of civil-military oppositions. The evidence suggests a gradual disintegration of the consensus that may have accompanied the military's accession to power and a kind of uneasy truce among different military factions in order to maintain the integrity of the institution. In most cases the military reserved for itself the final say in the implementation of the blueprint for transition. In retrospect this appears to have been more a defensive strategy than a firm resolve to dictate the outcome of the process at any cost.

Eventually, military officers sympathetic to the transition must prevail upon their more recalcitrant brethren and maintain the delicate balance among the different factions. In all cases reviewed herein a decision to devolve the government to civil society led inexorably to elections as the main avenue for extrication. Therefore, even though the military reserved the right to evaluate the outcomes of the process of transition in terms of national interest, the military paid very close attention to and respected the outcomes of the elections. Given the circumstances, the military hardly could afford to do otherwise.

It was precisely the outcome of these elections that precipitated the endgames of these transitions, for the elections forced the obstructionists to react and mount all-out efforts to derail the transition in order to prevent implementation of even more significant aspects of the agenda. These endgames were the key episodes of transition. Even though the military tolerated a degree of civilian obstructionism, it reacted more decisively, although not necessarily swiftly, to obstructionist behavior by any military faction. Generals Antônio Spínola and Otelo Saraiva de Carvalho, in Portugal; Milton Tavares de Souza and Newton de Oliveira e Cruz, in Brazil; Colonel Bolívar Jarrín, in Ecuador; and other military extremists found out that there were limits beyond which their colleagues would not allow them to go. These officers engaged in conduct that threatened the unity of the institution in the name of interests or ideological options outside the range compatible with an honorable retreat from power. In addition, such conduct was deemed intolerable because it implied a defiance of the principle of hierarchy and the notion of discipline and was predicated upon an alliance with civililans that only could come at the expense of institutional interests. Marcelo Caetano confronted the Portuguese military with the dilemma of the colonial wars. When this was compounded by possible changes in promotion patterns, Caetano was overthrown. In other cases—Argentina, Ecuador and Peru—the military institution removed a military government in order to implement a transition, or the military institution and government, although unable to justify their presence in power, were able to thwart the electoral advance of the opposition at a low cost to themselves.

Discovering intent is always problematic, especially when dealing with as secretive an institution as the military. But the evidence suggests ways in which the analyst may identify intent. For example, ability to implement the transition is the ultimate acid test of the military's willingness to extricate. The military either does or does not call for elections; it either begins to refrain from abusing state power or not; it either allows the opposition to claim its electoral victory or not. These outcomes are relatively clear. What is problematic is whether a failure to produce these outcomes in the early stages of a process of transition is a harbinger of failure. The evidence reviewed here would suggest it is not; one cannot talk about an unwavering, irreversible military commitment to civilian rule, imposed upon the institution by a military "founder." One must look instead for a pivotal role played by a key officer or group of officers who, motivated primarily by institutional concerns, is capable of creating consensus for the extrication and willing and able to see it through. This is a very tortuous, uncertain, and tentative process involving deliberations by very cautious "amateur" military politicians.

Finally, we know that most of these recent transitions, with the exception of Nicaragua and El Salvador, have not taken place in the middle of a civil war, nor have they been accompanied by very substantial changes in the political economy of the state. Quite clearly, they are reformist processes resulting in a drastic discontinuity in the type of government and in the nature of the political regime. That drastic discontinuity is not to be belittled. But neither can we gloat about its irreversibility. There is previous, ominous precedent and as Leonardo Morlino has suggested, we have not witnessed any strong consolidations of the new regimes, except perhaps in Portugal and Spain. How then can we call this process a success?

Electoral competition, even in the case of El Salvador, has produced outcomes favorable to democratization. In other words, obstructionism and continuism *always* have been defeated at the polls. These changes have been accompanied, at the level of the public, by very marked preferences in favor of peaceful solutions to political problems, a condemnation of military rule, and a new spirit of accommodation—although these are obviously not changes in political culture, not yet anyway. These processes have painted undemocratic obstructionists into a corner and have discredited them—this with the possible exception of El Salvador. This movement has created a new spirit of fellowship and solidarity, as reflected in a discourse of Ibero-American political leaders that is not utopian and maximalist but is instead eminently moderate and pragmatic. This discourse seems extraordinarily timely and refreshing to those who have lived with the consequences of the romantic vision of the revolutionaries and with the brave new world that the military technocracies put in place to prevent the revolution.

NOTES

1. Guillermo O'Donnell's concept of the BA has been alluded to in several of the chapters contained in this book. His most coherent discussion of this important concept in contemporary political analysis has been *1966–1973: El Estado Burocrático Autoritario: Triunfos, Derrotas y Crisis* (Buenos Aires: Editorial de Belgrano, 1982), Chapter 1. Unfortunately, O'Donnell continues to utilize the concept of BA in connection with the state, not the regime. This makes his analysis far less potent than it could be.

2. For the concept of "reactionary despotism," see Salvador Giner, "Economía política y legitimación cultural en los orígenes de la democracia parlamentaria: El caso de la Europa del Sur," in Julián Santamaría (ed.), *Transición a la Democracia en el Sur de Europa y América Latina* (Madrid: Centro de Investigaciones Sociológicas, 1981), pp. 19–39. For its application to Central America, see Enrique Baloyra-Herp, "Reactionary Despotism in Central America," *Jounral of Latin American Studies* 15, no. 2 (November 1983): 295–319; and Enrique A. Baloyra, "Reactionary Despotism in El Salvador," in Martin Diskin (ed.), *Trouble in Our Backyard: Central America and the United States in the Eighties* (New York: Pantheon Books, 1983), pp. 101–123.

3. The regime of Augusto Pinochet appears to have the characteristics of a classical personal dictatorship. However, Chapter 4 by Carlos Huneeus suggests that during 1985–1986, in order to reequilibrate the regime, General Pinochet found it necessary to give a more protagonistic political role to the Chilean armed forces. This could imply a more institutionalized role albeit very different from the BA model.

4. For more on this see Federico G. Gil, Enrique A. Baloyra and Lars Schoultz, "The Peaceful Transition to Democracy: Elections and The Restoration of Rights," Paper no. 1 (Washington, D.C.: Department of State Contract 1722-020083, August 1981), Part 3, pp. 112–131.

5. This is my reading of Paul Cammack's "The Political Economy of Contemporary Military Regimes in Latin America: From Bureaucratic Authoritarianism to Restructuring," in Philip O'Brien and Paul Cammack (eds.), *Generals in Retreat: The Crisis of Military Rule in Latin America* (Manchester: Manchester University Press, 1985), particularly pp. 25–26.

6. Elsewhere Carlos Huneeus has suggested that the semicompetitive and noncompetitive elections that take place in BA regimes are attempts to legitimize the regime through a degree of political mobilization. Huneeus sees in these elections an opportunity to gauge the mobilizational capacity of the regime. See "Elecciones no-competitives en las dictaduras burocrático-autoritarias en América Latina," *Revista Española de Investigaciones Sociológicas*, no. 13 (January-March 1981): 101–138.

7. See Enrique A. Baloyra, *El Salvador in Transition* (Chapel Hill: University of North Carolilna Press, 1982), Chapter 8; and Enrique A. Baloyra, "Dilemmas of Political Transition in El Salvador," *Journal of International Affairs* 38, no. 2 (Winter 1985): 236–238.

GLOSSARY

Note: All definitions refer to the usage introduced in Chapter 1 unless the author is identified.

Abertura (Port.), apertura (Span.): a process of genuine liberalization initiated but not necessarily controlled by a government; process of opening up the regime (Huneeus, Smith).

Aperturistas: political actors seeking to liberalize an authoritarian regime.

Breakdown: the collapse of a government followed by a marked discontinuity in the nature of the regime.

Consolidation: process whereby installed governments and inaugurated regimes are able to function and avoid or at least recover from deterioration.

Continuity: a situation in which a regime begins to change gradually by complying with the same rules envisioned by that regime for its internal self-transformation (Morlino).

Democracy: a regime in which the government cannot abuse its public powers because of the constraining effect of autonomous intermediary institutions; a set of institutions and rules that allows competition and participation for all citizens considered as equals (Morlino).

Democratization: implementing the substantive aspects of the agenda of political transition with outcomes favorable to a democratic inauguration; a process marked by the real recognition of civil and political rights and, where necessary, by the complete transformation toward the reconstruction of civil society (Morlino); establishment of institutional arrangements making possible the implementation of meaningful associational freedoms for all groups, universal adult suffrage in secret balloting, regular competitive elections with alternation in power, and executive accountability (Smith).

Deterioration: the loss by an incumbent government of its ability to cope with the policy agenda, particularly with matters affecting security and prosperity and other salient issues of high symbolic appeal to the public, and to justify its existence under the formula of political domination.

Discontinuity: change brought about when the rules of the previous regime are broken (Morlino).

Distensão (Port.): literally, "decompression," gradual exit of the military from direct responsibility for executive power (Smith).

Endgame: dynamics surrounding the crucial confrontation of a transition that changes the balance of power decisively in favor of the aperturists.

Establishment: the process of installing a set of structures and rules that are common to and recurring in democratic regimes (Morlino). See *inauguration*.

Government: a network of public officials identified with the chief executive who participate in the policymaking process as members of that network and whose tenure in office depends upon the tenure of that chief executive and/or upon his or her ability to govern effectively.

Implementation: how the protagonists of a process of change address the agenda of a political transition.

Inauguration: the crystallization of a new political regime; a formal announcement by a government of its commitment to consolidate a new type of regime; implementation of new political, social, and/or economic models opposed to the existing ones (Rial). See *establishment*.

Installation: the coming to power of a new government, whether by constitutional or extraordinary means; conventional formal date that is the starting point of a new regime (Rial).

Institutionalization: a property of consolidated regimes whereby they begin to function in consistent and predictable ways, there is a clear demarcation of responsibilities among their constituent units, their performance is evaluated in reference to norms of legitimacy, and the performance of the government is constrained.

Liberalization: a process of relaxing the harsher aspects of authoritarian rule; the process of concession from above of greater and larger civil and political rights, never too large and complete, but of such a nature that allows authoritarian elites to control the civil society, both at elite and mass levels (Morlino); a process of incorporating liberal values into the attitudinal structures of elites and the public and, at that, a necessary component of democratization (Floria); a curtailment of state repression and the reestablishment of basic rights—does not necessarily imply democratization (Smith).

Limited democracy: a democratic arrangement where there are partial constraints on or limits to political rights (Morlino).

Machtübergabe (Germ.): "handing over power" (Huneeus).

Machtübernahme (Germ.): "seizing power" (Huneeus).

Obstructionists: political actors resisting liberalization and the implementation of one or more aspects of the agenda of political transition.

Praetorianism: literally, "military interventionism"; as utilized here—as *mass praetorianism*—it refers to a situation in which the high intensity and broad scope of political participation overwhelm the channels provided by a regime that has a low level of institutionalization and/or is exclusionist.

Protected democracy: a democracy supported and conditioned by the military (Morlino).

Redemocratization: a democratic restoration; return to a previous democratic experience (Morlino).

Reequilibration: the process undergone by a regime surviving deterioration through government and/or policy changes.

Reforma (reform): see operational definition in Chapter 2.

Regime: the mode of government—that is, the manner in which public officials utilize state power in dealing with the society and the political community (including how they gain incumbency, how they formulate public policy, and how they deal with political opponents).

Restoration: a transition resulting in the inauguration of a regime inspired in a previously existing one.

Ruptura (rupture): a breakdown followed by a marked discontinuity in the nature of the state (see operational definition in Chapter 2).

Salida (Span.): literally, an "exit," that is, an escape; normally utilized as a *salida hacia adelante* (flight forward) to describe military retreats from power.

State: the formula of political domination utilized to invest an incumbent government with public powers and to legitimize how those powers may be used to regulate social and economic relations.

Transition: a political process that brings about a change in the nature of a political regime (see operational definition of democratic transition in Chapter 1); the ambiguous and intermediate period when the previous regime has abandoned some determining characteristics of its nondemocratic structures without having acquired all the characteristics of the new regime that eventually will be established (Morlino).

ABOUT THE CONTRIBUTORS

Enrique A. Baloyra is professor of political science and associate dean of the Graduate School of International Studies at the University of Miami, Coral Gables. He is the author of *El Salvador in Transition* and numerous articles on the politics of transition to democracy.

Carlos Alberto Floria directs the doctoral program in political science at the University of Belgrano and is a professor of law on the faculty of law and social sciences of the University of Buenos Aires. He is a member of the editorial board of *Criterio*, the author of *Guía para una Lectura de la Argentina Política*, and a coauthor of *Historia de los Argentinos* (2 vols.).

Carlos Huneeus is director of the Centro de Estudios de la Realidad Contemporánea of the Academia de Humanismo Cristiano in Santiago and is an adjunct professor of political science at the Pontificia Universidad Católica de Chile. He is the author of *Der Zusammernbruch der Demokratie in Chile* and *La Unión de Centro Democrático.*

Rafael López-Pintor is professor of industrial sociology at the Universidad Autónoma de Madrid. During 1978–1982 he directed the Centro de Investigaciones Sociológicas de la Presidencia del Gobierno and the Revista Española de Investigaciones Sociológicas. He is the author of *La Opinión Pública Española: Del Franquismo a la Democracia* and a coauthor of *Los Españoles de los Años Setenta.*

Leonardo Morlino is professor of political science on the faculty of political science of the University of Florence and editor of the *Rivista Italiana di Scienza Politica.* He is the author of *Come Cambiano i Regimi Politici* and of *Dalla Democrazia all'autoritarismo.*

Juan Rial is a historian and senior visiting fellow at the Kellogg Institute for International Studies of the University of Notre Dame. Previously, he was a senior research associate of the Centro de Informaciones y Estudios del Uruguay, where he wrote extensively on democratic transition, coedited *Uruguay y la Democracia* (3 vols.), and authored *Uruguay: Elecciones de 1984, Un Triunfo del Centro.*

William C. Smith is assistant professor of political science at the University of Miami, Coral Gables, and is book review editor of the *Journal of Interamerican Studies and World Affairs*. He was research associate at the Center for the Study of State and Society in Buenos Aires (1973–1975 and 1983) and at the Federal University of Minas Gerais (1981–1984). He has written extensively on Argentine and Brazilian politics and is currently completing "Crisis of the State, Authoritarian Politics, and Economic Transformation in Contemporary Argentina."

Waldino C. Suárez is a professor of political science at the University of Belgrano and until recently a research associate at the Centro Interdisciplinario de Estudios Sobre el Desarrollo Latinoamericano in Buenos Aires. He has written extensively on executive power and regime stability.

INDEX